Eliza Smith

The complete housewife

Eliza Smith

The complete housewife

ISBN/EAN: 9783741176425

Manufactured in Europe, USA, Canada, Australia, Japa

Cover: Foto ©Andreas Hilbeck / pixelio.de

Manufactured and distributed by brebook publishing software (www.brebook.com)

Eliza Smith

The complete housewife

Complete Housewife:
OR,
Accomplished Gentlewoman's
COMPANION.

BEING

A COLLECTION of upwards of Seven Hundred of the most approved RECEIPTS in

COOKERY,
PASTRY,
CONFECTIONARY,
POTTING,
COLLARING,
PRESERVING,
PICKLES,
CAKES,
CUSTARDS,

CREAMS.
PRESERVES,
CONSERVES,
SYRUPS,
JELLIES,
MADE WINES,
CORDIALS,
DISTILLING,
BREWING.

With COPPER PLATES, curiously engraven, for the regular Disposition or Placing of the various DISHES and COURSES.

AND ALSO,

BILLS of FARE for every Month in the Year.

To which is added,

A COLLECTION of above Three Hundred RECEIPTS of MEDICINES, consisting of Drinks, Syrups, Salves, Ointments, &c. which, after many Years Experience, have been proved to be innocent in their Application, and most salutary in their Use.

WITH

DIRECTIONS for MARKETING.

By E. SMITH.

The EIGHTEENTH EDITION, with ADDITIONS.

LONDON:

Printed for J. BUCKLAND, J. and F. RIVINGTON, J. HINTON, HAWES, CLARKE and COLLINS, W. JOHNSTON, S. CROWDER, T. LONGMAN, B. LAW, T. LOWNDES, S. BLADON, W. NICOLL, and C. and R. WARE. 1773.

PREFACE.

IT being now as unfashionable for a book to appear in public without a preface, as for a lady to be seen at a ball without a hoop-petticoat, I shall conform to custom for fashion sake, and not through any necessity: the subject being both common and universal, needs no arguments to introduce it, and being so necessary for the gratification of the appetite, stands in need of no encomiums to allure persons to the practice of it, since there are but few now-a-days who love not good eating and drinking.

Cookery, Confectionary, &c. like all other arts, had their infancy, and did not arrive at a state of maturity but by slow degrees, after various experiments, and a long track of time; for, in the infant age of the world, when its inhabitants contented themselves with the simple provision of nature, I mean, the vegetable diet, the fruits and productions of the earth, as they succeeded one another in their several peculiar seasons, the art of cookery was unknown: apples, nuts, and herbs, were both meat and sauce, and mankind stood in no need of additional sauces, ragoos, &c. to procure a good appetite; for a healthful and vigorous constitution, a clear, wholsome, odoriferous air, moderate exercise, and an exemption from anxious cares, always supplied them with it.

PREFACE.

We read of no palled appetites, but such as proceeded from the decays of nature by reason of an advanced old age; but on the contrary, a craving stomach, even upon a death-bed: no sicknesses, but those that were both the first and the last, which proceeded from the struggles of nature, and which abhorred the separation of soul and body; no physicians to prescribe for the sick, nor apothecaries to compound medicines, for two thousand years and upwards; in those days, food and physic were one and the same thing.

When man began to pass from a vegetable to an animal diet, and feed on flesh, fowls, and fish, then seasonings grew necessary, both to render it more palatable and savoury, and also to preserve that part, which was not immediately spent, from stinking and corruption; and probably salt was the first seasoning discovered.

Indeed, this seems to be necessary, especially for those who were advanced in age, whose palates, with their bodies, had lost their vigour as to taste; whose digestive faculty grew weak and impotent; and thence proceeded the use of soups and savoury messes; so that COOKERY *then began to be in use, though* LUXURY *had not brought it to the height of an* ART.

Whether the seasonings made use of in the infancy of the world were salt, savoury herbs, or roots only, or spices, the fruits of trees, such as pepper, cloves, nutmegs; bark, as cinnamon; roots, as ginger, &c. I shall not determine; but, as to the methods of the cookery of those times, boiling or stewing seems to have been the principal; broiling or roasting the next; besides which, I presume, scarce any other were used for more than two thousand years.

Cookery, however, did not long remain a bare piece of housewifery, or family œconomy; but in process of time, when luxury entered the world, it grew to an art, and soon after to a trade, as is evident from the sacred writings.

The

PREFACE.

The art of cookery, &c. is indeed diversified, according to the diversity of nations or countries; but, to treat of it in that latitude, would fill an unportable volume, and would rather confound than improve those who wish to receive instruction and advantage from perusing it: I shall, therefore, confine what I have to communicate within the limits of what is useful and pleasing; and thus, within the compass of a manual, shall neither burthen the hands to hold, the eyes to read, nor the mind to conceive.

What you will find in the following sheets, are directions generally for dressing after the best, most natural and wholsome manner, such provisions as are the product of our own country; and in such a manner as is most agreeable to English palates. I must confess that I have so far temporized, as, since we have, to our disgrace, grown so fond of the French tongue, French modes, and French messes, as to present you with a whole chapter on Foreign Cookery.

There are indeed already published various books that treat on this subject, and which bear great names, as cooks to kings, princes, and noblemen, and from which one might justly expect something more than many, if not most of those I have read, perform: but I found myself deceived in my expectations; for many of them to us are impracticable, others whimsical, others unpalatable, unless to depraved palates; some unwholsome; many things copied from old authors, and recommended, without (as I am persuaded) the copiers ever having had any experience of the palatableness, or any regard to the wholsomeness of them; which two things should be the standing rules, that no pretenders to cookery ought to deviate from; and I cannot but believe, that these celebrated performers, notwithstanding all their professions of having ingenuously communicated their art, industriously concealed their best receipts from the public.

What I here present the world with, is the product of my own experience, and that for the space of thirty years and upwards; during which time I have been constantly employed in fashionable and noble families, in which the provisions, ordered according to the following directions, have had the

general

PREFACE.

general approbation of such as have been at many noble entertainments.

These receipts are all suitable to English *constitutions, and* English *palates, wholsome, toothsome, all practicable and easy to be performed; here are those proper for a frugal, and also for a sumptuous table; and, if rightly observed, will prevent the spoiling of many a good dish of meat, the waste of many good materials, the vexation that frequently attends such mismanagements, and the curses not unfrequently bestowed on cooks, with the usual reflection, that whereas* God *sends good meat, the devil sends cooks.*

As to those parts that treat of confectionary, pickles, cordials, English *wines, &c. what I have said in relation to cookery, is equally applicable to them also.*

It is true, I have not been so numerous in receipts, as some who have gone before me; but I think I have made amends, in giving none but what are approved and practicable, and fit either for a genteel or a noble table; and though I have omitted odd and fantastical messes, yet I have set down a considerable number of receipts.

As for the receipts for medicines, salves, ointments, good in several diseases, wounds, hurts, bruises, aches, pains, &c. which amount to near three hundred, they are generally family receipts, that have never before been made public: excellent in their kind, and approved remedies, which have not been obtained by me, without much difficulty, and of such efficacy in distempers, &c. to which they are appropriated, that they have cured when all other means have failed; and a few of them, which I have communicated to a friend, have procured a very handsome livelihood.

These are very proper for those generous, charitable, and christian gentlewomen, who have a disposition to be serviceable to their poor country neighbours, labouring under any of the afflicting circumstances mentioned; who, by making the medicines, and generously contributing as occasions offer, may help the poor in their afflictions, gain their good will and wishes,
entitle

PREFACE.

entitle themselves to their blessings, and also have the pleasure of receiving that inexpressible satisfaction, which ever arises from acts of humanity.

As the whole of this collection has cost me much pains, and a thirty years diligent application, and as I have had experience of their use and efficacy, I hope they will be as kindly accepted, as by me they are generously offered to the public; and if they prove to the advantage of many, the end will be answered that is proposed by her, who is ever ready to serve the public to the utmost of her humble abilities.

As it must appear needless to pass any encomiums on a work, which has already gone through seventeen editions, we shall here confine ourselves solely to the improvements now offered in the eighteenth, to the candid inspection of the public.

The proprietors of this edition have been at a considerable expence in submitting the whole to a long and critical revision: in consequence of which it now appears in a new form, and in a dress very different from the former. The different receipts for making of one thing, which were before scattered up and down in various parts of the work, are now brought together into one view, and under distinct heads. The whole is divided into twelve parts, and each of those parts into as many chapters as the nature of it required. Thus, for instance, should the reader be in want of instructions for boiling either meat, poultry, fish, &c. in the first chapter of part the second, she will there find every thing on that head connected together, without the trouble of hunting in an index for every article separately. The same is done with respect to roasting, boiling, frying, &c. &c. as may be seen in the contents.

As new improvements are daily making in cookery, as well as in all other arts, we have been very assiduous to procure every information that could possibly contribute to complete our plan; and, if the present edition is wanting in a few of the old receipts, which were designedly omitted, the loss of them is amply repaid by the addition of near two hundred new ones.

PREFACE.

Part X. which treats of *medicines, salves,* &c. and which has always been considered as a valuable acquisition to the housewife, has had particular attention paid it. A very eminent gentleman of the faculty has perused it article by article, and expunged whatever appeared to him in the least degree either doubtful or dangerous. To make it still more useful, the Editor has reduced this part into alphabetical order, as nearly as the nature of the subject would admit. Thus the remedies for agues, bruises, coughs, dropsies, evils, fevers, &c. follow each other regularly, by which the various applications recommended for their cure may be found in an instant, and thus, seeing them all at one view, the afflicted will be the better enabled to make a prudent choice.

Most publications of this nature are confined to the business of the kitchen; but this enters on a more copious plan, and includes every article, which can add to the knowledge of the housewife. From the kitchen we step into the dairy, from the dairy to the farm-yard to view the poultry, and from the poultry to the brewhouse. In the Supplement we give the method of washing gauzes, muslins, laces, and cambrics; to take spots out of cloth or silk, and how to clean plate; besides many other articles of singular use. In short, we flatter ourselves that, after the kind reception of the former editions of this work, we shall now present the public with a book, which will have a just claim to the title of THE COMPLETE HOUSEWIFE, *or,* ACCOMPLISHED GENTLEWOMAN'S COMPANION.

A BILL *of* FARE *for every Season of the Year.*

For JANUARY.
First Course.
COLLAR of brawn
Bisque of fish
Soup with vermicelly
Orange pudding with patties
Chine and turkey
Lamb pasty
Roasted pullets with eggs
Oyster pye
Roasted lamb in joints
Grand sallad with pickles.
Second Course.
Wild fowl of all sorts
Chine of salmon boiled with smelts
Fruit of all sorts
Jole of sturgeon
Collared pig
Dried tongues with salt sallads
Marinated fish.
Another first Course.
Soup à-la-royal
Carp blovon
Tench stewed, with pitch-cocked eels
Rump of beef à-la-braise
Turkeys à-la-daube
Wild ducks comporté
Fricando of veal, with veal olives.
Another second Course.
Woodcocks
Pheasants
Salmagundi
Partridge poults
Bisque of lamb
Oyster loaves
Cutlets
Turkeys livers forced
Pippins stewed.

For FEBRUARY.
First Course.
SOUP la-reine
Turbot boiled, with oysters and shrimps
Grand patty
Hen turkeys with eggs
Marrow puddings
Stewed carps and broiled eels
Spring pye
Chine of mutton with pickles
Dish of Scotch collops
Dish of salmagundi.
Second Course.
Fat chickens and tame pigeons
Asparagus and lupines
Tansy and fritters
Dish of fruit of sorts
Dish of fried soles
Dish of tarts, custards, and cheesecakes.
Another first Course.
Soup à-la-princesse
Fish, the best you can get
Calf's-head hashed
Pullets à-la-royal
Kettle drums
Beef collops
French patties
Pupton of veal.
Another second Course.
Ducklings
Quails
Roasted lobsters
Potted lampreys
Blamange
Orange loaves
Morels and truffles ragooed
Green custard.

For MARCH.
First Course.
DISH of fish of all sorts
Soup de santé
Westphalia ham and pigeons
Battalia pye
Pole of ling
Dish of roasted tongues and udders
Pease soup
Almond pudding of sorts
Olives

A BILL *of* FARE *for*

Olives of veal à-la-mode
Dish of mullets boiled
  Second Course.
Broiled pike
Dish of notts, ruffs, and quails
Skerret pye
Dish of jellies of sorts
Dish of fruit of sorts
Dish of cream'd tarts.
  Another first Course.
Green puery soup
Fish of sorts
Tongue pye
Chine of mutton, or fillet of beef stuffed, larded and roasted
Pigeons comporté
Beef à-la-mode
Roasted ham and peepers.
  Another second Course.
Green geese
Sweetbreads roasted
Chickens à-la-crême
Cocks-combs and stones comporté
Crocande of pippins
Custard pudding
Fried oysters
Buttered cray-fish.

  For APRIL.
  First Course.
Westphalia ham and chickens
Dish of hashed carps
Bisque of pigeons
Lumber pye
Chine of veal
Grand sallad
Beef à-la-mode
Almond florendines
Fricasey of chickens
Dish of custards.
  Second Course.
Green geese and ducklings
Buttered crab, with smelts fry'd
Dish of sucking rabbets

Rock of snow and syllabubs
Dish of souced mullets
Buttered apple pye
March-pane.
  Another first Course.
Soup la reine
Salmon blovon
Breast of veal ragooed
Cutlets à-la-Maintenon
Pupton of pigeons
Bisque of sheep's tongues
Saddle of mutton
Almond pudding.
  Another second Course.
Turkey poults
Leverets
Green pease
Bisque of mushrooms
Tarts creamed
Ragoo of green morels
Lobsters serene
Fried smelts.

  For MAY.
  First Course.
Jole of salmon, &c.
Cray-fish soup
Dish of sweet puddings, of colours
Chicken pye
Calf's-head hashed
Chine of mutton
Grand sallad
Roasted fowls à-la-daube
Roasted tongues and udders
Ragoo of veal, &c.
  Second Course.
Dish of young turkeys larded, and quails
Dish of pease
Bisque of shell-fish
Roasted lobsters
Green geese
Dish of sweetmeats
Orangeado pye
Dish of lemon and chocolate creams
       Dish

every SEASON of the YEAR.

Dish of collared eels with cray-fish.

Another first Course.
Soup à-la-santé
Calvert salmon
Haunch of venison
Venison pasty
Roasted geese
Chine of veal, with fillets ragooed
Beef à-la-braise.

Another second Course.
Pheasants
Pease à-la-crême
Peepers roasted
Stewed asparagus
Codlin tart
Fruit of all sorts
Fried lamb-stones.

For JUNE.
First Course.
ROASTED pike and smelts
Westphalia ham and young fowls
Marrow puddings
Haunch of venison roasted
Ragoo of lamb-stones and sweetbreads
Fricasey of young rabbets, &c.
Umble pyes
Dish of mullets
Roasted fowls
Dish of custards.

Second Course.
Dish of young pheasants
Dish of fried soles and eels
Potatoe pye
Jole of sturgeon
Dish of tarts and cheesecakes
Dish of fruit of sorts
Syllabubs.

Another first Course.
Soups
Fish of sorts
Comporté of fowls
Pupton of sheep's trotters

Collared venison with ragoo
Chickens boiled, with lemon sauce
Mackarel
Leg of lamb forced, with the loin fricaseyed in the dish.

Another second Course.
Roasted lobsters
Pistachio pudding
White fricasey of rabbets
Goosberry tarts
Cray-fish
Salmagundi
Fish in jelly
Fried artichokes.

For JULY.
First Course.
COCK salmon with buttered lobsters
Dish of Scotch collops
Chine of veal
Venison pasty
Grand sallad
Roasted geese and ducklings
Patty royal
Roasted pig larded
Stewed carps
Dish of chickens boiled with bacon, &c.

Second Course.
Dish of partridges and quails
Dish of lobsters and prawns
Dish of ducks and tame pigeons
Dish of jellies
Dish of fruit
Dish of marinated fish
Dish of tarts of sorts.

Another first Course.
Rice soup with veal
A dish of trouts
A brown fricasey of fowls
A calf's-head boned, cleared, and stewed, with a ragoo of mushrooms
Mutton Maintenon

Rabbets

A BILL of FARE for

Rabbets with onions
Lumber pye
Ham pye.
    Another second Course.
A hare larded
Neck of venison
Partridges
Ragoo of artichokes
Cocks-combs à-la-crême
Fruit of sorts
Currant tarts
Apple puffs.

For AUGUST.
First Course.
Westphalia ham and chickens
Bisque of fish
Haunch of venison roasted
Venison pasty
Roasted fowls à-la-daube
Umble pyes
White fricasey of chickens
Roasted turkeys larded
Almond florendines
Beef à-la-mode.
Second Course.
Dish of pheasants and partridges
Roasted lobsters
Broiled pike
Creamed tart
Rock of snow and syllabubs
Dish of sweetmeats
Salmagundi.
Another first Course.
Stewed venison in soup
Haddock and soles
Leg of mutton à-la-daube
Rabbet patty
Chine of lamb
Beans and ham
Neck of mutton boned, and roasted with a ragoo of cucumbers.
Another second Course.
Bisque of lamb white

Turkeys roasted and larded
Sweetbreads and lamb-stones
Fruit of sorts
Morella cherry tarts
Strawberries and raspberries
Artichokes.

For SEPTEMBER.
First Course.
Boiled pullets with oysters, bacon, &c.
Bisque of fish
Battalia pye
Chine of mutton
Dish of pickles
Roasted geese
Lumber pye
Olives of veal with ragoo
Dish of boiled pigeons with bacon.
Second Course.
Dish of ducks and teal
Dish of fried soles
Buttered apple-pye
Jole of sturgeon
Dish of fruit
Marchpane.
Another first Course.
Green pease soup
Fish of sorts
Geese à-la-daube
Stewed hare
Bisque of pigeons
Breast of veal à-la-crême
Bisque of rabbets
Leg of veal with sorrel sauce.
Another second Course.
Pheasant larded, with celery sauce
Potted wheat-ears
Scolloped lobsters
Buttered crabs
Stewed mushrooms
Collared eels
Crocande of sweetmeats

every SEASON *of the* YEAR.

For OCTOBER.
First Course.
WESTPHALIA ham and fowls
Cod's-head with shrimps and oysters
Haunch of doe with udder à-la-force
Minced pyes
Chine and turkey
Bisque of pigeons
Roasted tongues and udders
Scotch collops
Lumber pye.
Second Course.
Wild fowl of sorts
Chine of salmon broiled
Artichoke pye
Broiled eels and smelts
Salmagundi
Dish of fruit
Dish of tarts and custards.
Another first Course.
Soup of beef bollin
Crimped cod and sentry
Pullets with oysters
Calf's-head à-la-crême
Venison pasty
Beef à-la-mode
Ox-cheek, with ragoo of herbs
Lemon torte.
Another second Course.
Teals and larks
Turkeys roasted
Tansy and black caps
Florendines
Scolloped oysters
Fried smelts
Cocks combs comporté
Fruit of sorts.

For NOVEMBER.
First Course.
BOILED fowls, with savoys, bacon, &c.
Dish of stewed carps and scolloped oysters
Chine of veal and ragoo
Sallad and pickles

Venison pasty
Roasted geese
Calf's-head hashed
Dish of gurnets
Grand patty
Roasted hen turkey with oysters.
Second Course.
Chine of salmon and smelts
Wild fowl of sorts
Potatoe pye
Sliced tongues with pickles
Dish of jellies
Dish of fruit
Quince pye.
Another first Course.
Harrico of mutton
Fish of sorts
Haunch of venison
Fillet of veal à-la-braise
Chine of mutton, with stewed celery
A pupton, with Maintenon cutlets.
Another second Course.
Roasted woodcocks
Roasted lobsters
Buttered crabs
Larks with brown crumbs
Fried oysters round two sweet-breads, larded and roasted
A pear tart
Crocande of sweetmeats.

For DECEMBER.
First Course.
WESTPHALIA ham and fowls
Soup with teal
Turbot, with shrimps and oysters
Marrow pudding
Chine of bacon and turkey
Battalia pye
Roasted tongue and udder, and hare
Pullets and oysters, sausages, &c.

Minced

A Bill of Fare, &c.

Minced pyes
Cod's-head with shrimps.
    Second Course.
Roasted pheasants and partridges
Bisque of shell-fish
Tansy
Dish of roasted ducks and teals
Jole of sturgeon
Pear tart creamed
Dish of sweetmeats
Dish of fruit of sorts.
    Another first Course.
Vermicelly soup
Fish of sorts.
Jugged hare

Beef à-la-royal
Scotch collops
French patty, with teal, &c.
Rice pudding.
    Another second Course.
Snipes, with a duck in the middle
Broiled chickens with mushrooms
Pickles of sorts
White fricasey of tripe
Pulled chickens
Stewed oysters
Stewed calves-feet
Cardoons.

The different Kinds of FRUITS and GARDEN STUFFS when in Season.

January Fruits yet lasting, are,

SOME grapes, the Kentish, russet, golden, French, kirton and Dutch pippins, John apples, winter queenings, the marigold and Harvey-apples, pom-water, golden-dorset, renneting, love's pearmain, and the winter pearmain; winter burgomot, winter boncretien, winter mask, winter Norwich, and great surrein pears. All garden things much the same as in December.

February Fruits yet lasting.

THE same as in January, except the golden-pippin and pom-water; also the pomery, and the winter-peppering and dagobent pear.

March Fruits yet lasting.

THE golden ducket-dauset, pippins, rennetings, love's pearmain and John apples. The latter boncretien, and double-blossom pear.

April Fruits yet lasting.

YOU have now in the kitchen-garden and orchard, autumn carrots, winter spinach, sprouts of cabbage and cauliflowers, turnip-tops, asparagus, young radishes, Dutch brown lettuce and cresses, burnet, young onions, scallions, leeks, and early kidney beans. On hot-beds, purslain, cucumbers, and mushrooms. Some cherries, green apricots, and gooseberries for tarts. Pippins, deuxans, Westbury apple, russeting, gilliflower, the latter boncretien, oak pear, &c.

May. The Product of the Kitchen and Fruit Garden.

ASPARAGUS, cauliflowers, imperial Silesia, royal and cabbage lettuces, burnet, purslain, cucumbers, nasturtium-flowers, pease

Fruits and Garden Stuffs in Season.

peafe and beans sown in October, artichokes, scarlet strawberries, and kidney beans. Upon the hot-beds, May cherries, May dukes. On walls, green apricots, and goosberries.

Pippins, devans, or John apple, Westbury apples, russeting, gilliflower apples, the codlin, &c.

The great karvile, winter-boncretien, black Worcester pear, surrein, and double blossom-pear. Now is the proper time to distil herbs, which are in their greatest perfection.

In June.

ASPARAGUS, garden beans and peafe, kidney beans, cauliflowers, artichokes, Battersea and Dutch cabbage, melons on the first ridges, young onions, carrots, and parsnips sown in February, purslain, borage, burnet, the flowers of nasturtium, the Dutch brown, the imperial, the royal, the Silesia and cofs lettuces, some blanched endive and cucumbers, and all sorts of pot-herbs.

Green groosberries, strawberries, some raspberries, currants white and black, duke cherries, red harts, the Flemish and carnation-cherries, codlins, jannatings, and the masculine apricot. And in the forcing frames all the forward kind of grapes.

In July.

RONCIVAL and sugared peafe, garden and kidney beans, cauliflowers, cabbages, artichokes, and their small suckers, all sorts of kitchen and aromatic herbs. Sallads, as cabbage-lettuce, purslain, burnet, young onions, cucumbers, blanched endive, carrots, turnips, beets, nasturtium-flowers, musk melons, wood-strawberries, currants, goosberries, raspberries, red and white jannatings, the Margaret apple, the primat-russet, summer-green chissel and pearl pears, the carnation-morella, great bearer, Morocco, origat, and begarreaux-cherries. The nutmeg, Isabella, Persian, Newington, violet, muscal, and rambouillet-peaches. Nectarines, the primordial, myrobalan, red, blue, amber, damask-pear, apricot, and cinnamon-plumbs; all the king's and lady Elizabeth's plumbs, &c. some figs and grapes. Walnuts in high season to pickle, and rock samphire. The fruit yet lasting of the last year is, the deuxans and winter-russeting.

In August.

CABBAGES and their sprouts, cauliflowers, artichokes, cabbage-lettuce, beets, carrots, potatoes, turnips, some beans, peafe, kidney-beans, and all sorts of kitchen-herbs, radishes,

horse-

FRUITS and GARDEN STUFFS in Seaſon.

horſe-radiſh, cucumbers, creſſes, ſome tarragon, onions, garlic, rocamboles, melons, and cucumbers for pickling.

Gooſberries, raſpberries, currants, grapes, figs, mulberries and filberts, apples, the Windſor ſovereign, orange burgamot ſliper, red Catharine, king-Catharine, penny-pruſſian, ſummer poppening, ſugar and louding pears. Crown Bourdeaux, lavur, diſput, ſavoy and wallacotta peaches; the muroy, tawny, red Roman, little green cluſter, and yellow nectarines.

Imperial blue dates, yellow late pear, black pear, white nutmeg late pear, great Antony or Turkey and Jane plumbs.

Cluſter, muſcadin, and cornelian grapes.

In September.

GARDEN and ſome kidney-beans, roncival peaſe, artichokes, radiſhes, cauliflowers, cabbage-lettuce, creſſes, chervil, onions, tarragon, burnet, celery, endive, muſhrooms, carrots, turnips, ſkirrets, beets, ſcorzonera, horſe-radiſh, garlic, eſchalots, rocambole, cabbage and their ſprouts, with ſavoys, which are better when more ſweetened with the froſt.

Peaches, grapes, figs, pears, plumbs, walnuts, filberts, almonds, quinces, melons, and cucumbers.

In October.

SOME cauliflowers, artichokes, peaſe, beans, cucumbers, and melons; alſo July ſown kidney-beans, turnips, carrots, parſnips, potatoes, ſkirrets, ſcorzonera, beets, onions, garlic, eſchalots, rocambole, chardones, creſſes, chervile, muſtard, raddiſh, rape, ſpinach, lettuce ſmall and cabbaged, burnet, tarragon, blanched celery and endive, late peaches and plumbs, grapes and figs. Mulberries, filberts, and walnuts. The bullace, pines, and arbuters; and great variety of apples and pears.

In November.

CAULIFLOWERS in the green-houſe, and ſome artichokes, carrots, parſnips, turneps, beets, ſkirrets, ſcorzonera, horſe-radiſh, potatoes, onions, garlic, eſchalots, rocambole, celery, parſley, ſorrel, thyme, ſavoury, ſweet-marjoram dry, and clary cabbages and their ſprouts, ſavoy-cabbage, ſpinach, late cucumbers. Hot herbs on the hot-bed, burnet, cabbage, lettuce, endive blanched; ſeveral ſorts of apples and pears.

Some bullaces, medlars, arbutas, walnuts, hazel nuts, and cheſnuts.

FRUITS and GARDEN STUFFS in Season.

In December.

MANY sorts of cabbages and savoys, spinach, and some cauliflowers in the conservatory, and artichokes in sand. Roots we have as in the last month. Small herbs on the hot-beds for sallads, also mint, tarragon, and cabbage-lettuce preserved under glasses; chervil, celery, and endive blanched. Sage, thyme, savoury, beet-leaves, tops of young beets, parsley, sorrel, spinach, leeks, and sweet-marjoram, marigold-flowers, and mint dried. Asparagus on the hot-bed, and cucumbers on the plants sown in July and August, and plenty of pears and apples.

CONTENTS.

PART I.

DIRECTIONS for MARKETING.

Chap. I. Of Butcher's Meat, &c.

To choose Beef　　Page 1
To choose Mutton and Lamb　　2
To choose Veal　　ibid.
To choose Pork　　3
To choose Brawn　　ibid.
To choose dried Hams and Bacon　　ibid.
To choose Venison　　ibid.

Chap. II. Of Poultry.

To know if a Capon be a true one or not, or whether it be young or old, new or stale　　4
To choose a Cock or Hen Turkey, Turkey Poults, &c.　　ibid.
To choose a Cock, Hen, &c.　　ibid.
To know if Chickens are new or stale　　ibid.
To choose a Goose, Wild Goose, and Bran-Goose　　5
To choose wild and tame Ducks　　ibid.
To choose the Bustard　　ibid.
To choose the Shuffler, Godwitz, Marle Knots, Gulls, Dotters, and Wheat-Ears　　ibid.
To choose the Pheasant Cock and Hen　　ibid.
To choose Heath and Pheasant Poults　　ibid.
To choose the Heath Cock and Hen　　ibid.
To choose the Woodcock and Snipe　　6
To choose the Partridge Cock or Hen　　ibid.
To choose Doves or Pigeons, Plovers, &c.　　ibid.
To choose Teal and Widgeon　　ibid.
To choose a Hare　　ibid.
To choose a Leveret　　ibid.
To choose a Rabbet　　7

Chap. III. Of Fish.

To choose the Turbot　　7
To choose Soals　　ibid.
To choose Plaise and Flounders　　ibid.
To choose Cod and Codling　　ibid.
To choose fresh Herrings and Mackerel　　8
To choose pickled Salmon　　ibid.
To choose pickled and red Herrings　　ibid.
To choose dried Ling　　ibid.
To choose pickled Sturgeon　　ibid.
To choose Lobsters　　8

CONTENTS.

To choose Crab-fish, great and small   9   To choose Prawns and Shrimps   ibid.

CHAP. IV. Of BUTTER, EGGS, and CHEESE.

To choose Butter and Eggs   9   To choose Cheese   10

PART II.
COOKERY.

CHAP. I. GENERAL DIRECTIONS for BOILING.

To boil a Tongue.	11	To boil Partridges	ibid.
To boil a Ham	ibid.	To boil Snipes or Woodcocks	15
To boil a Neck of Mutton	12	To boil a Pike	16
To boil a Haunch or Neck of Venison.	ibid.	To boil Mullet	ibid.
		To boil Sturgeon	ibid.
To boil a Leg of Mutton like Venison	ibid.	To boil a Turbot	ibid.
		To dress a Turtle	17
To boil a Lamb's-Head.	13	To dress a Turtle a hundred Weight	ibid.
To boil a Calf's-Head	ibid.	
To boil pickled Pork	ibid.	To dress a Turtle the West-Indian way	19
To boil Fowls and Cabbage	ibid.	
To boil a Duck or a Rabbet with Onions	14	To dress a mock Turtle	21
		To dress a Brace of Carp	ibid.
To boil Pheasants	ibid.		

CHAP. II. To dress GREENS, ROOTS, &c.

To dress Spinach	22	To dress Broccoli	24
To dress Carrots	23	To dress Asparagus	ibid.
To dress Cabbages	ibid.	To dress French Beans	ibid.
To dress Parsnips	ibid.	To dress Artichokes	ibid.
To dress Potatoes	ibid.	To dress Cauliflowers	25
To dress Turneps	ibid.		

CHAP. III. RULES to be observed in ROASTING.

To roast Mutton and Lamb	25	To roast Pork	ibid.
To roast a Breast of Mutton	26	To roast Venison	ibid.
To roast a Shoulder of Mutton in Blood	ibid.	To roast a Tongue, or Udder	29
		To roast Rabbets	ibid.
A Shoulder of Mutton in Epigram	ibid.	To roast a Goose	ibid.
		To dress a wild Duck the best way	ibid.
To stuff a Shoulder or Leg of Mutton with Oysters	27	
		Chickens roasted with Forcemeat and Cucumbers	30
Another Method	ibid.	
To roast Mutton like Venison	ibid.	To roast a Turkey	ibid.
To roast Beef	ibid.	To roast a Turkey the genteel way	ibid.
To roast a Rump of Beef	28	
To roast Veal	ibid.		

CONTENTS.

To roast a Hare 31	To barbicue a Pig 34
Another Method ibid.	To roast a pound of Butter ibid.
To roast Larks ibid.	To roast a Pike ibid.
To roast Pheasants ibid.	To roast a Pike in embers 35
To roast Partridges 32	To roast a Cod's-Head ibid.
To roast Woodcocks and Snipes ibid.	To roast Lobsters ibid.
To dress Ortolans ibid.	To roast a Fillet or Collar of Sturgeon ibid.
To roast a Pig ibid.	To roast an Eel 36
To roast a Pig with the hair on 33	To roast large Eels or Lampreys with a pudding in the belly ibid.
To roast a Pig with the skin on ibid.	To roast Ruffs and Rees 37

CHAP. IV. GENERAL DIRECTIONS for BROILING.

To broil Steaks 37	A second Way ibid.
To broil a Pigeon 38	To broil Haddocks, when they are in high season 39
Eels to broil ibid.	
To broil Haddocks or Whitings ibid.	To broil Cod-sounds ibid.

CHAP. V. DIRECTIONS for FRYING.

A very good way to fry Beef Steaks 39	Eels to fry 41
	Eels to pitchcock ibid.
To fry cold Veal ibid.	To force Eels with white Sauce ibid.
To fry Tripe 40	
Cauliflowers fried ibid.	To fry Lampreys ibid.
To fry Potatoes ibid.	To fry Carp 42
General Directions for frying Fish ibid.	To fry Herrings ibid.

CHAP. VI. DIRECTIONS for BAKING.

To bake a Rump of Beef 42	To bake Herrings ibid.
To bake a Leg of Beef 43	To bake a Carp ibid.
To bake a Pig ibid.	

CHAP. VII. SAUCES of various KINDS.

Sauce for boiled Ducks or Rabbets 44	Different sorts of Sauce for a Pig ibid.
Another for the same ibid.	Different Sauces for a Hare 47
Sauce for a boiled Goose 45	Sauce for Larks ibid.
Sauce for roast Venison ibid.	Sauce for a Woodcock ibid.
Gravy for a Fowl, when you have no meat or gravy ready ibid.	A standing Sauce for a Kitchen ibid.
Sauce for boiled Mutton ibid.	A rich and yet a cheap Sauce ibid.
Sauce for boiled Turkey or Chickens 46	Gravy to keep for Use 48
Sauce for Fish or Flesh ibid.	To make a cheap Gravy ibid.

CONTENTS.

To make the Mushroom Powder 49	To butter Shrimps ibid.
To make Mushroom Liquor and Powder ibid.	To butter Crabs or Lobsters ibid.
White Cucumber Sauce ibid.	Sauce for Fish in Lent, or at any Time ibid.
Brown Cucumber Sauce 50	To make Oyster Sauce 52
To fry Cucumbers for Mutton Sauce ibid.	Oyster Loaves ibid.
Savoury Balls ibid.	To make Anchovy Sauce ibid.
Another Way ibid.	To stuff a Fillet of Veal, or Calf's-Heart, with pickled Herrings 53
A Caudle for sweet Pyes ibid.	Stuffing, of pickled Herrings, for a roast Turkey ibid.
A Lear for savoury Pyes ibid.	Pickled Herring Pudding for a Hare ibid.
Fish Sauce, with Lobster 51	
To make Shrimp Sauce ibid.	

CHAP. VIII. Of SOUPS and BROTHS.

Rules to be observed in making Soups or Broths 53	Asparagus Soup, or green Pease 58
To make a Soup 54	To make Plumb Pottage ibid.
Another Receipt for Gravy Soup ibid.	A Soup or Pottage ibid.
Another for Gravy Soup ibid.	To make Pease Pottage 59
White Soup 55	Pease-Soup ibid.
Another excellent White Soup ibid.	To make green Pease Soup 60
To make White Soup a third Way ibid.	Another Way ibid.
	To make strong Broth to keep for use ibid.
A Fasting day Soup ibid.	To make Pocket Soup 61
To make a Soup 56	To make portable Soup ibid.
To make Soup à la Reine ibid.	Strong Broth 62
To make white Onion Soup 57	Oyster Soup ibid.
To make brown Onion Soup ibid.	A Cray-fish Soup 63
To make Partridge Soup ibid.	Another Cray-fish Soup ibid.
To make Asparagus Soup ibid.	To make Cray-fish or Lobster Soup 64
	Receipt for making pickled Herring Soup ibid.

CHAP. IX. Of MADE DISHES.

A fine Side-Dish 65	Veal Olives ibid.
Another 66	Beef Collops 69
To force a Leg of Veal, Mutton, or Lamb ibid.	An Amulet of Eggs the savoury Way ibid.
To make a savoury Dish of Veal ibid.	Artificial Potatoes for Lent: A Side-dish ibid.
Bombarded Veal 67	Scotch Collops 70
Veal Rolls ibid.	Three other Methods ibid.
To make Veal Cutlets ibid.	To dress a Fillet of Veal with Collops 71
Mutton Cutlets 68	A Calf's-Head Surprise ibid.
A pretty Side dish of Beef ibid.	To make Forcemeat ibid.
Beef Olives ibid.	Hog's

CONTENTS.

Hogs Ears forced 72
To force Cocks-Combs ibid.
How to force a Fowl ibid.
To make a Pulpatoon of Pigeons 73
To make a Bisk of Pigeons ibid.
To do Pigeons in Jelly ibid.
To make a Poloe 74
To make Pockets ibid.
To make artificial Venison ibid.
To keep Smelts in Jelly ibid.
Chickens forced with Oysters 75
To make Salamongundy ibid.
Another Way ibid.
To make a grand Dish of Eggs 76

Chap. X. Of Fricaseys.

A Fricasey of Lamb 77
To make a pale Fricasey ibid.
A Fricasey of Veal ibid.
A Fricasey of pulled Chickens 78
A Fricasey of Chickens ibid.
A brown Fricasey of Chickens or Rabbets ibid.
A white Fricasey of the same ibid.
A Fricasey of Rabbets ibid.
To fricasey Rabbets brown 79
To fricasey Rabbets white ibid.
To make a white Fricasey ibid.
Another Method ibid.
To fricasey a Pig 80
To fricasey Neats-Tongues ibid.
A Fricasey of Tripe ibid.
A Fricasey of double Tripe 81
A Fricasey of Ox-palates ibid.
Another ibid.
To make a Fricasey of Eggs 82
Another ibid.
To fricasey Artichoke-bottoms for a Side-dish ibid.
To make Skuets ibid.
To fricasey Soals white ibid.
To fricasey Soals brown 83
A Fricasey of great Plaice or Flounders ibid.
To fricasey Cod-founds ibid.
To fricasey Scate, or Thornback, white 84
To fricasey it brown ibid.
To fricasey Fish in general ibid.

Chap. XI. Of Ragoos.

To make a Ragoo of Lamb 85
To ragoo a Neck of Veal ibid.
To ragoo a Breast of Veal ibid.
Another 86
To ragoo a piece of Beef ibid.
A Ragoo for made Dishes 87
A Ragoo of Sweet-breads ibid.
Another ibid.
A Ragoo of Livers ibid.
To make a Ragoo of Pig's Ears 88
To ragoo Hogs Feet and Ears ibid.
A Ragoo of Eggs ibid.
To ragoo Endive 89
To ragoo Celery ibid.
To ragoo French Beans ibid.
To ragoo Mushrooms 90
To ragoo Cauliflowers ibid.
To make a Ragoo of Onions ibid.
A Ragoo of Asparagus ibid.
To ragoo Oysters 91
Another ibid.

Chap. XII. Of Hashes.

To make a Mutton-Hash 92
To hash roasted Mutton ibid.
To hash Mutton ibid.
To hash a Lamb's Pumice ibid.
To make a Calf's-Head Hash 93
Another Method ibid.
To hash a Calf's-Head White 94
To hash Venison ibid.
To hash a Turkey ibid.
To hash Fowls 95
To hash a Woodcock, or Partridge ibid.

CONTENTS.

CHAP. XIII. Various KINDS of STEWS.

To stew a Rump of Beef	95	To dress a Duck with green Pease	ibid.
To stew Beef Steaks	96	To stew a Duck with Cucumbers	102
To stew a Knuckle of Veal	ibid.	To stew Giblets	ibid.
To make Hodge Podge	ibid.	Another Way	ibid.
To stew a Head, Chine, and Neck of Venison	ibid.	To stew a Hare	103
To stew Mutton the Turkish Way	97	To jug a Hare	ibid.
To stew a Neck of Veal	ibid.	To jug Pigeons	ibid.
To stew a Pheasant	ibid.	To stew Pigs Petty-toes	104
To stew Plovers	98	To stew Golden Pippins	ibid.
To make Partridge Panes	ibid.	To stew Cucumbers	ibid.
To stew a Turkey brown	99	To stew Mushrooms	ibid.
To stew a Turkey brown the nice way	ibid.	To stew green Pease	105
To stew a Turkey or Fowl in celery sauce	100	To stew Carp	ibid.
		Another Method	ibid.
		Another Way to stew Carp	106
To stew Pigeons	ibid.	To stew Carp white	ibid.
Another Method	ibid.	Eels to stew	ibid.
Another Method	ibid.	To dress Eels with brown Sauce	107
To stew Pigeons with Asparagus	101	Soles to stew	ibid.
		To stew Oysters in French Rolls	ibid.
To mumble Rabbets and Chickens	ibid.	To stew Cod	108
		To make Water-sokey	ibid.

CHAP. XIV. Of PANCAKES and FRITTERS.

To make Pancakes	108	To make Parsnip Fritters	ibid.
Another Method	ibid.	To make Apple Fritters	ibid.
To make fine Pancakes	109	To make Hasty Fritters	ibid.
A second Sort of fine Pancakes	ibid.	To make fine Fritters	111
		Another Way	ibid.
A third Sort, called a Quire of Paper	ibid.	To make Fritters Royal	ibid.
		To make Skirret Fritters	ibid.
To make Rice Pancakes	ibid.	To make white Fritters	ibid.
To make Curd Fritters	ibid.	To make Water Fritters	112
To make fried Toasts	110		

CHAP. XV. All Sorts of PUDDINGS.

Rules to be observed in making Puddings, &c.	112	Another Hasty Pudding	ibid.
		To make stewed Pudding	ibid.
To make an Orange Pudding	113	A Bread and Butter Pudding for fasting Days	115
Another Sort of Orange Pudding	ibid.	To make a Quaking Pudding	ibid.
To make a Carrot Pudding	ibid.		
Puddings for little Dishes	ibid.	To make a French Barley Pudding	ibid.
A Hasty Pudding to butter itself	114	A good boiled Pudding	ibid.

To

CONTENTS.

To make an Oatmeal Pudding 116
Another ibid.
Another Method to make an Oatmeal Pudding ibid.
To make a Pith Pudding ibid.
To make a Curd Pudding 117
Orange Custard or Pudding ibid.
Buttered Crumbs ibid.
To make Hogs Puddings with Currants ibid.
Another Sort of Hogs Puddings ibid.
To make black Hogs Puddings 118
Very fine Hogs Puddings ibid.
To make Almond Hogs Puddings ibid.
To make an Almond Pudding 119
The Ipswich Almond Pudding ibid.
To make a brown Bread Pudding ibid.
A Rye-bread Pudding ibid.
To make a fine Bread Pudding 120
A baked Pudding ibid.
Another baked Bread Pudding ibid.
To make a baked Sack Pudding ibid.
To make a Cow-heel Pudding ibid.
To make a Calf's-foot Pudding 121
Another Method ibid.
To make a Spread-Eagle Pudding ibid.
To make New-College Puddings ibid.
To make an Oxford Pudding 122
To make a fine Hasty Pudding ibid.
To make a Sweetmeat Pudding ibid.
A Marrow Pudding ibid.
Another Method 123
Another Marrow Pudding ibid.
Lemon Pudding ibid.
Another 124
To make a Sweetmeat Pudding ibid.
To make a fine plain Pudding ibid.
A Rice Pudding ibid.
Another 125
A fine Rice Pudding ibid.
To make a cheap Rice Pudding ibid.
To make a Ratifia Pudding ibid.
Vermicelly Pudding ibid.
To make a Potatoe Pudding 126
An Apple Pudding ibid.
To make a Chesnut Pudding ibid.
To make a Marjoram Pudding ibid.
To make a Cabbage Pudding 127
A colouring Liquor for Puddings ibid.

CHAP. XVI. All Sorts of PYES.

To make an Olio Pye 127
To make an Olio Pye ibid.
To make a Florendine of Veal 128
A Veal Pye ibid.
A savoury Veal Pye ibid.
To make a savoury Lamb Pye ibid.
To make a sweet Lamb Pye 129
A Beef-steak Pye ibid.
A Ham Pye ibid.
A Battalia Pye, or Bride Pye 130
A Battalia Pye ibid.
To make Egg Pyes ibid.
To make a Lumber Pye ibid.
A sweet Chicken Pye 131
Another Chicken Pye ibid.
Another 132
To make a Hare Pye ibid.
Another Method ibid.
A Turkey Pye 133
A Codling Pye ibid.
A Pigeon Pye ibid.
To make a Giblet Pye 134
To make a Duck Pye ibid.
To make a Cheshire Pork Pye ibid.
To make a Devonshire Squab Pye ibid.
A Neat's-Tongue Pye 135
To make Mince Pyes the best way ibid.

To

CONTENTS.

To make Mince Pyes of Veal	135	To make a Cherry Pye	ibid.
To make a Potatoe Pye	136	A Fiſh Pye	ibid.
A fine Potatoe Pye for Lent	ibid.	To make an Eel Pye	139
To make an Onion Pye	ibid.	To make a Turbot Pye	ibid.
To make an Artichoke Pye	137	To make an Oyſter Pye	ibid.
To make a Skirret Pye	ibid.	To make a Salmon Pye	ibid.
To make a Cabbage-Lettuce Pye	ibid.	To make a Carp Pye	140
		To make a Soal Pye	ibid.
To make an Apple and a Pear Pye	138	To make a Flounder Pye	ibid.
		To make a Herring Pye	141

PART III.

New and approved RECEIPTS in CONFECTIONARY.

CHAP. I. The PREPARATION of SUGARS, of CANDIES, PRESERVES, &c.

To clarify Sugar	142	To make Gingerbread	148
To boil Sugar to the Degree called Smooth	ibid.	Another Method	ibid.
		Another Sort of Gingerbread	ibid.
The blown Sugar	143	Another	ibid.
The feathered Sugar	ibid.	To make Dutch Gingerbread	149
The crackled Sugar	ibid.	To make Wigs	ibid.
The Carmel Sugar	ibid.	Another Method	ibid.
To make little Things of Sugar, with Devices in them	ibid.	To make the light Wigs	ibid.
		To make very good Wigs	ibid.
To make Sugar of Roſes, and in all Sorts of Figures	144	To make Buns	150
		To make French Bread	ibid.
To make Orange Chips criſp	ibid.	To make brown French Loaves	ibid.
To preſerve Seville Orange liquid, as alſo Lemons	ibid.	To make March-pane unboiled	ibid.
To make a Compote of Oranges	145	To make March-pane	151
To make Orange Rings and Fagots	ibid.	To make a Jam of Raſpberries	ibid.
Zeſt of China Oranges	ibid.	To make a Jam of Cherries	ibid.
To candy Orange, Lemon, and Citron	146	To make a Jam of Gooſberries	ibid.
To candy Figs	ibid.	A Tanſy	ibid.
A grand Trifle	ibid.	To make a Tanſy to bake	152
To make artificial Fruit	147	To make a Gooſberry Tanſy	ibid.
To make Chocolate Almonds	ibid.	To make an Apple Tanſy	ibid.
To make Almond Loaves	ibid.	Balls for Lent	ibid.

CHAP. II. Of TARTS.

To make different Sorts of Tarts	153	To make Orange or Lemon Tarts	ibid.
To make a Chervil or Spinach Tart	ibid.	To make Puff-Paſte for Tarts	ibid.
		Another Paſte for Tarts	155
To make a Lemon Tart	154	Another	ibid.
		To Ice Tarts	ibid.

CHAP.

CONTENTS.

CHAP. III. Of PASTIES and PUFFS.

To make a Sweetbread Pasty to fry or bake 155	Apple Pasties to fry ibid.
To season and bake a Venison Pasty ibid.	Paste for Pasties 157
	To make Sugar Puffs ibid.
	To make Seed Puffs ibid.
A Venison Pasty 156	To make Lemon Puffs ibid.
To make Marrow Pasties ibid.	To make Almond Puffs ibid.
To make little Pasties to fry ibid.	To make Puff-Paste 158

CHAP. IV. Of CUSTARDS.

To make Custards 158	To make Hasty Puddings, to boil in Custard Dishes 159
Rice Custards ibid.	
To make Almond Tourt ibid.	To make a Custard Pudding ibid.
	Boiled Custards ibid.

CHAP. V. All Sorts of CAKES.

To make a rich great Cake 159	Another Seed Cake ibid.
To make an ordinary Seed Cake 160	A rich Seed Cake, called the Nun's Cake ibid.
To make the Marlborough Cake ibid.	To make Sugar Cakes 166
Another Sort of little Cakes 161	To make clear Cakes of Gooseberries ibid.
To make the white Cake ibid.	To Ice a great Cake ibid.
To make Orange Cakes ibid.	To make Cheesecakes ibid.
To make Shrewsbury Cakes ibid.	Another Way to make Cheesecakes 167
To make Almond Cakes 162	
To make Whetstone Cakes ibid.	Another ibid.
To make Portugal Cakes ibid.	Another Method ibid.
To make Jumbals ibid.	To make Cheesecakes without Rennet 168
To make a good Plumb Cake 163	To make Orange Cakes ibid.
Another Plumb Cake ibid.	To make Lemon Cakes ibid.
Another Plumb Cake with Almonds ibid.	Potatoe or Lemon Cheesecake ibid.
To make little Plumb Cakes 164	To make Lemon Cheesecakes 169
An ordinary Cake to eat with Butter ibid.	Another Method ibid.
	To make Cheesecakes without Curd ibid.
A French Cake to eat hot ibid.	
A good Seed Cake ibid.	To make Almond Cheesecakes ibid.
Another Seed Cake 165	
Another ibid.	

CHAP. VI. Of BISCUITS.

To make Drop Biscuits 170	To make little hollow Biscuits ibid.
To make little Cracknels ibid.	
To make the thin Dutch Biscuit 171	To make Ratafia Biscuits 172
	To make the hard Biscuit ibid.
Another Biscuit ibid.	To make Lemon Biscuit ibid.
Another ibid.	

CHAP.

CONTENTS.

CHAP. VII. Of elegant ORNAMENTS for the TABLE.

To spin a Silver Web for covering Sweetmeats	173	Hen and Chickens in Jelly	ibid.
To spin a Gold Web for covering Sweetmeats	174	To make a Desart Island	178
		To make a Floating Island	ibid.
To make a Desert of Spun Sugar	ibid.	Another Method	ibid.
		To make the Rocky Island	179
To make Flumery	175	To make Moonshine	ibid.
To make a Fish-pond	ibid.	To make Moon and Stars in Jelly	ibid.
To make a Hen's-nest	176		
To make Blomonge of Isinglass	ibid.	To make Eggs and Bacon in Flummery	180
Green Blomonge of Isinglass	ibid.	Solomon's Temple in Flummery	ibid.
Clear Blomonge	ibid.	To make a Dish of Snow	ibid.
Yellow Flummery	177	To make Black Caps	181
A good Green	ibid.	To make Green Caps	ibid.
Gilded Fish in Jelly	ibid.		

PART IV.

Of Preparing BACON, HAMS, and TONGUES; and Making BUTTER, CHEESE, &c.

CHAP. I. Of Preparing BACON, &c.

To salt Bacon	182	To dry Mutton to cut out in Shivers as Dutch Beef	ibid.
To make Westphalia Bacon	ibid.		
To salt and dry a Ham of Bacon	183	To prepare Hung Beef	ibid.
		Another Method	ibid.
To salt Hams, or Tongues, &c.	ibid.	To prepare the fine hanged Beef	186
Another Method	ibid.	A Pickle for Pork which is to be eat soon	ibid.
To dry Tongues	184		
To dry a Leg of Mutton like Pork	ibid.	To make Veal Hams	ibid.
		To make Beef Hams	ibid.
To make Sausages	ibid.	To recover Venison when it stinks	187
Very fine Sausages	ibid.		
To make Dutch Beef	185	Another and better Method	ibid.

CHAP. II. To make BUTTER, CHEESE, &c.

To make Butter	187	To make Mrs. Skynner's fresh Cheese	ibid.
To make Lemon Butter	188		
French Butter	ibid.	To make a Chedder Cheese	ibid.
To make a Summer Cream Cheese	ibid.	The Queen's Cheese	190
		To make a thick Cream Cheese	ibid.
To make a Newmarket Cheese to cut at two years old	ibid.	To make Slip-Coat Cheese	ibid.
		A Cream Cheese	ibid.
To make Lady Huncks's fresh Cheese	189	To make a fresh Cheese	191

To

CONTENTS.

To make Cream Cheese with old Cheshire 191
To make Rennet ibid.
To make a Rennet-Bag ibid.

PART V.
Of Foreign Dishes.

Chap. I. Of French Dishes.

To prepare Bouillion, or Broth 193
Beef A-la-mode 194
Another Method ibid.
Beef A-la-mode in Pieces ibid.
Beef Escarlot 195
Beef A-la-daub ibid.
A Piece of Beef trembling ibid.
To boil a Rump of Beef the French fashion 196
Sweet-breads A-la-daub ibid.
A Leg of Mutton A la-royal ibid.
A Goose, Turkey, or Leg of Mutton A-la-daube ibid.
Ducks A-la-mode 197
To boil Ducks the French Way ibid.
To stew a Hare ibid.
To dress a Pig the French Way 198
The best Method of dissecting, preparing, and dressing a Turtle ibid.
The Queen's Soup 199
To make Nantile Soup 200
To make Water Souchy ibid.
To make Herb Soup without Meat ibid.
A Matelotte of Chickens with Mushrooms 201
Rabbets collard with Sauce a l'Ivernoise ibid.
Hodge-podge of Beef, with Savoys 202
To make Pease Soup without Meat ibid.
Pease Françoise 203
To make a French Pye ibid.
Receipt to make French Bread ibid.

Chap. II. Of Jewish, Spanish, Dutch, German, and Italian Dishes.

To stew green Pease the Jews way 204
Marmalade of Eggs the Jews way 205
English Jews Puddings; an excellent dish for six or seven people, for the expence of six-pence ibid.
To dress Haddocks the Jews way ibid.
Artichoke Suckers dressed the Spanish way 206
Artichokes preserved the Spanish way ibid.
Spanish Pyes ibid.
Asparagus dressed the Spanish way ibid.
A Spanish Pease Soup 207
To make Onion Soup the Spanish way ibid.
Cauliflowers dressed the Spanish way ibid.
To dress Haddocks after the Spanish way ibid.
A Cake the Spanish way ibid.
Milk Soup the Dutch way 208
Carrrots and French Beans dressed the Dutch way ibid.
Red Cabbage dressed after the Dutch way ibid.
Minced Haddocks after the Dutch way ibid.
Beans dressed the German way ibid.
Fish Pasties the Italian way ibid.
To dress Mutton the Turkish way 209

To

CONTENTS.

To make a fricasey of Calves-feet and Chaldron, after the Italian way 209
To fricasey Pigeons the Italian way ibid.

PART VI.
Terms of Art for Carving.

Instructions for Carving according to the Terms of Art 210
To unjoint a Bittern ibid.
To cut up a Bustard ibid.
To souce a Capon ibid.
To unlace a Coney ibid.
To display a Crane 211
To unbrace a Duck ibid.
To rear a Goose ibid.
To dismember a Hern ibid.
To unbrace a Mullard 212
To wing a Partridge ibid.
To allay a Pheasant ibid.
To wing a Quail ibid.
To lift a Swan ibid.
To break a Teal ibid.
To cut up a Turkey ibid.
To thigh a Woodcock 213
General Directions to be observed before the cutting up a pickled Herring, which Way soever it is to be eat ibid.

PART VII.
Of Potting, Collaring, and Pickling.

Chap. I. Of Potting.

To pot Beef 214
Another Method ibid.
A fine Way to pot a Tongue 215
To pot Neats-Tongues ibid.
To pot Ducks or any Fowls, or small Birds ibid.
To pot a Swan 216
To pot Geese and Turkeys ibid.
To pot Venison ibid.
To pot a Hare 217
To pot Mushrooms ibid.
To pot Salmon ibid.
Another Method 218
Salmon or Mackarel to pot ibid.
Mackarel to caveack ibid.
To pot Lobsters 219
To pot Eels ibid.
To pot Herrings ibid.

Chap. II. Of Collaring.

To collar Beef 219
Another Method 220
To keep collared Beef ibid.
To collar Flat Ribs of Beef ibid.
Collared Mutton to eat hot 221
To collar a Breast of Mutton ibid.
To collar a Breast of Veal 222
Another Method ibid.
To collar a Calf's-Head ibid.
To grill a Calf's-Head 223
To collar Cow-heels ibid.
To collar a Pig ibid.
Another Method 224
To collar Venison ibid.
To collar Salmon 225
To collar Eels ibid.
To collar Mackarel ibid.

Chap. III. All Sorts of Pickles.

To pickle Hams or Ribs of Beef 226
To pickle a Buttock of Beef ibid.
To pickle Ox-Palates 227
To pickle Pigeons ibid.
To pickle Sparrows, or Squab-Pigeons ibid.

To

CONTENTS.

To pickle Mushrooms	228	To pickle Broom Buds	236
Another Method	ibid.	To pickle Purslane-Stalks	ibid.
Another excellent Method	ibid.	Another Method	ibid.
Another Method	229	To pickle Lemons	237
To pickle Walnuts	ibid.	To pickle small Onions	ibid.
Another Method	ibid.	To make Vinegar	ibid.
Another Method	230	To make Gooseberry Vinegar	238
To pickle Cucumbers	ibid.	To keep Artichokes in Pickle, to boil all Winter	ibid.
To pickle Cucumbers in Slices	231	The Lemon Sallad	ibid.
To mango Cucumbers	ibid.	To make English Catchup	239
To pickle Barberries	ibid.	Another Way	ibid.
Another Method	ibid.	Another Way	ibid.
To pickle Grapes	ibid.	To make Catchup to keep twenty Years	240
To pickle Gerkins	232		
To pickle Currants for present Use	233	A Pickle in imitation of Indian Bamboe	ibid.
To pickle Nasturtium-Buds	ibid.	To distil Verjuice for Pickles	ibid.
To keep Quinces in Pickle	ibid.	To pickle Salmon	ibid.
To pickle Asparagus	ibid.	To pickle Oysters	241
Cabbage Lettuce to keep	ibid.	Another Method	ibid.
To pickle Red Cabbage	234	To pickle Lobsters	ibid.
To pickle Pods of Radishes	ibid.	Tench to pickle	242
To pickle Ashen-keys	ibid.	To pickle Mackarel	ibid.
To pickle French Beans	ibid.	To pickle Sprats for Anchovies	ibid.
Another Method	ibid.		
French Beans to keep	235	To marinate Smelts	ibid.
To make Melon Mangoes	ibid.	To pickle Muscles or Cockles	243
To pickle Samphire	ibid.		
To pickle Asparagus	ibid.		

PART VIII.

PRESERVES, CONSERVES, SYRUPS, CREAMS, and JELLIES.

CHAP. I. Of PRESERVES.

To preserve Oranges whole	244	To preserve Apricots ripe	ibid.
Another Way	245	To preserve green Apricots	ibid.
Another Way to preserve Oranges	ibid.	Another Method	249
		To preserve Plumbs green	ibid.
The Dutchess of Cleveland's Receipts to preserve Lemons, Citrons and Oranges	246	Another Method	ibid.
		To preserve black Pear-Plumbs, or any black Plumb	250
How to take out the Seeds	ibid.	To preserve the great white Plumb	ibid.
To preserve whole Quinces white	ibid.	To preserve white Pear-Plumbs	ibid.
To preserve Gooseberries	ibid.		
To preserve Gooseberries in Hops	247	To preserve Damsons whole	251
		To preserve Cherries	ibid.
To preserve Gooseberries whole without stoning	ibid.	Another Method	ibid.
		To preserve Barberries	252
To preserve Apricots	248	Another Method	ibid.

To

CONTENTS.

To dry Barberries	252
A fine Way to preserve Raspberries	ibid.
To preserve Raspberries whole	253
To preserve Raspberries in Jelly	ibid.
To preserve Currants in Jelly	ibid.
To dry Currants in Bunches	254
To preserve small Cucumbers green	ibid.
To preserve green Cucumbers	ibid.
To preserve whole Pippins	ibid.
To preserve Mulberries whole	255
To preserve green Grapes	ibid.
To preserve or dry Samphire	256
To keep green Pease till Christmas	ibid.
To keep Artichokes all the Year	ibid.
To keep Walnuts all the Year	ibid.

CHAP. II. Of CONSERVES and SYRUPS.

To make Conserve of red Roses, or any other Flowers	257
To stew Apples	ibid.
To dry Plumbs or Apricots	ibid.
To dry Apricots like Prunello's	258
To dry Apricots	ibid.
To make Apricot Chips	ibid.
To make Marmalade of Apricots	ibid.
To make white Marmalade	259
To make white Quince Marmalade	ibid.
To make red Quince Marmalade	ibid.
To make red Quince Marmalade another way	ibid.
To make Orange Marmalade	260
Another Way to make Orange Marmalade	ibid.
To make Marmalade of Cherries	ibid.
To make Syrup of Orange-Peel	ibid.
To keep Orange-Flowers in Syrup	261
To keep Fruit in Syrup to candy	ibid.
To make Syrup of any Flowers	ibid.
To candy Orange-Flowers	ibid.
Another Method	262
Another Way	ibid.
To candy Orange Chips	ibid.
To candy Angelica	ibid.
To candy any Sort of Fruit	263
To candy Flowers	ibid.
To make Cakes of Flowers	ibid.
To make Wormwood Cakes	264
To scald Fruit for present Use	ibid.
To make Pastils	ibid.
To fricasey Almonds	ibid.
To dry Pears or Pippins without Sugar	265
To make Rose Drops	ibid.
To make a Paste of green Pippins	ibid.
To make white Quince Paste	ibid.
To dry Pears or Apples	266
To make clear Candy	ibid.
To make Sugar Plates	ibid.
To clear Sugar	267
To make brown Sugar	ibid.
To make Sugar of Roses	ibid.
To parch Almonds	ibid.

CHAP. III. Of CREAMS.

Lemon Cream	267
Another Lemon Cream	268
To make White Lemon Cream	ibid.
To make Orange Cream	ibid.
Another Method	ibid.
To make Gooseberry Cream	269
To make Barley Cream	ibid.
To make Steeple Cream	ibid.
To make whipped Cream	ibid.
To make White-wine Cream	270
To make Sack Cream	ibid.

To

CONTENTS.

To make Blanched Cream 270
To make Cream of any preserved Fruit ibid.
Lady Huncks's Spanish Cream ibid.
To make plain raw Cream thicker than usual 271
To make Crisp Cream ibid.
To make Sack Cream ibid.
To make Rice Cream ibid.
To make Pistachia Cream ibid.
To make Quince Cream 272
To make Almond Cream ibid.
To make Ratafia Cream ibid.

CHAP. IV. Of JELLIES, SYLLABUBS, &c.

To make Pippin Jelly 272
To make white Jelly of Quinces 273
To make Jelly of Currants ibid.
To make Jelly of white Currants ibid.
To make Jelly of Cherries ibid.
To make Jelly of Apricots 274
To make a strong Apple Jelly ibid.
To make Ribbon Jelly ibid.
To make Hart's-horn or Calves-feet Jelly without Lemons 275
To make Hart's-horn Jelly ibid.
To make Calves-feet Jelly ibid.
To make very fine Syllabubs ibid.
To make Lemon Syllabubs 276
To make whipped Syllabubs ibid.
King William's Posset ibid.
Lord Carlisle's Amber Posset ibid.
A Sack Posset without Eggs 277
A Sack Posset without Cream or Eggs ibid.
To make the Pope's Posset ibid.
To make a Snow Posset ibid.
To make a Jelly Posset 278
To make an Oatmeal Sack Posset ibid.
To make Oatmeal Caudle ibid.
To make Flummery Caudle ibid.
To make Tea Caudle 279
A fine Caudle ibid.
To make Spanish Pap ibid.
Buttered Oranges ibid.
To make white Leach ibid.
To make Strawberry or Raspberry Fool 280
To make Hart's-horn Flummery ibid.
To make Almond Butter ibid.
To make Salop ibid.

PART IX.

All SORTS of MADE WINES, and CORDIAL WATERS.

CHAP. I. Of MADE WINES, &c.

To make Apricot Wine 282
To make Damson Wine ibid.
To make Gooseberry Wine ibid.
Another Method 283
Another ibid.
Pearl Gooseberry Wine 284
To make Raisin Wine ibid.
Another Method ibid.
To make Orange Wine with Raisins ibid.
To make Cherry Wine 285
To make Morella Cherry Wine ibid.
To make Raspberry Wine ibid.
To make Raspberry Wine another Way ibid.
Another Sort of Raspberry Wine ibid.
To make Lemon Wine 286
To make Elder Wine ibid.
To make Clary Wine ibid.
To make Quince Wine 287
Another Method ibid.
To make Barley Wine ibid.
To make Plumb Wine 288
To make Orange Wine ibid.
To make Currant Wine ibid.

CONTENTS.

To make the fine Clary Wine 288
To make Wine of English Figs 289
To make Wine of Roses ibid.
To make Wine of Mulberries ibid.
To make Wine of Apples and Pears 290
To make Wines of Blackberries, Strawberries, or Dewberries ibid.
To make Sage Wine ibid.
Sage Wine another Way 291
Another Method ibid.
To make Sugar Wine ibid.
To make Cowslip Wine 292
Cyprus Wine imitated ibid.
Mountain Wine ibid.
Lemon Wine, or what may pass for Citron Water ibid.
To make Turnep Wine 293
To make Dr. Radcliffe's Stomach Wine ibid.
To make Frontiniac Wine ibid.
To make English Champaign, or the fine Currant Wine ibid.
To make Saragofa Wine, or English Sack 294
To fine Wine the Lisbon Way ibid.
To make Palermo Wine ibid.
To make Birch Wine ibid.
To make Mead 295
To make strong Mead ibid.
To make small white Mead ibid.
How to make Cyder 296
For fining Cyder ibid.
To make Turkish Sherbet ibid.
To make Cock Ale ibid.
To make Ebulum 297
To make Shrub ibid.
To make Cherry Brandy ibid.
To make Usquebaugh ibid.
To make Elder Ale 298
To make Elder-flower Water ibid.
To recover the lost Colour of White Wine, or Rhenish Wine ibid.
To prevent the Decay of lowering Wine ibid.
Of Racking Wine 299
To make Wines scent well, and give them a curious Flavour ibid.
To mend Wines that rope ibid.
To mend White, or Rhenish Wines ibid.

CHAP. II. All Sorts of CORDIAL WATERS.

To distil Caudle Water 300
To distil Milk Water ibid.
To make Hephnatick Water for the Gravel 301
To distil Pepper-Mint Water ibid.
To distil Elder-Flower Water ibid.
To distil Rose Water ibid.
To distil Penny-Royal Water ibid.
To distil Lavender Water 302
To distil Spirits of Wine ibid.
The great Palsey Water ibid.
To make Aqua Mirabilis 303
To make Orange-Flower Brandy ibid.
A Cordial Water that may be made in Winter ibid.
A Tincture of Ambergrease ibid.
To make Orange or Lemon Water 304
King Charles II's Surfeit Water ibid.
The Fever Water ibid.
Black Cherry Water for Children ibid.
To make Gripe Water 305
Lily of the Valley Water ibid.
To make Vertigo Water ibid.
Dr Burgess's Antidote against the Plague ibid.
To make Lime Water 306
Cock Water for a Consumption ibid.
Another Water against a Consumption ibid.
Another ibid.
Rue Water, good for Fits of the Mother ibid.
An opening Drink ibid.

PART

PART X.
MEDICINES, SALVES, &c.

CHAP. I. Of MEDICINES and SALVES; reduced to alphabetical Order, as nearly as the Nature of the Subject would admit.

An excellent Remedy for Agues, which has been often tried with very great Succefs 308
Three other Methods ibid.
Four other Methods 309
For a Tertain Ague, a never-failing Remedy ibid.
For an Afthma ibid.
For an old Ache or Strain 310
For the Bite of a mad Dog ibid.
Another Cure ibid.
An infallible Cure for the Bite of a mad Dog ibid.
Another for the Bite of a mad Dog, which has cured when the Perfon was difordered, and the falt Water failed 311
Dr. Mead's Receipt for the Bite of a Mad Dog ibid.
Cæfar's Cure for the Bite of a Rattle-Snake ibid.
An approved Remedy againft fpitting of Blood ibid.
A Receipt that cured a Gentleman, who had a long Time fpit Blood in a great Quantity, and was wafted with a Confumption 312
A fpecific Cure for ftopping Blood ibid.
For a violent Bleeding at the Nofe ibid.
To ftop Bleeding at the Nofe, or elfewhere 313
To ftop Bleeding inwardly ibid.
To ftop Bleeding in the Stomach ibid.
To ftop Bleeding ibid.
For fpitting Blood ibid.
To ftop Bleeding at Mouth, Nofe, or Ears ibid.
Another to ftop Bleeding ibid.
Lucatellus's Balfam 314
To make Lucatellus's Balfam to take inwardly ibid.

To take off Blackness by a Fall ibid.
To break a Bile ibid.
A bitter Draught ibid.
Another 315
To cure Blindnefs, when the Caufe proceeds from within the Eye ibid.
To raife a Blifter ibid.
Excellent for a Burn or Scald ibid.
For a Burn ibid.
Another Remedy 316
For a Cold, Dr. Radcliffe's Receipt ibid.
A Method to cure a Cold ibid.
For a Cold 317
For a Hoarfenefs with a Cold ibid.
An excellent Recipe to cure a Cold ibid.
An Ointment for a Cold on the Stomach ibid.
A Syrup for a Cough, or Afthma ibid.
To make Syrup of Balfam for a Cough 318
A Syrup for a Cough ibid.
Another ibid.
For a Cough ibid.
Another ibid.
Another Remedy for the fame 319
For an inveterate Cough ibid.
For a Cough fettled on the Stomach ibid.
The Tar-pills for a Cough ibid.
For a Chin-cough ibid.
For the fame ibid.
A Receipt for a Confumptive Cough ibid.
Excellent Lozenges for a Cough 320
An Electuary for a Cough ibid.
Another Remedy for a Cough ibid.

b 2 An

CONTENTS.

An excellent Remedy for Whooping Coughs 320
Water in a Consumption, or in Weakness after Sickness 321
An infallible Cure for the galloping Consumption ibid.
For the Cramp 322
Another Method ibid.
For Costiveness ibid.
For a Canker in the Mouth ibid.
An approved Remedy for a Cancer in the Breast ibid.
To keep a Cancer in the Breast from increasing ibid.
To cure a Cancer 323
A Medicine for the Cholic ibid.
Two other Remedies ibid.
Two other Remedies 324
A present Help for the Cholic ibid.
A Plaister for the Cholic ibid.
For Corns on the Feet ibid.
For Chilblains ibid.
To procure a good Colour ibid.
A Cere-cloth 325
To make Conserve of Hips ibid.
To cure a Dropsy ibid.
Another Method 326
A certain Cure for the Dropsy, if taken at the Beginning of the Distemper ibid.
Another Remedy for the same ibid.
An excellent Medicine for the Dropsy ibid.
Three other Medicines 327
For the Dropsy and Scurvy ibid.
An experienced Eye Water to strengthen the Sight, and prevent Cataracts 328
To draw a Rheum from the Eyes ibid.
To clear the Eyes ibid.
For a Pin or Web in the Eye ibid.
A Water for sore or weak Eyes ibid.
For Dimness of Sight and sore Eyes ibid.
A Powder that has restored Sight when almost lost 329
An Electuary for a Pain in the Stomach ibid.
An Electuary for a cold or windy Stomach ibid.
To make Stoughton's Elixir ibid.
To make Daffey's Elixir ibid.
To make the true Daffey's Elixir 330
To cure the Joint Evil ibid.
For a Drought in a Fever ibid.
Another for the same 331
To cure an intermitting Ague and Fever, without returning 330
An excellent Medicine for the spotted, and all other malignant Fevers ibid.
A very good Drink to to be used in all Sorts of Fevers 331
A Remedy for an inward Fever sometimes attending such as are poisoned ibid.
Symptoms attending such as are poisoned ibid.
A Drink for a Fever 332
For the Dysentery or bloody Flux ibid.
For the Bloody Flux ibid.
For a Flux ibid.
To prevent Fits in Children ibid.
Three other Methods 333
For Fits from Wind or Cold ibid.
A Powder for Convulsion Fits ibid.
To cure a pimpled Face ibid.
To cure a pimpled Face, and sweeten the Blood 334
For a Swelling in the Face ibid.
To take off Freckles ibid.
For the Gripes ibid.
A Receipt for the Gravel ibid.
For the Gout in the Stomach, Dr. Lower's constant Remedy ibid.
For the Gout ibid.
Another for the same 335
For Pains of the Gout ibid.
For the Hemorrhoids inflamed ibid.
For the Piles, a present Remedy ibid.
For the Piles ibid.
For an inveterate Head-ach ibid.
For the Hiccup ibid.
For the Jaundice 336
Three other Remedies ibid.
For the Yellow Jaundice ibid.
To cure the Yellow or Black Jaundice ibid.
To cure the Itch without Sulphur 337

Another

CONTENTS.

Another Cure for the Itch	337
To stay a Looseness	ibid.
For a Looseness	ibid.
For an inveterate Looseness	ibid.
Two other Remedies	ibid.
For Stuffing in the Lungs	338
To make Brimstone Lozenges for a short Breath	ibid.
To make Lozenges for the Heart-burn	ibid.
To make Cashew Lozenges	ibid.
For a sore Mouth in Children	ibid.
To increase Milk in Nurses	339
To take away Morphew	ibid.
The Bruise Ointment	ibid.
An Ointment for a scald Head	ibid.
An Ointment to cause Hair to grow	ibid.
An extraordinary Ointment for Burns or Scalds	ibid.
An Ointment for a Burn or Scald	340
An Ointment for a Blast	ibid.
A rare green Oil for Aches and Bruises	ibid.
For Obstructions	ibid.
A Plaister for a Weakness in the Back	341
A Drink for the same	ibid.
The Stomach Plaister	ibid.
The Leaden Plaister	ibid.
A Plaister for the Sciatica	ibid.
A Plaister for the Feet in a Fever	342
A Plaister for an Ague	ibid.
An excellent Plaister for any Pain occasioned by a Cold or Bruise	ibid.
A Poultice for a sore Breast, before it is broken	ibid.
A Poultice for a sore Breast, Leg, or Arm	ibid.
A Poultice to ripen Tumours	ibid.
A Poultice for a hard Swelling	343
To make Gascoign's Powder	ibid.
To make Pomatum	ibid.
For the Piles	ibid.
Another	ibid.
Pills to purge the Head	ibid.
A fine Purge	344
A purging Diet drink in the Spring	ibid.
For a Purge	ibid.
A good Purge	ibid.
A Purge for Hoarseness, or any Illness, on the Lungs	ibid.
A Purging Diet drink	ibid.
An excellent Medicine for a Pain in the Stomach	345
For a Pain in the Stomach	ibid.
To prevent After-Pains	ibid.
For a Pleurisy	ibid.
For a Pleurisy, if the Person cannot be blooded	ibid.
A Remedy for Pimples	ibid.
Another to take away Pimples	346
For Weakness in the Hands after a Palsey	ibid.
Receipt against the Plague	ibid.
A Remedy for rheumatic Pains	ibid.
For a Rheumatism	ibid.
Another Remedy for the same	347
To cure the Dropsy, Rheumatism, Scurvy, and Cough on the Lungs	ibid.
For the Rheumatism	ibid.
To make the right Angel-Salve	348
To make Lip-Salve	ibid.
A green Salve	ibid.
For a sore Breast, when it is broken	ibid.
The Black Salve	349
A Salve for a Burn or Scald	ibid.
A Salve for a Blast, Burn, or Scald	ibid.
A Salve for a Cere cloth for Bruises or Aches	ibid.
A Salve for a Sprain	350
A Salve for the King's Evil	ibid.
To make the Eye-Salve	ibid.
Sir Hans Sloane's Ointment for the Eyes	351
To make Spirit of Saffron	ibid.
To cure the Spleen or Vapours	ibid.
To make a Quilt for the Stomach	ibid.
To disperse Tumours	352
To cure a Place that is scalded	ibid.
For a Scald Head	ibid.
For the Falling Sickness	ibid.

To

CONTENTS.

To cure Spitting of Blood, if a Vein is broken 352
To take out the Redness and Scurf after the Small-Pox ibid.
To take out the Spots of the Small-Pox 353
For the Strangury ibid.
For the Scurvy ibid.
For the Scurvy or Dropsy ibid.
A Water for the Scurvy in the Gums ibid.
An excellent Medicine for Shortness of Breath ibid.
Another 354
To make Syrup of Garlic ibid.
To make Syrup of Marshmallows ibid.
To make Syrup of Saffron ibid.
To give Ease in a violent Fit of the Stone ibid.
An approved Medicine for the Stone 355
To give Ease in Fits of the Stone, &c. ibid.
How to make the Lime-Drink, famous for curing the Stone ibid.
A Receipt for the Cure of the Stone and Gravel, whether in the Kidneys, Ureters, or Bladder 356
A Wash for the Teeth, &c. ibid.
To preserve and whiten the Teeth 357
A good Remedy for a hollow aching Tooth ibid.
To cure the Tooth-ache ibid.
Another Method ibid.
For the Teeth ibid.
Pills to purge off a Rheum in the Teeth ibid.
A Powder for the Teeth 358
An admirable Powder for the Teeth ibid.
To make the Teeth white ibid.
An admirable Tincture for green Wounds ibid.
For the Trembling at the Heart 359
To kill a Tetter ibid.
For a Quinsey or Swelling in the Throat, so that the Patient cannot swallow ibid.
For a sore Throat ibid.
For a Thrush in Childrens Mouths ibid.
A Vomit ibid.
A good Vomit 360
Another Vomit ibid.
To stop Vomiting ibid.
Two other Remedies ibid.
To provoke Urine presently when stopped ibid.
To draw up the Uvula ibid.
A calcined Water to dry up Ulcers, and old Sores 361
For a Weakness in the Back or Reins ibid.
A rare Mouth Water ibid.
For the Worms ibid.
A Plaister for Worms in Children ibid.
A Clyster for the Worms 262
To know if a Child has Worms or not ibid.
Excellent Remedy for Worms in Children ibid.
Another Remedy ibid.
An excellent Prescription for the Cure of Worms ibid.
The Negro Cæsar's Cure for Poison 366
For Drink, during the Cure ibid.

CHAP. II. BROTHS, &c. for the SICK.

To make Broth of a Calf's-Head 366
To make Broth of a Knuckle or Scrag of Veal ibid.
To make strengthening Drink for very weak Persons 367
To make Chicken Broth ibid.
To boil a Chicken ibid.
To make Mutton Broth ibid.
To make Beef or Mutton Broth for very weak People, who take but little Nourishment ibid.
To make Beef Drink, which is ordered for weak People 368
A restorative Jelly for any one inclining to a Consumption ibid.
To make the Pectoral Drink ibid.
To make artifical Asses Milk ibid.
Another

CONTENTS.

Another Method	368	To make Panada	ibid.
To make Bread Jelly	369	To make Barley Water	ibid.
To boil Sago	ibid.	To make Water Gruel	ibid.
To make Sago Gruel	ibid.	To make Chicken Water	371
To make Sago with Milk	ibid.	To make Seed Water	ibid.
To make Barley Gruel	ibid.	To make white Caudle	ibid.
To mull Wine	370	To make brown Caudle	ibid.
To mull Ale	ibid.	To make Beef Tea	ibid.

PART XI.

DIRECTIONS for BREEDING all SORTS of POULTRY. 372

PART XII.

Of BREWING in General. 375

SUPPLEMENT.

Containing Directions for washing GAUZES, MUSLINS, LACES, &c. &c.

To wash Gauzes, Book-muslin, and Blond-lace	383	To keep English China clean	ibid.
		To make yellow Varnish	ibid.
To wash Cambricks, Muslins, and common Laces	385	To make white Varnish	390
		To boil Plate	ibid.
How to make Starch for starching small Linen	386	To clean and soften the Hands	ibid.
		The Italian Wash for the Neck	ibid.
An excellent Way of Washing, to save Soap, and whiten Cloaths	ibid.	A Water to wash the Face	391
To take Mildew out of Linen	ibid.	To whiten and clean the Hands	ibid.
To take Spots or Stains out of thin Silks, &c.	387	A Water to cure red or pimpled Faces	ibid.
To refresh Hangings, Tapestry, or Chairs	ibid.	A good Thing to wash the Face in	ibid.
To wash Gloves	ibid.	To make a sweet Bag for Linen	392
To take Spots out of white Silk, green or crimson Velvet	ibid.	To make the burning Perfume	ibid.
To take Spots of Ink or Wine out of Cloth	388	To make Paste for the Hands	ibid.
To take Pitch or Tar off Cloth	ibid.	The best Thing to wash Hands with instead of Washball, Soap, Almond-powder, or an Thing that can be invented for that Purpose	ibid.
To take a Spot of Oil out of Cloth	ibid.		
A Soap to take out all Spots from Cloth	ibid.		
To take out Grease and oily Spots	389	An excellent Liquid Blacking	393.
		To make Ink	ibid.
To wash Scarlet Cloaks, &c.	ibid.	A Receipt for destroying Bugs	ibid.
To wash black Silks	ibid.		

To

CONTENTS.

To cure Bugs 394
To kill Rats ibid.
To prevent Weefels, and other Vermin from deftroying Poultry ibid.
What Things are to be kept in the Houfe by fmall Families for Kitchen Ufe 395
To cure a mufty Pipe, Hogfhead, or any other Veffel of Wine ibid.
To make Pomatum ibid.
To make excellent Tinder ibid.
To boil up Plate to look like new 396
To make any Linen on the firft Appearance look like Diaper ibid.
A good Way to cement broken Glafs or China Ware ibid.
To raife a Sallad in two Hours at the Fire ibid.
A Marketing Table by the Pound 397
A Marketing Table by the Stone 398
A Table to caft up Expences, or Wages 399
Another 400

THE

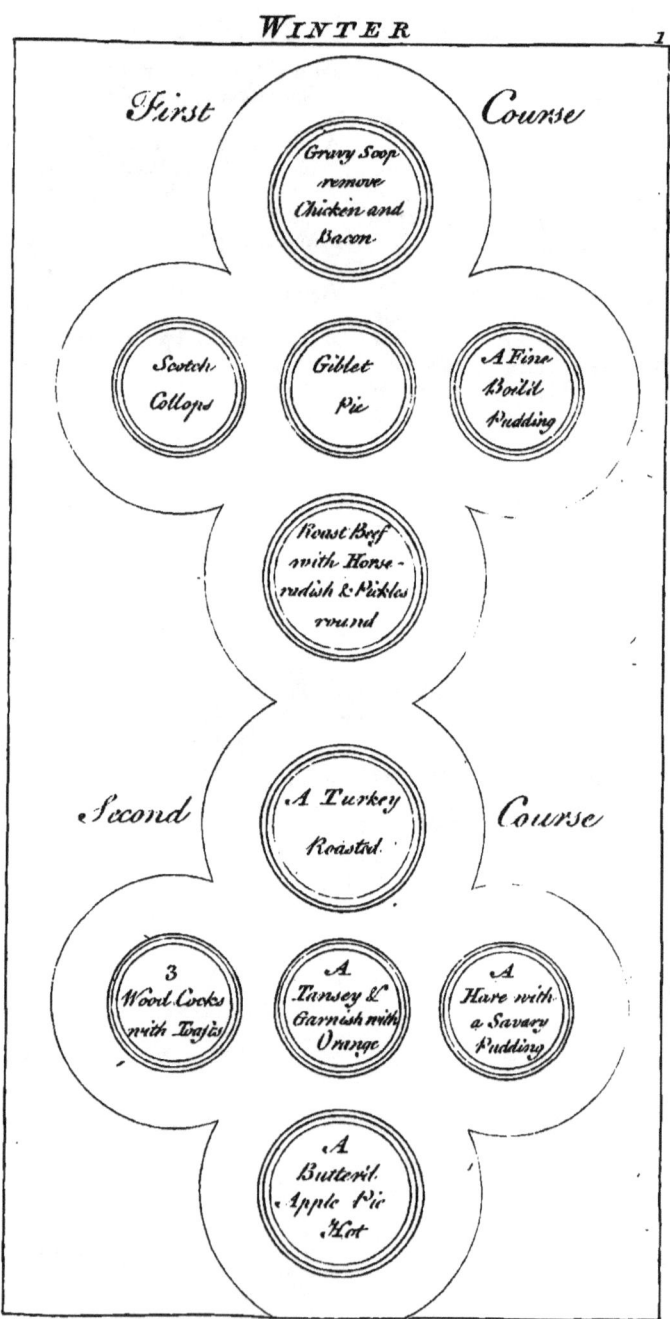

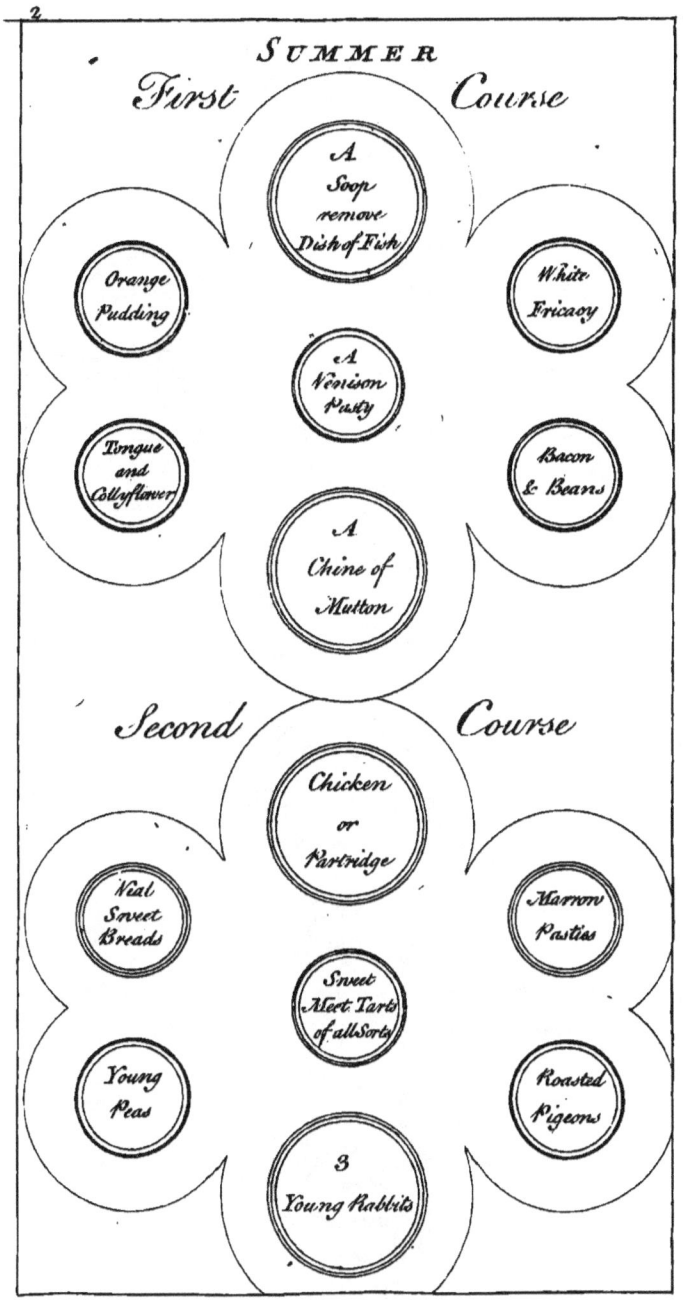

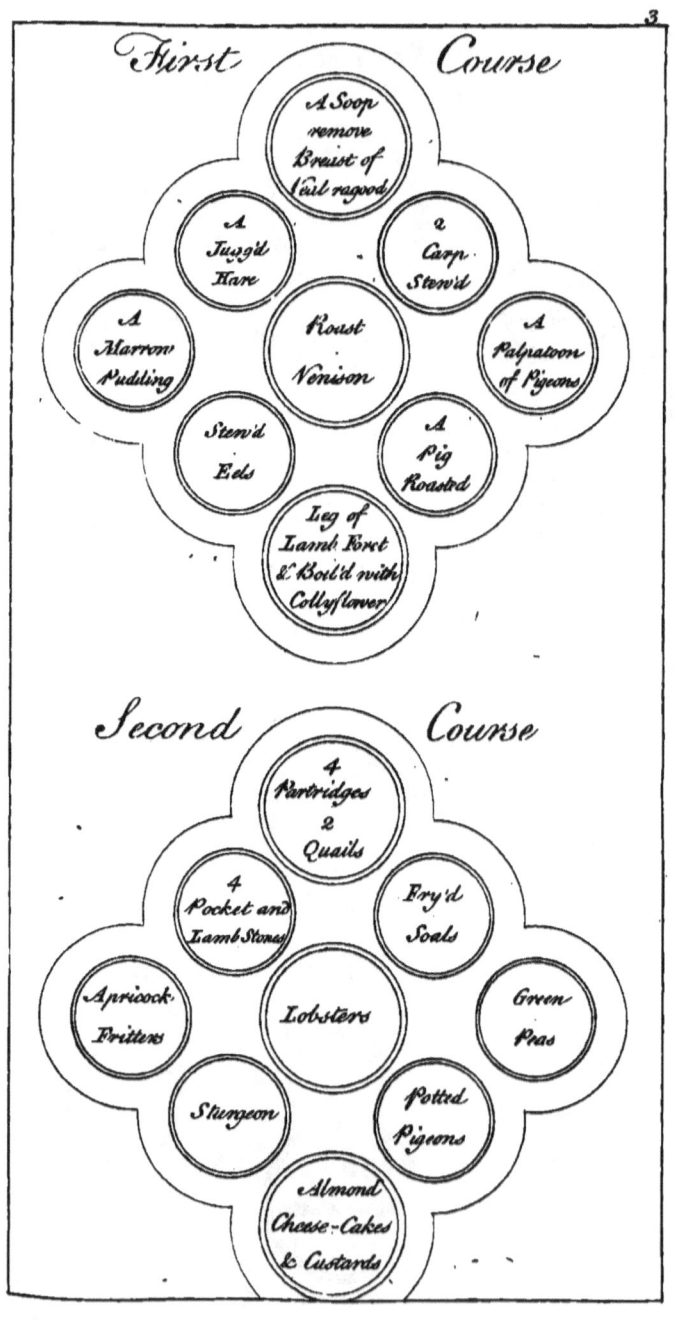

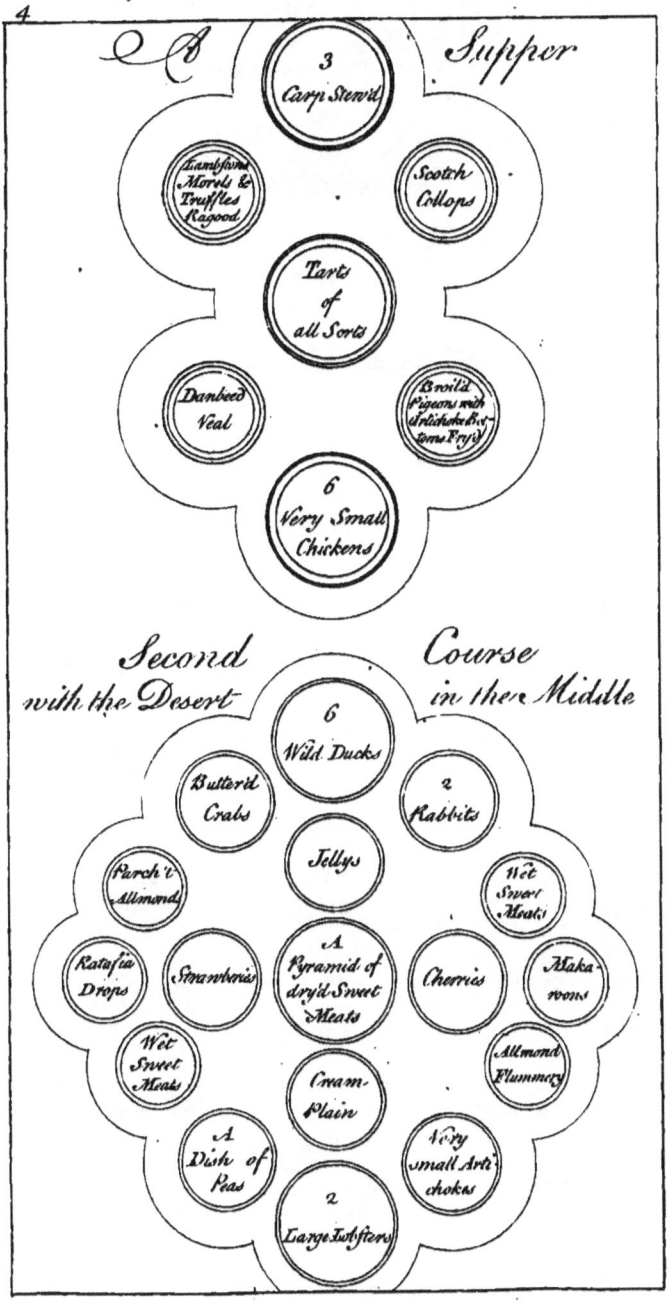

THE

Complete Housewife.

PART I.

DIRECTIONS *for* MARKETING.

CHAP. I.
OF BUTCHER's MEAT, &c.

To choose Beef.

IF it be true ox-beef, it will have an open grain, and the fat, if young, of a crumbling, or oily smoothness, except it be the brisket and neck pieces, with such others as are very fibrous. The colour of the lean should be of a pleasant carnation red, the fat rather inclining to white than yellow, (which seldom proves good) and the suet of a curious white colour.

Cow-beef is of a closer grain, the fat whiter, the bones less, and the lean of a paler colour. If it be young and tender, the dent you make with your finger by pressing it, will, in a little time, rise again.

Bull-beef is of a more dusky red, a closer grain, and firmer than either of the former; harder to be indented with your finger, and rising again sooner. The fat is very gross and fibrous, and of a strong rank scent. If it be old it will be so very tough, that if you pinch it you will scarce make any impression

pression in it. If it be fresh, it will be of a lively fresh colour; but if stale, of a dark dusky colour, and very clammy. If it be bruised, the part affected will look of a more dusky or blackish colour than the rest.

To choose Mutton and Lamb.

TAKE some of the flesh between your fingers and pinch it; if it feels tender, and soon returns to its former place, it is young; but if it wrinkles, and remains so, it is old. The fat will also, easily separate from the lean, if it be young; but if old it will adhere more firmly, and be very clammy and fibrous. If it be ram mutton, the fat will be spongy, the grain close, the lean rough, and of a deep red, and when dented by your finger will not rise again. If the sheep had the rot, the flesh will be palish, the fat a faint white, inclining to yellow; the meat will be loose at the bone, and, if you squeeze it hard, some drops of water, resembling a dew or sweat, will appear on the surface. [If it be a fore-quarter, observe the vein in the neck, for if it look ruddy, or of an azure colour, it is fresh; but if yellowish, it is near tainting, and if green, it is already so. As for the hind-quarter, smell under the kidney, and feel whether the knuckle be stiff or limber; for if you find a faint or ill scent in the former, or an unusual limberness in the latter, it is stale.] The sentences included in crotchets, will likewise be the marks for choosing lamb; and for choosing a lamb's head, mind the eyes, if they be sunk or wrinkled, it is stale; if plump and lively, it is new and sweet.

To choose Veal.

OBSERVE the vein in the shoulder; for if it be of a bright red, or looks blue, it is newly killed; but if greenish, yellowish, or blackish, or be more clammy, soft, and limber than usual, it is stale. Also, if it has any green spots about it, it is either tainting or already tainted. If it be wrapped in wet cloths, it is apt to be musty; therefore always observe to smell to it. The loin taints first under the kidney, and the flesh, when stale, will be soft and slimy. The neck and breast are first tainted at the upper end, and when so, will have a dusky, yellowish, or greenish appearance, and the sweet-bread on the breast will be clammy. The leg, if newly killed, will be stiff in the joint; but if stale, limber, and the flesh clammy, intermixed with green or yellowish specks. The flesh of a bull-calf is firmer grained and redder than that of a cow-calf, and the fat more curdled. In choosing the head, observe the same directions as above given for that of the lamb.

To choose Pork.

PINCH the lean between your fingers; if it breaks, and feels soft and oily, or if you can easily nip the skin with your nails, or if the fat be soft and oily, it is young; but if the lean be rough, the fat very spongy, and the skin stubborn, it is old. If it be a boar, or a hog gelded at full growth, the flesh will feel harder and rougher than usual, the skin thicker, the fat hard and fibrous, the lean of a dusky red, and of a rank scent. To know if it be fresh or stale, try the legs and hands at the bone, which comes out in the middle of the fleshy part, by putting in your finger; for as it first taints in those places, you may easily discover it by smelling to your finger; also the skin will be clammy and sweaty when stale, but smooth and cool when fresh.

To choose Brawn.

THE best method of knowing whether brawn be young or old, is by the extraordinary or moderate thickness of the rind, and the hardness and softness of it; for the thick and hard is old, but the moderate and soft is young. If the rind and fat be remarkably tender, it is not boar brawn, but barrow or sow.

To choose dried Hams and Bacon.

TAKE a sharp-pointed knife, run it into the middle of the ham on the inside under the bone, draw it out quickly and smell to it; if its flavour be fine and relishing, and the knife little daubed, the ham is sweet and good; but if, on the contrary, the knife be greatly daubed, has a rank smell, and a hogoo issues from the vent, it is tainted. Or you may cut off a piece at one end to look on the meat, if it appear white and be well scented, it is good; but if yellowish, or of a rusty colour, not well scented, it is either tainted or rusty, or at least will soon be so. A gammon of bacon may be tried in the same manner, and be sure to observe that the flesh sticks close to the bones, and the fat and lean to each other; for if it does not, the hog was not sound. Take care also that the extreme part of the fat near the rind be white, for if that be of a darkish or dirty colour, and the lean pale and soft, with some streaks of yellow, it is rusty, or will soon be so.

To choose Venison.

TRY the haunches, shoulders, and fleshy parts of the sides with your knife, in the same manner as before directed for ham, and in proportion to the sweet or rank smell it is new or stale.

stale. With relation to the other parts, obferve the colour of the meat; for if it be ftale or tainted, it will be of a black colour intermixed with yellowifh or greenifh fpecks. If it be old, the flefh will be tough and hard, the fat contracted, the hoofs large and broad, and the heel horny and much worn.

CHAP. II.

Of POULTRY.

To know if a Capon be a true one or not, or whether it be young or old, new or ftale.

IF a capon be young, his fpurs will be fhort and blunt, and his legs fmooth: if a true capon, it will have a fat vein on the fide of the breaft, a thick belly and rump, and its comb will be fhort and pale. If it be new, it will have a clofe hard vent; but if ftale, an open loofe vent.

To choofe a Cock or Hen Turkey, Turkey Poults, &c.

IF the fpurs of a turkey cock are fhort, and his legs black and fmooth, he is young; but if his fpurs be long, and his legs pale and rough, he is old. If long killed, his eyes will be funk into his head, and his feet feel very dry; but if frefh, his feet will be limber, and his eyes lively. For the hen, obferve the fame figns. If fhe be with egg, fhe will have an open vent; but if not, a clofe hard vent. The fame figns will ferve to difcover the newnefs or ftalenefs of turkey poults; and, with refpect to their age, you cannot be deceived.

To choofe a Cock, Hen, &c.

IF a cock be young, his fpurs will be fhort and dubbed; (but be fure to obferve that they are not pared or fcraped to deceive you) but if fharp and ftanding out, he is old. If his vent be hard and clofe, it is a fign of his being newly killed; but if he be ftale, his vent will be open. The fame figns will difcover whether a hen be new or ftale; and if old, her legs and comb will be rough; but if young, fmooth.

To know if Chickens are new or ftale.

IF they are pulled dry, they will be ftiff when new; but when ftale, they will be limber, and their vents green. If they are fcalded, or pulled wet, rub the breaft with your thumb or finger, and if they are rough and ftiff they are new; but if fmooth and flippery, ftale.

To choose a Goose, Wild-Goose, and Bran-Goose.

IF the bill and foot be red, and the body full of hairs, she is old; but if the bill be yellowish, and the body has but few hairs, she is young. If new, her feet will be limber, but if stale, dry. Understand the same of a wild-goose, and bran-goose.

To choose wild and tame Ducks.

THESE fowls are hard and thick on the belly, when fat, but thin and lean, when poor; limber-footed when new; but dry-footed when stale. A wild duck may be distinguished from a tame one, by its foot being smaller and reddish.

To choose the Bustard.

OBSERVE the same rules in choosing this curious fowl, as those already given for the turkey.

To choose the Shuffler, Godwitz, Marle Knots, Gulls, Dotters, and Wheat-Ears.

THESE birds, when new, are limber-footed; when stale, dry-footed: when fat, they have a fat rump; when lean, a close and hard one; when young, their legs are smooth; when old, rough.

To choose the Pheasant Cock and Hen.

THE spurs of the pheasant cock, when young, are short and dubbed; but long and sharp when old; when new, he has a firm vent, when stale an open and flabby one. The pheasant hen, when young, has smooth legs, and her flesh is of a fine and curious grain; but when old her legs are rough, and her flesh hairy when pulled. If she be with egg, her vent will be open, if not close. The same signs, as to newness or staleness, are to be observed as were before given for the cock.

To choose Heath and Pheasant Poults.

THE feet of these, when new, are limber, and their vents white and stiff; but when stale, are dry-footed, their vents green, and if you touch it hard, will peel

To choose the Heath Cock and Hen.

THE newness or staleness of these are known by the same signs as the foregoing; but when young their legs and bills are smooth; when old both are rough

To choose the Woodcock and Snipe.

THESE fowls are limber-footed when new; but stale, dry-footed: if fat, thick and hard; but if their noses are snotty, and their throats moorish and muddy, they are bad. A snipe, particularly, if fat, has a fat vent in the side under the wing, and in the vent feels thick.

To choose the Partridge Cock or Hen.

THESE fowls, when young, have black bills, and yellowish legs; when old, white bills and blueish legs; when new, a fast vent; when stale, a green and open one, which will peel with a touch: if they had fed lately on green wheat, and their crops be full, smell to their mouths, lest their crops be tainted.

To choose Doves or Pigeons, Plovers, &c.

THE turtle-dove is distinguished by a blueish ring round its neck, the other parts being almost white. The stock-dove exceeds both the wood-pigeon and ring-dove in bigness. The dove-house pigeons are red-leged when old: if new and fat, limber-footed, and feel full in the vent; but when stale, their vents are green and flabby.

After the same manner you may choose the gray and green plover, fieldfare, thrush, mavis, lark, blackbird, &c.

To choose Teal and Widgeon.

THESE, when new, are limber-footed; when stale, dry-footed; thick and hard on the belly, if fat; but thin and soft, if lean.

To choose a Hare.

IF the claws of a hare are blunt and rugged, and the clift in her lip spread much, she is old; but the opposite if young: if new and fresh killed, the flesh will be white and stiff; if stale, limber and blackish in many places. If the hare be young, the ears will tear like a sheet of brown paper; if old, they are dry and tough.

To choose a Leveret.

THE newness or staleness may be known by the same signs as the hare; but in order to discover if it be a real leveret, feel near the foot on its fore leg, if you find there a knob or small bone, it is a true leveret; but if not a hare.

To choose a Rabbet.

IF a rabbet be old, the claws will be very long and rough, and gray hairs intermixed with the wool; but if young, the claws and wool smooth; if stale, it will be limber, and the flesh will look blueish, having a kind of slime upon it; but if fresh, it will be stiff, and the flesh white and dry.

CHAP. III.
Of FISH.

To choose Salmon, Trout, Carp, Tench, Pike, Graylings, Barbel, Chub, Whiting, Smelt, Ruff, Eel, Shad, &c.

THE newness or staleness of these fish are known by the colour of their gills, their being hard or easy to be opened, the standing out or sinking of their eyes, their fins being stiff or limber, and by smelling to their gills. Eels taken in running water are better than those taken in ponds; of these the silver ones are most esteemed.

To choose the Turbot.

IF this fish be plump and thick, and its belly of a cream colour, it is good; but if thin, and of a blueish white on the belly, not so.

To choose Soals.

IF these are thick and stiff, and of a cream colour on the belly, they will spend well; but if thin, limber, and their bellies of a blueish white, they will eat very loose.

To choose Plaise and Flounders.

WHEN these fish are new they are stiff, and the eyes look lively, and stand out; but when stale, the contrary. The best plaise are blueish on the belly; but flounders of a cream colour.

To choose Cod and Codling.

CHOOSE those which are thick towards the head, and their flesh, when cut, very white.

To choose fresh Herrings and Mackerel.

IF these are new, their gills will be of a lively shining redness, their eyes sharp and full, and the fish stiff; but if stale, their gills will look dusky and faded, their eyes dull and sunk down, and their tails limber.

To choose pickled Salmon.

THE scales of this fish, when new and good, are stiff and shining, the flesh oily to the touch, and parts in fleaks without crumbling; but the opposite when bad.

To choose pickled and red Herrings.

TAKE the former and open the back to the bone, if it be white, or of a bright red, and the flesh white, oily, and fleaky, they are good. If the latter smell well, be of a good gloss, and part well from the bone, they are also good.

To choose dried Ling.

THE best sort of dried ling is that which is thickest in the pole, and the flesh of the brightest yellow.

To choose pickled Sturgeon.

THE veins and gristle of the fish, when good, are of a blue colour, the flesh white, the skin limber, the fat underneath of a pleasant scent, and you may cut it without its crumbling.

To choose Lobsters.

IF a lobster be new, it has a pleasant scent at that part of tail which joins to the body, and the tail will, when opened, fall smart like a spring; but when stale it has a rank scent, and the tail limber and flagging. If it be spent, a white scurf will issue from the mouth and roots of the small legs. If it be full, the tail about the middle will be full of hard reddish skin'd meat, which you may discover by thrusting a knife between the joints, on the bend of the tail. The heaviest are best if there be no water in them. The cock is generally smaller than the hen, of a deeper red when boiled, has no spawn or feed under its tail, and the uppermost fins within its tail, are stiff and hard.

To choose Crab-fish, great and small.

WHEN they are stale, their shells will be of a dusky red colour, the joints of their claws limber; they are loose and may be turned any way with the finger, and from under their throat will issue an ill smell; but if otherwise, they are good.

To choose Prawns and Shrimps.

IF they are hard and stiff, of a pleasant scent, and their tails turn strongly inward, they are new; but if they are limber, their colour faded, of a faint smell, and feel slimy, they are stale.

The seasons for eating all the above-mentioned articles may be seen in the foregoing bill of fare, for every month in the year.

CHAP. IV.
Of BUTTER, EGGS, AND CHEESE.

To choose Butter and Eggs.

WHEN you buy butter, taste it yourself at a venture, and do not trust to the taste they give you, lest you be deceived by a well tasted and scented piece artfully placed in the lump. Salt butter is better scented than tasted, by putting a knife into it, and putting it immediately to your nose; but, if it be a cask, it may be purposely packed, therefore trust not to the top alone, but unhoop it to the middle, thrusting your knife between the staves of the cask, and then you cannot be deceived.

When you buy eggs, put the great end to your tongue; if it feels warm, it is new; but if cold it is stale; and according to the heat or coldness of it, the egg is newer or staler. Or take the egg, hold it up against the sun or a candle, if the white appears clear and fair, and the yolk round, it is good; but if muddy or cloudy, and the yolk broken, it is nought. Or take the egg and put it into a pan of cold water; the fresher it is, the sooner it will sink to the bottom; but if it be rotten, or addled, it will swim on the surface of the water. The best way to keep them is in bran or meal; though some place their small ends downwards in fine wood-ashes. But for longer keeping, burying them in salt will preserve them almost in any climate.

To choose Cheese.

WHEN you buy cheese, observe the coat; for if the cheese be old, and its coat be rough, rugged, or dry at top, it indicates mites, or little worms. If it be spongy, moist, or full of holes, it is subject to maggots. If you perceive on the outside any perished place, be sure to examine its deepness, for the greater part may be concealed.

PART II.

COOKERY.

CHAP. I.

GENERAL DIRECTIONS *for* BOILING.

ET your pot be very clean; and, as a scum will arise from every thing, be sure to shake a small handful of flour into it, which will take all the scum up, and prevent any from falling down to make the meat black. All salt meat must be put in when the water is cold; but fresh meat, not till it boils; and as many pounds as your piece weighs, so many quarters of an hour it will require in boiling.

To boil a Tongue.

IF it be a dry tongue, it must be laid in warm water for six hours, then change your water, and let it lay three hours more; the second water must be cold. Then take it out and boil it three hours, which will be sufficient. If your tongue be just out of pickle, it must lay three hours in cold water, and boil it till it will peel.

To boil a Ham.

LAY your ham in cold water for two hours, wash it clean, and tie it up in clean hay; put it into fresh water, boil it very slow for one hour, and then very briskly an hour and an half more. Take it up in the hay, and let it lie in it till cold, then rub the rind with a clean piece of flannel.

To boil a Neck of Mutton.

TAKE the best end of a neck of mutton, cut it into steaks, and beat them with a rolling-pin; then strew some salt on them, and lay them in a frying pan; hold the pan over a slow fire, that may not burn them; turn them as they heat, and there will be gravy enough to fry them in till they are half enough; then put to them broth made thus: take the scrag end of the mutton, break it in pieces, and put it in a pipkin with three pints of water, an onion, and some salt; when it first boils skim it very well, cover it, and let it boil an hour; then put to it half a pint of white wine, a spoonful of vinegar, a nutmeg quartered, a little pepper, a bunch of sweet-herbs; cover it again, and let it boil till it comes to a pint; then strain it through a hair-sieve, and put this liquor in the frying-pan, and let it fry together till it is enough; then put in a good piece of butter, shake it together, and serve it up. Garnish with pickles.

To boil a Haunch or Neck of Venison.

LAY it in salt for a week, then boil it in a cloth well floured; for every pound of venison allow a quarter of an hour for the boiling. For sauce you must boil some cauliflowers, pulled into little sprigs in milk and water, some fine white cabbage, some turnips, cut into dice, with some beetroot cut into long narrow pieces, about an inch and a half long, and half an inch thick: lay a sprig of cauliflower, and some of the turnips mashed with some cream and a little butter; let your cabbage be boiled, and then beat in a saucepan with a piece of butter and salt, lay that next the cauliflower, then the turnips, then cabbage, and so on, till the dish is full; place the beetroot here and there, just as you fancy; it looks very pretty, and is a fine dish. Have a little melted butter in a cup, if wanted.

Note, A leg of mutton cut venison fashion, and dressed the same way, is a pretty dish: or a fine neck, with the scrag cut off. This eats well boiled or hashed, with gravy and sweet sauce the next day.

To boil a Leg of Mutton like Venison.

TAKE a leg of mutton cut venison fashion, boil it in a cloth well floured; and have three or four cauliflowers boiled, pulled into sprigs, stewed in a saucepan with butter, and a little pepper and salt; then have some spinach picked and washed clean, put it into a saucepan with a little salt, covered close, and stewed a little while; then drain the liquor, and pour in a quarter of a pint of good gravy, a good piece of butter rolled

in

in flour, and a little pepper and falt; when ftewed enough lay the fpinach in the difh, the mutton in the middle, and the cauliflower over it, then pour the butter the cauliflower was ftewed in over it all: but you are to obferve in ftewing the cauliflower, to melt your butter nicely, as for fauce, before the cauliflower goes in. This is a genteel difh for a firft courfe at bottom.

To boil a Lamb's Head.

BOIL the head and pluck tender, but do not let the liver be too much done. Take the head up, hack it crofs and crofs with a knife, grate fome nutmeg over it, and lay it in a difh before a good fire; then grate fome crumbs of bread, fome fweet-herbs rubbed, a little lemon-peel chopped fine, a very little pepper and falt, and bafte it with a little butter: then throw a little flour over it, and juft before it is done do the fame, bafte it and dredge it. Take half the liver, the lights, the heart and tongue, chop them very fmall, with fix or eight fpoonfuls of gravy or water; firft fhake fome flour over the meat, and ftir it together, then put in the gravy or water, a good piece of butter rolled in a little flour, a little pepper and falt, and what runs from the head in the difh; fimmer all together a few minutes, and add half a fpoonful of vinegar, pour it into your difh, lay the head in the middle of the mince-meat, have ready the other half of the liver cut thin, with fome flices of bacon broiled, and lay round the head. Garnifh the difh with lemon, and fend it to table.

To boil a Calf's Head.

SCALD the hair off, and take out the bones, then have in readinefs palates boiled tender, yolks of hard eggs, oyfters fcalded and forced-meat; ftuff all this into your head, and few it up clofe in a cloth; boil it three hours; make a ftrong gravy for fauce, and garnifh with fried bacon.

To boil pickled Pork.

WASH your pork, and fcrap it clean; then put it in when the water is cold, and boil it till the rind be tender.

To boil Fowls and Cabbage.

TAKE a well fhaped cabbage, peel off fome of the outfide leaves, and cut a piece out of the top; then fcoop out the infide, and fill the hole with favoury forced-meat beat up with two eggs; let it be tied up as a pudding in a cloth, but firft put on the top of the cabbage. When the outfide is tender, lay it

between

between two boned fowls, and on them all some melted butter and slices of fried bacon.

To boil a Duck or a Rabbet with Onions.

BOIL your duck or rabbet in a good deal of water, and be sure to skim your water, for there will always rise a scum, which if it boils down, will discolour your fowls, &c. They will take about half an hour boiling; for sauce, your onions must be peeled, and throw them into water as you peel them, then cut them into thin slices, boil them in milk and water, and skim the liquor. Half an hour will boil them. Throw them into a clean sieve to drain, put them into a saucepan and chop them small; shake in a little flour, put to them two or three spoonfuls of cream, a good piece of butter; stew all together over the fire till they are thick and fine, lay the duck or rabbet in the dish, and pour the sauce all o'er; if a rabbet, you must cut off the head, cut it in two, and lay it on each side the dish.

Or you may make this sauce for change: take one large onion, cut it small, half a handful of parsley clean washed and picked, chop it small, a lettuce cut small, a quarter of a pint of good gravy, a good piece of butter rolled in a little flour; add a little juice of lemon, a little pepper and salt, let all stew together for half an hour, then add two spoonfuls of red wine. This sauce is most proper for a duck; lay your duck in the dish, and pour your sauce over it.

To boil Pheasants.

TAKE a fine pheasant, boil it in a good deal of water, keep your water boiling; half an hour will do a small one, and three quarters of an hour a large one. Let your sauce be celery stewed and thickned with cream, and a little piece of butter rolled in flour; take up the pheasant, and pour the sauce all over. Garnish with lemon. Observe to stew your celery so, that the liquor will not be all wasted away before you put your cream in; if it wants salt, put in some to your palate.

To boil Partridges.

BOIL them in a good deal of water, let them boil quick, and fifteen minutes will be sufficient. For sauce, take a quarter of a pint of cream, and a piece of fresh butter as big as a large walnut; stir it one way till it is melted, and pour it into the dish.

Or this sauce: take a bunch of celery clean washed, cut all the white very small, wash it again very clean, put it into a saucepan with a blade of mace, a little beaten pepper, and a very little salt; put to it a pint of water, let it boil till the water is just wasted away, than add a quarter of a pint of cream,

and

The COMPLETE HOUSEWIFE. 15

and a piece of butter rolled in flour; stir all together, and when it is thick and fine pour it over the birds.

Or this sauce: take the livers and bruise them fine, some parsley chopped fine, melt a little nice fresh butter, and then add the livers and parsley to it, squeeze in a little lemon, just give it a boil, and pour over your birds.

Or this sauce: take a quarter of a pint of cream, the yolk of an egg beat fine, a little grated nutmeg, a little beaten mace, a piece of butter as big as a nutmeg, rolled in flour, and one spoonful of white wine; stir all together one way, when fine and thick pour it over the birds. You may add a few mushrooms.

Or this sauce: take a few mushrooms, fresh peeled, and wash them clean, put them in a saucepan with a little salt, put them over a quick fire, let them boil up, then put in a quarter of a pint of cream and a little nutmeg, shake them together with a very little piece of butter rolled in flour, give it two or three shakes over the fire, three or four minutes will do; then pour it over the birds.

Or this sauce: boil half a pound of rice very tender in beef gravy; season with pepper and salt, and pour over your birds. These sauces do for boiled fowls; a quart of gravy will be enough, and let it boil till it is quite thick.

To boil Snipes or Woodcocks.

BOIL them in good strong broth, or beef gravy made thus: take a pound of beef, cut it into little pieces, put it into two quarts of water, an onion, a bundle of sweet-herbs, a blade or two of mace, six cloves, and some whole pepper; cover it close, let it boil till about half wasted, then strain it off, put the gravy into a saucepan with salt enough to season it, take the snipes and gut them clean, (but take care of the guts) put them into the gravy and let them boil, cover them close, and ten minutes will boil them, if they keep boiling. In the mean time, chop the guts and liver small, take a little of the gravy the snipes are boiling in, and stew the guts in, with a blade of mace. Take some crumbs of bread, and have them ready fried in a little fresh butter crisp, of a fine light brown. You must take about as much bread as the inside of a stale roll, and rub them small into a clean cloth; when they are done, let them stand ready in a plate before the fire.

When your snipes are ready, take about half a pint of the liquor they are boiled in, and add to the guts two spoonfuls of red wine, and a piece of butter about as big as a walnut, rolled in a little flour; set them on the fire, shake your saucepan often (but do not stir it with a spoon) till the butter is all melted, then put in the crumbs, give your saucepan a shake, take up your birds, lay them in the dish, and pour this sauce over them. Garnish with lemon.

To boil a Pike.

CUT open the pike, gut it, and scour the outside and inside very well with salt, then wash it clean, and have in readiness the following pickle to boil it in; water, vinegar, mace, whole pepper, a bunch of sweet-herbs, and a small onion; there must be liquor enough to cover it; when the liquor boils put in the pike, and make it boil soon, (half an hour will boil a very large pike;) make y our sauce with white wine, a little of the liquor, two anchovies, some shrimps, lobster or crab; beat and mix with it grated nutmeg, and butter floured to thicken it; pour your sauce over the fish, garnish with horse-radish and sliced lemon.

To boil Mullet.

SCALE your fish, and wash them, saving their liver, or tripes, roes or spawn; boil them in water seasoned with salt, white wine vinegar, white wine, a bunch of sweet-herbs, a sliced lemon, one or two onions, some horse-radish; and when it boils up put in your fish; and for sauce, a pint of oysters with their liquor, a lobster bruised or minced, or shrimps, some white wine, two or three anchovies, some large mace, a quartered nutmeg, a whole onion; let these have a boil up, and thicken it with butter and the yolks of two or three eggs : serve it on sippets, and garnish with lemon.

To boil Sturgeon.

CLEAN your sturgeon, and prepare as much liquor as will just boil it. To two quarts of water a pint of vinegar, a stick of horse-radish, two or three bits of lemon-peel, some whole pepper, a bay-leaf, and a small handful of salt. Boil your fish in this, and serve it with the following sauce: melt a pound of butter, dissolve an anchovy in it, put in a blade or two of mace, bruise the body of a crab in the butter, a few shrimps or cray-fish, a little catchup, a little lemon-juice; give it a boil, drain your fish well and lay it in your dish. Garnish with fried oysters, sliced lemon, and scraped horse-radish; pour your sauce into boats or basons. So you may fry it, ragoo it, or bake it.

To boil a Turbot.

LAY it in a good deal of salt and water an hour or two, and if it is not quite sweet, shift your water five or six times; first put a good deal of salt in the mouth and belly.

In the mean time set on your fish-kettle, with clean water and salt, a little vinegar, and a piece of horse-radish. When the water

water boils, lay the turbot on a fish-plate, put it into the kettle, let it be well boiled, but take great care it is not too much done; when enough, take off the fish-kettle, set it before the fire, then carefully lift up the fish-plate, and set it across the kettle to drain in the mean time melt a good deal of fresh butter, bruise in either the body of one or two lobsters, and the meat cut small; then give it a boil, and pour it into basons. This is the best sauce; but you may make what you please. Lay the fish in the dish. Garnish with scraped horse-radish and lemon, and pour a few spoonfuls of sauce over it.

To dress a Turtle.

CUT his head off; cut it all around, and part the two shells, as you would a crab; leave some meat to the breast-shell, called the callapee; season that with some Cayan butter, pepper, spice, and force-meat balls between the flesh; and bake it with some meat in it, and baste it with some Madeira wine and butter. Take the deep shell called the callepash, take all the meat out of it, the guts, &c. open every gut, and clean it with a pen-knife, and cut them an inch long, and stew them four hours by themselves; cut the other meat in quarter of a pound pieces; take the fins and clean them as you would goose giblets, cut them in pieces like the other; stew the fins and meat together till they are tender, about an hour, and then strain them off, thickening your soup; put all your meat and guts into the soup as you would stewed giblets, season it with Cayan butter, spices, pepper and salt, eschalots, sweet-herbs, and Madeira wine, as you like it, and put it all into the deep shell, and send it to the oven and bake it. Then serve it up.

To dress a Turtle a hundred Weight.

CUT off the head, take care of the blood, and take off all the fins; lay them in salt and water, cut off the bottom shell, then cut off the meat that grows to it, which is the callepee, or fowl; take out the hearts, livers and lights, and put them by themselves; take out the bones, and the flesh out of the back shell, which is the callepash; cut the fleshy part into pieces, about two inches square, but leave the fat part, which looks green, and is called the monsieur; rub it first with salt, and wash it in several waters to make it come clean; then put in the pieces that you took out, with three bottles of Madeira wine, and four quarts of strong veal gravy, a lemon cut in slices, a bundle of sweet-herbs, a tea-spoonful of Cayan, six anchovies washed and picked clean, a quarter of an ounce of beaten mace, a tea-spoonful of mushroom powder, and half a pint of essence of ham, if you have it; lay over it a coarse paste,

paste, set it in the oven for three hours; when it comes out, take off the lid, and scum off the fat, and brown it with a salamander.—This is the bottom dish.

Then blanch the fins, cut them off at the first joint, fry the first pinions a fine brown, and put them into a tossing-pan with two quarts of strong brown gravy, a glass of red wine, and the blood of the turtle; a large spoonful of lemon pickle, the same of browning, two spoonfuls of mushroom catchup, Cayan and salt, an onion stuck with cloves, and a bunch of sweet-herbs; a little before it is enough put in an ounce of morels, the same of truffles, stew them gently over a slow fire for two hours; when they are tender, put them into another tossing-pan, thicken your gravy with flour and butter, and strain it upon them, give them a boil, and serve them up.—This is a corner dish.

Then take the thick or large part of the fins, blanch them in warm water, and put them in a tossing-pan, with three quarts of strong veal gravy, a pint of Madeira wine, half a tea-spoonful of Cayan, a little salt, half a lemon, a little beaten mace, a tea-spoonful of mushroom powder, and a bunch of sweet-herbs; let them stew till quite tender: they will take two hours at least; then take them up into another tossing-pan, strain your gravy, and make it pretty thick with flour and butter; then put in a few boiled forcemeat balls, which must be made of the vealy part of your turtle, left out for that purpose, one pint of fresh mushrooms, if you cannot get them, pickled ones will do, and eight artichoke bottoms boiled tender, and cut in quarters; shake them over the fire five or six minutes, then put in half a pint of thick cream, with the yolks of six eggs, beaten exceeding well; shake it over the fire again till it looks thick and white, but do not let it boil; dish up your fins with the balls, mushrooms, and artichoke-bottoms over and round them.—This is the top dish.

Then take the chicken part, and cut it like Scotch collops; fry them a light brown, then put in a quart of veal gravy, stew them gently a little more than half an hour, and put to it the yolks of four eggs boiled hard, a few morels, and a score of oysters; thicken your gravy, which must be neither white nor brown, but a pretty gravy colour; fry some oyster-patties and lay round it.—This is a corner dish to answer the small fins.

Then take the guts, (which are reckoned the best part of the turtle) rip them open, scrape and wash them exceeding well, rub them well with salt, wash them through many waters, and cut them in pieces two inches long; then scald the maw or paunch, take off the skin, scrape it well, cut it into pieces about half an inch broad and two inches long, put some of the filthy part of your turtle in it, set it over a slow charcoal fire, with two quarts of veal gravy, a pint of Madeira wine, a little mushroom catchup, a few shalots, a little Cayan, half a lemon,

and

and stew them gently four hours, till your gravy is almost consumed; then thicken it with flour, mixed with a little veal gravy, and put in half an ounce of morels, a few forcemeat balls, made as for the fins; dish it up, and brown it with a salamander, or in the oven.—This is a corner dish.

Then take the head, skin it and cut it in two pieces; put it into a stew-pot with all the bones, hearts, and lights, to a gallon of water, or veal broth, three or four blades of mace, one shalot, a slice of beef beaten to pieces, and a bunch of sweet-herbs, set them in a very hot oven, and let it stand an hour at least; when it comes out strain it into a tureen for the middle of the table.

Then take the hearts and lights, chop them very fine, put them in a stew-pan, with a pint of good gravy, thicken it and serve it up: lay the head in the middle, fry the liver, lay it round the head upon the lights, garnish with whole slices of lemon.—This is the fourth corner dish.

N. B. The first course should be of turtle only, when it is dressed in this manner; but when it is with other victuals, it should be in three different dishes. Observe to kill your turtle the night before you want it, or very early next morning, that you may have all your dishes going on at a time. Gravy for a turtle a hundred weight, will take two legs of veal, and two shanks of beef.

To dress a Turtle the West-Indian way.

TAKE the turtle out of water the night before you intend to dress it, and lay it on its back, in the morning cut its throat or the head off, and let it bleed well; then cut off the fins, scald, scale and trim them with the head, then raise the callepee (which is the belly or undershell) clean off, leaving to it as much meat as you conveniently can; then take from the back shell all the meat and intrails, except the monsieur, which is the fat, and looks green, that must be baked to and with the shell; wash all clean with salt and water, and cut it into pieces of a moderate size, taking from it the bones, and put them with the fins and head in a soup-pot, with a gallon of water, some salt, and two blades of mace. When it boils skim it clean, then put in a bunch of thyme, parsley, savoury, and young onions, and your veal part, except about one pound and a half, which must be made forcemeat of as for Scotch collops, adding a little Cayan pepper; when the veal has boiled in the soup about an hour, take it out and cut it in pieces, and put to the other part. The guts (which is reckoned the best part) must be split open, scraped and made clean, and cut in pieces about two inches long. The paunch or maw must be scalded and skinned, and cut as the other parts, the size you think proper; then put them with the guts and other parts, except the liver, with half a pound of good fresh butter, a few eschalots, a bunch of thyme, parsley, and a little savoury, seasoned with salt, white pepper, mace, three or four cloves beaten, a little Cayan pepper, and take care not to put too much; then let it stew about half an hour over a good charcoal fire, and put in a pint and a half of Madeira wine, and as much of the broth as will cover it, and let it stew till tender. It will take four or five hours doing. When almost enough, skim it, and thicken it with flour, mixt with some veal broth, about the thickness of a fricasey. Let your forcemeat balls be fried about the size of a walnut, and be stewed about half an hour with the rest; if any eggs, let them be boiled and cleaned as you do knots of pullets eggs; and if none, get twelve or fourteen yolks of hard eggs: then put the stew (which is the callepash) into the back shell with the eggs all over, and put it into the oven to brown, or do it with a salamander.

The callepee must be slashed in several places, and moderately seasoned, with pieces of butter, mixt with chopped thyme, parsley and young onions, with salt, white pepper and mace beaten, and a little Cayan pepper; put a piece on each slash, and then some over, and a dust of flour; then bake it in a tin or iron dripping-pan, in a brisk oven.

The back shell (which is called the callepash) must be seasoned as the callepee, and baked in a dripping-pan, set upright, with four brickbats, or any thing else. An hour and a half will bake it, which must be done before the stew is put in.

The fins, when boiled very tender, to be taken out of the soup, and put into a stew-pan, with some good veal gravy, not high coloured, a little Madeira wine, seasoned and thickened as the callepash, and served in a dish by itself.

The lights, heart and liver, may be done the same way, only a little higher seasoned; or the lights and heart may be stewed with the callepash, and taken out before you put it in the shell, with a little of the sauce, adding a little more seasoning, and dish it by itself.

The veal part may be made friandos, or Scotch collops of. The liver should never be stewed with the callepash, but always drest by itself, after any manner you like; except you separate the lights and heart from the callepash, and then always serve them together in one dish. Take care to strain the soup, and serve it in a turreen, or clean china bowl.

DISHES.
A Callepee,
Lights, &c.—Soop—Fins.
Callepash.

N. B. In the West-Indies they generally souse the fins, and eat them cold; omit the liver, and only send to table the callepee, callepash, and soup. This is for a turtle about sixty pounds weight.

To dress a mock Turtle.

TAKE a calf's-head, and scald off the hair as you would do off a pig; then clean it, cut off the horny part in thin slices, with as little of the lean as possible; put in a few chopped oysters, and the brains; have ready between a quart and three pints of strong mutton or veal gravy, with a quart of Madeira wine, a large tea-spoonful of Cayan butter, a large onion chopped very small; peel off an half of a large lemon shred as fine as possible, a little salt, the juice of four lemons, and some sweet-herbs cut small; stew all these together till the meat is very tender, which will be in about an hour and an half; and then have ready the back shell of a turtle, lined with a paste of flour and water, which you must first set in the oven to harden; then put in the ingredients, and set it into the oven to brown the top; and when that is done, suit your garnish at the top with the yolks of eggs boiled hard, and forcemeat balls.

N. B. This receipt is for a large head; if you cannot get the shell of a turtle, a china soup-dish will do as well; and if no oven is at hand, the setting may be omitted; and if no oysters are to be had, it is very good without.

It has been dressed with but a pint of wine, and the juice of two lemons.

When the horny part is boiled a little tender, then put in your white meat.

It will do without the oven, and take a fine knuckle of veal, cut off the skin, and cut some of the fine firm lean into small pieces, as you do the white meat of a turtle, and stew it with the other white meat above.

Take the firm hard fat which grows between the meat, and lay that into the sauce of spinach or sorrel, till half an hour before the above is ready; then take it out, and lay it on a sieve to drain; and put in juice to stew with the above. The remainder of the knuckle will help the gravy.

To dress a Brace of Carp.

FIRST knock the carp on the head, save all the blood you can, scale it, and then gut it; wash the carp in a pint of red wine, and the roes; have some water boiling, with a handful of salt, a little horse-radish, and a bundle of sweet-herbs; put in your carp, and boil it softly. When it is boiled, drain it well over the hot water; in the mean time strain the wine through a sieve, put it and the blood into a saucepan with a pint of good gravy, a little mace, twelve corns of black, and twelve of white pepper, six cloves, an anchovy, an onion, and a little bundle of sweet-herbs. Let them simmer very softly a quarter of an hour, then strain it, put it into the saucepan again, and add to two spoonfuls of catchup, and a quarter of a pound of butter rolled in a little flour, half a spoonful of mushroom-pickle, if you have it; if not, the same quantity of lemon-juice: stir it all together, and let it boil. Boil one half of the roes; the other half beat up with an egg, half a nutmeg grated, a little lemon peel cut fine, and a little salt. Beat all well together, and have ready some nice beef-dripping boiling in a stew-pan, into which drop your roe, and fry them in little cakes, about as big as a crown-piece, of a fine light brown, and some sippets cut three-corner-ways, and fried crisp; a few oysters, if you have them, dipped in a little batter and fried brown, and a handful of parsley fried green.

Lay the fish in the dish, the boiled roes on each side, the sippets standing round the carp; pour the sauce boiling hot over the fish; lay the fried roes and oysters, with parsley and scraped horse-radish and lemon between, all round the dish, the rest of the cakes and oysters lay in the dish, and send it to table hot. If you would have the sauce white, put in white wine, and good strong veal gravy, with the above ingredients.

As to dressing of pike, and all other fish, when you dress them with a pudding, you may add a little beef-suet cut very fine, and good gravy is the sauce. This is a better way than stewing them in the gravy.

CHAP. II.
To Dress GREENS, ROOTS, &c.

WHEN you have nicely picked and washed your greens, lay them in a colander to drain, for if any cold water hang to them they will be tough; then boil them alone in a saucepan, with a large quantity of water, for if any meat be boiled with them it will discolour them. But be sure not to put them in till the water boils.

To dress Spinach.

AFTER picking it very clean, wash it in several waters, put it into a saucepan with no more water than what hangs to it; when it boils up, pour the liquor from it, and put in a piece of butter and some salt; then boil it till the spinach falls to the bottom; take it up, press it very dry, and serve it up with melted butter.

To dress Carrots.

SCRAPE them very clean, and when the water boils, put them into your pot or saucepan; if they are young spring carrots, they will be boiled in half an hour, but if large, they will require an hour. Then take them out, slice them into a plate, and pour over them some melted butter.

To dress Cabbages.

CABBAGE, and all sorts of young sprouts, must be boiled in a great deal of water. When the stalks are tender, or fall to the bottom, they are enough; then take them off, before they lose their colour. Always throw salt in your water before you put your greens in. Young sprouts you send to table just as they are, but cabbage is best chopped and put into a saucepan with a good piece of butter, stirring it for about five or six minutes, till the butter is all melted, and then send it to table.

To dress Parsnips.

BOIL them in a large quantity of water, after they are cleanly scraped, and when they are enough, which may be known by their being soft, take them up, and separate from them all the sticky parts; then put them in a saucepan with some milk, a proper quantity of butter, and some salt; set them over the fire, stir them till they are thick, taking great care that they do not burn, and when the butter is melted send them to table.

To dress Potatoes.

PUT your potatoes into the saucepan with a proper quantity of water; and when they are enough, which may be known by their skins beginning to crack, drain all the water from them, and let them stand close covered up for two or three minutes; then peel them, place them in a plate, and pour over them a proper quantity of melted butter. Or after you have peeled them, lay them on a gridiron, and, when they are of a fine brown, send them to table. Or you may cut them into slices, fry them in butter, and season them with pepper and salt.

To dress Turneps.

THEY are best boiled in the pot: when they are enough put them into a pan with some butter and salt, and after you have mashed them send them to table. Or, after your turneps are pared, you may cut them into small pieces, and boil them in a saucepan with as much water as will just cover them; when they are enough, put them into a sieve to drain; then put them into a saucepan with a proper quantity of butter, and, after stirring them five or six minutes over the fire, send them to table.

To dress Broccoli.

AFTER you have separated the small branches from the large ones, and taken off the hard outside skin, throw them into water; then place your stew-pan, containing a sufficient quantity of water mixed with some salt, on the fire, and when your water boils put in your broccoli; when they are enough, which may be known by the stalks being tender, send them to table with melted butter in a cup.

To dress Asparagus.

LET all the stalks be carefully scraped till they look white, cut them of an equal length, and throw them into water; set your stew pan with a proper quantity of water, having some salt in it, on the fire, and when the water boils, put in your asparagus after being tied up in small bundles. When they are enough, which may be known by their being somewhat tender, take them up, for if they boil too long, they will lose both their colour and taste. Then cut a round off a small loaf, and having toasted it brown on both sides, dip it in the liquor of the asparagus, laying it in your dish. Melt some butter, and pour it on the toast, laying the asparagus on it round the dish, with the bottom part of the stalks outward. Put the remaining part of the butter in a bason, because pouring it over the asparagus makes them greasy: then send them to table.

To dress French Beans.

TAKE your beans, string them, cut them in two, and then across, or else into four, and then across, put them into water with some salt; set your saucepan full of water over the fire, cover them close, and when it boils put in your beans, with a little salt. They will be soon done, which you may know by their being tender; then take them up before they lose their fine green, and having put them in a plate, send them to table with butter in a cup.

To dress Artichokes.

AFTER you have twisted the heads from the stalks, put them into the saucepan with the water cold, placing their tops downwards,

downwards, by which means all the dust and sand contained between the leaves will boil out. When they have boiled about an hour and a half they will be enough; then take them up, and send them to table with melted butter in a bason.

To dress Cauliflowers.

CUT off all the green part from your flowers, and divide them into four parts, laying them in water for an hour. Put some milk and water into your saucepan, and set it over the fire, when it boils put in your cauliflowers, observing to skim your saucepan well. When they are enough, which you may know by the stalks being tender, take them up into a colander to drain. Take a quarter of a pound of butter, a spoonful of water, a little flour, and a little pepper and salt; put them into a stew-pan, place it on the fire, shaking it often till the butter is melted; then take half of the cauliflower, divide it into small pieces, and put them into the stew-pan, shaking it often for ten minutes; place the boiled round the sides of the plate, and the stewed in the middle; pour the butter you stewed it in over it, and send it to table.

CHAP. III.

RULES to be observed in ROASTING.

LET your fire be made in proportion to the piece you are to dress; that is, if it be a little or thin piece, make a little brisk fire, that it may be done quick and nice; but if a large joint, observe to lay a good fire to cake, and let it be always clear at the bottom.

When your meat is about half done, move it, and the dripping-pan, a little distance from the fire, which stir up and make it burn brisk; for the quicker your fire is, the sooner and better will your meat be done.

To roast Mutton and Lamb.

BEFORE you lay the mutton down, take care to have a clear quick fire; baste it often, and when it is almost done dredge it with a little flour. If it be a breast, skin it before you lay it down.

To roast a Breast of Mutton.

A BREAST of mutton dressed thus is very good: the forced-meat must be put under the skin at the end, and then the skin pinned down with thorns; before you dredge it, wash it over with a bunch of feathers dipt in eggs.

To roast a Shoulder of Mutton in Blood.

CUT the shoulder as you do venison, take off the skin, let it lie in the blood all night; then take as much powder of sweet-herbs as will lie on a six-pence, a little grated bread, some pepper, nutmeg and ginger, a little lemon-peel, the yolks of two eggs boiled hard, and about twenty oysters and salt; temper all together with some of the blood, and stuff the meat thick with it, and lay some of it about the mutton; then wrap the caul of the sheep round the shoulder; roast it, and baste it with blood till it is near roasted; then take off the caul, dredge it, and baste it with butter, and serve it to the table with venison-sauce in a bason. If you do not cut it venison-fashion, yet take off the skin, because it eats tough; let the caul be spread while it is warm, or it will not do well; and next day when you are to use it, wrap it up in a cloth that has been dipped in hot water: for sauce, take some of the bones of the breast, chop them, and put to them a whole onion, a bay-leaf, a piece of lemon-peel, two or three anchovies, with spice that please; stew these, then add some red wine, oysters and mushrooms.

A Shoulder of Mutton in Epigram.

ROAST it almost enough, then very carefully take off the skin about the thickness of a crown-piece, and the shank-bone with it at the end; then season that skin and shank-bone with pepper and salt, a little lemon-peel cut small, and a few sweet-herbs and crumbs of bread, then lay this on the gridiron, and let it be of a fine brown; in the mean time take the rest of the meat and cut it like a hash about the bigness of a shilling; save the gravy and put to it, with a few spoonfuls of strong gravy, half an onion cut fine, a little nutmeg, a little pepper and salt, a little bundle of sweet-herbs, some gerkins cut very small, a few mushrooms, two or three truffles cut small, two spoonfuls of wine, either red or white, and throw a little flour over the meat: let all these stew together very softly for five or six minutes, but be sure it do not boil; take out the sweet-herbs, and put the hash into the dish, lay the broiled upon it, and send it to table.

To stuff a Shoulder or Leg of Mutton with Oysters.

TAKE a little grated bread, some beef-suet, yolks of hard eggs, three anchovies, a bit of an onion, salt, pepper, thyme, winter-savoury, twelve oysters, and some nutmeg grated: mix all these together, shred them very fine, and work them up with raw eggs, like a paste; stuff your mutton under the skin in the thickest place, or where you please, and roast it; for sauce take some of the oyster liquor, some claret, two or three anchovies, a little nutmeg, a bit of onion, and the rest of the oysters: stew all these together, then take out the onion, and put it under the mutton.

Another Method.

STUFF a leg of mutton with mutton-suet, salt, pepper, nutmeg, and the yolks of eggs; then roast it, stick it all over with cloves, and when it is about half done, cut off some of the under-side of the fleshy end in little bits; put these into a pipkin with a pint of oysters, liquor and all, a little salt and mace, and half a pint of hot water: stew them till half the liquor is wasted, then put in a piece of butter rolled in flour, shake all together, and when the mutton is enough take it up; pour this sauce over it, and send it to table.

To roast Mutton like Venison.

TAKE a fat hind-quarter of mutton, and cut the leg like a haunch of venison, rub it well with salt-petre, hang it in a moist place for two days, wiping it two or three times a day with a clean cloth. Then put it into a pan, and having boiled a quarter of an ounce of all-spice in a quart of red wine, pour it boiling hot over your mutton, cover it close for two hours; take it out, spit it, lay it down to the fire, and constantly baste it with the same liquor and butter. If you have a good quck fire, and your mutton not prodigiously large, it will be ready in an hour and a half. Then take it up and send it to table with some good gravy in one cup, and sweet sauce in another.

To roast Beef.

IF the rib, sprinkle it with salt for half an hour, dry and flour it; then butter a piece of paper very thick, fasten it on the beef, with the buttered side next it. If a rump or sir-loin, do not salt it, but lay it a good distance from the fire; baste it once or twice with salt and water, then with butter, flour it, and keep it basting with what drops from it. Take three spoonfuls of vinegar, a pint of water, an eschalot, a small piece of horse-radish, two spoonfuls of catchup, and one glass of claret; baste it with this once or twice, then strain it and put it under your beef; garnish with horse-radish and red cabbage.

To roast a Rump of Beef.

LET your beef lie two days in salt, then wash it, and lay it one hour in a quart of red wine and a pint of elder vinegar, with which baste the beef very well while it is roasting; then take two pallets well boiled, and sliced thin; make your sauce with burnt butter, gravy, mushrooms, oysters; to which add the palates, and serve it up.

To roast Veal.

IF a shoulder, baste it with milk till half done, then flour it and baste it with butter. A fillet must be stuffed with thyme, marjoram, parsley, a small onion, a sprig of savoury, a bit of lemon-peel cut very small, nutmeg, pepper, mace, salt, crumbs of bread, four eggs, a quarter of a pound of butter or marrow, mixed with a little flour to make it stiff. Half of the above must be put into the udder, and the other into holes made in the fleshy part.

If it be a loin, paper the fat, that as little of it may be lost as possible. If it be the breast, you must cover it with the caul, and fasten the sweet-bread on the back side of it with a skewer. When it is almost done, take off the caul, baste and dredge it with a little flour. Send it up with melted butter, and garnished with lemon.

To roast Pork.

ALL pork must be floured thick, and laid at first a good distance from the fire; and when the flour begins to dry, wipe it clean. Then with a sharp knife cut the skin across. Heighten the fire, and put your meat near it; baste, and roast it as quick as you can. If a leg, you must cut it very deep. When almost done, fill the cuts with grated bread, sage, parsley, a small piece of lemon-peel cut small, a piece of butter, two eggs, a little pepper, salt and nutmeg, mixed together: when it is enough, send it to table with gravy and apple-sauce. If you roast a spare-rib, baste it with a little butter, flour, and sage shred small. When it is ready send it to table with apple-sauce.

To roast Venison.

WASH your venison in vinegar and water, dry it with a cloth, and cover it with the caul, or, instead of that a buttered

tered paper. Make a brisk fire, lay it down, and baste it with butter till it is almost done. Then take a pint of claret, boil it in a saucepan with some whole pepper, nutmeg, cloves and mace. Pour this liquor twice over your venison. Place your dish on a chafing-dish of coals to keep it hot. Then take it up, strain the liquor you poured over the venison, and serve it in the same dish with the venison, with good gravy in one bason, and sweet sauce in another

To roast a Tongue, or Udder.

TAKE your tongue or udder and parboil it; then stick into it ten or twelve cloves, and while it is roasting, baste it with butter. When it is ready, take it up, and send it to table with some gravy and sweet sauce.

To roast Rabbets.

WHEN you have lain your rabbets down to the fire, baste them with good butter, and then dredge them with flour. If they are small, and your fire quick and clear, half an hour will do them, but if large they will require three quarters of an hour. Melt some good butter, and having boiled the liver with a bunch of parsley, and chopped them small, put half into the butter, and pour it into the dish, garnishing it with the other half.

To roast a Goose.

TAKE a little sage, and a small onion chopped small, some pepper and salt, and a bit of butter; mix these together, and put it into the belly of the goose. Then spit it, singe it with a bit of white paper, dredge it with a little flour, and baste it with butter. When it is done, which may be known by the leg being tender, take it up, and pour through it two glasses of red wine, and serve it up in the same dish, and apple-sauce in a bason.

To dress a wild Duck the best way.

FIRST half roast it, then lay it in a dish, carve it, but leave the joints hanging together, throw a little pepper and salt, and squeeze the juice of a lemon over it, turn it on the breast, and press it hard with a plate, and add to it its own gravy, two or three spoonfuls of good gravy, cover it close with another dish, and set over a stove ten minutes; then send it to table hot in the dish it was done in, and garnish with lemon. You may add a little red wine, and an eschalot cut small, if you like it, but it is apt to make the duck eat hard, unless you first heat the wine and pour it in just as it is done.

Chickens roasted with Forcemeat and Cucumbers.

TAKE two chickens, dress them very neatly, break the breast-bone, and make forcemeat thus: take the flesh of a fowl and of two pigeons, with some slices of ham or bacon, chop them all well together, take the crumb of a penny loaf soaked in milk and boiled, then set to cool; when it is cool mix it all together, season it with beaten mace, nutmeg, pepper, and a little salt, a very little thyme, some parsley, and a little lemon-peel, with the yolks of two eggs; then fill your fowls, spit them, and tie them at both ends; after you have papered the breast, take four cucumbers, cut them in two, and lay them in salt and water two or three hours before; then dry them, and fill them with some of the forcemeat (which you must take care to save) and tie them with a packthread, flour them and fry them of a fine brown; when your chickens are enough, lay them in the dish and untie your cucumbers, but take care the meat do not come out; then lay them round the chickens with the fat side downwards, and the narrow end upwards. You must have some rich fried gravy, and pour into the dish; then garnish with lemon.

Note, One large fowl done this way, with the cucumbers laid round it, looks very pretty, and is a very good dish.

To roast a Turkey.

TAKE a quarter of a pound of lean veal, a little thyme, parsley, sweet marjoram, a sprig of winter savoury, a bit of lemon-peel, one onion, a nutmeg grated, a dram of mace, a little salt, and half a pound of butter; cut your herbs very small, pound your meat as small as possible, and mix all together with three eggs, and as much flour or bread, as will make it of a proper consistence. Then fill the crop of your turkey with it, paper the breast, and lay it down at a good distance from the fire. An hour and a quarter will roast it, if not very large.

To roast a Turkey the genteel way.

FIRST cut it down the back, and with a sharp penknife bone it, then make your forcemeat thus: take a large fowl, or a pound of veal, as much grated bread, half a pound of suet cut and beat very fine, a little beaten mace, two cloves, half a nutmeg grated, about a large tea-spoonful of lemon-peel, and the yolks of two eggs; mix all together, with a little pepper and salt, fill up the places where the bones came out, and fill

The COMPLETE HOUSEWIFE.

the body, that it may look just as it did before; sew up the back, and roast it. You may have oyster-sauce, celery-sauce, or any other you please; but good gravy in the dish, and garnish with lemon, is as good as any thing. Be sure to leave the pinions on.

To roast a Hare.

TAKE crumbs of bread, and suet cut small, of each half a pound; some parsley and thyme shred small; some salt, pepper, cloves, mace, and nutmegs pounded; three dried mushrooms cut small, two eggs, a glass of claret, two spoonfuls of cat hup; mix all these together, and sew it up in the belly of the hare; lay it down to a very slow fire, baste it with milk till it becomes very thick; then make a brisk fire, roast it for half an hour, baste it with butter, and dredge it with a little flour.

Another Method.

FLEA your hare, and lard it with bacon; take the liver, give it one boil; then bruise it small, and mix it with some marrow, or a quarter of a pound of beef-suet shred very fine, two anchovies chopped small, some sweet-herbs shred very small, some grated bread, a nutmeg grated, some salt, a little bit of eschalot cut fine; mix these together with the yolks of two or three eggs; then work it up in a good piece of butter; flour it, and when your hare is spitted, put this pudding in the belly, and sew it up, and lay it to the fire; put a dish under to receive what comes from the hare; baste it well with butter, and when it is enough, put in the dish with it a sauce made with strong broth, the gravy of your hare, the fat being taken off, and some claret; boil these up, and thicken it up with butter: when the hare is cut up, mix some of the pudding with your sauce. Garnish the dish with sliced lemon.

Some, instead of the pudding in the belly, roast a piece of bacon, with some thyme; and for sauce, have melted butter and thyme mixed with what comes from the hare.

To roast Larks.

SPIT them on a little bird-spit, roast them; when enough, have a good many crumbs of bread fried, and throw all over them; and lay them thick round the dish.

To roast Pheasants.

PICK and draw your pheasants, and singe them, lard one with bacon, but not the other, spit them, roast them fine, and paper them all over the breast; when they are just done, flour and baste them with a little nice butter, and let them have a fine
white

white froth; then take them up, and pour good gravy in the dish and bread-sauce in plates.

Or you may put water-cresses nicely picked and washed, and just scalded, with gravy in the dish, and lay the cresses under the pheasants.

Or you may make celery-sauce stewed tender, strained and mixed with cream, and poured into the dish.

If you have but one pheasant, take a large fine fowl about the bigness of a pheasant, pick it nicely with the head on, draw it and truss it with the head turned as you do a pheasant's, lard the fowl all over the breast and legs with a large piece of bacon cut in little pieces; when roasted put them both in a dish, and no body will know it. They will take an hour doing, as the fire must not be too brisk. A Frenchman would order fish-sauce to them, but then you quite spoil your pheasants.

To roast Partridges.

LET them be nicely roasted, but not too much; dredge them with a little flour, and baste them moderately; let them have a fine froth, let there be good gravy-sauce in the dish, and bread-sauce in basons made thus: take a pint of water, put in a good thick piece of bread, some whole pepper, a blade or two of mace; boil it five or six minutes till the bread is soft; then take out all the spice, and pour out all the water, only just enough to keep it moist; beat it soft with a spoon; throw in a little salt, and a good piece of fresh butter; stir it well together, set it over the fire for a minute or two, then put it into a boat.

To roast Woodcocks and Snipes.

PUT them on the spit without taking any thing out of them; baste them with butter, and when the tail begins to drop, put into the dish to receive it a round of a three-penny loaf toasted brown. When they are done put the toast into the dish, with about a quarter of a pint of good gravy; put the woodcocks on it, and set it over a lamp or chafing-dish of coals for about three minutes, and send them to table.

To dress Ortolans.

SPIT them sideways, with a bay leaf between; baste them with butter, and have fried crumbs of bread round the dish. Dress quails the same way.

To roast a Pig.

LAY your pig in warm milk for a quarter of an hour, and wipe it very dry. Take of butter and crumbs of bread, of each a quarter of a pound, a little sage, thyme, parsley, sweet marjoram,

marjoram, pepper, salt, and nutmeg, the yolks of two eggs; mix these together, and sew it up in the belly. Flour it very thick; then spit it, and lay it to the fire, taking care that your fire burns well at both ends, or till it does, hang a flat iron in the middle of the grate. When you find the crackling grows hard, wipe it clean with a cloth wet in salt and water, and baste it with butter. As soon as the gravy begins to run, put basons in the dripping-pan to receive it. When the pig is enough, take about a quarter of a pound of butter, put it into a coarse cloth, and, having made a brisk fire, rub the pig all over with it, till the crackling is quite crisp, and then take it from the fire. Cut off the head, and cut the pig in two, before you take it from the spit. Then having cut the ears off, and placed one at each end, and also the under jaw in two, and placed one part on each side, take some good butter, melt it, mix it with the gravy, the brains bruised, and some sage shred small, and send it to table.

To roast a Pig with the hair on.

DRAW you pig very clean at the vent, then take out the guts, liver, and lights; cut off his feet; and truss him, prick up his belly, spit him, lay him down to the fire, but take care not to scorch him: when the skin begins to rise up in blisters, pull off the skin, hair and all: when you have cleared the pig of both, scorch him down to the bones, and baste him with butter and cream, or half a pound of butter, and a pint of milk, put it into the dripping-pan, and keep basting it well; then throw some salt over it, and dredge it with crumbs of bread till it is half an inch or an inch thick. When it is enough, and of a fine brown, but not scorched, take it up, lay it in your dish, and let your sauce be good gravy, thickened with butter rolled in a little flour; or else make the following sauce: take half a pound of butter and a pint of cream, put them on the fire, and keep them stirring one way all the time; when the butter is melted, and the sauce thickened, pour it into your dish. Don't garnish with any thing, unless some raspings of bread; and then with your finger figure it as you fancy.

To roast a Pig with the skin on.

LET your pig be newly killed, draw him, flay him, and wipe him very dry with a cloth; then make a hard meat with a pint of cream, the yolks of six eggs, grated bread, and beef-suet, seasoned with salt, pepper, mace, nutmeg, thyme, and lemon-peel; make of this a pretty stiff pudding, stuff the belly of the pig, and sew it up; then spit it, and lay it down to roast. Let your dripping-pan be very clean, then pour into it a pint of red wine, and grate some nutmeg all over it; throw a little
salt

salt over, a little thyme, and some lemon-peel minced; when it is enough shake a little flour over it, and baste it with butter, to have a fine froth. Take it up and lay it in a dish, cut off the head, take the sauce which is in your dripping-pan, and thicken it with a piece of butter; then take the brains, bruise them, mix them with the sauce, rub in a little dried sage, pour it into your dish, and serve it up. Garnish with hard eggs cut into quarters, and if you have not sauce enough, add half a pint of good gravy.

Note, You must take great care no ashes fall into the dripping-pan, which may be prevented by having a good fire, that will not want any stirring.

To barbicue a Pig.

DRESS a pig of ten weeks old as if it were to be roasted, make a forcemeat of two anchovies, six sage leaves, and the liver of the pig, all chopped very small; then put them into a marble mortar, with the crumbs of half a penny loaf, four ounces of butter, half a tea spoonful of Cayan pepper, and half a pint of red wine; beat them altogether to a paste, put it in your pig's belly and sew it up; lay your pig down at a good distance before a large brisk fire, singe it well, put in your dripping-pan three bottles of red wine, and baste it with the wine all the time it is roasting; when it is half roasted, put under your pig two penny loaves; if you have not wine enough, put in more; when your pig is near enough, take the loaves and sauce out of your dripping-pan, put to the sauce one anchovy chopped small, a bundle of sweet-herbs, and half a lemon, and boil it a few minutes; then draw your pig, put a small lemon or apple in the pig's mouth, and a loaf on each side; strain your sauce, and pour it on them boiling hot; lay barberries and slices of lemon round it, and send it up whole to the table.——It is a grand bottom dish. It will take four hours roasting.

To roast a pound of Butter.

LAY it in salt and water two or three hours, then spit it, and rub it all over with crumbs of bread, with a little grated nutmeg, lay it to the fire, and as it roasts, baste it with the yolks of two eggs, and then with crumbs of bread all the time it is roasting; but have ready a pint of oysters stewed in their own liquor, and lay in the dish under the butter; when the bread has soaked up all the butter, brown the outside, and lay it on your oysters. Your fire must be very slow.

To roast a Pike.

TAKE a large pike, gut it, clean it, and lard it with eel and bacon, as you lard a fowl; then take thyme, savoury, salt, mace, nutmeg, some crumbs of bread, beef-suet, and parsley; shred all very fine, and mix it up with raw eggs; make it in a long pudding, and put it in the belly of your pike; sew up the belly, and dissolve the anchovies in butter, basting it with it; put two splints on each side the pike, and tie it to the spit; melt butter thick for the sauce, or if you please, oyster-sauce, and bruise the pudding in it. Garnish with lemon.

To roast a Pike in embers.

WHEN your fish is scaled, and well dried in a cloth, make a pudding with sweet-herbs, grated bread, and onion, wrapt up in butter; put it into the belly, and sew it up, turn the tail into the mouth, and roll it up in white paper, and then in brown, wet them both, and tie them round with packthread; then rake it up in the embers, and let it lie two or three hours; then take it up, and take the pudding out of the belly; mix it with sauce, such as is usually made for fish, and serve it up.

To roast a Cod's Head.

TAKE the head, wash and scour it very clean, then scotch it with a knife, strew a little salt on it, and lay it on a stew-pan before the fire, with something behind it; throw away the water that runs from it the first half hour, then strew on it some nutmeg, cloves, mace and salt, and baste it often with butter, turning it till it is enough. If it be a large head it will take four or five hours roasting; then take all the gravy of the fish, as much white wine, and more meat gravy, some horse-radish, one or two eschalots, a little sliced ginger, some whole pepper, cloves, mace, and nutmeg, a bay-leaf or two; beat this liquor up with butter and the liver of the fish boiled, broke, and strained into it with the yolks of two or three eggs, some oysters and shrimps, balls made of fish and fried fish round it. Garnish with lemon and horse-radish.

To roast Lobsters.

TIE your lobsters to the spit alive, baste them with water and salt till they look very red, and are enough; then baste them with butter and salt, take them up, and set little dishes round with the sauce, some plain melted butter, and oyster-sauce.

To roast a Fillet or Collar of Sturgeon.

TAKE a piece of fresh sturgeon, scale it, gut it, take out the bones and cut in lengths about seven or eight inches; then provide some shrimps and oysters chopped small; an equal quantity

quantity of crumbs of bread, and a little lemon-peel grated, some nutmeg, a little beaten mace, a little pepper and chopped parsley, a few sweet-herbs, an anchovy, mix it together. When it is done, butter one side of your fish, and strew some of your mixture upon it; then begin to roll it up as close as possible, and when the first piece is rolled up, roll upo that another, prepared in the same manner, and bind it round with a narrow fillet, leaving as much of the fish apparent as may be; but you must mind that the roll must not be above four inches and an half thick, for else one part will be done before the inside is warm; therefore we often parboil the inside roll before we roll it. When it is enough, lay it in your dish, and prepare sauce as above. Garnish with lemon.

To roast an Eel.

TAKE a large eel, and scour him well with salt; skin him almost to the tail; then gut, and wash, and dry him; take a quarter of a pound of suet, shred as fine as possible; put to it sweet-herbs, an eschalot likewise shred very fine, and mix it together, with some salt, pepper, and grated nutmeg; scotch your eel on both sides, the breadth of a finger's distance, and wash it with yolks of eggs, and strew some seasoning over it, and stuff the belly with it; then draw the skin over it, put a long skewer through it, and tie it to the spit, baste it with butter, and make the sauce anchovy and butter melted.

To roast large Eels or Lampreys with a pudding in the belly.

SKIN your eels or lampreys, cut off the head, take the guts out and scrape the blood clean from the bone; then make a good forcemeat of oysters or shrimps chopped small, the crumbs of half a penny loaf, a little nutmeg and lemon-peel shred fine, pepper, salt, and the yolks of two eggs; put them in the belly of your fish, sew it up, and turn it round on your dish; put over it flour and butter, pour a little water in your dish, and bake it in a moderate oven; when it comes out take the gravy from under it, and skim off the fat; then strain it through a hair sieve, add to it a tea spoonful of lemon pickle, two of browning, a meat spoonful of walnut catchup, a glass of white wine, one anchovy, and a slice of lemon; let it boil ten minutes, thicken it with butter and flour, send it up in a sauceboat, dish your fish: garnish it with lemon and crisp parsley.

This is a pretty dish for either corner or side for a dinner.

To roast Ruffs and Rees.

THE best way to feed these birds, which are seldom met with any where but in Lincolnshire, is with white bread boiled in milk: they must have separate pots, for two will not eat out of one. They will be fat in eight or ten days; when you kill them, slip the skin off the head and neck with the feathers on, then pluck and draw them. When you roast them, put them a good distance from the fire; if the fire be good, they will take about twelve minutes; when they are roasted, slip the skin on again with the feathers on, send them up with gravy under them, made the same as for the pheasant, and bread-sauce, in a boat, or crisp crumbs of bread round the edge of the dish.

CHAP. IV.
General DIRECTIONS for BROILING.

First, TAKE care that your fire be very clear, before you lay your meat on the gridiron.

Secondly, Turn your meat, when it is down, quick, having, at the same time, a dish placed on a chafing-dish of hot coals to put your meat in as fast as it is ready, and carry it to the table covered hot.

Thirdly, Observe never to baste any thing on the gridiron, for that causes it to be both smoked and burnt.

To broil Steaks.

WHEN you have made a clear brisk fire, make your gridiron very clean, put some hot coals from the fire into a chafing-dish, and place a dish over them, in order to receive your steaks when ready; take rump steaks, which should be about half an inch thick; after you have thrown over them a little pepper and salt, place them on the gridiron, and do not turn them till that side be done; when you have turned them you will soon perceive a fine gravy lying on the upper part of the steak, which you must carefully preserve, by taking the steaks, when ready, warily from your gridiron, and placing them in your dish: then covering your dish, send them hot to table with the cover on. Some, before they take the steak from the gridiron, cut into the dish an eschalot or two, or a little onion, and a little vinegar.

To broil a Pigeon.

YOU may either split and broil them with a little pepper and salt; or you may take a small piece of butter, a little pepper and salt, and having put it into their bellies, tie both ends close. Then lay them on your gridiron, taking care to place it high, that they may not burn; and when they are ready, send them to table with a little melted butter in a cup.

Eels to broil.

TAKE a large eel, skin it and make it clean. Open the belly, cut it in four pieces, take the tail-end, strip off the flesh, beat it in a mortar, season it with a little beaten mace, a little grated nutmeg, pepper and salt, a little parsley and thyme, a little lemon-peel, an equal quantity of crumbs of bread, roll it in a little piece of butter; then mix it again with the yolk of an egg, roll it up again, and fill the three pieces of belly with it. Cut the skin of the eel, wrap the pieces in, and sew up the skin. Broil them well, have butter and an anchovy for sauce, with the juce of lemon.

To broil Haddocks or Whitings.

GUT and wash your haddocks or whitings; dry them with a cloth, and rub a little vinegar over them, as it will keep the skin on better; dust them well with flour, rub your gridiron with butter, and let it be very hot when you lay the fish on, or they will stick; turn them two or three times on the gridiron; when enough, serve them up, and lay pickles round them, with plain melted butter, or cockle sauce: they are a pretty dish for supper.

A second Way.

WHEN you have cleaned your haddocks or whitings, as above, put them in a tin oven, and set them before a quick fire; when the skins begin to rise, take it off, beat an egg, rub it over them with a feather, and strew over them a few bread crumbs; dredge them well with flour; when your gridiron is hot, rub it well with butter or suet, for it must be very hot before you lay the fish on; when you have turned them, rub a little cold butter over them; turn them as your fire requires until they are enough and a little brown; lay round them cockles, muscles, or red cabbage: you may either have shrimp sauce or melted butter.

To broil Haddocks, when they are in high season.

SCALE them, gut and wash them clean, don't rip open their bellies, but take the guts out with the gills; dry them in a clean cloth very well: if there be any roe or liver, take it out, but put it in again; flour them well, and have a clear good fire. Let your gridiron be hot and clean, lay them on, turn them quick two or three times for fear of sticking; then let one side be enough, and turn the other side. When that is done, lay them in a dish, and have plain butter in a cup.

They eat finely salted a day or two before you dress them, and hung up to dry, or boiled with egg-sauce. Newcastle is a famous place for salted haddocks. They come in barrels, and keep a great while.

To broil Cod-sounds.

YOU must first lay them in hot water a few minutes; take them out and rub them well with salt, to take off the skin and black dirt, then they will look white, then put them in water, and give them a boil. Take them out and flour them well, pepper and salt them, and broil them. When they are enough, lay them in your dish, and pour melted butter and mustard into the dish. Broil them whole.

CHAP. V.
DIRECTIONS for FRYING.

A very good way to fry Beef Steaks.

CUT your steaks as for broiling, put them into a stew-pan with a good lump of butter, set them over a very slow fire, keep turning them till the butter is become a thick white gravy, pour it into a bason, and put more butter to them; when they are almost enough, pour all the gravy into your bason, and put more butter into your pan, fry them a light brown over a quick fire, take them out of the pan, put them in a hot pewter dish, slice an eschalot among them, put a little in your gravy that was drawn from them, and pour it hot upon them: I think this is the best way of dressing beef steaks. Half a pound of butter will dress a large dish.

To fry cold Veal.

CUT it in pieces about as thick as half a crown, and as long as you please, dip them in the yolk of an egg, and then in

D 4 crumbs

crumbs of bread, with a few sweet-herbs, and shred lemon-peel in it; grate a little nutmeg over them, and fry them in fresh butter. The butter must be hot, just enough to fry them in: in the mean time, make a little gravy of the bone of the veal; when the meat is fried take it out with a fork, and lay it in a dish before the fire, then shake a little flour into the pan, and stir it round; then put in a little gravy, squeeze in a little lemon, and pour it over the veal. Garnish with lemon.

To fry Tripe.

CUT your tripe into pieces about three inches long, dip them in the yolk of an egg and a few crumbs of bread, fry them of a fine brown, and then take them out of the pan and lay them in a dish to drain. Have ready a warm dish to put them in, and send them to table, with butter and mustard in a cup.

Cauliflours fried.

TAKE two fine cauliflowers, boil them in milk and water, then leave one whole, and pull the other to pieces; take half a pound of butter, with two spoonfuls of water, a little dust of flour, and melt the butter in a stew-pan; then put in the whole cauliflower cut in two, and the other pulled to pieces, and fry it till it is of a very light brown. Season it with pepper and salt. When it is enough, lay the two halves in the middle, and pour the rest all over.

To fry Potatoes.

CUT them into thin slices, as big as a crown-piece, fry them brown, lay them in the plate or dish, pour melted butter, and sack and sugar over them. These are a pretty corner-plate.

General DIRECTIONS for frying FISH.

OBSERVE always in the frying of any sort of fish, that you dry your fish very well in a clean cloth, then flour it. Let your stew pan you fry them in be very nice and clean, and put in as much beef-dripping, or hog's lard, as will almost cover your fish; and be sure it boils before you put in your fish. Let it fry quick, and let it be of a fine light brown, but not too dark a colour. Have your fish-slice ready, and if there is occasion turn it; when it is enough, take it up, and lay a coarse cloth on a dish, on which lay your fish, to drain all the grease from it; if you fry parsley, do it quick, and take great care to whip it out of the pan so soon as it is crisp, or it will lose its fine colour. Take great care that your dripping be very nice and clean.

Some love fish in batter; then you must beat an egg fine, and dip your fish in just as you are going to put it in the pan; or as good a batter as any, is a little ale and flour beat up, just as you are ready for it, and dip the fish, so fry it.

Eels to fry.

MAKE them very clean, cut them into pieces, season them with pepper and salt, flour them and fry them in butter. Let your sauce be plain butter melted, with the juice of lemon. Be sure they be well drained from the fat before you lay them in the dish.

Eels to pitchcock.

YOU must split a large eel down the back, and joint the bones, cut it in two or three pieces, melt a little butter, put in a little vinegar and salt, let your eel lay in two or three minutes; then take the pieces up one by one, turn them round with a little fine skewer, roll them in crumbs of bread, and broil them of a fine brown. Let your sauce be plain butter, with the juice of lemon.

To force Eels with white Sauce.

SKIN and clean your eel well, pick off all the flesh clean from the bone, which you must leave whole to the head. Take the flesh, cut it small and beat it in a mortar; then take half the quantity of crumbs of bread, beat it with the fish, season it with nutmeg and beaten pepper, an anchovy, a good deal of parsley chopped fine, a few truffles boiled tender in a very little water, chop them fine, put them into the mortar with the liquor and a few mushrooms: beat it well together, mix in a little cream, then it take out and mix it well together in your hand, lay it round the bone in the shape of the eel, lay it on a buttered pan, dredge it well with fine crumbs of bread, and bake it. When it is done, lay it carefully in your dish, have ready half a pint of cream, a quarter of a pound of fresh butter, stir it one way till it is thick, pour it over your eels, and garnish with lemon.

To fry Lampreys.

BLEED them and save the blood, then wash them in hot water to take off the slime, and cut them to pieces. Fry them in a little fresh butter not quite enough, pour out the fat, put in a little white wine, give the pan a shake round, season it with whole pepper, nutmeg, salt, sweet-herbs and a bay-leaf, put in

a few

a few capers, a good piece of butter rolled up in flour, and the blood; give the pan a shake round often, and cover them close. When you think they are enough take them out, strain the sauce, then give them a boil quick, squeeze in a little lemon and pour over the fish. Garnish with lemon, and dress them just what way you fancy.

To fry Carp.

FIRST scale and gut them, wash them clean, lay them in a cloth to dry, then flour them, and fry them of a fine light brown. Fry some toast cut three-corner-ways, and the roes; when your fish is done, lay them on a coarse cloth to drain. Let your sauce be butter and anchovy, with the juice of lemon. Lay your carp in the dish, the roes on each side, and garnish with the fried toast and lemon.

To fry Herrings.

CLEAN them as above, fry them in butter, have ready a good many onions peeled and cut thin. Fry them of a light brown with the herrings; lay the herrings in your dish, and the onions round, butter and mustard in a cup. You must do them with a quick fire.

CHAP. VI.
DIRECTIONS for BAKING.

To bake a Rump of Beef.

BONE a rump of beef, beat it very well with a rolling-pin, cut off the sinew, and lard it with large pieces of bacon; roll your lards in seasoning, which is pepper, salt, and cloves; lard athwart the meat, that it may cut handsomely; then season it all over the meat with pepper and salt pretty thick, tie it with packthread cross and cross, and put the top under the bottom, and tie it up tight; put it in an earthen pot, break all the bones, and put in the sides and cover, to keep it fast that it cannot stir; then put in half a pound of butter, some bay-leaves, whole pepper, an eschalot or two, and some sweet-herbs; cover the top of the pot with coarse paste; put it in the oven, and let it stand eight hours. Serve it up with its own liquor, and some dried sippets.

To bake a Leg of Beef.

TAKE a leg of beef, cut it and break the bones; put it into an earthen pan with a spoonful of whole pepper, a few cloves and blades of mace, two onions, and a bundle of sweet-herbs; cover it with water, and having tied the pot down close with brown paper, put it into the oven to bake. When it is enough, strain it thro' a sieve, and pick out all the fat and sinews, putting them into a saucepan with a little gravy, and a piece of butter rolled in flour. Set the saucepan on the fire, shaking it often; and, when it is thoroughly hot, pour it into the dish, and send it to table. Ox's cheek is done in the same manner.

To bake a Pig.

TAKE your pig, flour it well, and having buttered your dish, lay your pig into it, and put it into the oven. When it is ready, and you have drawn it out of the oven, rub it all over with a buttery cloth; then put it again into the oven, and when it is dry take it out, lay it in your dish, and cut it up. Take the gravy which remains in the dish you baked it in, after you have skimmed off the fat; mix it with some good gravy, a sufficient quantity of butter rolled in flour, and a glass of white wine; set it on the fire, and as soon as it boils, pour it into the dish with the brains and the sage which was roasted in its belly.

To bake Herrings.

TAKE thirty herrings, scale them, cut off their heads, pull out their roes, wash them very clean, and lay them to drain four or five hours; roll them in a dry cloth, season them with pepper and salt, and lay them in a long venison pot at full length; when you have laid one row, shred a large onion very small, and mix it with a little cloves, mace and ginger cut small, and strew it all over the herrings; and then another row of herrings, and seasoning; and so do till all is in the pot, let it stand seasoned an hour before it is put in the oven; then put in a quart of claret, and tie it over with paper, and bake it with household bread.

To bake a Carp.

SCALE, wash, and clean a brace of carp very well; take an earthen pan deep enough to lie cleverly in, butter the pan a little, lay in your carp; season it with mace, cloves, nutmeg, and black and white pepper, a bundle of sweet-herbs, an onion, and anchovy; pour in a bottle of white wine, cover it close, and let them bake an hour in a hot oven, if large; if small, a less time

time will do them. When they are enough, carefully take them up and lay them in a dish; set it over hot water to keep it hot, and cover it close, then pour all the liquor they were baked in into a saucepan; let it boil a minute or two, then strain it, and add half a pound of butter rolled in flour. Let it boil, keep stirring it, squeeze in the juice of half a lemon, and put in what salt you want; pour the sauce over the fish, lay the roes round, and garnish with lemon. Observe to skim all the fat off the liquor.

CHAP. VII.
SAUCES of various KINDS.

Sauce for boiled Ducks or Rabbets.

TAKE a sufficient quantity of onions, peel them, and boil them in a large quantity of water: when they are about half boiled, throw that water away and fill your saucepan with half milk and half water, in which let them boil till they are enough; then take them up into a colander, and when they are drained, chop them with a knife; put them into a saucepan with a piece of butter rolled in flour; set the saucepan over the fire, shaking it often till the butter is melted, then pour it over your boiled ducks or rabbets, and send them to table.

Another for the same.

TO boiled ducks or rabbets, you must pour boiled onions over them, which do thus: take the onions, peel them, and boil them in a great deal of water; shift your water, then let them boil about two hours, take them up and throw them into a colander to drain, then with a knife chop them on a board; put them into a saucepan, just shake a little flour over them, put in a little milk or cream, with a good piece of butter; set them over the fire, and when the butter is melted they are enough. But if you would have onion-sauce in half an hour, take your onions, peel them, and cut them in thin slices, put them into milk and water, and when the water boils they will be done in twenty minutes, then throw them into a colander to drain, and chop them and put them into a saucepan; shake in a little flour, with a little cream if you have it, and a good piece of butter; stir all together over the fire till the butter is melted, and they will be very fine. This sauce is very good with roast mutton, and it is the best way of boiling onions.

Sauce for a boiled Goose.

YOU may either make onion-sauce, as directed for boiled ducks, &c. or you may boil some cabbage, and then stew it a small time in butter.

Sauce for roast Venison.

TAKE a pound of lean beef, and a quarter of a pound of lean bacon, cut into small pieces; put it into a stew-pan with three pints of water, a bunch of sweet-herbs, and an onion; boil it till half is consumed. Strain it, and add to it two spoonfuls of catchup, as much oyster-liquor, and thicken it with brown butter. Or,

Take half the crumb of a halfpenny loaf, a large stick of cinnamon, some mace and nutmeg, and a race of ginger, put these into a saucepan with a pint of water; boil it, beat it very fine, and strain it through a sieve, adding to it half a pint of red wine, and sweeten it to your taste.

Gravy for a Fowl, when you have no meat nor gravy ready.

TAKE the neck, liver, and gizzard, boil them in half a pint of water, with a little piece of bread toasted brown, a little pepper and salt, and a little bit of thyme. Let them boil till there is about a quarter of a pint, then pour in half a glass of red wine, boil it and strain it, then bruise the liver well in, and strain it again; thicken it with a little piece of butter rolled in flour, and it will be very good.

An ox's kidney makes good gravy, cut all to pieces, and boiled with spice, &c. as in the foregoing receipts.

You have a receipt in the beginning of the book, in the preface for gravies.

Sauce for boiled Mutton.

TAKE a piece of liver as big as a pigeon's egg and boil it tender, with half a handful of parsley and a few sprigs of pot thyme, with the yolks of three or four eggs boiled hard; bray them with a spoon till they are dissolved; then add one anchovy washed and stripped from the bone, thyme, beaten pepper and grated nutmeg, with a little salt; put all these together in a saucepan, with a glass of white wine, and the gravy that has drained from your leg of mutton after it is taken out of the pot, or a quarter of a pint of the liquor the mutton is boiled in: mix it all together, and give it a boil, then beat it up with three ounces of butter: you may add a tea-spoonful of vinegar, which

takes

takes off a sweetness it is apt to have: it is best to make the sauce thick, or it will be too thin when the mutton is cut.

Sauce for boiled Turkey or Chickens.

BOIL a spoonful of the best mace very tender, and the liver of the turkey, but not too much, for then it will be hard; bray the mace with a few drops of a liquor to a very fine pulp, then bray the liver, and put about half of it to the mace with a little pepper, and some salt, if you please you may put the yolk of an egg boiled hard and dissolved; to this add by degrees a little of the liquor that drains from the turkey, or some other gravy; put these liquors to the pulp, and boil them some time; then take half a pint of oysters, and boil them no longer than till they will break; and last put in white wine and butter wrapt in flour: let it boil but a little, lest the wine make the oysters hard, and just at the last scald four or five spoonfuls of thick new cream, with a few drops of lemon or vinegar; mushrooms pickled do well, but then leave out the other acids; some like this sauce best thickened with yolks of eggs and no butter.

Sauce for Fish or Flesh.

TAKE a quart of verjuice, and put it into a jug; then take Jamaica pepper whole, some sliced ginger, some mace, a few cloves, some lemon-peel, horse-radish root sliced, some sweet-herbs, six eschalots peeled, and eight anchovies; two or three spoonfuls of shred capers; put all these into a linen bag, and put the bag into your verjuice; stop the jug close, and keep it for use; a spoonful cold or mixed in sauce for fish or flesh.

Different sorts of Sauce for a Pig.

NOW you are to observe there are several ways of making sauce for a pig. Some do not love any sage in the pig, only a crust of bread; but then you should have a little dried sage rubbed and mixed with the gravy and butter. Some love bread-sauce in a bason, made thus: take a pint of water, put in a good piece of crumb of bread, a blade of mace, and a little whole pepper; boil it for about five or six minutes, and then pour the water off: take out the spice, and beat up the bread with a good piece of butter. Some love a few currants boiled in it, a glass of wine, and a little sugar: but that you must do just as you like it. Others take half a pint of good beef gravy, and the gravy which comes out of the pig, with a piece of butter rolled in flour, two spoonfuls of catchup, and boil them all together; then take the brains of the pig and bruise them fine, with two eggs boiled hard and chopped; put all these together,

with

with the sage in the pig, and pour into your dish. It is a very good sauce. When you have not gravy enough comes out of your pig with the butter for sauce, take about half a pint of veal gravy and add to it: or stew the petty-toes, and take as much of that liquor as will do for sauce, mixed with the other.

Different Sauces for a Hare.

TAKE some good gravy, and a proper quantity of butter rolled in flour; when it is melted pour it into your dish. Or take half a pound of butter, put it into a saucepan, set it over the fire, keeping it continually stirred till the butter is melted, and the sauce thick; then take it from the fire and pour it into the dish. Or take a pint of red wine and half a pound of sugar, and after it has simmered about a quarter of an hour over the fire, pour it into the dish.

Sauce for Larks.

TAKE for every dozen of larks, a quarter of a pound of butter, the crumb of a halfpenny loaf rubbed small; when the butter is melted put in your bread, keeping it constantly stirring till it becomes brown; then drain it through a sieve, and place it round your larks.

Sauce for a Woodcock.

TAKE a very little claret, some good gravy, a blade of mace, some whole pepper, an eschalot; let these stew a little, then thicken it up with butter; roast the guts in the woodcock, and let them run on sippets, or a toast of white bread, and lay it under your woodcock, and pour the sauce into the dish.

A standing Sauce for a Kitchen.

TAKE a quart of claret or white wine, put it in a glazed jar, with the juice of two lemons, five large anchovies, some Jamaica pepper whole, some sliced ginger, some mace, a few cloves, a little lemon-peel, horse-radish sliced, some sweet-herbs, six eschalots, two spoonfuls of capers, and their liquor; put all these in a linen bag, and put it into the wine; stop it close, and set the vessel in a kettle of hot water for an hour, and keep it in a warm place. A spoonful or two of this liquor is good in any sauce.

A rich and yet a cheap Sauce.

TAKE a large deep stew-pan, half a pound of bacon, fat and lean together, cut the fat and lay it over the bottom of
the

the pan; then take a pound of veal, cut it into thin slices, beat it well with the back of a knife, lay it all over the bacon; then have six penny-worth of the coarse lean part of the beef cut thin and well beat, lay a layer of it all over, with some carrot, then the lean of the bacon cut thin and laid over that: then cut two onions and strew over, a bundle of sweet-herbs, four or five blades of mace, six or seven cloves, a spoonful of whole pepper, black and white together, half a nutmeg beat, a pigeon beat all to pieces, lay that all over, half an ounce of truffles and morels, the rest of your beef, a good crust of bread toasted very brown and dry on both sides: you may add an old cock beat to pieces; cover it close, and let it stand over a slow fire two or three minutes, then pour in boiling water, enough to fill the pan, cover it close, and let it stew till it is as rich as you would have it, and then strain off all that sauce. Put all your ingredients together again, fill the pan with boiling water, put in a fresh onion, a blade of mace, and a piece of carrot; cover it close, and let it stew still it is as strong as you want it. This will be full as good as the essence of ham for all sorts of fowls, or indeed most made dishes, mixed with a glass of wine, and two or three spoonfuls of catchup. When your first gravy is cool, skim off all the fat, and keep it for use.

Gravy to keep for Use.

TAKE a piece of coarse beef, cover it with water; when it has boiled some time, take out the meat; beat it very well, and cut it in pieces to let out the gravy; then put it in again, with a bunch of sweet-herbs, an onion stuck with cloves, a little salt, and some whole pepper; let it stew, but not boil; when it is of a brown colour it is enough; take it up; put it in an earthen-pot, and let it stand to cool; when it is cold skim off the fat: it will keep a week unless the weather be very hot. If for a brown fricasee, put some butter in your frying-pan, and shake in it a little flour as it boils, and put in some gravy, with a glass of claret, and shake up the fricasee in it. If for a white fricasee, then melt your butter in the gravy, with a little white wine, a spoonful or two of cream, and the yolks of eggs.

To make a cheap Gravy.

TAKE twelve penny-worth of coarse lean beef, which will be six or seven pounds, cut it all to pieces, flour it well, take a quarter of a pound of good butter, put it into a little pot or large deep stew-pan, and put in your beef: keep stirring it, and when it begins to look a little brown, pour in a pint of boiling water; stir it all together, put in a large onion, a bundle of sweet-herbs, two or three blades of mace, five or six cloves,

The COMPLETE HOUSEWIFE.   49

cloves, a spoonful of whole pepper, a crust of bread toasted, and a piece of carrot; then pour in four or five quarts of water, stir all together, cover close, and let it stew till it is as rich as you would have it; when enough, strain it off, mix with it two or three spoonfuls of catchup, and half a pint of white wine; then put all the ingredients together again; and put in two quarts of boiling water, cover it close, and let it boil till there is about a pint; strain it off well, add it to the first, and give it a boil all together. This will make a great deal of rich good gravy.

To make the Mushroom Powder.

TAKE the large mushrooms, wash them clean from grit; cut off the stalks, but do not peel or grill them; so put them into a kettle over the fire, but no water; put a good quantity of spice of all sorts, two onions stuck with cloves, a handful of salt, some beaten pepper, and a quarter of a pound of butter; let all these stew, till the liquor is dried up in them; then take them out, and lay them on sieves to dry, till they will beat to powder; press the powder hard down in a pot, and keep it for use, what quantity you please at a time in sauce.

To make Mushroom Liquor and Powder.

TAKE a peck of mushrooms, wash and rub them clean with a piece of flannel, cutting out all the gills, but not peeling off the skins; put to them sixteen blades of mace, four cloves, six bay-leaves, twice as much beaten pepper as will lie on a half-crown, a handful of salt, a dozen onions, a piece of butter as big as an egg, and half a pint of vinegar; stew them up as fast as you can, keeping them stirring till the liquor is out of your mushrooms; drain them through a colander, save the liquor and spice, and when cold, bottle it up for use; dry the mushrooms first on a broad pan in the oven, afterwards put them on sieves till they are dry enough to pound to powder. This quantity usually makes about half a pound.

White Cucumber Sauce.

TAKE six or eight cucumbers for six chickens, according as they are in bigness; pare and slice them with a piece of onion, some pepper and salt, and as much water as will stew them till they are tender; then toss them up in some butter rolled in flour; it must be as thick as you can well make it, without burning it, which it is subject to; you may strain it through a thin colander into another saucepan, to take out the seeds, then heat it, and you may pour it upon the chickens, rabbets, or neck of veal.

Brown Cucumber Sauce.

PARE and slice them with a piece of onion, then put a piece of butter in the frying-pan, and when it is hot put in your cucumbers with flour on them, and stew them till they are brown; then take them out of the pan with a slice, and put them into a saucepan, with a little sauce made of broth or gravy, that is savoury; when you have so done, burn a piece of butter in a pan, and when it is sufficiently burnt, put your cucumber sauce in by degrees, and season it with salt to your taste.

To fry Cucumbers for Mutton Sauce.

YOU must brown some butter in a pan, and cut the cucumbers in thin slices; drain them from the water, then fling them into the pan, and when they are fried brown, put in a little pepper and salt, a bit of onion and gravy, and let them stew together, and squeeze in some juice of lemon; shake them well, and put them under your mutton.

Savoury Balls.

TAKE part of a leg of lamb or veal, and scrape it fine, with the same quantity of minced beef suet, a little lean bacon, sweet-herbs, an eschalot, and anchovies; beat it in a mortar till it is as smooth as wax: season it with savoury spice, and make it into little balls.

Another Way.

TAKE the flesh of a fowl, beef suet, and marrow, the same quantity; six or eight oysters, lean bacon, sweet-herbs, and savoury spices; pound it, and make it into little balls.

A Caudle for sweet Pyes.

TAKE sack and white wine alike in quantity, a little verjuice and sugar, boil it, and brew it with two or three eggs, as buttered ale; when the pyes are baked, pour it in with a funnel, and shake it together.

A Lear for savoury Pyes.

TAKE claret, gravy, oyster-liquor, two or three anchovies, a faggot of sweet-herbs and an onion; boil it up and thicken it with brown butter, then pour it into your savoury pyes when called for.

Fish

Fish Sauce, with Lobster.

FOR salmon or turbot, broiled cod or haddock, &c. nothing is better than fine butter melted thick; and take a lobster, bruise the body of the lobster in the butter, and cut the flesh into little pieces; stew it all together, and give it a boil. If you would have your sauce very rich, let one half be rich beef gravy, and the other half melted butter with the lobster; but the gravy, I think, takes away the sweetness of the butter and lobster, and the fine flavour of the fish.

To make Shrimp Sauce.

TAKE a pint of beef gravy, and half a pint of shrimps, thicken it with a good piece of butter rolled in flour. Let the gravy be well seasoned, and let it boil.

To butter Shrimps.

STEW a quart of shrimps in half a pint of white wine, a nutmeg grated, and a good piece of butter; when the butter is melted, and they are hot through, beat the yolks of four eggs, with a little white wine, and pour it in; shake it well, till it is of the thickness you like; then dish it on sippets, and garnish with sliced lemon.

To butter Crabs or Lobsters.

YOUR crabs and lobsters being boiled and cold, take all the meat out of the shells and body, break the claws, and take out all their meat, mince it small, and put it all together, adding to it two or three spoonfuls of claret, a very little vinegar, a nutmeg grated; let it boil up till it is thorough hot; then put in some butter melted, with some anchovies and gravy, and thicken up with the yolks of an egg or two; when it is very hot put it in the large shell, and stick it with toasts.

Sauce for Fish in Lent, or at any Time.

TAKE a little thyme, horse-radish, a bit of onion, lemon-peel, and whole pepper; boil them in a little fair water; then put in two anchovies, and four spoonfuls of white wine; strain them out, and put the liquor into the same pan again, with a pound of fresh butter; when it is melted take it off the fire, and stir in the yolks of two eggs well beaten, with three spoonfuls of white wine; set it on the fire again, and keep it stirring till it is the thickness of cream, and pour it hot over your fish. Garnish them with lemon and horse-radish.

To make Oyster Sauce.

TAKE half a pint of large oysters, liquor and all; put them into a saucepan, with two or three blades of mace, and twelve whole pepper-corns; let them simmer over a slow fire, till the oysters are fine and plump, then carefully with a fork take out the oysters from the liquor and spice, and let the liquor boil five or six minutes; then strain the liquor, wash out the saucepan clean, and put the oysters and liquor in the saucepan again, with half a pint of gravy, and half a pound of butter just rolled in a little flour. You may put in two spoonfuls of white wine, keep it stirring till the sauce boils, and all the butter is melted.

Oyster Loaves.

TAKE a quart of middling oysters, and wash them in their own liquor; then strain them through a flannel, and put them on the fire to warm; then take three quarters of a pint of gravy and put to the oysters, with a blade of mace, a little white pepper, a little horse-radish, a piece of lean bacon, and half a lemon; then stew them leisurely. Take three penny loaves, and pick out the crumb clean; then take a pound of butter, and set on the fire in a saucepan that will hold the loaves, and when it is melted, take it off the fire, and let it settle; then pour off the clear, and set it on the fire again with the loaves in it, turning them about till you find them crisp; then put a pound of butter in a frying-pan, and with a dredging-box dust in flour till you find it of a reasonable thickness, then mix that and the oysters together; when they are stewed enough take out the bacon, and put the oysters into the loaves; then put them into a dish, and garnish the loaves with the oysters you cannot get in, and with slices of lemon; and when you have thickened the liquor, squeeze in lemon to your taste; or you may fry the oysters with batter to garnish the leaves.

To make Anchovy Sauce.

TAKE a pint of gravy, put in an anchovy, take a quarter of a pound of butter rolled in a little flour, and stir all together till it boils. You may add a little juice of a lemon, catchup, red wine, and walnut liquor, just as you please.

Plain butter melted thick, with a spoonful of walnut-pickle, or catchup, is good sauce, or anchovy.

To stuff a Fillet of Veal, or Calf's-Heart, with pickled Herrings.

TAKE two herrings, skin, bone, and wash them in several waters. Chop them very small, with a quarter of a pound of suet. Add a handful of bread grated fine; and the like quantity of parsley, cut very small. Throw in a little thyme, nutmeg, and pepper, to your taste; and mix all together, with two eggs.

Half the quantity of the above stuffing is exceedingly good for a calf's-heart.

Stuffing, of pickled Herrings, for a roast Turkey.

WASH, in several waters, two pickled herrings; which afterwards skin, and take the bone out carefully. Take half a pound of suet, and two large handfuls of bread grated. Chop the herrings, suet, and bread (separately) very small. Beat these all together in a marble mortar, with the white of an egg, after throwing in a little nutmeg and white pepper.

Pickled Herring Pudding for a Hare.

TAKE half a pound of the lean of fine veal, which clear of the skin and strings; two pickled herrings, which wash in two or three waters; then skin, and clear them of the bones; a quarter of a pound of suet, two handfuls of bread grated fine, a handful of parsley; chop all the above (separately) then mix them, throwing in half a nutmeg grated, a little thyme, sweet-marjoram, and one egg: beat the whole together in a marble mortar.

CHAP. VIII.
Of SOUPS and BROTHS.

Rules to be observed in making Soups or Broths.

FIRST take great care the pots or saucepans and covers be very clean and free from all grease and sand, and that they be well tinned, for fear of giving the broths and soups any brassy taste. If you have time to stew as softly as you can, it will both have a finer flavour, and the meat will be tenderer. But then observe, when you make soups or broths for present use, if it is to be done softly, don't put much more water than you intend to have soup or broth; and if you have the convenience of an earthen pan or pipkin, set it on wood embers till it boils, then skim it, and put in your seasoning; cover it close, and set it on embers, so that it may do very softly for some time, and both the meat and broths will be delicious. You must observe in all broths and soups that one thing does not taste more than another; but that the taste be equal, and it has a fine agreeable relish, according to what you design it for; and you must be sure, that all the greens and herbs you put in be cleaned, washed, and picked.

To make a Soup.

TAKE twelve pounds of beef, a scrag of mutton, and knuckle of veal; it must be neck-beef, and the sticking-piece, put your beef in a saucepan, and half fry it with a bit of butter; then put all in a pot, with nine quarts of water, a good handful of salt, a piece of bacon, boil and skim it, then season it with three onions stuck with cloves, whole pepper, Jamaica pepper, and a bunch of sweet-herbs; let it boil five or six hours close covered; then strain it out, and put it in your dish, with stewed herbs and toasted bread.

Another Receipt for Gravy Soup.

TAKE the bones of a rump of beef, and a piece of the neck, and boil it till you have all the goodness out of it; then strain it off, and take a good piece of butter, and put it in a stew-pan and brown it, then put to it an onion stuck with cloves, some celery, endive, and spinach; then take your gravy, and put to it some pepper, salt, and cloves, and let it boil all together; then put in sippets of bread dried by the fire; and you may put in a glass of red wine. Serve it up with a French roll toasted in the middle.

Another Gravy Soup.

TAKE a leg of beef, and a piece of the neck, boil it till you have all the goodness out of it; then strain it from the meat; take half a pound of fresh butter, put it in a stew-pan, and brown it, adding an onion stuck with cloves, some endive, celery and spinach, and your strong broth, seasoning it to your palate with salt, pepper, and spices; let it boil together, put in chips of French bread dried by the fire, and serve it with a French roll toasted in the middle.

White

White Soup.

TAKE some liquor that has had a leg of mutton boiled in it, in which you may stew a knuckle of veal, an onion, and a bay-leaf; strain it off, and put it again into your stew-pan, with a handful of shred celery, and a good quantity of oysters; let them boil till they will break, then put in such a quantity of buttered crumbs as will make it thick; you may boil in this some vermicelly; grate in half a nutmeg, salt it to your taste; some celery if you please.

Another excellent White Soup.

TO six quarts of water put in a knuckle of veal, a large fowl, and a pound of lean bacon, and half a pound of rice, with two anchovies, a few pepper-corns, two or three onions, a bundle of sweet-herbs, three or four heads of celery in slices, stew all together, till your soup is as strong as you chuse it, then strain it through a hair sieve into a clean earthen pot, let it stand all night, then take off the scum, and pour it clear off into a tossing pan, put in half a pound of Jordan almonds beat fine, boil it a little and run it through a lawn sieve, then put in a pint of cream and the yolk of an egg.——Make it hot, and send it to the table.

To make White Soup a third Way.

BOIL a knuckle of veal and a fowl, with a little mace, two onions, a little pepper and salt to a strong jelly, then strain it and scum off all the fat, have ready the yolks of six eggs well beat, put them in and keep stirring it or it will curdle, put it in your dish with boiled chicken and toasted bread cut in pieces; if you do not like the eggs, you may put in a large handful of vermicelly half an hour before you take it off the fire.

A Fasting-day Soup.

TAKE spinach, sorrel, chervil, and lettuce, and chop them a little; then brown some butter, and put in your herbs, keep them stirring, that they do not burn; then, having boiling water over the fire, put to it a very little pepper, and some salt, a whole onion stuck with cloves, a French roll cut in slices and dried very hard, some pistachia kernels, blanched and shred fine, and let all boil together; then beat up the yolks of eight eggs with a little white wine and the juice of a lemon; mix it with your broth, toast a whole French roll, and put it in the middle of your dish, pouring your soup over it; garnish your dish with ten or twelve poached eggs, and scalded spinach.

To make a Soup.

TAKE a leg of beef, and boil it down with some salt, a bundle of sweet-herbs, an onion, a few cloves, a bit of nutmeg; boil three gallons of water to one; then take two or three pounds of lean beef cut in thin slices; then put in your stew-pan a piece of butter as big as an egg, and flour it, and let the pan be hot, and shake it till the butter be brown; then lay your beef in your pan over a pretty quick fire, cover it close, give it a turn now and then, and strain in your strong broth, with an anchovy or two, a handful of spinach and endive boiled green, and drained and shred gross; then have pallets ready boiled and cut in pieces, and toasts fried and cut like dice, and forced-meat balls fried: take out the fried beef, and put all the rest together with a little pepper, and let it boil a quarter of an hour, and serve it up with a knuckle of veal, or a fowl boiled in the middle.

To make Soup à la Reine.

TAKE a knuckle of veal and three or four pounds of lean beef, put to it six quarts of water with a little salt, when it boils scum it well, then put in six large onions, two large carrots, a head or two of celery, a parsnip, one leek, and a little thyme, boil them all together till the meat is boiled quite down, then strain it through a hair sieve, and let it stand about half an hour, then scum it well, and clear it off gently from the settlings into a clear pan; boil half a pint of cream, and pour it on the crumbs of a halfpenny loaf, and let it soak well; take half a pound of almonds, blanch and beat them as fine as possible, putting in now and then a little cream to prevent them from oiling, then take the yolks of six hard eggs, and the roll that is soaked in the cream, and beat them all together quite fine, then make your broth hot and pour it to your almonds, strain it through a fine hair sieve, rubbing it with a spoon till all the goodness is gone through into a stew-pan, and add more cream to make it white; set it over the fire, keep stirring it till it boils, scum off the froth as it rises, soak the tops of two French rolls in melted butter in a stew-pan till they are crisp, but not brown, then take them out of the butter, and lay them on a plate before the fire; and, a quarter of an hour before you send it to the table, take a little of the soup hot, and put it to the roll in the bottom of the tureen; put your soup over the fire, keep stirring it till ready to boil, then pour it into your tureen, and serve it up hot; be sure you take all the fat off the broth

The COMPLETE HOUSEWIFE. 57

broth before you put it to the almonds or it will spoil it, and take care it does not curdle.

To make white Onion Soup

TAKE thirty large onions, boil them in five quarts of water with a knuckle of veal, a blade or two of mace, and a little whole pepper; when your onions are quite soft take them up, and rub them through a hair sieve, and work half a pound of butter with flour in them; when the meat is boiled so as to leave the bone, strain the liquor to the onions, and boil it gently for half an hour, serve it up with a coffee cup full of cream and a little salt; be sure you stir it when you put in the flour and butter, for fear of its burning.

To make Brown Onion Soup.

SKIN and cut roundways in slices six large Spanish onions, fry them in butter till they are a nice brown, and very tender, then take them out and lay them on a hair sieve to drain out the butter, when drained put them in a pot with five quarts of boiling water, boil them one hour and stir them often, then add pepper and salt to your taste, rub the crumbs of a penny loaf through a colander, put it to the soup, stir it well to keep it from being in lumps, and boil it two hours more; ten minutes before you send it up beat the yolks of two eggs with two spoonfuls of vinegar and a little of the soup, pour it in by degrees, and keep stirring it all the time one way, put in a few cloves if you chuse it.—N. B. It is a fine soup, and will keep three or four days.

To make Partridge Soup.

TAKE off the skin of two old partridges, cut them into small pieces with three slices of ham, two or three onions sliced and some celery, fry them in butter till they are as brown as they can be made without burning, then put them into three quarts of water with a few black pepper-corns, boil it slowly till a little more than a pint is consumed, then strain it, put in some stewed celery and fried bread.

To make Asparagus-Soup

TAKE twelve pounds of lean beef, cut in thin slices; then put a quarter of a pound of butter in a stew-pan over the fire, and put your beef in; let it boil up thick till it begins to brown; then put in a pint of brown ale, and a gallon of water; cover

it

it close, and let it stew gently for an hour and a half; put in what spice you like in the stewing, and strain out the liquor, and skim off all the fat; then put in some vermicelly, some celery washed and cut small, half a hundred of asparagus cut small, and palates boiled tender and cut; put all these in, and let them boil gently till tender; just as it is going up fry a handful of spinach in butter, and throw in a French roll.

Asparagus Soup, or green Pease.

TAKE some strong broth of beef, mutton, or both, boil in it a large brown toast, a little flour sifted from oatmeal, and three or four handfuls of asparagus cut small, so far as they are green (or green pease) some spinach, white beets, and what herbs you like, a little celery, and a few sprigs of parsley; toast little white toasts, butter them, and pour your soup upon them; the brown bread ought to be strained off before your asparagus goes in; season it with salt to your taste.

To make Plumb Pottage.

TAKE a leg and shin of beef to ten gallons of water, boil it very tender, and when the broth is strong, strain it out; wipe the pot, and put in the broth again; slice six penny loaves thin, cutting off the top and bottom; put some of the liquor to it, cover it up, and let it boil a quarter of an hour, and then put it in your pot; let it boil a quarter of an hour, then put in five pounds of currants; let them boil a little, and put in five pounds of raisins, and two pounds of prunes, and let them boil till they swell, then put in three quarters of an ounce of mace, half an ounce of cloves, two nutmegs, all of them beat fine, and mix it with a little liquor cold, and put them in a very little while; then take off the pot, and put in three pounds of sugar, a little salt, a quart of sack, a quart of claret, and the juice of two or three lemons; you may thicken with sago instead of bread, if you please; pour them into earthen pans, and keep them for use.

A Soup or Pottage.

TAKE several knuckles of mutton, a knuckle of veal, a shin of beef, and put to these twelve quarts of water; cover the pot close, and set it on the fire; let it not boil too fast; skim it well, and let it stand on the fire twenty-four hours; then strain it thro' a colander, when it is cold take off the fat, set it on the fire again, and season it with salt, a few cloves, pepper, a blade of mace, a nutmeg quartered, a bunch of sweet herbs, and a pint of gravy; let all these boil up for half an hour, and then strain it; put spinach, sorrel, green peafe, asparagus, or artichoke bottoms, according to the time of the year; then thicken it up with the yolks of three or four eggs; have in readiness some sheep's tongues, cocks-combs and sweet-breads, sliced thin and fried, and put them in, some mushrooms, and French bread dried and cut in little bits, some forcemeat balls, and some very thin slices of bacon; make all these very hot, and garnish the dish with coleworts and spinach scalded green.

To make Peafe-Pottage.

TAKE a quart of white peafe, a piece of neck-beef, and four quarts of fair water; boil them till they are all to pieces, and strain them through a colander; then take a handful or two of spinach, a top or two of young coleworts, and a very small leek; shred the herbs a little, and put them into a frying-pan, or stew-pan, with three quarters of a pound of fresh butter, but the butter must be very hot before you put in your herbs; let them fry a little while, then put in your liquor, and two or three anchovies, some salt and pepper to your taste, a sprig of mint rubbed in small, and let it all boil together till you think it is thick enough; then have in readiness some forcemeat, and make three or fourscore balls, about the bigness of large peafe, fry them brown, and put them in the dish you serve it in, and fry some thin slices of bacon; put some into the dish, and some on the rim of the dish, with scalded spinach; fry some toasts after the balls are brown and hard, and break them into the dish; then pour your pottage over all, and serve to the table.

Peafe-Soup.

TAKE the broth of a leg of beef, and boil in it a piece of bacon and a sheep's-head, to mash with a good quantity of peafe; strain the broth from the husks, then take half a nutmeg, four cloves, and a race of ginger, some pepper, a pretty deal of mint, some sweet marjoram and thyme; bruise the spice, powder the herbs, and put them into the soup; boil leeks in two or three waters till they are tender, and the rankness out of them; put in what other herbs you please, as spinach, lettuce, beets, &c. forget not to boil an onion or two in the broth at first. Some will burn butter in a stew-pan, and when it is boiling put in a large plate of sliced onions; let them boil till they are tender, keeping them stirring all the time, and boil them in a soup; others will scrape a little Cheshire cheese, and strew in the butter and onions; it ought to be old Cheshire cheese; if you put in the onions mentioned last, they must be fried in butter, brown, before they are put into the soup; when you

put

put them into the frying-pan flour them well, put in celery and turneps, if you like the taste, but strain the turneps out: to throw an old pigeon in with the meat at first, gives a high taste, or a piece of lean bacon dried.

To make green Peafe-Soup.

TAKE half a bushel of the youngest peafe, divide the great from the small; boil the smallest in two quarts of water, and the biggest in one quart; when they are well boiled, bruise the biggest, and when the thin is drained from it boil the thick in as much cold water as will cover it; then rub away the skins, and take a little spinach, mint, sorrel, lettuce, parsley, and a good quantity of marigolds; wash, shred, and boil these in half a pound of butter, and drain the small peafe; save the water, and mingle all together, with a spoonful of whole pepper; then melt a quarter of a pound of butter, shake a little flour into it, and let it boil; put the liquor to the butter, and mingle all well together, and let them boil up; so serve it with dried bread.

Another Way.

MAKE strong broth of a leg of beef, a knuckle or scrag end of veal, and scrag of mutton; clear it off; then chop some cabbage, lettuce, spinach, and a little sorrel; then put half a pound of butter in a flat saucepan, dredge in some flour, put it over the fire until it is brown: then put in your herbs and tofs them up a little over the fire; then put in a pint and a half of green peafe half boiled before, adding your strong broth, and let it just simmer over the fire half an hour: then cut some French bread very thin, dry it well before the fire, put it in, and let it stew half an hour longer; feason your broth with pepper, salt, and a few cloves and mace. Garnish the dish with spinach scalded green, and some very thin bits of bacon toasted before the fire.

To make strong Broth to keep for use.

TAKE part of a leg of beef, the scrag end of a neck of mutton, break the bones in pieces, put to it as much water as will cover it, and a little salt; when it boils skim it clean, and put into it a whole onion stuck with cloves, a bunch of sweet-herbs, some pepper, and a nutmeg quartered; let these boil till the meat is boiled in pieces, and the strength is boiled out of it; then put to it two or three anchovies; when they are dissolved, strain it out, and keep it for any sort of hash or fricasee.

To make Pocket Soup.

TAKE a leg of veal, strip off all the skin and fat, then take all the muscular or fleshy parts clean from the bones. Boil this flesh in three or four gallons of water till it comes to a strong jelly, and that the meat is good for nothing. Be sure to keep the pot close covered, and not do too fast; take a little out in a spoon now and then, and when you find it is a good rich jelly, strain it through a sieve into a clean earthen pan. When it is cold, take off all the skin and fat from the top, then provide a large deep stew-pan with water boiling over a stove; take some deep china cups, or well-glazed earthen-ware, and fill these cups with the jelly, which you must take clear from the settling at the bottom, and set them in the stew-pan of water. Take great care that none of the water gets into the cups; if it does, it will spoil it. Keep the water boiling gently all the time, till the jelly becomes as thick as glue, take them out, and let them stand to cool; then turn the glue out into some new coarse flannel, which draws out all the moisture; turn them in six or eight hours on fresh flannel, and so do till they are quite dry. Keep it in a dry warm place, and in a little time it will be like a dry hard piece of glue, which you may carry in your pocket without getting any harm. The best way is to put it into little tin boxes. When you use it, boil about a pint of water, and pour it on a piece of glue about as big as a small walnut, stirring it all the time till it is melted. Season with salt to your palate; and if you chuse any herbs, or spice, boil them in the water first, and then pour the water over the glue.

To make portable Soup.

TAKE two legs of beef, about fifty pounds weight, take off all the skin and fat as well as you can, then take all the meat and sinews clean from the bones, which meat put into a large pot, and put to it eight or nine gallons of soft water; first make it boil, then put in twelve anchovies, an ounce of mace, a quarter of an ounce of cloves, an ounce of whole pepper black and white together, six large onions peeled and cut in two, a little bundle of thyme, sweet-marjoram, and winter-savoury, the dry hard crust of a two-penny loaf, stir it all together and cover it close, lay a weight on the cover to keep it close down, and let it boil softly for eight or nine hours, then uncover it, and stir it together; cover it close again, and let it boil till it is a very rich good jelly, which you will know by taking a little out now and then, and letting it cool. When you think it is a thick jelly, take it off, strain it through a coarse hair bag, and press it hard; then strain it through a hair sieve into a large earthen pan; when it is quite cold, take off the skum and fat, and take the fine jelly

clear

clear from the settlings at bottom, and then put the jelly into a large deep well tinned stew-pan. Set it over a stove with a slow fire, keep stirring it often, and take great care it neither sticks to the pan or burns. When you find the jelly very stiff and thick, as it will be in lumps about the pan, take it out, and put it into large deep china cups, or well-glazed earthen-ware. Fill the pan two-thirds full of water, and when the water boils, set in your cups. Be sure no water gets into the cups, and keep the water boiling softly all the time till you find the jelly is like a stiff glue; take out the cups, and when they are cool, turn out the glue into a coarse new flannel. Let it lie eight or nine hours, keeping it in a dry warm place, and turn it on fresh flannel till it is quite dry, and the glue will be quite hard; put it into clean new stone pots, keep it close covered from dust and dirt, in a dry place, and where no damp can come to it.

When you use it, pour boiling water on it, and stir it all the time till it is melted. Season it with salt to your palate. A piece as big as a large walnut will make a pint of water very rich; but as to that you are to make it as good as you please; if for soup, fry a French roll and lay it in the middle of the dish, and when the glue is dissolved in the water, give it a boil and pour it into a dish. If you chuse it for change, you may boil either rice or barley, vermicelly, celery cut small, or truffles or morels; but let them be very tenderly boiled in the water before you stir in the glue, and then give it a boil all together. You may, when you would have it very fine, add forcemeat balls, cocks-combs, or a palate boiled very tender, and cut into little bits; but it will be very rich and good without any of these ingredients.

If for gravy, pour the boiling water on to what quantity you think proper; and when it is dissolved, add what ingredients you please, as in other sauces. This is only in the room of a rich good gravy. You may make your sauce either weak or strong, by adding more or less.

Strong Broth.

TAKE twelve quarts of water, two knuckles of veal, a leg or two shins of beef, two pair of calves-feet, a chicken, a rabbet, two onions, cloves, mace, pepper, salt, a bunch of sweet-herbs; cover it close, and let it boil till six quarts are consumed; strain it out, and keep it for use.

Oyster-Soup.

TAKE a quart of small oysters, put them into a colander to drain; then strain the liquor through a muslin rag, and put to it half a pint of water, and a quarter of a pint of white wine; let them stew with a few sprigs of parsley, and a little thyme, a little eschalot or onion, a little lemon-peel, a few cloves,

cloves, a blade of mace, and a little whole pepper; let them stew gently a pretty while; take a quarter of a pound of butter and put into a pan, but flour it well first, then fry it till it has done hissing; dry the oysters in a cloth, and flour them; put them into the butter, and fry them till they are plump; then take one anchovy and dissolve in the liquor; add some fresh wine, the yolks of two eggs, well beaten; put all into the pan together, and give it a scald, keeping it stirring all the time it is on the fire; before you put the soup into the dish, lay the crust of a French loaf, or a toast, at the bottom, which must soak with some of the liquor over coals. Before you put in the whole, you may add strong broth or fried gravy if not in Lent. This soup must be thick with buttered crumbs: you may add burnt butter or sago, but that you must boil in several waters, the more, the whiter it looks. Vermicelly is good in this, but that must boil but little time. Cray-fish and shrimps do well in this soup: if you have shrimps, the fewer oysters will do.

A Cray-fish Soup.

TAKE a gallon of water, and set it a boiling; put in it a bunch of sweet-herbs, three or four blades of mace, an onion stuck with cloves, pepper, and salt; then have about two hundred cray-fish, save about twenty, then pick the rest from the shells, save the tails whole; the body and shells beat in a mortar, with a pint of pease green or dry, first boiled tender in fair water, put your boiling water to it, and strain it boiling hot through a cloth till you have all the goodness out of it: set it over a slow fire or stew-hole, have ready a French roll cut very thin, and let it be very dry, put it to your soup, let it stew till half is wasted, then put a piece of butter as big as an egg into a saucepan, let it simmer till it has done making a noise, shake in two tea-spoonfuls of flour, stirring it about, and an onion; put in the tails of the fish, give them a shake round, put to them a pint of good gravy, let it boil four or five minutes softly, take out the onion, and put to it a pint of the soup; stir it well together, and pour it all together, and let it simmer very softly a quarter of an hour; fry a French roll very nice and brown, and the twenty cray-fish, pour your soup into the dish, and lay the roll in the middle, and cray-fish round the dish.

Fine cooks boil a brace of carp and tench, and may be a lobster or two, and many more rich things, to make a cray-fish soup; but the above is full as good, and wants no addition.

Another Cray-fish Soup.

BOIL half a hundred of fresh cray-fish, pick out all the meat, which you must save, take a fresh lobster and pick out all the meat, which you must likewise save, pound the shells

of

of the cray-fish and lobster fine in a marble mortar, and boil them in four quarts of water with four pounds of mutton, a pint of green split peafe, nicely picked and washed, a large turnip, carrot, onion, mace, cloves, anchovy, a little thyme, pepper and falt. Stew them on a flow fire till all the goodness is out of the mutton and shells, then strain it through a sieve, and put in the tails of your cray-fish and the lobster meat, but in very small pieces, with the red coral of the lobster, if it has any; boil it half an hour, and just before you serve it up, add a little butter melted thick and smooth, stir it round several times, when you put it in, send it up very hot, but don't put too much spice in it.——N. B. Pick out all the bags and the woolly part of your cray-fish before you pound them.

To make Cray-fish or Lobster-Soup.

TAKE whitings, flounders, and grigs, put them in a gallon of water, with pepper, falt, cloves, mace, a bunch of sweet-herbs, a little onion, and boil them to pieces, and strain them out of the liquor; then take a large carp, cut off one side of it, put some eel to it, make forcemeat of it, and lay it on the carp as before; dredge grated bread over it, butter a dish well, put it in an oven, and bake it; take an hundred of cray-fish, break all the shells of the claws and tails, and take out the meat as whole as you can; then break all the shells small, and the spawn of a lobster, putting them to the foup, and if you please, some gravy; give them a boil together, and strain the liquor out into another faucepan, with the tops of French rolls dried, beat and sifted, and give it a boil up to thicken; then brown some butter, put in the tails and claws of your cray-fish, and some of your forcemeat made into balls, putting your baked carp into the middle of the dish, and pouring your foup on boiling hot, and your cray-fish or lobster in it; garnish the dish with lemon and scalded greens.

Receipt for making pickled Herring-Soup.

TAKE a quart of split peafe; put to them four quarts of cold water, a quarter of an ounce of whole Jamaica pepper, two large onions, three pickled herrings (washed in two or three waters, and the roes out) skinned, and cut to pieces.

Boil all together till a quart is diminished. Pour in a pint of boiling water, and let the whole boil a quarter of an hour. Take it off, and strain it through a colander. Throw into the foup seven or eight handfuls of celery, three heads of endive, all of them cut very small; (but if on ship-board, where endive is not to be had, a larger number of onions may be employed in its stead) together with a handful of dried mint passed through a lawn sieve. Set all these on a fire, and boil the whole near three quarters

quarters of an hour, ſtirring the ſoup perpetually, to prevent burning to, which it will do in a moment, and therefore the pot ſhould ſtand on a trivet.

Bread, cut into diamonds, and fried criſp in butter, muſt be thrown into the ſoup, which then may be ſerved up.

CHAP. IX.
Of MADE DISHES.

BE careful that the toſſing-pan is well tinned, quite clean, and not gritty, and put every ingredient into your white ſauce; have it of a proper thickneſs, and well boiled, before you put in eggs and cream, for they will not add much to the thickneſs, nor ſtir them with a ſpoon after they are in, nor ſet your pan on the fire, for it will gather at the bottom and be in lumps, but hold your pan a good height from the fire, and keep ſhaking the pan round one way; this will keep the ſauce from curdling, and be ſure you do not let it boil; it is the beſt way to take up your meat, collops, or haſh, or any other kind of diſh you are making, with a fiſh-ſlice, and ſtrain your ſauce upon it, for it is almoſt impoſſible to prevent little bits of meat from mixing with the ſauce; and by this method the ſauce will look clear.

In the brown made diſhes, take ſpecial care no fat is on the top of the gravy, but ſkim it clean off, and that it be of a fine brown, and taſte of no one thing particular; if you uſe any wine put it in ſome time before your diſh is ready, to take off the rawneſs, for nothing can give a made diſh a more diſagreeable taſte than raw wine, or freſh anchovy: when you uſe fried forcemeat balls, put them on a ſieve to drain the fat from them, and never let them boil in your ſauce, as it will give them a greaſy look, and ſoften the balls; the beſt way is to put them in after your meat is diſhed up.

You may uſe pickled muſhrooms, artichoke-bottoms, morels, truffles, and forcemeat balls, in almoſt every made diſh; and in ſeveral, you may uſe a roll of forcemeat inſtead of balls, and where you can uſe it, it is much handſomer than balls, eſpecially in a mock turtle, collared or ragooed breaſt of veal, or any large made diſh.

A fine Side-Diſh.

TAKE veal, chicken, or rabbet, with as much marrow, or beef ſuet, as meat; a little thyme, lemon-peel, marjoram, two anchovies, waſhed and boned; a little pepper, ſalt, mace, and cloves; bruife the yolks of hard eggs, fome oyfters, or mufh-rooms; mix all thefe together, chop them, and beat them in a mortar very fine; then fpread the caul of a breaft of veal on a table, and lay a layer of this, and a layer of middling bacon, cut in thin fmall pieces, rolling it up hard in the caul; roaft or bake it as you like; cut it into thin flices, and lay it in your difh, with a rich gravy fauce.

Another.

TAKE half a pound of almonds, blanch and beat them very fine; put to them a little rofe or orange-flower-water in the beating; then take a quart of fweet thick cream, and boil it with whole cinnamon, and mace, and quartered dates; fweeten your cream with fugar to your tafte, and mix it with your almonds, and ftir it well together, and ftrain it out through a fieve. Let your cream cool, and thicken it with the yolks of fix eggs; then garnifh a deep difh, lay pafte at the bottom, and then put in fliced artichoke-bottoms, being firft boiled, and upon that a layer of marrow, fliced citron, and candied orange; fo do till your difh is near full; then pour in your cream, and bake it without a lid; when it is baked, fcrape fugar on it, and ferve it up hot. Half an hour will bake it.

To force a Leg of Veal, Mutton, or Lamb.

TAKE out all the meat, and leave the fkin whole; then take the lean of it and make it into forcemeat thus: to two pounds of your lean meat, three pounds of beef fuet; take away all fkins from the meat and fuet; then fhred both very fine, and beat it with a rolling-pin, till you know not the meat from the fuet; then mix with it four fpoonfuls of grated bread, half an ounce of cloves and mace beaten, as much pepper, fome falt, a few fweet-herbs fhred fmall; mix all thefe together with fix raw eggs, and put into the fkin again, and few it up. If you roaft it, ferve it with anchovy-fauce; if you boil it, lay cauliflower or French beans under it. Garnifh with pickles, or ftew oyfters and put under it, with forcemeat balls, or faufages fried in butter.

To make a favoury Difh of Veal.

CUT large collops out of a leg of veal, fpread them abroad on a dreffer, hack them with the back of a knife, dip them in the yolks of eggs, and feafon them with cloves, mace, nutmeg, falt, and pepper; then make forcemeat with fome of your veal, beef fuet, oyfters chopped, fweet-herbs fhred fine, and the aforefaid fpice, and ftrew all thefe over your collops; roll and tie them up, put them on fkewers, tie them to a fpit, and roaft roast them; to the rest of your forcemeat add the yolk of an egg or two, make it up in balls, and fry them; put them in the dish with your meat when roasted, and make the sauce with strong broth, or anchovy, an eschalot, and a little white wine and spice; let it stew, and thicken it up with butter.

Bombarded Veal.

YOU must get a fillet of veal, cut out of it five lean pieces as thick as your hand, round them up a little, then lard them very thick on the round side with little narrow thin pieces of bacon, and lard five sheeps tongues (being first boiled and blanched) lard them here and there with very little bits of lemon-peel, and make a well-seasoned forcemeat of veal, bacon, ham, beef suet, and an anchovy beat well; make another tender forcemeat of veal, beef suet, mushrooms, spinach, parsley, thyme, sweet-marjoram, winter savoury, and green onions. Season with pepper, salt, and mace; beat it well, make a round ball of the other forcemeat and stuff in the middle of this, roll it up in a veal caul, and bake it; what is left, tie up like a Bologna sausage, and boil it, but first rub the caul with the yolk of an egg; put the larded veal into a stew-pan with some good gravy, and when it is enough skim off the fat, put in some truffles and morels, and some mushrooms. Your forcemeat being baked enough, lay it in the middle, the veal round it, and the tongues fried, and laid between, the boiled cut into slices, and fried, and throw all over. Pour on them the sauce. You may add artichoke-bottoms, sweet-breads, and cocks-combs, if you please. Garnish with lemon.

Veal Rolls.

TAKE ten or twelve little thin slices of veal, lay on them some forcemeat according to your fancy, roll them up, and tie them just across the middle with coarse thread, put them on a bird-spit, rub them over with the yolks of eggs, flour them, and baste them with butter. Half an hour will do them. Lay them into a dish, and have ready some good gravy, with a few truffles and morels, and some mushrooms. Garnish with lemon.

To make Veal Cutlets.

CUT your veal steaks thin, hack them, and season them with pepper and salt, and sweet herbs; wash them over with eggs, and strew over them some forcemeat; put two steaks together, and lard them with bacon; wash them over with melted butter, and wrap them in white papers buttered; roast them on a lark-spit, or bake them; when they are enough, unpaper them, and serve them with good gravy and sliced lemon.

Mutton Cutlets.

CUT a neck of mutton bone by bone, and beat it flat with your cleaver; have ready seasoning, with grated bread, a little thyme rubbed to powder, shred parsley, with grated nutmeg, and some lemon-peels minced; then beat up two eggs, flour your cutlets on both sides; dip them in the eggs beat up with a little salt, and roll them in the grated bread and seasoning; put some butter in your frying-pan, and when it is hot lay in your cutlets, and fry them brown on both sides. For sauce, take gravy or strong broth, an onion, some spice, a bit of bacon and a bay-leaf, and boil them well together; then beat it up with an anchovy, or some oysters, and a quarter of a pint of red wine; strew upon your cutlets pickled walnuts in quarters, barberries, samphire or cucumbers, and a little sliced lemon.

A pretty side-dish of Beef.

ROAST a tender piece of beef, lay fat bacon over it, and roll it in paper; baste it, and when it is roasted cut about two pounds in thin slices, lay them in a stew-pan, and take six large cucumbers, peel them, and chop them small, lay over them a little pepper and salt, stew them in butter for about ten minutes, then drain out the butter, and shake some flour over them; toss them up, pour in half a pint of gravy, let them stew till they are thick, and dish them up.

Beef Olives.

CUT a rump of beef into steaks half a quarter long, about an inch thick, and square; lay on some good forcemeat made with veal, roll them, tie them once round with a hard knot, dip them in egg, crumbs of bread, and grated nutmeg, and a little pepper and salt. The best way is to roast them, or fry them brown in fresh butter; lay them every one on a bay-leaf, and cover them every one with a piece of bacon toasted, have some good gravy, a few truffles and morels, and mushrooms; boil all together, pour into the dish, and send it to table.

Veal Olives.

THEY are good done the same way, only roll them narrow at one end and broad at the other. Fry them of a fine brown. Omit the bay-leaf, but lay little bits of bacon about two inches long on them. The same sauce. Garnish with lemon.

Beef Collops.

CUT them into thin pieces about two inches long, beat them with the back of a knife very well, grate some nutmeg, flour them a little, lay them in a stew-pan, put in as much water as you think will do for sauce, half an onion cut small, a little piece of lemon-peel cut small, a bundle of sweet-herbs, a little pepper and salt, a piece of butter rolled in a little flour. Set them on a slow fire: when they begin to simmer, stir them now and then; when they begin to be hot, ten minutes will do them, but take care they do not boil. Take out the sweet-herbs, pour it into the dish, and send it to table.

Note, You may do the inside of a sirloin of beef in the same manner, the day after it is roasted, only do not beat them, but cut them thin.

N. B. You may do this dish between two pewter dishes: hang them between two chairs, take six sheets of white-brown paper, tear them into slips, and burn them under the dish, one piece at a time.

An Amulet of Eggs the savoury way.

TAKE a dozen of eggs, beat them very well, season them with salt and a little pepper, then have your frying pan ready with a good deal of fresh butter in it, and let it be thoroughly hot; then put in your eggs, with four spoonfuls of strong gravy, and have ready parsley, and a few chives cut, and throw them over it, and when it is enough turn it; and when done, dish it, and squeeze orange or lemon over it.

Artificial Potatoes for Lent: A Side Dish.

TAKE a pound of butter, put it into a stone mortar, with half a pound of Naples biscuit grated, and half a pound of Jordan almonds beat small after they are blanched, eight yolks of eggs, four whites, a little sack and orange-flower-water; sweeten to your taste; pound all together till you do not know what it is, and with a little fine flour make it into stiff paste, lay it on a table, and have ready about two pounds of fine lard in your pan, let it boil very fast, and cut your paste the bigness of chesnuts, and throw them into the boiling lard, and let them boil till they are of a yellow brown; when they are enough, take them up in a sieve to drain the fat from them; put them in a dish, pour sack and melted butter; strew double refined sugar over the brim of the dish.

Scotch Collops.

CUT your collops off a fillet of veal; cut them thin, hack them and fry them in fresh butter; then take them out and brown your pan with butter and flour, as you do for a soup. Do not make it too thick; put in your collops and some bacon cut thin and fried, and some forcemeat balls fried, some mushrooms, oysters, artichoke-bottoms, sliced lemon, and sweet-breads, or lamb-stones; some strong broth, gravy, and thick butter; toss up all together. Garnish the dish with sliced lemon.

Another Method.

CUT thin slices out of a leg of veal, as many as you think will serve for a dish, hack them, and lard some with bacon, and fry them in butter; then take them out of the pan, and keep them warm; clean the pan, and put into it half a pint of oysters, with their liquor, some strong broth, one or two eschalots, a glass of white wine, two or three anchovies minced, some grated nutmeg; let these have a boil up, and thicken it with four or five eggs and a piece of butter; then put in your collops, and shake them together till it is thick; put dried sippets on the bottom of the dish, and put your collops in, and so many as you please of the things in your hash.

Another Method.

TAKE the skin from a fillet of veal, and cut it in thin collops, hack and scotch them with the back of a knife, lard half of them with bacon, and fry them with a little brown butter; then take them out, and put them into another tossing-pan; then set the pan they were fried in over the fire again, and wash it out with a little strong broth, rubbing it with your ladle, then pour it to the collops; do this every pan full till all are fried; then stew and toss them up with a pint of oysters, two anchovies, two shivered palates, cocks-combs, lamb-stones, and sweet-breads, blanched and sliced, savoury balls, onions, a faggot of sweet-herbs; thicken it with brown butter, and garnish it with lemons.

Another Method.

CUT thin slices off a fillet of veal, and hack them; then take the yolks of four eggs; beat a little melted butter, a little salt, and some nutmeg, or lemon-peel grated in it; then dip in each collop, lay them in a pewter-dish, flour them, and let them lie till you want them. Put a bit of butter in the frying-pan, and your collops, and fry them quick, shaking them all

the

the while to keep the butter from oiling; then pour it into a stew-pan covered close, and keep it warm; then put to them some good gravy, some mushrooms, or what else you like, a bit of butter, toss it up thick, and squeeze an orange over it.

To dress a Fillet of Veal with Collops.

FOR an alteration, take a small fillet of veal, cut what collops you want, then take the udder and fill it with forcemeat; roll it round, tie it with a packthread across, and roast it; lay your collops in the dish, and lay your udder in the middle. Garnish your dishes with lemon.

A Calf's Head Surprise.

YOU must bone it, but not split it, cleanse it well, fill it with a ragoo (in the form it was before) made thus: take two sweetbreads, each sweetbread being cut into eight pieces, an ox's palate boiled tender and cut into little pieces, some cockscombs, half an ounce of truffles and morels, some mushrooms, some artichoke-bottoms, and asparagus-tops; stew all these in half a pint of good gravy, season it with two or three blades of mace, four cloves, half a nutmeg, a very little pepper, and some salt, pound all these together, and put them into the ragoo: when it has stewed about half an hour, take the yolks of three eggs beat up with two spoonfuls of cream and two of white wine, put it to the ragoo, keep it stirring one way for fear of turning, and stir in a piece of butter rolled in flour; when it is very thick and smooth fill the head, make a forcemeat with half a pound of veal, half a pound of beef suet, as much crumbs of bread, a few sweet-herbs, a little lemon-peel, and some pepper, salt, and mace, all beat fine together in a marble mortar; mix it up with two eggs, make a few balls, (about twenty) put them into the ragoo in the head, then fasten the head with fine wooden skewers, lay the forcemeat over the head, do it over with the yolks of two eggs, and send it to the oven to bake. It will take about two hours baking. You must lay pieces of butter all over the head, and then flour it. When it is baked enough, lay it in your dish, and have a pint of good fried gravy. If there is any gravy in the dish the head was baked in, put it to the other gravy, and boil it up; pour it into your dish, and garnish with lemon. You may throw some mushrooms over the head.

To make Forcemeat.

TAKE a piece of a leg of veal, the lean part, and some lean bacon; mince them very fine, and add a double quantity of suet; put it all in a marble mortar, beat it well, sprinkle it with a little water in the beating; season it with pepper, salt, and a little cloves and mace, to your taste; shred spinach very fine if you would have it look green, or else without; make it up as you use it, with an egg or two, and roll it in long or round balls.

Hogs Ears forced.

TAKE four hogs ears, and half boil them, or take them soused; make a forcemeat thus: take half a pound of beef suet, as much crumbs of bread, an anchovy, some sage, boil and chop very fine a little parsley; mix all together with the yolk of an egg, a little pepper, slit your ears very carefully to make a place for your stuffing, fill them, flour them, and fry them in fresh butter till they are of a fine brown; then pour out all the fat clean, and put to them half a pint of gravy, a glass of white wine, three tea-spoonfuls of mustard, a piece of butter as big as a nutmeg rolled in flour, a little pepper, a small onion whole; cover them close, and let them stew softly for half an hour, shaking your pan now and then. When they are enough, lay them in your dish, and pour your sauce over them; but first take out the onion. This makes a very pretty dish; but if you would make a fine large dish, take the feet, and cut all the meat in small thin pieces, and stew with the ears. Season with salt to your palate.

To force Cocks-Combs.

PARBOIL your cocks-combs, then open them with a point of a knife at the great end: take the white of a fowl, as much bacon and beef marrow, cut these small, and beat them fine in a marble mortar; season them with salt, pepper, and grated nutmeg, and mix it with an egg; fill the cocks-combs, and stew them in a little strong gravy softly for half an hour, then slice in some fresh mushrooms and a few pickled ones; then beat up the yolk of an egg in a little gravy, stirring it. Season with salt. When they are enough, dish them up in little dishes or plates.

How to force a Fowl.

TAKE a good fowl, kill, pull and draw it; slit the skin down the back, take off the flesh from the bones, mince it very small, and mix it with one pound of beef suet shred, and a pint of large oysters chopped, two anchovies, an eschalot, a little grated bread, some sweet-herbs; shred all these very well, mix them, and make it up with the yolks of eggs; put all these ingredients on the bones again, and draw the skin over again;

few up the back, and put the fowl in a bladder; boil it an hour and a quarter; then stew some more oysters in gravy, bruise in a little of your forcemeat, and beat it up with fresh butter; put the fowl in the middle; pour on the sauce and garnish with sliced lemon.

To make a Pulpatoon of Pigeons.

TAKE mushrooms, palates, oysters, sweet-breads, and fry them in butter; then put all these into a strong gravy; give them a heat over the fire, and thicken up with an egg and a bit of butter; then half roast six or eight pigeons, and lay them in a crust of forcemeat, as follows: scrape a pound of veal, and two pounds of marrow, and beat it together in a stone mortar, after it is shred very fine; then season it with salt, pepper, spice, and put in hard eggs, anchovies, and oysters; beat all together, and make the lid and sides of your pye of it; first, lay a thin crust in your pattlpan, then put in your forcemeat, then lay an exceeding thin crust over them, then put in your pigeons and other ingredients, with a little butter on the top; bake it two hours.

To make a Bisk of Pigeons.

TAKE twelve pigeons, fill the bellies with forcemeat, and half roast them, or half boil them in strong broth; then have slices of French bread, toasted hard and stewed in strong broth; and have in readiness some lamb-stones, sweet-breads, and palates, they being first boiled tender; then stew them with your pigeons in your strong broth; add balls of forcemeat first stewed or fried; lay your pigeons in a dish; lay on them thin slices of broiled bacon, and your other ingredients, and pour in your strong broth, and garnish with lemon. You may leave out the sweet-breads, palates, and lamb-stones, and put in scalded herbs; as for soups, and turneps half boiled, cut like dice, and fried brown, and so serve it like a soup, and but six pigeons.

To do Pigeons in Jelly.

TAKE a knuckle of veal, and a good piece of ising-glass, and make a strong jelly; season it with mace, white pepper, salt, bay-leaves, and lemon-peel; then truss your pigeons as for boiling, and boil them in the jelly; when they are cold, put them in the dish you serve them in; then add the juice of a lemon to your jelly, clarify it with the whites of eggs, run it through a jelly bag into a pan, and keep it till it is cold: with a spoon lay it in heaps, on and between your pigeons. Garnish with sliced lemon and bay-leaves.

To

To make a Poloe.

TAKE a pint of rice, boil it in as much water as will cover it; when your rice is half boiled put in your fowl, with a small onion, a blade or two of mace, some whole pepper, and some salt; when it is enough, put the fowl in the dish, and pour the rice over it.

To make Pockets.

CUT three slices out of a leg of veal, the length of a finger, the breadth of three fingers, the thickness of a thumb, with a sharp pen-knife; give it a slit through the middle, leaving the bottom and each side whole, the thickness of a straw, then lard the top with small fine lards of bacon; then make a forcemeat of marrow, sweet-breads, and lamb-stones just boiled; make it up after it is seasoned and beaten together with the yolks of two eggs, and put it into your pockets, as if you were filling a pincushion; then sew up the top with fine thread, flour them, put melted butter on them, and bake them; roast three sweet-breads to put between, and serve them with gravy-sauce.

To make artificial Venison.

BONE a rump of beef, or a large shoulder of mutton; then beat it with a rolling-pin; season it with pepper and nutmeg, lay it twenty-four hours in sheep's-blood, then dry it with a cloth, and season it again with pepper, salt, and spice. Put your meat in the form of a paste, and bake it as a venison-pasty, and make a gravy with the bones, to put in when it is drawn out of the oven.

To keep Smelts in Jelly.

TAKE smelts alive, if you can get them; chuse out the firmest without spawn, set them a boiling in a gallon of water, a pint of wine vinegar, two handfuls of salt, and a bunch of sweet-herbs, and lemon-peel; let them boil three or four walms, and take them up before they break. The jelly make thus: take a quart of the liquor, a quart of vinegar, a quart of white wine, one ounce of ising-glass, some cloves, mace, sliced ginger, whole pepper, and salt; boil these over a gentle fire till a third part be consumed, and the ising-glass be melted; then set it by till almost cold: lay your smelts in a china-plate one by one, then pour it on your smelts; set it in a cool place; it will jelly by next day.

Chickens forced with Oysters.

LARD and truss them; make a forcing with oysters, sweet-breads, parsley, truffles, mushrooms, and onions; chop these together, and season it; mix it with a piece of butter and the yolk of an egg; then tie them at both ends and roast them; then make for them a ragoo, and garnish them with sliced lemon.

To make Salamongundy.

TAKE two or three Roman or cabbage lettuces, and when you have washed them clean, swing them pretty dry in a cloth; then beginning at the open end, cut them cross-ways, as fine as a good big thread, and lay the lettuces so cut, about an inch thick, all over the bottom of a dish. When you have thus garnished your dish, take two cold roasted pullets or chickens, and cut the flesh off the breasts and wings into slices, about three inches long, a quarter of an inch broad, and as thin as a shilling: lay them upon the lettuce round the end to the middle of the dish, and the other towards the brim; then having boned and cut six anchovies, each into eight pieces, lay them all between each slice of the fowls, then cut the lean meat off the legs into dice, and cut a lemon into small dice; then mince the yolks of four eggs, three or four anchovies, and a little parsley, and make a round heap of these in your dish, piling it up in the form of a sugar-loaf, and garnish it with onions, as big as the yolks of eggs, boiled in a good deal of water very tender and white. Put the largest of the onions in the middle on the top of the salamongundy, and lay the rest all round the brim of the dish, as thick as you can lay them; then beat some sallad oil up with vinegar, salt, and pepper, and pour over it all. Garnish with grapes just scalded, or French beans blanched, or nasturtium-flowers, and serve it up for a first course.

Another Way.

MINCE two chickens, either boiled or roasted, very fine, or veal, if you please; also mince the yolks of hard eggs very small, and mince the whites very small by themselves; shred the pulp of two or three lemons very small, then lay in your dish a layer of mincemeat, and a layer of yolks of eggs, a layer of whites, a layer of anchovies, a layer of your shred lemon-pulp, a layer of pickles, a layer of sorrel, a layer of spinach and eschalots shred small. When you have filled a dish with the ingredients, set an orange or lemon on the top; then garnish with horse-radish scraped, barberries, and sliced lemon. Beat up some oil, with the juice of lemon, salt, and mustard, thick and

and serve it up for a second course, side-dish, or middle-dish, for supper.

To make a grand Dish of Eggs.

YOU must break as many eggs as the yolks will fill a pint bason, the whites by themselves, tie the yolks by themselves in a bladder round: boil them hard, then have a wooden bowl that will hold a quart, made like two butter-dishes, but in the shape of an egg, with a hole through one at the top. You are to observe, when you boil the yolks, to run a packthread through, and leave a quarter of a yard hanging out. When the yolk is boiled hard, put it into the bowl-dish; but be careful to hang it so as to be in the middle. The string being drawn through the hole, then clap the two bowls together and tie them tight, and with a funnel pour in the whites through the hole; then stop the hole close, and boil it hard. It will take an hour. When it is boiled enough, carefully open it, and cut the string close. In the mean time take twenty eggs, beat them well, the yolks by themselves, and the whites by themselves; divide the whites into two, and boil them in bladders the shape of an egg. When they are boiled hard, cut one in two long-ways and one cross-ways, and with a fine sharp knife cut out some of the white in the middle; lay the great egg in the middle, the two long halves on each side, with the hollow part uppermost, and the two round flat between. Take an ounce of truffles and morels, cut them very small, boil them in half a pint of water till they are tender, then take a pint of fresh mushrooms clean picked, washed, and chopped small, and put into the truffles and morels. Let them boil, add a little salt, a little beaten nutmeg, a little beaten mace, and add a gill of pickled mushrooms chopped fine. Boil sixteen of the yolks hard in a bladder, then chop them and mix them with the other ingredients; thicken it with a lump of butter rolled in flour, shaking your saucepan round till hot and thick, then fill the round with this, turn them down again, and fill the two long ones; what remains, save to put into the saucepan. Take a pint of cream, a quarter of a pound of butter, the other four yolks beat fine, a gill of white wine, a gill of pickled mushrooms, a little beaten mace, and a little nutmeg; put all into the saucepan to the other ingredients, and stir all well together one way till it is thick and fine; pour it over all, and garnish with notched lemon.

This is a grand dish at a second course. Or you may mix it up with red wine and butter, and it will do for a first course.

CHAP. X.
Of FRICASEYS.

A Fricasey of Lamb.

CUT an hind quarter of lamb into slices, season it with savoury spice, sweet-herbs, and an eschalot; then fry them, and toss them up in strong broth, white wine, oysters, balls and palates, a little brown butter to thicken it, or a bit of butter rolled up in flour.

To make a pale Fricasey.

TAKE lamb, chicken, or rabbets, cut in pieces, wash it well from the blood, then put it in a broad pan or stew-pan; put in as much fair water as will cover it; add salt, a bunch of sweet-herbs, some pepper, an onion, two anchovies, and stew it till it is enough; then mix in a porringer six yolks of eggs, a glass of white wine, a nutmeg grated, a little chopped parsley, a piece of fresh butter, and three or four spoonfuls of cream; beat all these together, and put it in a stew-pan, shaking it together till it is thick. Dish it on sippets, and garnish with sliced lemon.

A Fricasey of Veal.

CUT a fillet of veal in thin slices, a little broader than a crown-piece, beat them with a rolling-pin to make them tender; then steep them in milk three hours, take a blade or two of mace, a few corns of pepper, a small sprig of thyme, a little piece of lemon-peel, a bone of mutton, and the veal bones; stew them gently all together for sauce; if you have no mutton, a little piece of beef; if no beef, a spoonful of gravy at least; then drain the milk from the veal, and put fresh milk into a stew-pan, and stew the veal in it without salt, for that curdles the milk; stew it till it is enough, or you may half stew it, and fry it as pale as possible; then drain it, and strain the sauce, which beat up with some salt, flour, and butter, a pretty deal of cream, and some white wine: just at the last you may shred a little parsley, and scalding it, strew it upon the veal, and squeeze a little lemon, which will thicken the sauce. You may make the same sauce for this as you do for the boiled turkey, if you like it better.

A Fricafey of pulled Chickens.

BOIL fix chickens near enough; flea them, and pull the white flefh all off from the bones; put it in a ftew-pan with half a pint of cream, made fcalding hot, the gravy that runs from the chickens, a few fpoonfuls of that liquor they were boiled in; to this add fome raw parfley fhred fine, give them a tofs or two over the fire, and duft a little flour upon fome butter, and fhake up with them. Chicks done this way muft be killed the night before, and a little more than half boiled, and pulled in pieces as broad as your finger, and half as long; you may add a fpoonful of white wine.

A Fricafey of Chickens.

AFTER you have drawn and wafhed your chickens, half boil them; then take them up, cut them in pieces, put them into a frying-pan, and fry them in butter; then take them out of the pan, clean it, and put in fome ftrong broth, fome white wine, fome grated nutmeg, a little pepper, falt, a bunch of fweet-herbs, and an efchalot or two; let thefe, with two or three anchovies, ftew on a flow fire and boil up; then beat it up with butter and eggs till it is thick; put your chickens in, and tofs them well together; lay fippets in the difh, and ferve it up with fliced lemon and fried parfley.

A brown Fricafey of Chickens or Rabbets.

CUT them in pieces, and fry them in butter; then having ready hot a pint of gravy, a little claret, white wine, ftrong broth, two anchovies, two fhivered palates, a faggot of fweet-herbs, favoury balls and fpice, thicken it with brown butter, and fqueeze on it a lemon.

A white Fricafey of the fame.

CUT them in pieces, wafh them from the blood, and fry them on a flow fire; then put them in a toffing-pan, with a little ftrong broth; feafon them, and tofs them up with mufh-rooms, and oyfters; when almoft enough, put to them a pint of cream, thicken it with a bit of butter rolled up in flour.

A Fricafey of Rabbets.

CUT and wafh your rabbets very well; put them in a frying-pan, with a pound of butter, an onion ftuck with cloves, a bunch of fweet-herbs, and fome falt; let it ftew till it is enough; then beat up the yolks of fix eggs, with a glafs of

white

white wine, a little parsley shred, a nutmeg grated, and mix it by degrees with the liquor in your pan; shake it till it is thick, and serve it up on sippets. Garnish the dish with sliced lemon.

To fricasey Rabbets brown.

CUT up your rabbets as for eating, fry them in butter a light brown, put them into a tossing-pan, with a pint of water, a tea-spoonful of lemon-pickle, a large spoonful of mushroom catchup, one anchovy, a slice of lemon, Cayan pepper, and salt to your taste; stew them over a slow fire till they are enough, thicken your gravy, and strain it, dish up your rabbets, and pour the gravy over.

To fricasey Rabbets white.

CUT your rabbets as before, and put them into a tossing-pan, with a pint of veal gravy, a tea-spoonful of lemon-pickle, one anchovy, a slice of lemon, a little beaten mace, Cayan pepper, and salt; stew them over a slow fire: when they are enough, thicken your gravy with flour and butter, and strain it; then add the yolks of two eggs mixed with a large tea-cupful of thick cream, and a little nutmeg grated in it. Do not let it boil, and serve it up.

To make a white Fricasey.

YOU must take two or three rabbets or chickens, skin them, and lay them in warm water, and dry them with a clean cloth. Put them into a stew-pan with a blade or two of mace, a little black and white pepper, an onion, a little bundle of sweet-herbs, and do but just cover them with water: stew them till they are tender, then with a fork take them out, strain the liquor, and put them into the pan again with half a pint of the liquor and half a pint of cream, the yolks of two eggs beat well, half a nutmeg grated, a glass of white wine, a little piece of butter rolled in flour, and a gill of mushrooms; keep stirring all together, all the while one way, till it is smooth and of a fine thickness, and then dish it up. Add what you please.

Another Method.

TAKE three chickens, skin them, cut them into small pieces; that is, every joint asunder; lay them in warm water, for a quarter of an hour, take them out and dry them with a cloth, then put them into a stew-pan with milk and water, and boil them tender: take a pint of good cream, a quarter of a pound of butter, and stir it till it is thick, then let it stand till it is cool, and put to it a little beaten mace, half a nutmeg grated

grated, a little salt, a gill of white wine, and a few mushrooms; stir all together, then take the chickens out of the stew-pan, throw away what they are boiled in, clean the pan and put in the chickens and sauce together: keep the pan shaking round till they are quite hot, and dish them up. Garnish with lemon. They will be very good without wine.

To fricasey a Pig.

HALF roast your pig, then take it up, and take off the coat, pull the meat in flakes from the bones, and put it in a stew-pan, with some strong broth, some white wine, a little vinegar, an onion stuck with cloves, some mace, a bunch of sweet-herbs, and some salt, and lemon-peel; when it is almost done, take out the onions, herbs, and lemon peel, and put in some mushrooms, and thicken it with cream and eggs. The head must be roasted whole, and set in the middle, and the fricasey round it. Garnish with lemon.

To fricasey Neats-tongues.

TAKE neats-tongues, boil them tender, peel them, cut them into thin slices, and fry them in fresh butter; then pour out the butter, put in as much gravy as you shall want for sauce, a bundle of sweet-herbs, an onion, some pepper and salt, and a blade or two of mace; simmer all together half an hour, then take out your tongue, strain the gravy, put it with the tongue in the stew-pan again, beat up the yolks of two eggs with a glass of white wine, a little grated nutmeg, a piece of butter as big as a walnut rolled in flour, shake all together for four or five minutes, dish it up, and send it to table.

A Fricasey of Tripe.

TAKE lean tripes, cut and scrape them from all the loose stuff; cut them in pieces two inches square, and then cut them across from corner to corner, or in what shape you please; put them into a stew-pan, with half as much white wine as will cover them, sliced ginger, whole pepper, a blade of mace, a little sprig of rosemary, a bay-leaf, an onion, or a small clove of garlic; when it begins to stew, a quarter of an hour will do it; then take out the herbs and onion, and put in a little shred parsley, the juice of a lemon, and a little piece of anchovy shred small, a few spoonfuls of cream, the yolk of an egg, or a piece of butter: salt it to your taste: when it is in the dish, you may lay on a little boiled spinach and sliced lemon.

A Fricasey of double Tripe.

CUT your tripe in slices two inches long, and put it into a stew-pan; put to it a quarter of a pound of capers, as much samphire shred, half a pint of strong both, as much white wine, a bunch of sweet-herbs, a lemon shred small; stew all these together till it is tender; then take it off the fire, and thicken up the liquor with the yolks of three or four eggs, a little parsley boiled green and chopped, some grated nutmeg and salt, shake it well together, serve it on sippets, garnish with lemon. You may add white walnut pickle, or mushrooms, in the room of capers, just to add tartness to your sauce.

A Fricasey of Ox-palates.

MAKE the gravy thus: Take two pounds of beef, cut it in little bits, and put it in a saucepan, with a quart of water, some salt, some whole pepper, an onion, an eschalot or two, two or three anchovies, a bit of horse-radish; let all these stew till it is strong gravy; then strain it out, and set it by; then have ten or twelve ox-palates, boil them till they are tender, peel them, and cut them in square pieces; then flay and draw two or three chickens, cut them between every joint, season them with a little nutmeg, salt, and shred thyme, put them in a pan, and fry them with butter; when they are half fried, put in half your gravy, and all your palates, and let them stew together; put the rest of your gravy into a saucepan, and when it boils, thicken it up with the yolks of three or four eggs, beaten with a glass of white wine, a piece of butter, and three or four spoonfuls of thick cream; then pour all into your pan, shake it well together, and dish it up; garnish with pickled grapes.

Another.

AFTER boiling your palates very tender, (which you must do by setting them on in cold water, and letting them do softly) then blanch them and scrape them clean; take mace, nutmeg, cloves, and pepper beat fine, rub them all over with those, and with crumbs of bread; have ready some butter in a stew-pan, and when it is hot, put in the palates; fry them brown on both sides, then pour out the fat, and put to them some mutton or beef gravy, enough for sauce, an anchovy, a little nutmeg, a little piece of butter rolled in flour, and the juice of a lemon: let it simmer all together for a quarter of an hour, dish it up, and garnish with lemon.

To make a Fricasey of Eggs.

BOIL your eggs hard, and take out a good many of the yolks whole, then cut the rest in quarters, yolks and whites together. Set on some gravy, with a little shred thyme and parsley in it, give it a boil or two; then put in your eggs, with a little grated nutmeg; shake it up with a bit of butter, till it be as thick as another fricasey: then fry artichoke-bottoms in thin slices, and serve it up. Garnish with eggs shred small.

Another.

BOIL six eggs hard, slice them in round slices, then stew some morels in white wine, with an eschalot, two anchovies, a little thyme, a few oysters or cockles, and salt to your taste; when they have stewed well together, put in your eggs and a bit of butter; toss them up together till it is thick, and then serve it up.

To fricasey Artichoke-bottoms for a Side-dish.

BOIL your artichokes tender, take off the leaves and choke; when cold split every bottom, dredging them with flour; then dip them in beaten eggs, with some salt and grated nutmeg; then roll them up in grated bread; fry them in butter; make gravy sauce thickened with butter, and pour under them.

To make Skuets.

TAKE fine, long, and slender skewers; then cut veal sweet-breads into pieces like dice, and some fine bacon in thin square bits; season them with forcemeat, and then spit them on the skewers, a bit of sweet-bread, a bit of bacon, till all is on; roast them, and lay them round a fricasey of sheeps-tongues.

To fricasey Soals white.

SKIN, wash, and gut your soals very clean, cut off their heads, dry them in a cloth, then with your knife very carefully cut the flesh from the bones and fins on both sides. Cut the flesh long-ways, and then across, so that each soal will be in eight pieces: take the heads and bones, then put them into a saucepan with a pint of water, a bundle of sweet-herbs, an onion, a little whole pepper, two or three blades of mace, a little salt, a very little piece of lemon-peel, and a little crust of bread. Cover it close, let it boil till half is wasted, then strain it through a fine sieve, put it into a stew-pan, put in the soals and half a pint of white wine, a little parsley chopped fine, a few mushrooms cut small, a piece of butter as big as an hen's egg rolled in flour,

grate

grate in a little nutmeg, set all together on the fire, but keep shaking the pan all the while till the fish is enough. Then dish it up, and garnish with lemon.

To fricasey Soals brown.

CLEANSE and cut your soals, boil the water as in the foregoing receipt, flour your fish, and fry them in fresh butter of a fine light brown. Take the flesh of a small soal, beat it in a mortar, with a piece of bread as big as an hen's egg soaked in cream, the yolks of two hard eggs, and a little melted butter, a little bit of thyme, a little parsley, an anchovy, season it with nutmeg, mix all together with the yolk of a raw egg and with a little flour, roll it up into little balls and fry them, but not too much. Then lay your fish and balls before the fire, pour out all the fat of the pan, pour in the liquor which is boiled with the spice and herbs, stir it round in the pan, then put in half a pint of red wine, a few truffles and morels, a few mushrooms, a spoonful of catchup, and the juice of half a small lemon. Stir it all together and let it boil, then stir in a piece of butter rolled in flour; stir it round, when your sauce is of a fine thickness, put in your fish and balls, and when it is hot dish it up, put in the balls, and pour your sauce over it. Garnish with lemon. In the same manner dress a small turbot, or any flat fish.

A Fricasey of great Plaice or Flounders.

RUN your knife all along upon the bone on the back-side of your plaice, then raise the flesh on both sides from the head to the tail, and take out the bone clear; then cut your plaice in six collops, dry it very well from the water, sprinkle it with salt, flour it well, and fry it in a very hot pan of beef-dripping, so that it may be crisp; take it out of the pan, and keep it warm before the fire; then make clean the pan, and put into it oysters and their liquor, some white wine, the meat of the shell of a crab or two: mince half the oysters, some grated nutmeg, three anchovies; let all these stew up together; then put in half a pound of butter, and put in your plaice; toss them well together, dish them on sippets, and pour the sauce over them; garnish the dish with yolks of hard eggs minced, and sliced lemon. After this manner do salmon, or any firm fish.

To fricasey Cod-sounds.

CLEAN them very well, as above, then cut them into little pretty pieces, boil them tender in milk and water, then throw them into a colander to drain, pour them into a clean saucepan, season them with a little beaten mace and grated nutmeg, and a very little salt; pour to them just cream enough for sauce, and a good piece of butter rolled in flour, keep shaking your saucepan round all the time, till it is thick enough; then dish it up, and garnish with lemon.

To fricasey Scate, or Thornback, white.

CUT the meat clean from the bone, fins, &c. and make it very clean. Cut it into little pieces, about an inch broad and two inches long, lay it in your stew-pan. To a pound of the flesh put a quarter of a pint of water, a little beaten mace, and grated nutmeg, a little bundle of sweet-herbs, and a little salt; cover it, and let it boil three minutes. Take out the sweet-herbs, put in a quarter of a pint of good cream, a piece of butter as big as a walnut rolled in flour, a glass of white wine, keep shaking the pan all the while one way, till it is thick and smooth; then dish it up, and garnish with lemon.

To fricasey it brown.

TAKE your dish as above, flour it and fry it of a fine brown, in fresh butter; then take it up, lay it before the fire to keep warm, pour the fat out of the pan, shake in a little flour, and with a spoon stir in a piece of butter as big as an egg; stir it round till it is well mixed in the pan, then pour in a quarter of a pint of water, stir it round, shake in a very little beaten pepper, a little beaten mace; put in an onion, and a little bundle of sweet-herbs, an anchovy, shake it round and let it boil; then pour in a quarter of a pint of red wine, a spoonful of catchup, a little juice of lemon, stir it all together, and let it boil. When it is enough, take out the sweet-herbs and onion, and put in the fish to heat. Then dish it up, and garnish with lemon.

To fricasey Fish in general.

MELT butter, according to the quantity of fish you have; melt it thick, cut your fish in pieces in length and breadth three fingers; then put them and your butter into a frying or stew-pan: it must not boil too fast, for fear of breaking the fish, and turning the butter into oil; turn them often till they are enough; put in a bunch of sweet-herbs at first, an onion, two or three anchovies cut small, a little pepper, nutmeg, mace, lemon-peel, two or three cloves; when all these are in, put in some claret, and let them stew all together; beat up six yolks of eggs and put them in, with such pickles as you please, as oysters, mushrooms, and capers; shake them well together that they do not curdle; if you put the spice in whole, take it out when it is done; the seasoning ought to be stewed first in a little water, and then the butter melted in that and wine before you put the fish in. Jacks do best this way.

CHAP.

CHAP. XI.

Of RAGOOS.

To make a Ragoo of Lamb.

TAKE a fore-quarter of lamb, cut the knuckle-bone off, lard it with little thin bits of bacon, flour it, fry it of a fine brown, and then put it into an earthen pot or stew-pan; put to it a quart of broth or good gravy, a bundle of herbs, a little mace, two or three cloves, and a little whole pepper; cover it close, and let it stew pretty fast for half an hour, pour the liquor all out, strain it, keep the lamb hot in the pot till the sauce is ready. Take half a pint of oysters, flour them, fry them brown, drain out all the fat clean that you fried them in, skim all the fat off the gravy, then pour it into the oysters, put in an anchovy, and two spoonfuls of either red or white wine; boil all together, till there is just enough for sauce, add some fresh mushrooms (if you can get them) and some pickled ones, with a spoonful of the pickle, or the juice of half a lemon. Lay your lamb in the dish, and pour the sauce over it. Garnish with lemon.

To ragoo a Neck of Veal.

CUT a neck of veal into steaks, flatten them with a rolling-pin, season them with salt, pepper, cloves and mace, lard them with bacon, lemon-peel and thyme, dip them in the yolks of eggs, make a sheet of strong cap-paper up at the four corners in the form of a dripping-pan; pin up the corners, butter the paper and also the gridiron, and set it over a fire of charcoal; put in your meat, let it do leisurely; keep it basting and turning to keep in the gravy; and when it is enough have ready half a pint of strong gravy, season it high, put in mushrooms and pickles, forcemeat balls dipped in the yolks of eggs, oysters stewed and fried, to lay round and at the top of your dish, and then serve it up. If for a brown ragoo, put in red wine. If for a white one, put in white wine, with the yolks of eggs beat up with two or three spoonfuls of cream.

To ragoo a Breast of Veal.

TAKE your breast of veal, put it into a large stew pan, put in a bundle of sweet-herbs, an onion, some black and white pepper, a blade or two of mace, two or three cloves, a very little piece of lemon-peel, and just cover it with water: when it is tender take it up, bone it, put in the bones, boil it up till the gravy is very good, then strain it off, and if you have a little rich beef gravy add a quarter of a pint, put in half an ounce of truffles and morels, a spoonful or two of catchup, two or three spoonfuls of white wine, and let them all boil together: in the mean time flour the veal, and fry it in butter till it is of a fine brown, then drain out all the butter and pour the gravy you are boiling to the veal, with a few mushrooms: boil all together till the sauce is rich and thick, and cut the sweet-bread into four. A few forcemeat balls is proper in it. Lay the veal in the dish, and pour the sauce all over it, Garnish with lemon.

Another.

YOU may bone it nicely, flour it, and fry it of a fine brown, then pour the fat out of the pan, and the ingredients as above, with the bones; when enough, take it out, and strain the liquor, then put in your meat again, with the ingredients, as before directed.

To ragoo a piece of Beef.

TAKE a large piece of the flank, which has fat at the top cut square, or any piece that is all meat, and has fat at the top, but no bones. The rump does well. Cut all nicely off the bone (which makes fine soup) then take a large stew pan, and with a good piece of butter fry it a little brown all over, flouring your meat well before you put it into the pan, then pour in as much gravy as will cover it, made thus: Take about a pound of coarse beef, a little piece of veal cut small, a bundle of sweet-herbs, an onion, some whole black pepper and white pepper, two or three large blades of mace, four or five cloves, a piece of carrot, a little piece of bacon steeped in vinegar a little while, a crust of bread toasted brown; put to this a quart of water, and let it boil till half is wasted. While this is making, pour a quart of boiling water into the stew pan, cover it close, and let it be stewing softly; when the gravy is done strain it, pour it into the pan where the beef is, take an ounce of truffles and morels cut small; some fresh or dried mushrooms cut small, two spoonfuls of catchup, and cover it close. Let all this stew till the sauce is rich and thick: then have ready some artichoke-bottoms cut into four, and a few pickled mushrooms, give them a boil or two, and when your meat is tender and your sauce quite rich lay the meat into a dish and pour the sauce over it. You may add a sweet-bread cut in six pieces, a palate stewed tender cut into little pieces, some cocks-combs, and a few forcemeat balls. These are a great addition, but it will be good without.

The COMPLETE HOUSEWIFE.   87

Note, For variety, when the beef is ready and the gravy put to it, add a large bunch of celery cut small and washed clean, two spoonfuls of catchup, and a glass of red wine. Omit all the other ingredients. When the meat and celery are tender, and the sauce rich and good, serve it up. It is also very good this way: take six large cucumbers, scoop out the seeds, pare them, cut them into slices, and do them just as you do the celery.

A Ragoo for made Dishes.

TAKE claret, gravy, sweet-herbs, and savoury spice, toss up in it lamb-stones, cocks-combs, boiled, blanched, and sliced, with sliced sweet-meats, oysters, mushrooms, truffles, and morels; thicken these with brown butter, and use it when called for.

A Ragoo of Sweet-breads.

TAKE your sweet-breads and skin them; put some butter in the frying-pan, brown it with flour, and put the sweet breads in; stir them a little, and turn them; then put in some strong broth and mushrooms, some pepper, salt, cloves and mace; let them stew half an hour; then put in some forcemeat balls, some artichoke-bottoms cut small and thin; make it thick, and serve it up with sliced lemon.

Another.

RUB them over with the yolk of an egg, strew over them bread crumbs and parsley, thyme and sweet marjoram shred small, and pepper and salt; make a roll of forcemeat like a sweet-bread, and put it in a veal caul, and roast them in a Dutch oven; take some brown gravy, and put to it a little lemon-pickle, mushroom catchup, and the end of a lemon; boil the gravy, and when the sweet-breads are enough, lay them in a dish, with the forcemeat in the middle; take the end of the lemon out, and pour the gravy in the dish, and serve them up.

A Ragoo of Livers.

TAKE as many livers as you would have for you dish: a turkey's liver and six fowls livers will make a pretty dish. Pick the galls from them, and throw them into cold water; take the six livers, put them in a saucepan with a quarter of a pint of gravy, a spoonful of mushrooms, either pickled or fresh, a spoonful of catchup, a little bit of butter as big as a nutmeg rolled in flour; season them with pepper and salt to your palate. Let them

them stew softly ten minutes: in the mean while broil the turkey's liver nicely, lay it in the middle, and the stewed livers round. Pour the sauce all over, and garnish with lemon.

To make a Ragoo of Pig's Ears.

TAKE a quantity of pig's ears, and boil them in one half wine and the other water; cut them in small pieces, then brown a little butter, and put them in, and a pretty deal of gravy, two anchovies, an eschalot or two, a little mustard, and some slices of lemon, some salt and nutmeg; stew all these together, and shake it up thick. Garnish the dish with barberries.

To ragoo Hogs Feet and Ears.

TAKE your feet and ears out of the pickle they are soused in, or boil them till they are tender, then cut them into little long thin bits about two inches long, and about a quarter of an inch thick: put them into your stew-pan with half a pint of good gravy, a glass of white wine, a good deal of mustard, a good piece of butter rolled in flour, and a little pepper and salt: stir all together till it is of a fine thickness, and then dish it up.

Note, They make a very pretty dish fried with butter and mustard, and a little good gravy, if you like it. Then only cut the feet and ears in two. You may add half an onion, cut small.

A Ragoo of Eggs.

BOIL twelve eggs hard, take off the shells, and with a little knife very carefully cut the white across long-ways, so that the white may be in two halves, and the yolks whole. Be careful neither to break the whites nor yolks, take a quarter of a pint of pickled mushrooms chopped very fine, half an ounce of truffles and morels, boiled in three or four spoonfuls of water, save the water, and chop the truffles and morels very small, boil a little parsley, chop it fine, mix them together, with the truffle-water you saved, grate a little nutmeg in, a little beaten mace, put it into a saucepan with three spoonfuls of water, a gill of red wine, one spoonful of catchup, a piece of butter as big as a large walnut, rolled in flour, stir all together, and let it boil. In the mean time get ready your eggs, lay the yolks and whites in order in your dish, the hollow parts of the whites uppermost, that they may be filled; take some crumbs of bread, and fry them brown and crisp, as you do for larks, with which fill up the whites of the eggs as high as they will lie, then pour in your sauce all over, and garnish with fried crumbs of bread. This is a very genteel pretty dish, if it be well done.

To ragoo Endive.

TAKE some fine white endive, three heads, lay them in salt and water two or three hours, take a hundred of asparagus, cut off the green heads, chop the rest as far as is tender small, lay it in salt and water, take a bunch of celery, wash it and scrape it clean, cut it in pieces about three inches long, put it into a saucepan, with a pint of water, three or four blades of mace, some whole pepper tied in a rag, let it stew till it is quite tender; then put in the asparagus, shake the saucepan, let it simmer till the grass is enough. Take the endive out of the water, drain it, leave one large head whole, the other leaf by leaf, put it into a stew-pan, put to it a pint of white wine; cover the pan close, let it boil till the endive is just enough, then put in a quarter of a pound of butter rolled in flour, cover it close, shaking the pan when the endive is enough. Take it up, lay the whole head in the middle, and with a spoon take out the celery and grass and lay round, the other part of the endive over that: then pour the liquor out of the saucepan into the stew-pan, stir it together, season it with salt, and have ready the yolks of two eggs, beat up with a quarter of a pint of cream, and half a nutmeg grated in. Mix this with the sauce, keep it stirring all one way till it is thick: then pour it over your ragoo, and send it to table hot.

To ragoo Celery.

WASH and make a bunch of celery very clean, cut it in pieces, about two inches long, put it into a stew-pan with just as much water as will cover it, tie three or four blades of mace, two or three cloves, about twenty corns of whole pepper in a muslin rag loose, put it into the stew-pan, a little onion, a little bundle of sweet-herbs; cover it close, and let it stew softly till tender; then take out the spice, onion and sweet-herbs, put in half an ounce of truffles and morels, two spoonfuls of catchup, a gill of red wine, a piece of butter as big as an egg rolled in flour, six farthing French rolls, season with salt to your palate, stir it all together, cover it close, and let it stew till the sauce is thick and good. Take care that the roll do not break, shake your pan often; when it is enough, dish it up, and garnish with lemon. The yolks of six hard eggs, or more, put in with the rolls, will make it a fine dish. This for a first course.

If you would have it white, put in white wine instead of red, and some cream for a second course.

To ragoo French Beans.

TAKE a few beans, boil them tender, then take your stew-pan, put in a piece of butter, when it is melted shake in some flour,

flour, and peel a large onion, flice it and fry it brown in that butter; then put in the beans, fhake in a little pepper and a little falt; grate a little nutmeg in, have ready the yolk of an egg and fome cream; ftir them all together for a minute or two, and difh them up.

To ragoo Mufhrooms.

PEEL and fcrape the flaps, put a quart into a faucepan, a very little falt, fet them on a quick fire, let them boil up, then take them off, put to them a gill of red wine, a quarter of a pound of butter rolled in a little flour, a little nutmeg, a little beaten mace, fet it on the fire, ftir it now and then; when it is thick and fine, have ready the yolks of fix eggs hot and boiled in a bladder hard, lay it in the middle of your difh, and pour the ragoo over it. Garnifh with boiled mufhrooms.

To ragoo Cauliflowers.

LAY a large cauliflower in water, then pick it to pieces, as if for pickling: take a quarter of a pound of butter, with a fpoonful of water, and melt it in a ftew-pan, then throw in you cauliflowers, and fhake them about often till they are quite tender; then fhake in a little flour, and tofs the pan about. Seafon them with a little pepper and falt, pour in half a pint of good gravy, let them ftew till the fauce is thick, and pour it all into a little difh. Save a few little bits of cauliflower, when ftewed in the butter, to garnifh with.

To make a Ragoo of Onions.

TAKE a pint of fmall young onions, peel them, and take four large ones, peel them and cut them very fmall; put a quarter of a pound of good butter into a ftew-pan, when it is melted and done making a noife, throw in your onions, and fry them till they begin to look a little brown: then fhake in a little flour, and fhake them round till they are thick; throw in a little falt, a little beaten pepper, a quarter of a pint of good gravy, and a tea-fpoonful of muftard. Stir all together, and when it is well tafted and of a good thicknefs pour it into your difh, and garnifh it with fried crumbs of bread and rafpings. They make a pretty little difh, and are very good. You may ftew rafpings in the room of flour, if you pleafe.

A Ragoo of Afparagus.

SCRAPE a hundred of grafs very clean, and throw it into cold water. When you have fcraped all, cut as far as is good and green, about an inch long, and take two heads of endive clean

The COMPLETE HOUSEWIFE. 91

washed and picked, cut it very small, a young lettuce clean washed and cut small, a large onion peeled and cut small; put a quarter of a pound of butter into a stew-pan, when it is melted throw in the above things: tofs them about, and fry them ten minutes; then season them with a little pepper and salt, shake in a little flour, tofs them about, then pour in half a pint of gravy. Let them stew till the sauce is very thick and good; then pour all into your dish. Save a few of the little tops of the grafs to garnish the dish.

To ragoo Oysters.

TAKE a quart of the largest oysters you can get, open them, save the liquor, and strain it through a fine sieve; wash your oysters in warm water; make a batter thus: Take two yolks of eggs, beat them well, grate in half a nutmeg, cut a little lemon-peel small, a good deal of parsley, a spoonful of the juice of spinach, two spoonfuls of cream or milk, beat it up with flour to a thick batter, have ready some butter in a stew-pan, dip your oysters one by one into the batter, and have ready crumbs of bread, then roll them in it, and fry them quick and brown; some with the crumbs of bread, and some without. Take them out of the pan, and set them before the fire, then have ready a quart of chesnuts shelled and skinned, fry them in the butter; when they are enough take them up, pour the fat out of the pan, shake a little flour all over the pan, and rub a piece of butter as big as a hen's egg all over the pan with your spoon, till it is melted and thick; then put in the oyster-liquor, three or four blades of mace, stir it round, put in a few pistacho nuts shelled, let them boil, then put in the chesnuts, and half a pint of white wine, have ready the yolks of two eggs beat up with four spoonfuls of cream; stir all well together, when it is thick and fine, lay the oysters in the dish, and pour the ragoo over them. Garnish with chesnuts and lemon.

You may ragoo muscles the same way. You may leave out the pistacho nuts, if you don't like them; but they give the sauce a fine flavour.

Another.

PUT into your stew-pan a quarter of a pound of butter, and let it boil; then take a quart of oysters, strain them from their liquor, and put them to the butter; let them stew with a bit of eschalot shred very fine, some grated nutmeg, and a little salt; then beat the yolks of three or four eggs with the oyster-liquor, and half a pound of butter; shake all very well together till it is thick, and serve it up with sippets, and garnish it with sliced lemon.

CHAP.

CHAP. XII.
Of HASHES.

To make a Mutton-Hash.

CUT your mutton in little bits as thin as you can, strew a little flour over it, have ready some gravy (enough for sauce) wherein sweet-herbs, onion, pepper and salt, have been boiled; strain it, put in your meat, with a little piece of butter rolled in flour, and a little salt, an eschalot cut fine, a few capers and gerkins chopped fine, and a blade of mace; toss all together for a minute or two, have ready some bread toasted and cut into thin sippets, lay them round the dish, and pour in your hash. Garnish you dish with pickles and horse-radish.

Note, Some like a glass of red wine, or walnut pickle. You may put just what you will into a hash. If the sippets are toasted it is better.

To hash roasted Mutton.

TAKE your mutton half roasted, and cut it in pieces as big as a half-crown; then put into your saucepan half a pint of claret, as much strong broth or gravy, (or water, if you have not the other) one anchovy, an eschalot, a little whole pepper, some nutmeg sliced, salt to your taste, some oyster-liquor, a pint of oysters; let these stew a little, then put in the meat, and a few capers and samphire shred; when it is hot through, thicken it up with a piece of fresh butter rolled in flour; toast sippets, and lay in your dish, and pour your meat on them. Garnish with lemon.

To hash Mutton.

CUT your mutton in slices, put a pint of gravy or broth into a tossing-pan, with one spoonful of mushroom catchup, and one of browning; slice in an onion, a little pepper and salt, put it over the fire, and thicken it with flour and butter; when it boils, put in your mutton, keep shaking it till it is thoroughly hot, put it in a soup-dish, and serve it up.

To hash a Lamb's Pumice.

BOIL the head and neck at most a quarter of an hour, the heart five minutes, and the lights half an hour, the liver boiled or fried in slices (but not hashed) slice all the rest very thin, put in the gravy that runs from it, and a quarter of
a pint

The COMPLETE HOUSEWIFE. 93

a pint of the liquor they are boiled in, a few spoonfuls of walnut liquor, or a little elder vinegar, a little catchup, pepper, salt, and nutmeg, the brains a little boiled and chopped, with half a spoonful of flour, and a piece of butter as big as a walnut mixed up with them; but before you put in the butter, put in four middling cucumbers sliced thin and stewed a little time, or you may fry them in butter before you put them into the hash, and shake them up together; but they are excellent good if only stewed; at the time of the year, green gooseberries scalded, and in grape time, green grapes, to strew on the top.

To make a Calf's Head Hash.

CLEAN your calf's head exceedingly well, and boil it a quarter of an hour; when it is cold cut the meat into thin broad slices, and put it into a tossing-pan, with two quarts of gravy; when it has stewed three quarters of an hour, add to it one anchovy, a little beaten mace, and Cayan to your taste, two tea-spoonfuls of lemon-pickle, two meat-spoonfuls of walnut catchup, half an ounce of truffles and morels, a slice or two of lemon, a bundle of sweet-herbs, and a glass of white wine; mix a quarter of a pound of butter with flour, and put it in a few minutes before the head is enough; take your brains and put them into hot water, it will make them skin sooner, and beat them fine in a bason; then add to them two eggs, one spoonful of flour, a bit of lemon-peel shred fine, chop small a little parsley, thyme, and sage, beat them very well together, and strew in a little pepper and salt; then drop them in little cakes into a panful of boiling hog's-lard, and fry them a light brown, then lay them on a sieve to drain; take your hash out of the pan with a fish-slice, and lay it on your dish, and strain your gravy over it; lay upon it a few mushrooms, forcemeat balls, the yolks of four eggs boiled hard, and the brain-cakes: garnish with lemon and pickles.

It is proper for a top or side-dish.

Another Method.

BOIL the head almost enough, then take the best half, and with a sharp knife take it nicely from the bone, with the two eyes. Lay it in a little deep dish before a good fire, and take great care no ashes fall into it, and then hack it with a knife cross and cross: grate some nutmeg all over, a very little pepper and salt, a few sweet-herbs, some crumbs of bread, and a little lemon-peel chopped very fine, baste it with a little butter, then baste it again, and pour over it the yolks of two eggs; keep the dish turning that it may be all brown alike: cut the other half

half and tongue into little thin bits, and set on a pint of drawn gravy in a saucepan, a little bundle of sweet-herbs, an onion, a little pepper and salt, a glass of red wine, and two eschalots; boil all these together a few minutes, then strain it through a sieve, and put it into a clean stew-pan with the hash. Flour the meat before you put it in, and put in a few mushrooms, a spoonful of the pickle, two spoonfuls of catchup, and a few truffles and morels; stir all these together for a few minutes, then beat up half the brains, and stir into the stew-pan, and a little piece of butter rolled in flour. Take the other half of the brains and beat them up with a little lemon-peel cut fine, a little nutmeg grated, a little beaten mace, a little thyme shred small, a little parsley, the yolk of an egg, and have some good dripping boiling in a stew-pan; then fry the brains in little cakes, about as big as a crown-piece. Fry about twenty oysters dipped in the yolk of an egg, toast some slices of bacon, fry a few forcemeat balls, and have ready a hot dish; if pewter, over a few clear coals; if china, over a pan of hot water. Pour in your hash, then lay in your toasted head, throw the forcemeat balls over the hash, and garnish the dish with fried oysters, the fried brains, and lemon; throw the rest over the hash, lay the bacon round the dish, and send it to table.

To hash a Calf's Head White.

TAKE half a pint of gravy, a large wine-glass of white wine, a little beaten mace, a little nutmeg, and a little salt; throw into your hash a few mushrooms, a few truffles and morels first parboiled, a few artichoke-bottoms, and asparagus-tops, if you have them, a good piece of butter rolled in flour, the yolks of two eggs, half a pint of cream, and one spoonful of mushroom catchup; stir it all together very carefully till it is of a fine thickness; then pour it into your dish, and lay the other half of the head as before-mentioned, in the middle, and garnish it as before directed, with fried oysters, brains, lemon, and forcemeat balls fried.

To hash Venison.

CUT your venison in thin slices, put a large glass of red wine into a tossing-pan, a spoonful of mushroom catchup, an onion stuck with cloves, and half an anchovy chopped small; when it boils, put in your venison, let it boil three or four minutes, pour it into a soup-dish, and lay round it currant jelly or red cabbage.

To hash a Turkey.

TAKE off the legs, cut the thighs in two pieces, cut off the pinions and breast in pretty large pieces, take off the skin or it will give the gravy a greasy taste, put it into a stew pan, with a pint of gravy, a tea-spoonful of lemon pickle, a slice off the end of a lemon, and a little beaten mace; boil your turkey six or seven minutes, (if you boil it any longer it will make it hard); then put it on your dish, thicken your gravy with flour and butter, mix the yolks of two eggs with a spoonful of thick cream, put it in your gravy, shake it over your fire till it is quite hot, but do not let it boil, strain it, and pour it over your turkey: lay sippets round, serve it up, and garnish with lemon or parsley.

To hash Fowls.

CUT up your fowl as for eating, put it in a tossing-pan, with half a pint of gravy, a tea-spoonful of lemon-pickle, a little mushroom catchup, a slice of lemon, thicken it with flour and butter; just before you dish it up, put in a spoonful of good cream: lay sippets round your dish, and serve it up.

To hash a Woodcock, or Partridge.

CUT your woodcock up as for eating, work the entrails very fine with the back of a spoon, mix it with a spoonful of red wine, the same of water, cut an onion in slices, and pull it into rings; roll a little butter in flour, put them all in your tossing-pan, and shake it over the fire till it boils; then put in your woodcock, and when it is thoroughly hot, lay it in your dish with sippets round it; strain the sauce over the woodcock, and lay on the onion in rings; it is a pretty corner-dish for dinner or supper.

CHAP. XIII.

Various Kinds of STEWS.

To stew a Rump of Beef.

SEASON your rump of beef with two nutmegs, some pepper and salt, and lay the fat side downward in your stew-pan; put to it a quarter of a pint of vinegar, a pint of claret, three pints of water, three whole onions stuck with a few cloves, and a bunch of sweet-herbs; cover it close, and let it stew over a gentle fire four or five hours; skim off the fat from the liquor. Lay your meat on sippets, and pour your liquor over it. Garnish your dish with scalded greens.

To

To stew Beef Steaks.

TAKE rump steaks, pepper and salt them, lay them in a stew-pan, pour in half a pint of water, a blade or two of mace, two or three cloves, a little bundle of sweet-herbs, an anchovy, a piece of butter rolled in flour, a glass of white wine, and an onion; cover them close, and let them stew softly till they are tender, then take out the steaks, flour them, fry them in fresh butter, and pour away all the fat, strain the sauce they were stewed in, and pour into the pan: toss it all up together till the sauce is quite hot and thick. If you add a quarter of a pint of oysters, it will make it the better. Lay the steaks into the dish, and pour the sauce over them. Garnish with any pickle you like.

To stew a Knuckle of Veal.

CUT your veal in proper pieces, season it with salt, whole pepper, and large mace, and put the bone chopped amongst the meat; fill it a little more than half full with water; stew it slowly near an hour; then take up the meat, and cover it up warm; strain the spice and bones, bray the mace with a little of the liquor, and put in a quarter of a pint of thick cream and the yolk of an egg; if you have no cream, put some butter dipped in flour; scald it in well over the fire with the rest of the liquor, then pour it upon the veal, and serve it.

To make Hodge Podge.

TAKE a piece of beef, fat and lean together about a pound, a pound of veal, a pound of scrag of mutton, cut all into little pieces, set it on the fire, with two quarts of water, an ounce of barley, an onion, a little bundle of sweet-herbs, three or four heads of celery washed clean and cut small, a little mace, two or three cloves, some whole pepper, tied all in a muslin rag, and put to the meat three turneps pared and cut in two, a large carrot scraped clean and cut in six pieces, a little lettuce cut small, put all in the pot and cover it close. Let it stew very softly over a slow fire five or six hours; take out the spice, sweet-herbs, and onion, and pour all into a soup-dish, and send it to table; first season it with salt. Half a pint of green pease, when it is the season for them, is very good. If you let this boil fast, it will waste too much; therefore you cannot do it too slow, if it does but simmer.

To stew a Head, Chine, and Neck of Venison.

FIRST take off all the fat, then cut it in pieces to your liking, and season it with your compound seasoning, an onion or two quartered, and two or three bay-leaves; put them in a stew-pan, with water near enough to cover them; let it stew till it is almost enough, and then put in a bottle of stale beer, or half red wine and half beer; it may stew two hours before this is in, and one after; burn a quarter of a pound of butter pretty thick with the liquor of the venison, and mix it with it when you serve it: the fat taken off must be put in some time before the venison has done stewing. If you put in beer instead of red wine, boil it and skim it before you put it in.

To stew Mutton the Turkish Way.

FIRST cut your meat into thin slices, then wash it in vinegar, and put it into a pot or saucepan that has a close cover to it, put in some rice, whole pepper, and three or four whole onions; let all these stew together, skimming it frequently: when it is enough, take out the onions, and season it with salt to your palate, lay the mutton in the dish, and pour the rice and liquor over it.

Note, The neck or leg are the best joints to dress this way. Put into a leg four quarts of water, and a quarter of a pound of rice: to a neck two quarts of water, and two ounces of rice. To every pound of meat allow a quarter of an hour, being close covered. If you put in a blade or two of mace, and a bundle of sweet-herbs, it will be a great addition. When it is just enough put in a piece of butter, and take care the rice don't burn to the pot. In all these things you should lay skewers at the bottom of the pot to lay your meat on, that it may not stick.

To stew a Neck of Veal.

CUT your neck of veal in steaks; beat them flat and season them with salt, grated nutmeg, thyme and lemon-peel, shred very fine; when you put it into your pan, put to it some thick cream, according to the quantity you do, and let it stew softly till enough; then put into your pan two or three anchovies, a little gravy, or strong broth, a bit of butter and some flour dusted in, and toss it up till it is thick, then dish it. Garnish with lemon.

To stew a Pheasant.

TAKE your pheasant and stew it in veal gravy, take artichoke-bottoms parboiled, some chesnuts roasted and blanched: when your pheasant is enough (but it must stew till there is just enough for sauce, then skim it) put in the chesnuts and artichoke-bottoms, a little beaten mace, pepper, and salt, just enough to season it, and a glass of white wine; and if you don't
think

think it thick enough, thicken it with a little piece of butter rolled in flour; squeeze in a little lemon, pour the sauce over the pheasant, and have some forcemeat balls fried and put into the dish.

Note, A good fowl will do full as well, trussed with the head on like a pheasant. You may fry sausages instead of forcemeat balls.

To stew Plovers.

TO two plovers take two artichoke-bottoms boiled, some chesnuts roasted and blanched, some skirrets boiled, cut all very small, mix it with some marrow or beef suet, the yolks of two hard eggs, chop all together, season with pepper, salt, nutmeg, and a little sweet-herbs; fill the bodies of the plovers, lay them in a saucepan; put to them a pint of gravy, a glass of white wine, a blade or two of mace, some roasted chesnuts blanched, and artichoke-bottoms cut into quarters, two or three yolks of eggs, and a little juice of lemon; cover them close, and let them stew very softly an hour. If you find the sauce is not thick enough, take a piece of butter rolled in flour, and put into the sauce, shake it round, and when it is thick take up your plovers and pour the sauce over them. Garnish with roasted chesnuts.

Ducks are very good done this way.

Or you may roast your plovers as you do any other fowl, and have gravy-sauce in the dish.

Or boil them in good celery-sauce, either white or brown, just as you like.

The same way you may dress wigeons.

To make Partridge Panes.

TAKE two roasted partridges and the flesh of a large fowl, a little parboiled bacon, a little marrow or sweet suet chopped very fine, a few mushrooms and morels chopped fine, truffles, and artichoke-bottoms, season with beaten mace, pepper, a little nutmeg, salt, sweet-herbs chopped fine, and the crumb of a two-penny loaf soaked in hot gravy; mix all well together with the yolks of two eggs, make your panes on paper, of a round figure, and the thickness of an egg, at a proper distance one from another, dip the point of a knife in the yolk of an egg, in order to shape them; bread them neatly, and bake them a quarter of an hour in a quick oven: observe that the truffles and morels be boiled tender in the gravy you soak the bread in. Serve them up for a side-dish, or they will serve to garnish the above dish, which will be a very fine one for a first course.

Note, When you have cold fowls in the house, this makes a pretty addition in an entertainment.

To stew a Turkey brown.

TAKE your turkey, after it is nicely picked and drawn, fill the skin of the breast with forcemeat, and put an anchovy, an eschalot, and a little thyme in the belly, lard the breast with bacon, then put a good piece of butter in the stew-pan, flour the turkey, and fry it just of a fine brown; then take it out, and put it into a deep stew-pan, or little pot, that will just hold it, and put in as much gravy as will barely cover it, a glass of red wine, some whole pepper, mace, two or three cloves, and a little bundle of sweet-herbs; cover it close, and stew it for an hour, then take up the turkey, and keep it hot covered by the fire, and boil the sauce to about a pint, strain it off, add the yolks of two eggs, and a piece of butter rolled in flour; stir it till it is thick, and then lay your turkey in the dish, and pour your sauce over it. You may have ready some little French loaves, about the bigness of an egg, cut off the tops, and take out the crumbs; then fry them of a fine brown, fill them with stewed oysters, lay them round the dish, and garnish with lemon.

To stew a Turkey brown the nice way.

BONE it, and fill it with forcemeat made thus: Take the flesh of a fowl, half a pound of veal, and the flesh of two pigeons, with a well-pickled or dry tongue, peel it, and chop it all together, then beat in a mortar, with the marrow of a beef bone, or a pound of the fat of a loin of veal; season it with two or three blades of mace, two or three cloves, and half a nutmeg dried at a good distance from the fire, and pounded, with a little pepper and salt: mix all these well together, fill your turkey, fry them of a fine brown, and put it into a little pot that will just hold it; lay four or five skewers at the bottom of the pot, to keep the turkey from sticking; put in a quart of good beef and veal gravy, wherein was boiled spice and sweet-herbs, cover it close, and let it stew half an hour; then put in a glass of red wine, one spoonful of catchup, a large spoonful of pickled mushrooms, and a few fresh ones, if you have them, a few truffles and morels, a piece of butter as big as a walnut rolled in flour; cover it close, and let it stew half an hour longer; get the little French rolls ready fried, take some oysters, and strain the liquor from them; then put the oysters and liquor into a saucepan, with a blade of mace, a little white wine, and a piece of butter rolled in flour; let them stew till it is thick, then fill the loaves, lay the turkey in the dish, and pour the sauce over it. If there is any fat on the gravy take it off, and lay the loaves on each side of the turkey. Garnish with lemon when you have no loaves, and take oysters dipped in batter and fried.

Note, The same will do for any white fowl.

To stew a Turkey or Fowl in celery-sauce.

YOU must judge according to the largeness of your turkey or fowl, what celery or sauce you want. Take a large fowl, put it into a saucepan or pot, and put to it one quart of good broth or gravy, a bunch of celery washed clean and cut small, with some mace, cloves, pepper, and allspice tied loose in a muslin-rag; put in an onion and a sprig of thyme; let these stew softly till they are enough, then add a piece of butter rolled in flour; take up your fowl, and pour the sauce over it. An hour will do a large fowl, or a small turkey; but a very large turkey will take two hours to do it softly. If it is overdone or dry it is spoiled; but you may be a judge of that, if you look at it now and then. Mind to take out the onion, thyme, and spice, before you send it to table.

Note, A neck of veal done this way is very good, and will take two hours doing.

To stew Pigeons.

SEASON eight pigeons with pepper and salt only; take a middling cabbage cut across the middle, and lay the bottom with the thick pieces in the stew-pan; then lay on your pigeons, and cover them with the top of your cabbage; pour in a pint of red wine, and a pint of water; let it stew slowly an hour or more.

Another Method.

SEASON your pigeons with pepper, salt, cloves, and mace, with some sweet-herbs; wrap a seasoning up in a bit of butter, and put it in their bellies, then tie up the neck and vent, and half roast them; then put them in a stew-pan, with a quart of good gravy, a little white white, some pickled mushrooms, a few pepper-corns, three or four blades of mace, a bit of lemon-peel, a bunch of sweet-herbs, a bit of onion, some oyster-pickle: let them stew till they are enough; then thicken it up with butter and the yolks of eggs. Garnish with lemon. Do ducks the same way. You may put forcemeat in their bellies, or shred thyme wrapped up in butter. Put forcemeat balls in both.

Another Method.

STUFF your pigeons with sweet-herbs chopped small, some bacon minced small, grated bread, spice, butter, and yolk of an egg; sew them up top and bottom, and stew them in strong broth, with half a pint of white wine to six pigeons, and as much broth as will cover them well, with nutmeg, whole pepper,
mace,

mace, salt, a little bundle of sweet-herbs, a bit of lemon-peel, and an onion; when they are almost done, put in some artichoke-bottoms ready boiled and fried in brown butter, or asparagus-tops ready boiled; thicken up the liquor with the stuffing out of the pigeons, and a bit of butter rolled in flour: take out the lemon-peel, bunch of herbs, and onion. Garnish the dish with sliced lemon, and very thin bits of bacon toasted before the fire.

To stew Pigeons with Asparagus.

DRAW your pigeons, and wrap up a little shred parsley, with a very few blades of thyme, some salt and pepper in a piece of butter; put some in the belly, some in the neck, and tie up the vent and the neck, and half roast them; then have some strong broth and gravy, put them together in a stew-pan; stew the pigeons till they are full enough; then have tops of asparagus boiled tender, and put them in, and let them have a walm or two in the gravy, and dish it up.

To mumble Rabbets and Chickens.

PUT into the bellies of your rabbets, or chickens, some parsley, an onion, and the liver; set it over the fire in a stew pan with as much water mixed with a little salt as will cover them; when they are half boiled take them out, and shred the parsley, liver, and onion; tear the flesh from the bones of the rabbet in small flakes, and put it into the stew-pan again with a very little of the liquor it was boiled in, a pint of white wine, some gravy, half a pound or more of butter, and some grated nutmeg; when it is enough shake in a little flour, and thicken it up with butter. Serve it on sippets.

To dress a Duck with green Pease.

PUT a deep stew-pan over the fire, with a piece of fresh butter; singe your duck and flour it, turn it in the pan two or three minutes, then pour out all the fat, but let the duck remain in the pan; put to it half a pint of good gravy, a pint of pease, two lettuces cut small, a small bundle of sweet-herbs, a little pepper and salt, cover them close, and let them stew for half an hour, now and then give the pan a shake; when they are just done, grate in a little nutmeg, and put in a very little beaten mace, and thicken it either with a piece of butter rolled in flour, or the yolk of an egg beat up with two or three spoonfuls of cream; shake it all together for three or four minutes, take out the sweet-herbs; lay the duck in the dish, and pour the sauce over it. You may garnish with boiled mint chopped, or let it alone.

To stew a Duck with Cucumbers.

TAKE three or four cucumbers, pare them, take out the seeds, cut them into little pieces, lay them in vinegar for two or three hours before, with two large onions peeled and sliced, then do your duck as above; then take the duck out, and put in the cucumbers and onions; first drain them in a cloth, let them be a little brown, shake a little flour over them, in the mean time let your duck be stewing in the saucepan with half a pint of gravy for a quarter of an hour, then add to it the cucumbers and onions, with pepper and salt to your palate, a good piece of butter rolled in flour, and two or three spoonfuls of red wine; shake all together, and let it stew together for eight or ten minutes, then take up your duck, and pour the sauce over it.

Or you may roast your duck, and make this sauce and pour over it, but then a quarter of a pint of gravy will be enough.

To stew Giblets.

LET them be nicely scalded and picked, break the two pinion bones in two, cut the head in two, and cut off the nostrils; cut the liver in two, the gizzard in four, and the neck in two; slip off the skin of the neck, and make a pudding with two hard eggs chopped fine, the crumb of a French roll steeped in hot milk two or three hours, then mix it with the hard egg, a little nutmeg, pepper, salt, and a little sage chopped fine, a very little melted butter, and stir it together: tie one end of the skin, and fill it with ingredients, tie the other end tight, and put all together in the saucepan, with a quart of good mutton broth, a bundle of sweet-herbs, an onion, some whole pepper, mace, two or three cloves tied up loose in a muslin-rag, and a very little piece of lemon-peel; cover them close, and let them stew till quite tender, then take a small French roll toasted brown on all sides, and put it into the saucepan, give it a shake, and let it stew till there is just gravy enough to eat with them, then take out the onion, sweet-herbs, and spice, lay the roll in the middle, the giblets round, the pudding cut into slices and laid round, and then pour the sauce over all.

Another Way.

TAKE the giblets clean picked and washed, the feet skinned and bill cut off, the head cut in two, the pinion bones broke into two, the liver cut in two, the gizzard cut into four, the pipe pulled out of the neck, the neck cut in two: put them into a pipkin with half a pint of water, some whole pepper, black and white, a blade of mace, a little sprig of thyme, a small onion, a little cruft of bread, then cover them clofe, and fet them on a very flow fire. Wood-embers is beft. Let them ftew till they are quite tender, then take out the herbs and onions, and pour them into a little difh. Seafon them with falt.

To ftew a Hare.

CUT it into pieces, and put it into a ftew-pan, with a blade or two of mace, fome whole pepper black and white, an onion ftuck with cloves, an anchovy, a bundle of fweet-herbs, and a nutmeg cut to pieces, and cover it with water; cover the ftew-pan clofe, let it ftew till the hare is tender, but not too much done: then take it up, and with a fork take out the hare into a clean pan, ftrain the fauce through a coarfe fieve, empty all out of the pan, put in the hare again with fauce, take a piece of butter as big as a walnut rolled in flour, and put in likewife one fpoonful of catchup, and one of red wine; ftew all together (with a few frefh mufhrooms, or pickled ones if you have any) till it is thick and fmooth; then difh it up, and fend it to table. You may cut a hare in two, and ftew the fore-quarters thus, and roaft the hind-quarters with a pudding in the belly.

To jug a Hare.

CUT a hare in pieces, but do not wafh it; feafon it with half an onion fhred very fine, a fprig of thyme, a little parfley all fhred, beaten pepper and falt, as much as will lie on a fhilling, half a nutmeg, and a little lemon-peel; ftrew all thefe over your hare, and cut half a pound of fat bacon into thin flices; then put your hare into a jug, a layer of hare, and the flices of bacon on it: fo do till all is in the jug; ftop the jug clofe that not any fteam can go out; then put it in a pot of cold water, lay a tile on the top, and let it boil three hours; take the jug out of the kettle, put half a pound of butter in it, and fhake it together till the butter is melted; then pour it in your difh. Garnifh with lemon.

To jug Pigeons.

PULL, crop, and draw your pigeons, but not wafh them; fave the livers, put them in fcalding water, and fet them on the fire for a minute or two; then take them out, and bruife them fmall with the back of a fpoon; mix them with a little pepper, falt, grated nutmeg, lemon-peel fhred very fine, chopped parfley, two yolks of eggs very hard, and bruifed as you did the liver, fuet fhaved exceeding fine, and fome grated bread; work thefe together with raw eggs, roll it in butter, putting a bit into the crop and belly of your pigeon, and few up the neck and vent;

vent; then dip your pigeons in water, seasoning them with pepper and salt, as for a pye; then put them into your jug with a piece of celery; stop them up close, set them in a kettle of cold water, with a tile on the top, and let it boil three hours; then take them out of the jug, and put them in your dish; take out the celery, and put in a piece of butter rolled in flour; shake it till it is thick, and put it on your pigeons. Garnish with lemon.

To stew Pigs Petty-toes.

PUT your petty-toes into a saucepan, with half a pint of water, a blade of mace, a little whole pepper, a bundle of sweet-herbs, and an onion. Let them boil five minutes, then take out the liver, lights, and heart, mince them very fine, grate a little nutmeg over them, and shake a little flour on them; let the feet do till they are tender, then take them out and strain the liquor; put all together with a little salt, and a piece of butter as big as a walnut, shake the saucepan often, let it simmer five or six minutes, then cut some toasted sippets and lay round the dish, lay the mincemeat and sauce in the middle, and the petty-toes split round it. You may add the juice of half a lemon, or a very little vinegar.

To stew Golden Pippins.

PARE your pippins, scoop out the cores, and throw them into the water to preserve their colour; to a pound of pippins thus prepared, take half a pound of double refined sugar, and a pint of water; boil them, and strain the syrup before you put the pippins in; when they are in, let them boil a little to make them clear, and when they rise put in a little lemon-peel, and the juice of a lemon to your taste.

To stew Cucumbers.

PARE twelve cucumbers, slice them as for eating, put them to drain, and lay them in a coarse cloth till they are dry; flour them, and fry them brown in butter; then put to them some gravy, a little claret, some pepper, cloves and mace, and let them stew a little; then roll a bit of butter in flour, and toss them up; put them under mutton or lamb roasted.

To stew Mushrooms.

TAKE some strong broth, season it with a bunch of sweet-herbs, some spice and anchovies, setting it over the fire till it is hot; then put in the mushrooms, and just let them boil up; then

then take the yolks of eggs, with a little minced thyme, parsley, and some grated nutmeg; and stir it over the fire till it is thick. Serve it up with sliced lemon.

To stew green Peafe.

TAKE five pints of young green peafe, put them into a dish with a little spring-water, savoury, some sweet-marjoram, thyme, and onion, a few cloves and a little whole pepper; melt half a pound of sweet butter, with a piece of dried fat bacon the bigness of an egg, in a stew-pan, and let it boil till it is brown; take the white part of three hard lettuces cut very small, and put them into the butter; set it again on the fire for half a minute, stirring the lettuces four or five times; then put in the peafe, and after you have given them five or six tosses, put in as much strong broth as will stew them; then add half a pint of cream, and let them boil till the liquor is almost wasted; bruife them a little with a spoon, and put a quarter of a pint of more cream to them; tofs them five or six times, and dish them. Any good gravy may be added.

To stew Carps.

SCALE and gut your carp, and wash the blood out of their bellies with vinegar; then flour them well, and fry them in butter till they are thorough hot, then put them into your stew-pan, with a pint of claret, two anchovies, an onion stuck with three or four cloves, two or three blades of mace, a bunch of fweet-herbs, and a pound of fresh butter; put them over a soft fire, three quarters of an hour will do them; then take your fish up, and put them in the dish you serve them in; if your fauce is not thick enough, boil it a little longer; then strain it over your carp. This is a very good way to stew eels, only cut them in pieces, and not fry them. Garnish with horseradish and lemon.

Another Method.

TAKE a live carp, cut him in the neck and tail, and save the blood; then open him in the belly; take care you do not break the gall; put a little vinegar in the belly, to wash out the blood; stir all the blood with your hand; then put your carp into a stew-pan; if you have two carps, you may cut off one of their heads an inch below the gills, and flit the body in two, and put it into your stew pan after you have rubbed them with salt; but before you put them in, your liquor must boil, a quart of claret, or as much as will cover them, the blood you saved, an onion stuck with cloves, a bunch of fweet-herbs, some gravy,

three

three anchovies. When this liquor boils up, put in your fish, cover it close, and let it stew up for about a quarter of an hour; then turn it and let it stew a little longer; then put your carp into a dish, and beat up the sauce with butter melted in oyster-liquor, and pour your sauce over it. Your milt, spawn, and rivets must be laid on the top: garnish the dish with fried smelts, oysters, or pitchcock-eel, lemon and fried parsley.

Another Way to stew Carp.

TAKE two carps, scale and rub them well with salt; cut them in the nape of the neck and round the tail, to make him bleed; cut up the belly, take out the liver and guts, and if you please to cut each carp in three pieces, they will eat the firmer; then put them in a stew-pan, with their blood, a quart of claret, a bunch of sweet-herbs, an onion, one or two eschalots, a nutmeg, a few cloves, mace, whole pepper; cover them close and let them stew till they are half enough, then turn them, and put half a pound of fresh butter, four anchovies, the liver and guts, taking out the gall, and let them stew till they are enough; then beat the yolks of five or six eggs with a little verjuice, and by degrees mix it with the liquor the carp was stewed in; just give it a scald to thicken it; then put your carp in a dish, and pour this over it; garnish the dish with a sliced lemon.

To stew Carp white.

WHEN the carp are scaled, gutted, and washed, put them into a stew-pan, with two quarts of water, half a pint of white wine, a little mace, whole pepper, and salt, two onions, a bunch of sweet-herbs, a stick of horse-radish; cover the pan close, and let it stand an hour and a half over a slow stove; then put a gill of white wine into a saucepan, with two anchovies chopped, an onion, a little lemon-peel, a quarter of a pound of butter rolled in flour, a little thick cream, and a large tea-cupful of the liquor the carp was stewed in; boil them a few minutes, and drain your carp; add to the sauce the yolks of two eggs, mixed with a little cream; when it boils up, squeeze in the juice of half a lemon; dish up your carp, and pour your sauce hot upon it.

Eels to stew.

SKIN, gut, and wash them very clean in six or eight waters, to wash away all the sand; then cut them in pieces, about as long as your finger, put just water enough for sauce; put in a small onion stuck with cloves, a little bundle of sweet herbs, a blade or two of mace, and some whole pepper in a thin muslin-rag. Cover it close, and let them stew very softly.

Look at them now and then, put in a little piece of butter rolled in flour, and a little chopped parsley. When you find they are quite tender and well done, take out the onion, spice, and sweet-herbs. Put in salt enough to season it. Then dish them up with the sauce.

To dress Eels with brown Sauce.

SKIN and clean a large eel very well, cut it in pieces, put it into a saucepan or stew-pan, put to it a quarter of a pint of water, a bundle of sweet herbs, an onion, some whole pepper, a blade of mace and a little salt. Cover it close, and when it begins to simmer, put in a gill of red wine, a spoonful of mushroom pickle, a piece of butter as big as a walnut rolled in flour: cover it close, and let it stew till it is enough, which you will know by the eel being very tender. Take up your eel, lay it in a dish, strain your sauce, give it a boil quick, and pour it over your fish. You must make sauce according to the largeness of your eel, more or less. Garnish with lemon.

Soles to stew.

WHEN your soles are washed, and the fins cut off, put them into a stew-pan, with no liquor but a quarter of a pint of white wine, some mace, whole pepper and salt; when they are half stewed, put in some thick cream, and a little piece of butter dipped in flour; when that is melted, put in some oysters with their liquor; keep them often shaking, till the fish and oysters are enough, or that the oysters will break; squeeze in a little piece of lemon, give them a scald, and pour it into the dish.

To stew Oysters in French Rolls.

TAKE a quart of large oysters; wash them in their own liquor, strain it, and put them in it with a little salt, some pepper, mace, and sliced nutmeg; let the oysters stew a little with all these things, and thicken them up with a great deal of butter; then take six French rolls, cut a piece off the top, and take out the crumbs; take your oysters boiling hot, and fill the rolls full, set them near the fire on a chafing-dish of coals, and let them be hot through; as the liquor soaks in, fill them up with more, if you have it, or some hot gravy: so serve them up instead of a pudding.

To stew Cod.

CUT your cod in thin slices, and lay them one by one in the bottom of a dish; put in a pint of white wine, half a pound of butter, some oysters and their liquor, two or three blades of mace, a few crumbs of bread, some pepper and salt, and let it stew till it is enough. Garnish the dish with lemon.

To make Water-sokey.

TAKE some of the smallest plaice or flounders you can get, wash them clean, cut the fins close, put them into a stew-pan, put just water enough to boil them in, a little salt, and a bunch of parsley; when they are enough send them to table in a soup-dish, with the liquor to keep them hot. Have parsley and butter in a cup.

CHAP. XIV.
Of PANCAKES and FRITTERS.

To make Pancakes.

TAKE a pint of cream, and eight eggs, whites and all, a whole nutmeg grated, and a little salt; then melt a pound of rare dish butter, and a little sack; before you fry them, stir it in: it must be made as thick with three spoonfuls of flour, as ordinary batter, and fried with butter in the pan, the first pancake, but no more: strew sugar, garnish with orange, turn it on the backside of a plate.

Another Method.

TAKE a quart of milk, beat in six or eight eggs, leaving half the whites out; mix it well till your batter is of a fine thickness. You must observe to mix your flour first with a little milk, then add the rest by degrees; put in two spoonfuls of beaten ginger, a glass of brandy, a little salt; stir all together, make your stew-pan very clean, put in a piece of butter as big as a walnut, then pour in a ladleful of batter, which will make a pancake, moving the pan round that the batter be all over the pan; shake the pan, and when you think that side is enough, toss it; if you can't, turn it cleverly, and when both sides are

done,

The COMPLETE HOUSEWIFE. 109

done, lay it in a dish before the fire, and so do the rest. You must take care they are dry; when you send them to table strew a little sugar over them.

To make fine Pancakes.

TAKE half a pint of cream, half a pint of sack, the yolks of eighteen eggs beat fine, a little salt, half a pound of fine sugar, a little beaten cinnamon, mace, and nutmeg; then put in as much flour as will run thin over the pan, and fry them in fresh butter. This sort of pancake will not be crisp, but very good.

A second Sort of fine Pancakes.

TAKE six new-laid eggs well beat, mix them with a pint of cream, a quarter of a pound of sugar, some grated nutmeg, and as much flour as will make the batter of a proper thickness. Fry these fine pancakes in small pans, and let your pans be hot. You must not put above the bigness of a nutmeg of butter at a time into the pan.

A third Sort, called a Quire of Paper.

TAKE a pint of cream, six eggs, three spoonfuls of fine flour, three of sack, one of orange-flower-water, a little sugar, and half a nutmeg grated, half a pound of melted butter almost cold; mingle all well together, and butter the pan for the first pancake; let them run as thin as possible; when they are just coloured they are enough: and so do with all the fine pancakes.

To make Rice Pancakes.

TAKE a quart of cream and three spoonfuls of the flour of rice, boil it till it is as thick as pap, and as it boils stir in half a pound of butter, a nutmeg grated; then pour it out into an earthen pan, and when it is cold, put in three or four spoonfuls of flour, a little salt, some sugar, nine eggs well beaten; mix all well together, and fry them in a little pan, with a small piece of butter; serve them up four or five in a dish.

To make Curd Fritters.

BOIL a handful of curds, a handful of flour, ten eggs well beaten and strained, some sugar, some cloves, mace, nutmeg, and a little saffron; stir all well together, and fry them in very hot beef dripping; drop them in the pan by spoonfuls;

stir

stir them about till they are of a fine yellow brown; drain them from the suet, and scrape sugar on them, when you serve them up.

To make fried Toasts.

CHIP a manchet very well, and cut it round-ways into toasts; then take cream and eight eggs, seasoned with sack, sugar and nutmeg; and let these toasts steep in it about an hour; then fry them in sweet butter, serve them up with plain melted butter, or with butter, sack and sugar, as you please.

To make Parsnep Fritters.

BOIL your parsneps very tender, peel them and beat them in a mortar; rub them through a hair-sieve, and mix a good handful of them with some fine flour, six eggs, some cream, and new milk, salt, sugar, a little nutmeg, a small quantity of sack and rose-water; mix all well together a little thicker than pancake batter; have a frying-pan ready with good store of hog's-lard very hot over the fire, and put in a spoonful in a place, till the pan be so full as you can fry them conveniently; fry them a light brown on both sides. For sauce, take sack and sugar, with a little rose-water or verjuice; strew sugar on them when in the dish.

To make Apple Fritters.

TAKE the yolks of eight eggs, the whites of four, beat them well together, and strain them into a pan; then take a quart of cream, warm it as hot as you can endure your finger in it; then put to it a quarter of a pint of sack, three quarters of a pint of ale, and make a posset of it; when your posset is cool, put to it your eggs, beating them well together; then put in the nutmeg, ginger, salt, and flour to your liking: your batter should be pretty thick; then put in pippins sliced or scraped; fry them in good store of hot lard with a quick fire.

To make Hasty Fritters.

TAKE a stew-pan, put in some butter, and let it be hot; in the mean time take half a pint of all-ale, not bitter, and stir in some flour by degrees in a little of the ale; put in a few currants, or chopped apples, beat them up quick, and drop a large spoonful at a time all over the pan. Take care they don't stick together, turn them with an egg-slice, and when they are of a fine brown, lay them in a dish, and throw some sugar over them. Garnish with orange cut into quarters.

To make fine Fritters.

PUT to half a pint of thick cream four eggs well beaten, a little brandy, some nutmeg and ginger. Make this into a thick batter with flour, and your apples must be golden pippins pared and chopped with a knife; mix all together, and fry them in butter. At any time you may make an alteration in the fritters with currants.

Another Way.

DRY some of the finest flour well before the fire: mix it with a quart of new milk, not too thick, six or eight eggs, a little nutmeg, a little mace, a little salt, and a quarter of a pint of sack or ale, or a glass of brandy. Beat them well together, then make them pretty thick with pippins, and fry them dry.

To make Fritters Royal.

TAKE a quart of new milk, put it into a skillet or saucepan, and as the milk boils up, pour in a pint of sack, let it boil up, then take it off, and let it stand five or six minutes, then skim off all the curd, and put it into a bason; beat it up well with six eggs, season it with nutmeg, then beat it up with a whisk, add flour to make it as thick as batter usually is, put in some fine sugar, and fry them quick.

To make Skirret Fritters.

TAKE a pint of pulp of skirrets and a spoonful of flour, the yolks of four eggs, sugar and spice, make it into a thick batter, and fry them quick.

To make white Fritters.

HAVING some rice, wash it in five or six several waters, and dry it very well before the fire; then beat it in a mortar very fine, and sift it thro' a lawn-sieve, that it may be very fine. You must have at least an ounce of it, then put it into a saucepan, just wet it with milk, and when it is well incorporated with it, add to it another pint of milk; set the whole over a stove or a very slow fire, and take care to keep it always moving; put in a little sugar, and some candied lemon-peel grated, keep it over the fire till it is almost come to the thickness of a fine paste, flour a peal, pour it on it, and spread it abroad with a rolling-pin. When it is quite cold cut it into little morsels, taking care that they stick not one to the other; flour your

hands

hands and roll up your fritters handsomely, and fry them. When you serve them up, pour a little orange-flower-water over them, and sugar. These make a pretty side-dish; or are very pretty to garnish a fine dish with.

To make Water Fritters.

TAKE a pint of water, put into a saucepan a piece of butter as big as a walnut, a little salt, and some candied lemon-peel minced very small. Make this boil over a stove, then put in two good handfuls of flour, and turn it about by main strength till the water and flour be well mixed together, and none of the last stick to the saucepan; then take it off the stove, mix in the yolks of two eggs, mix them well together, continuing to put in more, two by two, till you have stirred in ten or twelve, and your paste be very fine; then dredge a peal thick with flour, and dipping your hand into the flour, take out your paste bit by bit, and lay it on a peal. When it has lain a little while roll it, and cut it into little pieces, taking care that they stick not one to another; fry them of a fine brown, put a little orange flower-water over them, and sugar all over.

CHAP. XV.
All Sorts of PUDDINGS.

Rules to be observed in making Puddings, &c.

IN boiled puddings, take great care the bag or cloth be very clean, not soapy, but dipped in hot water, and well floured. If a bread pudding, tie it loose; if a batter pudding, tie it close, and be sure the water boils when you put the pudding in, and you should move the puddings in the pot now and then, for fear they stick. When you make a batter pudding, first mix the flour well with a little milk, then put in the ingredients by degrees, and it will be smooth and not have lumps; but for a plain batter pudding, the best way is to strain it through a coarse hair-sieve, that it may neither have lumps, nor the treadles of the eggs: and all other puddings, strain the eggs when they are beat. If you boil them in wooden bowls, or china dishes, butter the inside before you put in your batter; and for all baked puddings, butter the pan or dish before the pudding is put in.

To

To make an Orange Pudding.

TAKE two large Seville oranges, and grate off the rind, as far as they are yellow; then put your oranges in fair water, and let them boil till they are tender, shift the water three or four times to take out the bitterness; when they are tender cut them open, take away the seeds and strings, and beat the other part in a mortar, with half a pound of sugar, till it is a paste; then put in the yolks of six eggs, three or four spoonfuls of thick cream, half a Naples biscuit grated; mix these together, and melt a pound of very good fresh butter, and stir it well in; when it is cold, put a bit of fine puff-paste about the brim and bottom of your dish; put it in, and bake it about three quarters of an hour.

Another Sort of Orange Pudding.

TAKE the outside rind of three Seville oranges, boil them in several waters till they are tender; then pound them in a mortar with three quarters of a pound of sugar; then blanch and beat half a pound of almonds very fine, with rose-water to keep them from oiling; then beat sixteen eggs, but six whites, and a pound of fresh butter; beat all these together very well till it is light and hollow; then put it in a dish with a sheet of puff-paste at the bottom, and bake it with tarts; scrape sugar on it, and serve it up hot.

To make a Carrot Pudding.

TAKE raw carrots, and scrape them clean, grate them with a grater without a back. To half a pound of carrots, take a pound of grated bread, a nutmeg, a little cinnamon, a very little salt, half a pound of sugar, half a pint of sack, eight eggs, a pound of butter melted, and as much cream as will mix it well together; stir it and beat it well up, and put it in a dish to bake; put puff-paste at the bottom of your dish.

Puddings for little Dishes.

YOU must take a pint of cream and boil it, and slit a half-penny loaf, and pour the cream hot over it, and cover it close till it is cold; then beat it fine, and grate in half a large nutmeg, a quarter of a pound of sugar, the yolks of four eggs, but two whites well beat, beat it all well together. With the half of this fill four little wooden dishes; colour one yellow with saffron, one red with cochineal, green with the juice of spinach, and blue with syrup of violets; the rest mix with an ounce of sweet almonds blanched and beat fine, and fill a dish. Your dishes must be small, and tie your covers over very close with packthread. When your pot boils, put them in. An hour will boil them; when enough, turn them out in a dish, the white one in the middle, and the four coloured ones round: When they are enough, melt some fresh butter with a glass of sack, and pour over, and throw sugar all over the dish. The white pudding-dish must be of a larger size than the rest; and be sure to butter your dishes well before you put them in, and don't fill them too full.

A Hasty Pudding to butter itself.

SET a quart of thick cream upon the fire, put into it the crumb of a penny white loaf grated, boil it pretty thick together, with often stirring it; a little before you take it up, put in the yolks of four eggs, with a spoonful of sack or orange-flower-water and some sugar; boil it very slow, keeping it stirring; some make it with grated Naples biscuit, and put no eggs in; you may know when it is enough, by an oil round the edge of the skillet, and soon all over it; then pour it out; it will require half an hour or more before it is enough; some put a few almonds blanched, and beat very fine, with a spoonful of wine, to keep them from oiling.

Another Hasty Pudding.

BREAK an egg into fine flour, and with your hand work up as much as you can into as stiff a paste as possible; then mince it as small as if it were to be sifted; then set a quart of milk a boiling, and put in your paste, so cut as before-mentioned; put in a little salt, some beaten cinnamon and sugar, a piece of butter as big as a walnut, and keep it stirring all one way, till it is as thick as you would have it; and then stir in such another piece of butter; and when it is in the dish stick it all over with little bits of butter.

To make stewed Pudding.

GRATE a two-penny loaf, and mix it with half a pound of beef suet finely shred, and three quarters of a pound of currants, and a quarter of a pound of sugar, a little cloves, mace, and nutmeg; then beat five or six eggs, with three or four spoonfuls of rose-water, beat all together, and make them up in little round balls the bigness of an egg; some round and some long, in the fashion of an egg, then put a pound of butter in a pewter dish, when it is melted and thorough hot, put in your puddings, and let them stew till they are brown; turn them,

and

and when they are enough, serve them up with sack, butter, and sugar for sauce.

A Bread and Butter Pudding for fasting Days.

TAKE a two-penny loaf, and a pound of fresh butter; spread it in very thin slices, as to eat; cut them off as you spread them, and stone half a pound of raisins, and wash a pound of currants; then put puff-paste at the bottom of a dish, and lay a row of your bread and butter, and strew a handful of currants, a few raisins, and some little bits of butter, and so do till your dish is full: then boil three pints of cream, and thicken it when cold with the yolks of ten eggs, a grated nutmeg, a little salt, near half a pound of sugar, and some orange flower-water; pour this in just as the pudding is going into the oven.

To make a Quaking Pudding.

TAKE a pint of cream, and boil it with nutmeg, cinnamon and mace; take out the spice, when it is boiled; then take the yolks of eight eggs, and four of the whites, beat them very well with some sack; then mix your eggs and cream, with a little salt and sugar, and a stale half-penny white loaf, one spoonful of flour, and a quarter of a pound of almonds blanched and beat fine, with some rose-water; beat all these well together; then wet a thick cloth, flour it, and put it in when the pot boils; it must boil an hour at least; melt butter, sack and sugar for the sauce; stick blanched almonds and candied orange-peel on the top.

To make a French Barley Pudding.

TAKE a quart of cream, and put to it six eggs well beaten, but three of the whites; then season it with sugar, nutmeg, a little salt, orange-flower-water, and a pound of melted butter; then put to it six handfuls of French barley that has been boiled tender in milk: butter a dish, and put it in, and bake it. It must stand as long as a venison-pasty, and it will be as good.

A good boiled Pudding.

TAKE a pound and a quarter of beef suet, after it is skinned, and shred very fine; then stone three quarters of a pound of raisins, and mix with it, as also a grated nutmeg, a quarter of a pound of sugar, a little salt, a little sack, four eggs, four spoonfuls of cream, and about half a pound of fine flour; mix these well

well together pretty stiff, tie it in a cloth, and let it boil four hours; melt butter thick for sauce.

To make an Oatmeal Pudding.

TAKE a pint of great oatmeal, beat it very small, then sift it fine; take a quart of cream, boil it and your oatmeal together, stirring it all the while until it is pretty thick; then put it in a dish, cover it close, and let it stand a little; then put into it a pound and a half of fresh butter, and let it stand two hours before you stir it; put to it twelve eggs, a nutmeg grated, a little salt, sweeten it to your taste; a little sack, or orange-flower-water; stir all very well together, put paste at the bottom of your dish, and put in your pudding-stuff, the oven not too hot; an hour will bake it.

Another.

A WINE pint of oatmeal picked from the blacks, a pint and a quarter of milk warmed; let it steep one night; three quarters of a pound of beef suet shred, one nutmeg, three spoonfuls of sugar, a small handful of flour, four eggs, and salt to your taste; make two puddings, and boil them three hours; if the oatmeal be too large, beat it, and if you make it into but one pudding, boil it four hours.

Another Method to make an Oatmeal Pudding.

TAKE a pint of fine oatmeal, boil it in three pints of new milk, stirring it till it is as thick as a hasty pudding; take it off, and stir in half a pound of fresh butter, a little beaten mace and nutmeg, and gill of sack; then beat up eight eggs, half the whites, stir all well together, lay puff-paste all over the dish, pour in the pudding, and bake it half an hour. Or you may boil it with a few currants.

To make a Pith Pudding

TAKE a quantity of the pith of an ox, and let it lie all night in water to soak out the blood; the next morning strip it out of the skins, and beat it with the back of a spoon in orange-flower-water till it is as fine as pap; then take three blades of mace, a nutmeg quartered, a stick of cinnamon; then take half a pound of the best Jordan almonds, blanched in cold water, beat them with a little of the cream, and as they dry put in more cream, and when they are all beaten, strain the cream from them to the pith; then take the yolks of ten eggs, the whites of but two, beat them very well, and put them to the

ingredients;

ingredients; then take a spoonful of grated bread, or Naples biscuit; mingle all these together, with half a pound of fine sugar, the marrow of four large bones, and a little salt; fill them in small ox or hogs guts, or bake it with puff-crust.

To make a Curd Pudding.

TAKE the curd of a gallon of milk, whey it well, and rub it through a sieve; then take six eggs, a little thick cream, three spoonfuls of orange-flower-water, one nutmeg grated, grated bread and flour, of each three spoonfuls, a pound of currants and stoned raisins; mix all these together; butter a thick cloth, and tie it up in it; boil it an hour; for sauce, melt butter with orange-flower-water and sugar.

Orange Custard or Pudding.

TAKE Seville oranges, and rub the outside with a little salt very well, pare them, and take half a pound of the peel, and lay them in several waters till the bitterness is abated; beat them small in a stone or wooden mortar, then put in ten yolks of eggs and a quart of thick cream, mix them well, and sweeten them to your taste; melt half a pound of butter, and stir it well in, if you design it for a pudding, and pour it into a dish covered with paste; if for custards, leave out the butter, and pour it into china cups, and bake it to eat cold.

Buttered Crumbs.

PUT a piece of butter into a saucepan, and let it run to oil; then skim it clean, and pour it off from the settlement; to this clear oil put grated crumbs of bread, and keep them stirring till they are crisp.

To make Hogs Puddings with Currants.

TAKE three pounds of grated bread to four pounds of beef suet finely shred, two pounds of currants, cloves, mace, and cinnamon, of each half an ounce beaten fine, a little salt, a pound and a half of sugar, a pint of sack, a quart of cream, a little rose-water, twenty eggs well beaten, but half the whites; mix all these well together, and fill the guts half full; boil them a little, and prick them as they boil, to keep them from breaking the guts; take them up on clean cloths.

Another Sort of Hogs Puddings.

TO half a pound of grated bread put half a pound of hogs liver boiled, cold, and grated, a pound and a half of suet finely

finely shred, a handful of salt, a handful of sweet-herbs, chopped small, some spice; mix all these together, with six eggs well beaten, and a little thick cream; fill your guts and boil them; when cold, cut them in round slices an inch thick; fry them in butter, and garnish your dish of fowls, hash, or fricasey.

To make black Hogs Puddings.

BOIL all the hog's harslet in about four or five gallons of water till it is very tender, then take out all the meat, and in that liquor steep near a peck of groats; put in the groats as it boils, and let them boil a quarter of an hour; then take the pot off the fire, and cover it up very close, and let it stand five or six hours; chop two or three handfuls of thyme, a little savoury, some parsley, and pennyroyal, some cloves and mace beaten, a handful of salt; mix all these with half the groats and two quarts of blood; put in most part of the leaf of the hog; cut it in square bits like dice, and some in long bits; fill your guts, and put in the fat as you like it; fill the guts three quarters full, put your puddings into a kettle of boiling water, let them boil an hour, and prick them with a pin, to keep them from breaking; lay them on clean straw when you take them up.

The other half of the groats you may make into white puddings for the family; chop all the meat very small, and shred two handfuls of sage very fine, an ounce of cloves and mace finely beaten, and some salt; work all together very well with a little flour, and put into the large guts; boil them about an hour, and keep them and the black near the fire till used.

Very fine Hogs Puddings.

SHRED four pounds of beef suet very fine, mix with it two pounds of fine sugar powdered, two grated nutmegs, some mace beat, a little salt, and three pounds of currants washed and picked; beat twenty-four yolks, twelve whites of eggs, with a little sack; mix all well together, and fill your guts, being clean, and steeped in orange-flower-water; cut your guts a quarter and a half long, fill them half full; tie at each end, and again thus occo; boil them as others, and cut them in balls when sent to table.

To make Almond Hogs Puddings.

TAKE two pounds of beef suet, or marrow, shred very small, a pound and a half of almonds blanched, and beaten very small, with rose-water, one pound of grated bread, a pound and a quarter of fine sugar, a little salt, one ounce of mace, nutmeg and cinnamon, twelve yolks of eggs, four whites, a pint of fack, a pint and a half of thick cream, some rose or orange-flower-water; boil the cream, tie a little saffron in a rag, and dip it in the cream to colour it; first beat your eggs very well, then stir in your almonds, then the spice, salt and suet; then mix all your ingredients together; fill your guts but half full, put some bits of citron in the guts as you fill them; tie them up, and boil them about a quarter of an hour.

To make an Almond Pudding.

TAKE a pound of the best Jordan almonds blanched in cold water, and beat very fine with a little rose-water; then take a quart of cream boiled with whole spice, and taken out again, and when it is cold, mix it with the almonds, and put to it three spoonfuls of grated bread, one spoonful of flour, nine eggs, but three whites, half a pound of sugar, and a nutmeg grated; mix and beat these well together, put some puff-paste at the bottom of a dish: put your stuff in, and here and there stick a piece of marrow in it. It must bake an hour, and when it is drawn, scrape sugar on it, and serve it up.

The Ipswich Almond Pudding.

STEEP somewhat above three ounces of the crumb of white bread sliced, in a pint and a half of cream, or grate the bread; then beat half a pound of blanched almonds very fine till they do not glister, with a small quantity of perfumed water, beat up the yolks of eight eggs, and the whites of four; mix all well together, put in a quarter of a pound of white sugar; then set it into the oven, but stir in a little melted butter before you let it in; let it bake but half an hour.

To make a brown Bread Pudding.

TAKE half a pound of brown bread, and double the weight of it in beef suet, a quarter of a pint of cream, the blood of a fowl, a whole nutmeg, some cinnamon, a spoonful of sugar, six yolks of eggs, three whites; mix it all well together, and boil it in a wooden dish two hours; serve it with sack and sugar, and butter melted.

A Rye-bread Pudding.

TAKE half a pound of sour rye-bread grated, half a pound of beef suet finely shred, half a pound of currants clean washed, half a pound of sugar, a whole nutmeg grated; mix all well together, with five or six eggs: butter a dish, boil it an hour and a quarter, and serve it up with melted butter.

To make a fine Bread Pudding.

TAKE three pints of milk and boil it; when it is boiled, sweeten it with half a pound of sugar, a small nutmeg grated, and put in half a pound of butter; when it is melted, pour in it a pan, over eleven ounces of grated bread; cover it up; the next day put to it ten eggs well beaten, stir all together, and when the oven is hot, put it in your dish, three quarters of an hour will bake it; boil a bit of lemon-peel in the milk, take it out before you put your other things in.

A baked Pudding.

BLANCH half a pound of almonds and beat them fine with sweet water, ambergrease dissolved in orange-flower-water, or in some cream; then warm a pint of thick cream, and melt in it half a pound of butter; then mix it up with your beaten almonds, a little salt, a grated nutmeg, and sugar, and the yolks of six eggs; beat it up together, and put it in a dish with puff-paste, the oven not too hot; scrape sugar on it just before it goes into the oven.

Another baked Bread Pudding.

TAKE a penny loaf, cut it in thin slices, then boil a quart of cream or new milk, and put in your bread, and break it very fine; put five eggs to it, a nutmeg grated, a quarter of a pound of sugar, and half a pound of butter; stir all these well together; butter your dish, and bake it an hour.

To make a baked Sack Pudding.

TAKE a pint of cream, and turn it to a curd with sack; bruise the curd very small with a spoon, and grate in two Naples biscuits, or the inside of a stale penny loaf; mix it well with the curd, and half a nutmeg grated, some fine sugar, and the yolks of four eggs, the whites of two, beaten with two spoonfuls of sack; then melt half a pound of fresh butter, and stir all together till the oven is hot; butter a dish, put it in, and sift some sugar over it just as it is going into the oven; half an hour will bake it.

To make a Cow-heel Pudding.

TAKE a large cow-heel, and cut off all the meat but the black toes; put them away, but mince the rest very small, and shred it over again, with three quarters of a pound of beef suet; put to it a penny loaf grated, cloves, mace, nutmeg, sugar, a little salt, some sack, and rose-water; mix these well together

The COMPLETE HOUSEWIFE. 121

together with six raw eggs well beaten; butter a cloth, put it in, and boil it two hours; for sauce, melt butter, sack and sugar.

To make a Calf's-foot Pudding.

TAKE two calves-feet finely shred; then take of biscuits grated, and stale mackaroons broken small, the quantity of a penny loaf; then add a pound of beef suet very finely shred, half a pound of currants, a quarter of a pound of sugar; some cloves, mace, and nutmeg, beat fine; a very little salt, some sack and orange-flower-water, some citron and candied orange-peel; work all these well together with yolks of eggs; if you boil it, put it in the caul of a breast of veal, and tie it over with a cloth; it must boil four hours. For sauce, melt butter, with a little sack and sugar; if you bake it, put some paste in the bottom of the dish, but none on the brim; then melt half a pound of butter, which mix with your stuff, and put it in your dish, sticking lumps of marrow in it: bake it three or four hours; scrape sugar over it, and serve it hot.

Another Method.

TAKE calves-feet, shred them very fine, and mix them with a penny loaf grated and scalded with a pint of cream; put to it half a pound of shred beef suet, eight eggs, and a handful of plumped currants; season it with sweet-spice and sugar, a little sack, orange-flower-water, and the marrow of two bones; then put it in a veal caul, being washed over with batter of eggs; then wet a cloth and put it therein; tie it close up; when the pot boils, put it in; boil it about two hours, and turn it in a dish, sticking in it sliced almonds and citron; let the sauce be sack and orange-flower-water, with lemon-juice, sugar and drawn butter.

To make a Spread-Eagle Pudding.

CUT off the crust of three halfpenny rolls, and slice them into your pan; then set three pints of milk over the fire, make it scalding hot, but not boil, put it over your bread, cover it close, and let it stand an hour; then put in a good spoonful of sugar, a very little salt, a nutmeg grated, a pound of suet after it is shred, half a pound of currants washed and picked, four spoonfuls of cold milk, ten eggs, but five whites; and when all is in stir it, but not till all is in; then mix it well, butter a dish; less than an hour will bake it.

To make New-College Puddings.

GRATE a penny stale loaf, put to it a like quantity of beef suet finely shred, a nutmeg grated, a little salt, and some currants;

currants; then beat some eggs in a little sack, and some sugar; mix all together, knead it as stiff as for a manchet, and make it up in the form and size of a turkey egg, but a little flatter; then take a pound of butter, put it in a dish, set the dish over a clear fire in a chafing-dish, and rub your butter about the dish till it is melted; put your puddings in, and cover the dish, but often turn your puddings, until they are all brown alike, and when they are enough, scrape sugar over them, and serve them up hot for a side dish.

You must let the paste lie a quarter of an hour before you make up your puddings.

To make an Oxford Pudding.

A QUARTER of a pound of biscuit grated, a quarter of a pound of currants clean washed and picked, a quarter of a pound of suet shred small, half a large spoonful of powder-sugar, a very little salt, and some grated nutmeg; mix all well together, then take two yolks of eggs, and make it up in balls as big as a turkey's egg. Fry them in fresh butter of a fine light brown; for sauce have melted butter and sugar, with a little sack or white wine. You must mind to keep the pan shaking about, that they may be all of a fine light brown.

To make a fine Hasty Pudding.

BREAK an egg into fine flour, and with your hand work up as much as you can into as stiff paste as is possible, then mince it as small as herbs to the pot, as small as if it were to be sifted; then set a quart of milk a boiling, and put it in the paste so cut: put in a little salt, a little beaten cinnamon and sugar, a piece of butter as big as a walnut, and stirring all one way. When it is as thick as you would have it, stir in such another piece of butter, then pour it into your dish, and stick pieces of butter here and there. Send it to table hot.

To make a Sweetmeat Pudding.

PUT a thin puff-paste at the bottom of your dish, then have of candied orange, lemon, and citron-peel, of each an ounce; slice them thin, and put them in the bottom on your paste; then beat eight yolks of eggs, and two whites, near half a pound of sugar, and half a pound of butter melted; mix and beat all well together, and when the oven is ready, pour it on your sweetmeats in the dish. An hour or less will bake it.

A Marrow Pudding.

BOIL a quart of cream or milk, with a stick of cinnamon, a quartered nutmeg, and a large blade of mace; then mix it

with

with eight eggs well beat, a little salt, sugar, sack, and orange-flower-water; strain it; then put to it three grated biscuits, an handful of currants, as many raisins of the sun, the marrow of two bones, all in four large pieces; put it into a dish, having the brim thereof garnished with puff paste, and raised in the oven; then lay on the four pieces of marrow, knots and pastes, sliced citron and lemon-peel.

Another Method.

TAKE a quart of cream, and three Naples biscuits grated, a nutmeg grated, the yolks of ten eggs, the whites of five well beaten, and sugar to your taste; mix all well together, and put a little bit of butter in the bottom of your saucepan; then put in your stuff, and set it over the fire, and stir it till it is pretty thick; then put it into your pan, with a quarter of a pound of currants that have been plumped in hot water; stir it together, and let it stand all night. The next day put some fine paste rolled very thin at the bottom of your dish, and when the oven is ready, pour in your stuff, and on the top lay large pieces of marrow. Half an hour will bake it.

Another Method.

TAKE out the marrow of three or four bones, and slice it in thin pieces; and take a penny loaf, cut off the crust, and slice it in as thin slices as you can, and stone half a pound of raisins of the sun; then lay a sheet of thin paste in the bottom of a dish; so lay a row of marrow, or bread, and of raisins till the dish is full; then have in readiness a quart of cream boiled, and beat five eggs, and mix with it; put to it nutmeg grated, and half a pound of sugar. When it is just going into the oven, pour in your cream and eggs; bake it half an hour, scrape sugar on it when it is drawn, and serve it up.

Lemon Pudding.

GRATE the peels of three large lemons, only the yellow, then take two lemons more, and the three you have grated, and roll them under your hand on a table till they are very soft; but be careful not to break them; then cut and squeeze them, and strain the juice from the seeds to the grated peels, then grate the crumb of three halfpenny loaves, (or ten ounces of crumb, white loaves) into a bason, and make a pint of white wine scalding hot, pour it to your bread, and stir it well together to soak, then put to it the grated peel and juice; beat the yolks of eight eggs and four whites together, and mingle with the rest three quarters of a pound of butter that is fresh and melted, and almost a pound of white sugar, beat it will together till it

be

be thoroughly mixed, then lay a sheet of puff-paste at the bottom and brim, cutting it into what form you please; the paste that is left roll out, and with a jagging iron cut them out in little stripes, neither so broad or long as your little finger, and bake them on a floured paper; let the pudding bake almost an hour, when it comes out of the oven stick the pieces of paste on the top of it to serve it to table. It eats well either hot or cold.

Another.

TAKE two clear lemons, grate off the outside rinds; then grate two Naples biscuits, and mix with your grated peel, adding to it three quarters of a pound of fine sugar, twelve yolks and six whites of eggs, well beat, three quarters of a pound of butter melted, and half a pint of thick cream; mix these well together, put in a sheet of paste at the bottom of the dish, and just as the oven is ready put your stuff in the dish; sift a little double-refined sugar over it before you put it in the oven; an hour will bake it.

To make a Sweetmeat Pudding.

PUT a thin puff-paste all over your dish; then have candied orange and lemon-peel, and citron, of each an ounce, slice them thin, and lay them all over the bottom of your dish; then beat eight yolks of eggs and two whites, near half a pound of sugar, and half a pound of melted butter. Beat all well together; when the oven is ready, pour it on your sweetmeats. An hour or less will bake it. The oven must not be too hot.

To make a fine plain Pudding.

GET a quart of milk, put into it six laurel leaves, boil it, then take out your leaves, and stir in as much flour as will make it a hasty pudding pretty thick, take it off, and then stir in half a pound of butter, then a quarter of a pound of sugar, a small nutmeg grated, and twelve yolks and six whites of eggs well beaten. Mix all well together, butter a dish, and put in your stuff. A little more than half an hour will bake it.

A Rice Pudding.

TAKE two large handfuls of rice well beaten and searced: then take two quarts of milk or cream, set it over the fire with the rice, put in cinnamon and mace, let it boil a quarter of an hour; it must be as thick as hasty pudding; then stir in half a pound of butter while it is over the fire; then take it off to cool,

cool, and put in sugar, and a little salt; when it is almost cold put in ten or twelve eggs, take out four of the whites; butter the dish; an hour will bake it; searce sugar over it.

Another.

SET a pint of thick cream over the fire, and put into it three spoonfuls of the flour of rice, stir it, and when it is pretty thick, pour it into a pan, adding to it half a pound of fresh butter; stir it till it is almost cold; then add to it a grated nutmeg, a little salt, some sugar, a little sack, the yolks of six eggs; stir it well together; put some puff paste in the bottom of the dish, pour it in; an hour or less will bake it.

A fine Rice Pudding.

TAKE of the flour of rice six ounces, put it in a quart of milk, and let it boil till it is pretty thick, stirring it all the while; then pour it into a pan, and stir in it half a pound of fresh butter, and a quarter of a pound of sugar, or sweeten it to your taste; when it is cold, grate in a nutmeg, and beat six eggs, with a spoonful or two of sack, and beat and stir all well together; put a little fine paste at the bottom of your dish, and bake it.

To make a cheap Rice Pudding.

GET a quarter of a pound of rice and half a pound of raisins stoned, and tie them in a cloth. Give the rice a great deal of room to swell. Boil it two hours: when it is enough turn it into your dish, and pour melted butter and sugar over it, with a little nutmeg.

To make a Ratafia Pudding.

TAKE a quart of cream, boil it with four or five laurel leaves; then take them out, and break in half a pound of Naples biscuit, half a pound of butter, some sack, nutmeg, and salt; take it off the fire, and cover it up; when it is almost cold put in two ounces of almonds blanched, and beaten fine, with the yolks of five eggs; mix all well together, and bake it in a moderate oven half an hour; scrape sugar on it as it goes into the oven.

Vermicelly Pudding.

BOIL five ounces of vermicelly in a quart of milk till it is tender, with a blade of mace, and a rind of lemon or Seville orange, sweeten it to your taste, the yolks of six eggs, and
four

four whites; have a dish ready covered with paste, and just before you set it into the oven, stir in half a pound of melted butter, a very little salt does well; if you have no peels, put in a little orange-flower-water.

To make a Potatoe Pudding.

TAKE a quart of potatoes, boil them soft, peel them and mash them with the back of a spoon, and rub them through a sieve, to have them fine and smooth; take half a pound of fresh butter melted, half a pound of fine sugar, so beat them well together till they are very smooth, beat six eggs, whites and all, stir them in, and a glass of sack or brandy. You may add half a pound of currants, boil it half an hour, melt butter with a glass of white wine; sweeten with sugar, and pour over it. You may bake it in a dish, with puff-paste all round the dish, and at the bottom.

An Apple Pudding.

PEEL and quarter eight golden rennets, or twelve golden pippins; put them into water, in which boil them as you do apple-sauce; sweeten them with loaf sugar, squeeze in two lemons, and grate in their peels; break eight eggs, and beat them all well together; pour it into a dish covered with puff-paste, and bake it an hour in a slow oven.

To make a Chesnut Pudding.

TAKE a dozen and a half of chesnuts, put them in a skillet of water, and set them on the fire till they will blanch; then blanch them, and when cold, put them in cold water, then stamp them in a mortar, with orange-flower-water and sack till they are very small; mix them in two quarts of cream, and eighteen yolks of eggs, the whites of three or four; beat the eggs with sack, rose-water, and sugar, put it in a dish with puff paste; stick in some lumps of marrow or fresh butter, and bake it.

To make a Marjoram Pudding.

TAKE the curd of a quart of milk finely broken, a good handful or more of sweet-marjoram chopped as small as dust, and mingle with the curd five eggs, but three whites, beaten with rose-water, some nutmeg and sugar, and half a pint of cream; beat all these well together, and put in three quarters of a pound of melted butter; put a thin sheet of paste at the bottom of your dish; then pour in your pudding, and with a spur cut out little slips of paste the breadth of a little finger, and

lay

lay them over crofs and crofs in large diamonds; put fome fmall bits of butter on the top, and bake it. This is old fafhioned, and not good.

To make a Cabbage Pudding.

TAKE two pounds of the lean part of a leg of veal, of beef fuet the like quantity, chop them together, then beat them together in a ftone mortar, adding to it half a little cabbage fcalded, and beat that with your meat; then feafon it with meat and nutmeg, a little pepper and falt, fome green goofberries, grapes, or barberries in the time of the year; in the winter put in a little verjuice, then mix all well together, with the yolks of four or five eggs well beaten; wrap it up in green cabbage leaves, tie a cloth over it, boil it an hour; melt butter for fauce.

A colouring Liquor for Puddings.

BEAT an ounce of cochineal very fine, put it in a pint of water in a fkillet, and a quarter of an ounce of roach allum, boil it till the goodnefs is out, ftrain it into a phial, with two ounces of fine fugar; it will keep fix months.

CHAP. XVI.
All Sorts of PYES.

To make an Olio Pye.

TAKE a fillet of veal, cut it in large thin flices, and beat it with a rolling-pin; have ready fome forcemeat made with veal and fuet, grated bread, grated lemon-peel, fome nutmeg, the yolks of two or three hard eggs; fpread the forcemeat all over your collops, and roll them up, and place them in your pye, with yolks of hard eggs, lumps of marrow, and fome water; lid it and bake it; when it is done, put in a caudle of ftrong gravy, white wine and butter.

To make an Olio Pye.

MAKE your pye ready; then take the thin collops of the but end of a leg of veal, as many as you think will fill your pye; hack them with the back of a knife, and feafon them with pepper, falt, cloves, and mace: wafh over your collops with a bunch of feathers dipped in eggs, and have in readinefs a good handful of fweet-herbs fhred fmall; the herbs muft be

thyme,

thyme, parsley, and spinach; the yolks of eight hard eggs minced, and a few oysters parboiled and chopped: some beef suet shred very fine. Mix these together, and strew them over your collops, and sprinkle a little orange-flower-water on them, and roll the collops up very close, and lay them in your pye, strewing the seasoning that is left over them; put butter on the top, and close up your pye; when it is drawn, put in gravy, and one anchovy dissolved in it, and pour it in very hot: you may put in artichoke-bottoms, and chesnuts, if you please, or sliced lemon, or grapes scalded, or what else is in season: but if you will make it a right savoury pye, leave them out.

To make a Florendine of Veal.

TAKE the kidney of a loin of veal, fat and all, and mince it very fine; then chop a few herbs, and put to it, and add a few currants; season it with cloves, mace, nutmeg, and a little salt; and put in some yolks of eggs, and a handful of grated bread, a pippin or two chopped, some candied lemon-peel minced small, some sack, sugar, and orange-flower-water. Put a sheet of puff-paste at the bottom of your dish; put this in, and cover it with another, close it up, and when it is baked, scrape sugar on it, and serve it hot.

A Veal Pye.

RAISE an high pye, then cut a fillet of veal into three or four slices, season it with savoury spice, a little minced sage and sweet-herbs; lay it in the pye with slices of bacon at the bottom, and betwixt each piece lay on butter, and close the pye.

A savoury Veal Pye.

TAKE a breast of veal, cut it into pieces, season it with pepper and salt, lay it all into your crust, boil six or eight eggs hard, take only the yolks, put them into the pye here and there, fill your dish almost full of water, put on the lid, and bake it well.

To make a savoury Lamb Pye.

SEASON your lamb with pepper, salt, cloves, mace, and nutmeg: so put it into your coffin with a few lamb-stones, and sweet-breads seasoned as your lamb; also some large oysters, and savoury forcemeat balls, hard yolks of eggs, and the tops of asparagus two inches long, first boiled green: then put butter all over the pye, lid it, and set it in a quick oven an hour and a half; then make the liquor with oyster liquor, as much gravy,

gravy, a little claret, with one anchovy it, a grated nutmeg. Let thefe have a boil, thicken it with yolks of two or three eggs, and when the pye is drawn, pour it in hot.

To make a fweet Lamb Pye.

CUT your lamb into fmall pieces, and feafon it with a little falt, cloves, mace, and nutmeg; your pye being made, put in your lamb or veal; ftrew on it fome ftoned raifins and currants, and fome fugar; then lay on it fome forcemeat balls made fweet, and in the fummer fome artichoke-bottoms boiled, and fcalded grapes in the winter. Boil Spanifh potatoes cut in pieces; candied citron, candied orange and lemon-peel, and three or four large blades of mace; put butter on the top; clofe up your pye and bake it. Make the caudle of white wine, juice of lemon and fugar: thicken it with the yolks of two or three eggs, and a bit of butter; and when your pye is baked, pour in the caudle as hot as you can, and fhake it well in the pye, and ferve it up.

A Beef-fteak Pye.

TAKE fine rump-fteaks, beat them with a rolling-pin, then feafon them with pepper and falt, according to your palate. Make a good cruft, lay in your fteaks, fill your difh, then pour in as much water as will half fill the difh. Put on the cruft, and bake it well.

A Ham Pye.

TAKE fome cold boiled ham, and flice it about half an inch thick, make a good thick cruft over the difh, and lay a layer of ham, fhake a little pepper over it, then take a large young fowl clean picked, gutted, wafhed, and finged: put a little pepper and falt in the belly, and rub a very little falt on the outfide; lay the fowl on the ham, boil fome eggs hard, put in the yolks, and cover all with ham, then fhake fome pepper on the ham, and put on the top-cruft. Bake it well, have ready, when it comes out of the oven, fome very rich beef gravy, enough to fill the pye; lay on the cruft again, and fend it to table hot. A frefh ham will not be fo tender; fo that I always boil my ham one day and bring it to table, and the next day make a pye of it. It does better than an unboiled ham. If you put two large fowls in, they will make a fine pye; but that is according to your company, more or lefs. The larger the pye, the finer the meat eats. The cruft muft be the fame you make for a venifon pafty. You fhould pour a little ftrong gravy into the pye when you make it, juft to bake the meat, and then fill it up when it

K comes

comes out of the oven. Boil some truffles and morels and put into the pye, which is a great addition, and some fresh mushrooms, or dried ones.

A Battalia Pye, or Bride Pye.

TAKE young chickens as big as black-birds, quails, young partridges, larks, and squab-pigeons, truss them, and put them in your pye; then have ox-palates boiled, blanched, and cut in pieces, lamb-stones, sweet-breads, cut in halves or quarters, cocks-combs blanched, a quart of oysters dipped in eggs, and dredged over with grated bread and marrow: sheeps-tongues boiled, peeled, and cut in slices; season all with salt, pepper, cloves, mace, and nutmegs, beaten and mixed together; put butter at the bottom of the pye, and place the rest in with the yolks of hard eggs, knots of eggs, forcemeat balls; cover all with butter, and close up the pye; put in five or six spoonfuls of water when it goes into the oven, and when it is drawn pour it out and put in gravy.

A Battalia Pye.

TAKE four small chickens, four squab-pigeons, four sucking rabbets; cut them in pieces, season them with savoury spice, and lay them in a pye, with four sweet-breads sliced, and as many sheeps-tongues, two shivered palates, two pair of lamb-stones, twenty or thirty cocks-combs, with savoury balls and oysters. Lay on butter, and close the pye. A lear.

To make Egg Pyes.

TAKE the yolks of two dozen of eggs boiled hard, and chopped with double the quantity of beef suet, and half a pound of pippins pared, cored, and sliced; then add to it one pound of currants washed and dried, half a pound of sugar, a little salt, some spice beaten fine, the juice of a lemon, and half a pint of sack, candied orange and citron cut in pieces, of each three ounces, some lumps of marrow on the top, fill them full; the oven must not be too hot; three quarters of an hour will bake them; put the marrow only on them that are to be eaten hot.

To make a Lumber Pye.

TAKE a pound and a half of veal, parboil it, and when it is cold chop it very small, with two pounds of beef suet, and some candied orange-peel, some sweet-herbs, as thyme, sweet-marjoram; and a handful of spinach; mince the herbs small before

fore you put them to the other; chop all together, and a pippin or two, then add a handful or two of grated bread, a pound and a half of currants washed and dried, some cloves, mace, nutmeg, a little salt, sugar, and sack, adding to all these as many yolks of raw eggs, and whites of two, as will make it a moist forcemeat; work it with your hands into a body, and make it into balls as big as a turkey's egg, then having your coffin made, put in your balls; take the marrow out of three or four bones as whole as you can; let your marrow lie a little in water, to take out the blood and splinters; then dry it, and dip it in yolks of eggs; season it with a little salt, nutmeg grated, and grated bread; lay it on and between your forcemeat balls, and over that sliced citron, candied orange and lemon, eringo-roots, and preserved barberries; then lay on sliced lemon, and thin slices of butter over all; then lid your pye, and bake it; and when it is drawn, have in readiness a caudle made of white wine and sugar, and thickened with butter and eggs, and pour it hot into your pye.

A sweet Chicken Pye.

TAKE five or six small chickens, pick, draw, and truss them for baking; season them with cloves, mace, nutmeg, cinnamon, and a little salt; wrap up some of the seasoning in butter, and put it in their bellies: and your coffin being made, put them in; put over and between them pieces of marrow, Spanish potatoes and chesnuts, both boiled, peeled, and cut, a handful of barberries stripped, a lemon sliced, some butter on the top; so close up the pye and bake it, and have in readiness a caudle made of white wine, sugar, nutmeg; beat it up with yolks of eggs and butter; have a care it does not curdle; pour the caudle in, shake it well together, and serve it up hot.

Another Chicken Pye.

SEASON your chickens with pepper, salt, cloves, mace, nutmeg, a little shred parsley, and thyme, mixed with the other seasoning; wrap up some in butter, put it in the bellies of the chickens, and lay them in your pye; strew over them lemon cut like dice, a handful of scalded grapes, artichoke-bottoms in quarters; put butter on it, and close it up; when it is baked, put in a lear of gravy, with a little white wine, a grated nutmeg, thicken it up with butter, and two or three eggs; shake it well together, and serve it up hot.

Another.

MAKE a puff-paste crust, take two chickens, cut them to pieces, season them with pepper and salt, a little beaten mace, lay a forcemeat made thus round the side of the dish: take half a pound of veal, half a pound of suet, beat them quite fine in a marble mortar, with as many crumbs of bread, season it with a very little pepper and salt, an anchovy with the liquor, cut the anchovy to pieces, a little lemon-peel cut very fine and shred small, a very little thyme, mix all together with the yolk of an egg, make some into round balls, about twelve, the rest lay round the dish. Lay in one chicken over the bottom of the dish, take two sweet-breads, cut them into five or six pieces, lay them all over, season them with pepper and salt, strew over them half an ounce of truffles and morels, two or three artichoke-bottoms cut to pieces, a few cocks-combs, if you have them, a palate boiled tender and cut to pieces; then lay on the other part of the chicken, put half a pint of water in, and cover the pye; bake it well, and when it comes out of the oven, fill it with good gravy, lay on the crust, and send it to table.

To make a Hare Pye.

SKIN your hare, wash her, dry her, and bone her; season the flesh with pepper, salt, and spice, beaten fine in a stone mortar; do a young pig at the same time in the same manner; then make your pye, and lay a layer of pig and a layer of hare till it is full; put butter at the bottom and on the top; bake it three hours: it is good hot or cold.

Another Method.

BONE your hare as whole as you can, then lard it with the fat of bacon, first dipt in vinegar and pepper, then season it with pepper, salt, a little mace, and a clove or two; put it into a dish with puff paste, and have in readiness gravy or strong broth made with the bones, and put it in just before you set it in the oven; when it comes out, pour in some melted butter with strong broth and wine; but before you pour it in, taste how the pye is seasoned, and if it wants, you may season the liquor accordingly; if you please, you may lay slices of butter upon the hare before it goes into the oven, which I think best, instead of the melted butter: after, a glass of claret does well, just before you serve it. To seven pounds of lean venison without bones, put two ounces and a half of salt, and half an ounce of pepper, to season this in proportion; some chuse to put in the legs and wings with the bones; divide them at every joint,

and

and take the bones of the body, only cracking the other bones in the limbs.

A Turkey Pye.

BONE the turkey, ſeaſon it with favoury ſpice, and lay it in the pye with two capons, or two wild-ducks cut in pieces to fill up the corners; lay on butter, and cloſe the pye.

A Codling Pye.

GATHER ſmall codlings, put them in a clean braſs pan with ſpring water, lay vine leaves on them, and cover them with a cloth wrapped round the cover of the pan to keep in the ſteam; when they grow ſoftiſh, peel off the ſkin, and put them in the ſame water with the vine leaves; hang them a great height over the fire to green, and when you ſee them a fine green, take them out of the water and put them in a deep diſh, with as much powder or loaf ſugar as will ſweeten them; make the lid of rich puff-paſte, and bake it; when it comes from the oven, take off the lid, and cut it in little pieces like ſippets, and ſtick them round the inſide of the pye with the points upward, pour over your codlings a good cuſtard made thus:—— Boil a pint of cream, with a ſtick of cinnamon, and ſugar enough to make it a little ſweet; let it ſtand till cold, and then put in the yolks of four eggs well beaten, ſet it on the fire and keep ſtirring it till it grows thick, but do not let it boil, left it curdle; then pour it into your pye, pare a little lemon thin, cut the peel like ſtraws, and lay it on your codlings over the top.

A Pigeon Pye.

LET your pigeons be nicely picked and cleaned, ſeaſon them with pepper and ſalt, and put a good piece of fine freſh butter, with pepper and ſalt in their bellies; lay them in your pan, and the necks, gizzards, livers, pinions, and hearts, lay between; put as much water as will almoſt fill the diſh, lay on the top-cruſt, and bake it well. This is the beſt way to make a pigeon pye; but the French fill the pigeons with a very high forcemeat, and lay forcemeat balls round the inſide, with aſparagus-tops, artichoke-bottoms, muſhrooms, truffles and morels, and ſeaſon high; but that is according to different palates. To the former ſimple method ſome add the yolk of an egg boiled hard, and a beef-ſteak in the middle.

To make a Giblet Pye.

TAKE two pair of giblets nicely cleaned, put all but the livers into a saucepan, with two quarts of water, twenty corns of whole pepper, three blades of mace, a bundle of sweet-herbs, and a large onion; cover them close, and let them stew very softly till they are quite tender, then have a good crust ready, cover your dish, lay a fine rump-steak at the bottom, seasoned with pepper and salt; then lay in your giblets with the livers, and strain the liquor they were stewed in. Season it with salt, and pour it into your pye; put on the lid, and bake it an hour and a half.

To make a Duck Pye.

MAKE a puff-paste crust, take two ducks, scald them and make them very clean, cut off the feet, the pinions, the neck, and head, all clean picked and scalded, with the gizzards, livers and hearts; pick out all the fat of the inside, lay a crust all over the dish, season the ducks with pepper and salt, inside and out; lay them in your dish, and the giblets at each end seasoned; put in as much water as will almost fill the pye, lay on the crust, and bake it, but not too much.

To make a Cheshire Pork Pye.

TAKE a loin of pork, skin it, cut it into steaks, season it with salt, nutmeg, and pepper; make a good crust, lay a layer of pork, then a large layer of pippins pared and cored, a little sugar, enough to sweeten the pye, then another layer of pork; put in half a pint of white wine, lay some butter on the top, and close your pye. If your pye be large, it will take a pint of white wine.

To make a Devonshire Squab Pye.

MAKE a good crust, cover the dish all over, put at the bottom a layer of sliced pippins, strew over them some sugar, then a layer of mutton-steaks cut from the loin, well seasoned with pepper and salt, then another layer of pippins; peel some onions and slice them thin, lay a layer all over the apples, then a layer of mutton, then pippins and onions, pour in a pint of water; so close your pye and bake it.

A Neat's-Tongue Pye.

HALF boil the tongues, blanch and flice them; feafon them with favoury fpice, with balls, fliced lemon and butter, and clofe the pye. When it is baked pour into it a ragoo.

To make Mince Pyes the beft way.

TAKE three pounds of fuet fhred very fine, and chopped as fmall as poffible, two pounds of raifins ftoned, and chopped as fine as poffible, two pounds of currants nicely picked, wafhed, rubbed, and dried at the fire, half a hundred of fine pippins, pared, cored, and chopped fmall, half a pound of fine fugar pounded fine, a quarter of an ounce of mace, a quarter of an ounce of cloves, two large nutmegs, all beat fine; put all together into a great pan, and mix it well together with half a pint of brandy, and half a pint of fack; put it down clofe in a ftone-pot, and it will keep good four months. When you make your pyes, take a little difh, fomething bigger than a foupplate, lay a very thin cruft all over it, lay a thin layer of meat, and then a thin layer of citron cut very thin, then a layer of mincemeat, and a thin layer of orange-peel cut thin, over that a little meat, fqueeze half the juice of a fine Seville orange or lemon, and pour in three fpoonfuls of red wine; lay on your cruft, and bake it nicely. Thefe pyes eat finely cold. If you make them in little patties, mix your meat and fweetmeats accordingly. If you chufe meat in your pyes, parboil a neat's-tongue, peel it, and chop the meat as fine as poffible, and mix with the reft; or two pounds of the infide of a firloin of beef boiled.

To make Mince Pyes of Veal.

FROM a leg of veal cut off four pounds of the flefhy part in thick pieces, put them in fcalding water, and let it juft boil; then cut the meat in fmall thin pieces, and fkin it; it muft be four pounds after it is fcalded and fkinned; to this quantity put nine pounds of beef fuet well fkinned; fhred them very fine with eight pippins pared and cored, and four pounds of raifins of the fun ftoned; when it is fhred very fine put it in a large pan, or on a table to mix, and put to it one ounce of nutmegs grated, half an ounce of cloves, as much mace, a large fpoonful of falt, above a pound of fugar, the peel of a lemon fhred exceeding fine; when you have feafoned it to your palate, put in feven pounds of currants, and two pounds of raifins ftoned and fhred; when you fill your pyes, put into every one fome fhred lemon with its juice, fome candied lemon-peel and citron in slices; and just as the pyes go into the oven, put into every one a spoonful of sack and a spoonful of claret, so bake them.

To make a Potatoe Pye.

BOIL three pounds of potatoes, peel them, make a good crust and lay in your dish; lay at the bottom half a pound of butter, then lay in your potatoes, throw over them three tea-spoonfuls of salt, and a small nutmeg grated all over, six eggs boiled hard chopped fine, throw all over, a tea-spoonful of pepper strewed all over, then half a pint of white wine. Cover your pye, and bake it half an hour, or till the crust is enough.

A fine Potatoe Pye for Lent.

FIRST make your forcemeat, about two dozen of small oysters just scalded, and when cold chopped small, a stale roll grated, and six yolks of eggs boiled hard, and bruised small with the back of a spoon; season with a little salt, pepper, and nutmeg, some thyme and parsley, both shred small; mix these together well, pound them a little, and make it up in a stiff paste, with half a pound of butter and an egg worked in it; just flour it to keep it from sticking, and lay it by till your pye is fit, and put a very thin paste in your dish, bottom and sides; then put your forcemeat, of an equal thickness, about two fingers broad, about the sides of your dish, as you would do a pudding crust; dust a little flour on it, and put it down close; then fill your pye, a dozen of potatoes, about the bigness of a small egg, finely pared, just boiled a walm or two, a dozen yolks of eggs boiled hard, a quarter of a hundred of large oysters just scalded in their own liquor and cold, six morels, four or five blades of mace, some whole pepper, and a little salt butter on the bottom and top; then lid your pye, and bake it an hour; when it is drawn, pour in a caudle made with half a pint of your oyster liquor, three or four spoonfuls of white wine, and thickened up with butter and eggs; pour it in hot at the hole on the top, and shake it together, and serve it.

To make an Onion Pye.

WASH and pare some potatoes, and cut them in slices, peel some onions, cut them in slices pare some apples and slice them, make a good crust, cover your dish, lay a quarter of a pound of butter all over, take a quarter of an ounce of mace beat fine, a nutmeg grated, a tea-spoonful of beaten pepper, three tea-spoonfuls of salt, mix all together, strew some over the butter, lay a layer of potatoes, a layer of onion, a layer of apple, and a layer of eggs, and so on till you have filled your pye,

strewing

strewing a little of the seasoning between each layer, and a quarter of a pound of butter in bits, and six spoonfuls of water. Close your pye, and bake it an hour and a half.

To make an Artichoke Pye.

BOIL the bottoms of eight or ten artichokes, scrape and make them clean from the core; cut each of them into six parts; season them with cinnamon, nutmeg, sugar, and a little salt; then lay your artichokes in your pye. Take the marrow of four or five bones, dip your marrow in yolks of eggs and grated bread, and season it as you did your artichokes, and lay it on the top and between your artichokes; then lay on sliced lemon, barberries and large mace; put butter on the top, and close up your pye; then make your lear of white wine, sack, and sugar; thicken it with yolks of eggs, and a bit of butter; when your pye is drawn, pour it in, shake it together, and serve it hot.

To make a Skirret Pye.

BOIL your biggest skirrets, blanch them, and season them with cinnamon, nutmeg, and a very little ginger and sugar. Your pye being ready, lay in your skirrets; season also the marrow of three or four bones with cinnamon, sugar, a little salt, and grated bread. Lay the marrow in your pye, and the yolks of twelve hard eggs cut in halves, a handful of chesnuts boiled and blanched, with some candied orange-peel in slices. Lay butter on the top, and lid your pye. Let your caudle be white wine, verjuice, some sack and sugar; thicken it with the yolks of eggs, and when the pye is baked, pour it in, and serve it hot. Scrape sugar on it.

To make a Cabbage-Lettuce Pye.

TAKE some of the largest and hardest cabbage-lettuces you can get, boil them in salt and water till they are tender, then lay them in a colander to drain; have your paste laid in your pattipan ready, and lay butter on the bottom; then lay in your lettuce, some artichoke-bottoms, some large pieces of marrow, the yolks of eight hard eggs, and some scalded sorrel; bake it, and when it comes out of the oven, cut open the lid, and pour in a caudle made with white wine and sugar, thickened with eggs; so serve it hot.

To make an Apple and a Pear Pye.

MAKE a good puff-paste crust, lay some round the sides of the dish, pare and quarter your apples, and take out the cores, lay a row of apples thick, throw in half the sugar you design for your pye, mince a little lemon-peel fine, throw over and squeeze a little lemon over them, then a few cloves, here and there one, then the rest of your apples and the rest of your sugar. You must sweeten to your palate, and squeeze a little more lemon. Boil the peeling of the apples and the cores in some fair water, with a blade of mace, till it is very good; strain it and boil the syrup with a little sugar, till there is but very little and good, pour it into your pye, put on your upper crust and bake it. You may put in a little quince or marmalade, if you please.

Thus make a pear pye, but don't put in any quince. You may butter them when they come out of the oven; or beat up the yolks of two eggs and half a pint of cream, with a little nutmeg, sweetened with sugar, take off the lid and pour in the cream. Cut the crust in little three corner pieces, stick about the pye and send it to table.

To make a Cherry Pye.

MAKE a good crust, lay a little round the sides of your dish, throw sugar at the bottom, and lay in your fruit and sugar at top. A few red currants does well with them; put on your lid, and bake in a slack oven.

Make a plumb pye the same way and a gooseberry pye. If you would have it red, let it stand a good while in the oven, after the bread is drawn. A custard is very good with the gooseberry pye.

A Fish Pye.

TAKE of soles, or thick flounders, gut and wash them, and just put them in scalding water to get off the black skin; then cut them in scollops, or indented, so that they will join and lie in the pye as if they were whole; have you pattipans in readiness, with puff-paste at the bottom, and a layer of butter on it; then season your fish with a little pepper, salt, cloves, mace, and nutmeg, and lay it in your pattipans, joining the pieces together as if the fish had not been cut; then put in forcemeat balls made with fish, slices of lemon with the rind on, whole yolks of hard eggs, and pickled barberries; then lid your pye and bake it; when it is drawn, make a caudle of oyster liquor

and

and white wine thickened up with yolks of eggs and a bit of butter; serve it hot.

To make an Eel Pye.

MAKE a good crust, clean, gut, and wash your eels very well, then cut them in pieces half as long as your finger; season them with pepper, salt, and a little beaten mace to your palate, either high or low. Fill your dish with eels, and put as much water as the dish will hold; put on your cover and bake them well.

To make a Turbot Pye.

GUT, wash, and boil your turbot; season it with a little pepper, salt, cloves, mace, nutmeg, and sweet-herbs shred fine; then lay it in your pye, or pattipan, with the yolks of six eggs boiled hard; a whole onion, which must be taken out when it is baked. Put two pounds of fresh butter on the top; close it up; when it is drawn, serve it hot or cold: it is good either way.

To make an Oyster Pye.

MAKE good puff-paste, and lay a thin sheet in the bottom of your pattipan; then take two quarts of large oysters, wash them well in their own liquor, take them out of it, dry them, and season them with salt, spice, and a little pepper, all beaten fine; lay some butter in the bottom of your pattipan, then lay in your oysters and the yolks of twelve hard eggs whole, two or three sweet-breads cut in slices, or lamb-stones, or for want of these a dozen of larks, two marrow-bones, the marrow taken out in lumps, dipped in the yolks of eggs, and seasoned as you did your oysters, with some grated bread dusted on it, and a few forcemeat balls: when all these are in put some butter on the top, and cover it over with a sheet of puff-paste, and bake it; when it is drawn out of the oven, take the liquor of the oysters, boil it, skim it, and beat it up thick with butter, and the yolks of two or three eggs; pour it hot into your pye, shake it well together, and serve it hot.

To make a Salmon Pye.

MAKE a good puff-paste, and lay it in your pattipan, then take the middle piece of salmon, season it pretty high with pepper, salt, cloves and mace, cut it in three pieces, then lay a layer of butter, and a layer of salmon, till all is in; make forcemeat balls of an eel, chop it fine with the yolks of hard eggs,

two

two or three anchovies, marrow, (or, if for a fasting-day, butter) sweet-herbs, some grated bread, and a few oysters and grated nutmeg, some small pepper, and a little salt; make it up with raw eggs into balls, some long, some round, and lay them about your salmon: put butter over all, and lid your pye; an hour will bake it.

To make a Carp Pye.

TAKE a large carp, scale, wash, and gut it clean; take an eel, boil it just a little tender, pick off all the meat and mince it fine, with an equal quantity of crumbs of bread, a few sweet-herbs, a little lemon-peel cut fine, a little pepper, salt, and grated nutmeg, an anchovy, half a pint of oysters parboiled and chopped fine, the yolks of three hard eggs cut small, roll it up with a quarter of a pound of butter, and fill the belly of the carp. Make a good crust, cover the dish, and lay in your carp; save the liquor you boil your eel in, put in the eel bones, boil them with a little mace, whole pepper, an onion, some sweet-herbs, and an anchovy. Boil it till there is about half a pint, strain it, add to it a quarter of a pint of white wine, and a lump of butter mixed in a very little flour; boil it up, and pour into your pye. Put on the lid, and bake it an hour in a quick oven. If there be any forcemeat left after filling the belly, make balls of it, and put into the pye. If you have not liquor enough, boil a few small eels, to make enough to fill your dish.

To make a Soal Pye.

MAKE a good crust, cover your dish, boil two pounds of eels tender, pick all the flesh clean from the bones, throw the bones into the liquor you boil the eels in, with a little mace and salt, till it is very good, and about a quarter of a pint, then strain it. In the mean time cut the flesh of your eel fine, with a little lemon-peel shred fine, a little salt, pepper, and nutmeg, a few crumbs of bread, chopped parsley, and an anchovy; melt a quarter of a pound of butter, and mix with it, then lay it in the dish, cut the flesh of a pair of large soals, or three pair of very small ones, clean from the bones and fins, lay it on the forcemeat and pour in the broth of the eels you boiled; put the lid of the pye on, and bake it. You should boil the bones of the soals with the eel bones, to make it good. If you boil the soal bones with one or two little eels, without the forcemeat, your pye will be very good. And thus you may do a turbot.

To make a Flounder Pye.

GUT some flounders, wash them clean, dry them in a cloth, just boil them, cut off the meat clean from the bones, lay a good crust

cruſt over the diſh, and lay a little freſh butter at the bottom, and on that the fiſh; ſeaſon them with pepper and ſalt to your mind. Boil the bones in the water your fiſh was boiled in, with a little bit of horſe-radiſh, a little parſley, a very little bit of lemon-peel and a cruſt of bread. Boil it till there is juſt enough liquor for the pye, then ſtrain it, and put it into your pye; put on the top-cruſt, and bake it.

To make a Herring Pye.

SCALE, gut, and waſh them very clean, cut off the heads, fins, and tails. Make a good cruſt, cover your diſh, then ſeaſon your herrings with beaten mace, pepper, and ſalt; put a little butter in the bottom of your diſh, then a row of herrings, pare ſome apples and cut them in thin ſlices all over, then peel ſome onions, and cut them in ſlices all over thick, lay a little butter on the top, put in a little water, lay on the lid, and bake it well.

PART III.

NEW *and* APPROVED RECEIPTS *in* CONFECTIONARY.

CHAP. I.
The Preparation of SUGARS, of CANDIES, PRESERVES, &c.

To clarify Sugar.

BREAK into your preserving-pan the white of an egg, put in four quarts of water, beat it up to a froth with a whisk, then put in twelve pounds of sugar; mixed together, set it over the fire, and when it boils put in a little cold water; so do for four or five times, till the scum appears thick on the top; then remove it from the fire, and let it settle; then take off the scum, and pass it through your straining-bag.

Note, If the sugar do not appear very fine, you must boil it again before you strain it; otherwise, in boiling it to a height, it will rise over the pan.

To boil Sugar to the Degree called Smooth.

WHEN your sugar is thus clarified, put what quantity you have occasion for over the fire, to boil smooth; the which you will prove by dipping your skimmer into the sugar, and then touching it with your fore-finger and thumb; in opening them you will see a small thread drawn betwixt, which immediately breaks, and remains in a drop on your thumb; thus it is a little smooth: then boiling more, it will draw into a larger string; then it is become very smooth.

The blown Sugar.

BOIL your sugar longer than the former, and try it thus, viz. dip in your skimmer, and take it out, shaking off what sugar you can into the pan, and then blow with your mouth strongly through the holes; and if certain bubbles or bladders blow through, it is boiled to the degree called blown.

The feathered Sugar.

THIS is a higher degree of boiling sugar; which is to be proved by dipping the skimmer, when it has boiled somewhat longer; shake it first over the pan, then give it a sudden flirt behind you: if it be enough, the sugar will fly off like feathers.

The crackled Sugar.

IS proved by letting it boil somewhat longer; and then dipping a stick into the sugar, which immediately remove into a pot of cold water, standing by for that purpose, drawing off the sugar that cleaves to the stick; if it becomes hard, and will snap in the water, it is enough; if not, you must boil it till it comes to that degree.

Note, Your water must be always very cold or it will deceive you.

The Carmel Sugar.

IS known by boiling yet longer; and is proved by dipping a stick, as aforesaid, first in the sugar and then in the water: but this you must observe, when it comes to the carmel height, it will snap like glass the moment it touches the cold water, which is the nighest and last degree of boiling sugar.

Note, Observe that your fire be not very fierce when you boil this, lest, flaming up the sides of your pan, it should cause the sugar to burn, and so discolour it.

To make little Things of Sugar, with Devices in them.

TAKE gum-dragant steeped in rose water, have some double refined sugar searced, and make it up into paste; some of your pastes you may colour with powders and juices, what colour you please, and make them up in what shapes you like; colours by themselves or with white, or white without the colours; in the middle of them have little pieces of paper, with some pretty smart sentences wrote on them; they will in company make much mirth.

To make Sugar of Roses, and in all Sorts of Figures.

CLIP off the white from the red bud, and dry it in the sun; to one ounce of that finely powdered, take one pound of loaf sugar; wet the sugar in rose-water, (but, if in season, take the juice of roses) boil it to a candy height, put in your powder of roses, and the juice of a lemon; mince all well together, put it on a pye-plate, and cut it into lozenges, or make it into any figures you fancy, as men, women, or birds; and if you want for ornaments in your desert, you may gild or colour them, as in the wormwood cakes.

To make Orange Chips crisp.

PARE your oranges very thin, leaving as little white on the peel as possible; throw the rinds into fair water as you pare them off, then boil them therein very fast till they are tender, still filling up the pan with boiling water as it wastes away; then make a thin syrup with part of the water they were boiled in, and put the rinds therein, and just let them boil; then take them off, and let them lie in the syrup three or four days; then boil them again, till you find the syrup begins to draw between your fingers; then take them off from the fire, and let them drain through a colander; take out but a few at a time, because, if they cool too fast, it will be difficult to get the syrup from them, which must be done by passing every piece of peel through your fingers, and laying them single on a sieve, with the rind uppermost; the sieves may be set in a stove, or before the fire; but in summer the sun is hot enough to dry them; three pounds of sugar will make syrup to do the peels of twenty-five oranges.

To preserve Seville Oranges liquid, as also Lemons.

TAKE the best Seville oranges and pare them very neatly, and put them into salt and water for about two hours, then boil them very tender, till a pin will go into them easily, then drain them well from the water, and put them into your preserving-pan, putting as much clarified sugar to them as will cover them, laying a trencher or plate on them to keep them down; then set them over a fire, and by degrees heat them till they boil; let them have a quick boil, till the sugar comes all over them in a froth; then set them by till next day, when you must drain the syrup from them, and boil it till it becomes very smooth, adding some more clarified sugar; put it upon the oranges, and give them a boil; then set them by till next day, when you must do as the day before. The fourth day drain them, and strain
your

your syrup thro' a bag, and boil it till it becomes very smooth; then take some other clarified sugar, boil it till it blows very strong, and take some jelly of pippins, as I shall hereafter express, with the juice of some other oranges; after they are preserved as above directed, take two pounds of clarified sugar, boil it to blow very strong; then one pint and a half of pippin jelly, and the juice of four or five oranges; boil all together; then put in the syrup that has been strained and boiled to be very smooth, and give all a boil; then put your oranges into your pots, or glasses, and fill them up with the above made jelly; when cold cover them and set them by for use.

Note, Be sure in all your boilings to clear away the scum, otherwise you will endanger their working; and if you find they will swim above your jelly, you must bind them down with the sprig of a clean whisk.

To make a Compote of Oranges.

CUT the rind off your oranges into ribs, leaving part of the rind on; cut them into eight parts, and throw them into boiling water; when a pin will easily go through the rind, drain and put them into as much sugar, boiled, till it becomes smooth, as will cover them; give all a boil together, adding some juice of oranges to what sharpness you please; you may put a little pippin jelly into the boiling; when cold, they make pretty plates.

To make Orange Rings and Faggots.

PARE your oranges as thin and as narrow as you can; put the parings into water whilst you prepare the rings, which are done by cutting the oranges, so pared, into as many rings as you please; then cut out the meat from the inside, and put the rings and faggots into boiling water; boil them till they are tender, then put them into as much clarified sugar as will cover them; set them by till next day, then boil them all together, and set them by till the day after; then drain the syrup and boil it till very smooth, then return your oranges into it, and give all a boil; the next day boil the syrup till it rises up to almost the top of your pan; then return your oranges into it, give them a boil, and put them by in some pot to be candied, whenever you shall have occasion.

Zest of China Oranges.

PARE off the outward rind of the oranges very thin, and only strew it with fine powder sugar as much as their own moisture will take, and dry them in a hot stove.

L

To candy Orange, Lemon, and Citron.

DRAIN what quantity you will candy clean from the syrup, wash it in lukewarm water, and lay it on a sieve to drain; then take as much clarified sugar as you think will cover what you will candy; boil it till it blows very strong, then put in your rings, and boil them till it blows again; then take it from the fire, let it cool a little, and, with the back of a spoon, rub the sugar against the inside of your pan, till you see the sugar becomes white; then with a fork, take out the rings one by one, and lay them on a wire grate to drain; then put in your faggots, and boil them as before directed; then rub the sugar, and take them up in bunches, having somebody to cut them with a pair of scissars to what bigness you please, laying them on your wire to drain.

Note, Thus you may candy all sorts of oranges, lemon-peels, or chips; lemon-rings and faggots are done the same way, with this distinction only, that the lemons ought to be pared twice over, that the ring may be the whiter; so will you have two sorts of faggots, but you must be sure to keep the outward rind from the other, otherwise it will discolour them.

To candy Figs.

TAKE your figs when they are ripe, weigh them, and to every pound of figs add a pound of loaf sugar, wetted so as to make a syrup; put the figs in when the syrup is made, that is, melted; let it not be too hot when you put them in; boil them gently, till they are tender, and put them up in pots. To keep them too long candied they lose their beauty; but when you are desirous to use them, and you take any out of the pots, you must take care to add as much loaf sugar, boiled to a candy height, as will cover those remaining in the pots; but before you put the figs into the sugar, they must be washed in warm water, and dried with a clean cloth; let not your syrup be boiled above a syrup candy height; let the figs lie a day or two, then take them up, and lay them upon glasses to dry; they will candy in one hour's lying in the syrup; but it is better that they lie longer.

A grand Trifle.

TAKE a very large china dish or glass, that is deep, first make some very fine rich calves-feet jelly, with which fill the dish about half the depth; when it begins to jelly, have ready some Naples biscuits, macaroons, and the little cakes called matrimony; take an equal quantity of these cakes, break them in pieces, and stick them in the jelly before it be stiff, all over very thick; pour over that a quart of very thick sweet cream,
then

then lay all round, currant jelly, rafpberry jam, and fome calves-feet jelly, all cut in little pieces, with which garnifh your difh thick all round, intermixing them, and on them lay macaroons, and the little cakes, being firft dipped in fack.

Then take two quarts of the thickeft cream you can get, fweeten it with double refined fugar, grate into it the rinds of three fine large lemons, and whifk it up with a whifk; take off the froth as it rifes, and lay it in your difh as high as you can poffibly raife it; this is fit to go to the king's table, if well made, and very excellent when it comes to be all mixed together.

To make artificial Fruit.

FIRST take care at a proper time of the year, to fave the ftalks of the fruit with the ftones to them; then get fome neat pretty tins made in the fhape of the fruit you intend to make, leaving a hole at the top to put in the ftone and ftalk, and they muft be fo contrived as to open in the middle to take out the fruit; there muft be made alfo a frame of wood to fix them in, and in the making of the tins, care muft be taken to make them extremely fmooth in the infide, left by their roughnefs they mark the fruit; as alfo that they are made of exact fhape to what they reprefent; becaufe, a defect in either will not only give deformity to the artificial fruit, but likewife rob the artift of the honour fhe would otherwife acquire, and for which the lady would undoubtedly ftand admired.

Then take two cow-heels and a calve's-foot; boil them in a gallon of foft water, till all boil to rags; when you have a full quart of jelly, ftrain it through a fieve, put it in a faucepan, fweeten it, put in fome lemon-peel with perfume, and colour it to the fruit you intend to imitate; ftir all together, give it a boil, and fill your tins; put in your ftones and the ftalks juft as the fruit grows; when the jelly is quite cold, open your tins for the bloom, and carefully duft powder-blue; an ingenious clever perfon may make great improvements on this artificial fruit, as it requires great nicety in the doing it; a little practice will perfect them in it.

To make Chocolate Almonds.

TAKE a pound of chocolate finely grated, and a pound and a half of the beft fugar finely fifted; then foak gum-dragant in orange-flower-water, and work them into what form you pleafe; the pafte muft be ftiff; dry them in a ftove.

To make Almond Loaves.

BLANCH your almonds in hot water, and throw them into cold; then take their weight in double refined fugar finely

fearced,

fearced, beat them together till they come to a paste; make them up into little loaves, and ice them over with some white of egg and sugar; bake them on paper; if you please you may throw your almonds into orange-flower-water, instead of cold water.

To make Gingerbread.

TAKE a pound and a half of treacle, two eggs beaten, half a pound of brown sugar, one ounce of ginger beaten and sifted; of cloves, mace and nutmegs altogether half an ounce, beaten very fine, coriander-seeds and carraway-seeds of each half an ounce, two pounds of butter melted; mix all these together, with as much flour as will knead it into a pretty stiff paste; then roll it out, and cut it into what form you please; bake it in a quick oven on tin plates; a little time will bake it.

Another Method.

TAKE three pounds of fine flour, and the rind of a lemon dried and beaten to powder, half a pound of sugar or more, as you like it, and an ounce and a half of beaten ginger; mix all these well together, and wet it pretty stiff with nothing but treacle, make it into long rolls or cakes, as you please; you may put candied orange-peel and citron in it: butter your paper you bake it on, and let it be baked hard.

Another Sort of Gingerbread.

TAKE half a pound of almonds, blanch and beat them till they have done shining; beat them with a spoonful or two of orange-flower-water, put in half an ounce of beaten ginger, and a quarter of an ounce of cinnamon powdered; work it to a paste with double refined sugar beaten and sifted; then roll it out, and lay it on papers to dry in an oven after pyes are drawn.

Another.

TO one pound of flour, three quarters of a pound of sugar, and an ounce of nutmegs, ginger and cinnamon together, beaten and sifted; a quarter of a pound of candied orange-peels or fresh peel cut in small stripes; two ounces of sweet butter rubbed in flour; take the yolks of two eggs, beat with eight spoonfuls of sack, and six of yeast, make it up in a stiff paste; roll it thin, and cut it with a glass; bake them and keep them dry.

To make Dutch Gingerbread.

TAKE four pounds of flour, and mix with it two ounces and a half of beaten ginger, then rub in a quarter of a pound of butter, and add to it two ounces of carraway-feeds, as much orange-peel dried and rubbed to powder, a few coriander-feeds bruifed, and two eggs; mix all up into a ftiff pafte with two pounds and a quarter of treacle; beat it very well with a rolling-pin, and make it up into thirty cakes; put in a candied citron; prick them with a fork; butter papers, three double, one white, and two brown; wafh them over with the white of an egg; put them into an oven not too hot, for three quarters of an hour.

To make Wigs.

TAKE three pounds and a half of flour, and three quarters of a pound of butter, and rub it into the flour till none of it be feen; then take a pint or more of new milk, and make it very warm, and half a pint of new ale-yeaft, then make it into a light pafte; put in carraway-feeds, and what fpice you pleafe; then make it up and lay it before the fire to rife; then work in three quarters of a pound of fugar, and then roll them into what form you pleafe, pretty thin, and put them on tin plates, and hold them before the oven to rife again, before you fet them in; your oven muft be pretty quick.

Another Method.

TAKE two pounds of flour, and a quarter of a pound of butter, as much fugar, a nutmeg grated, a little cloves and mace, and a quarter of an ounce of carraway-feeds, cream and yeaft as much as will make it up into a pretty light pafte; make them up, and fet them by the fire to rife till the oven be ready, they will quickly be baked.

To make the light Wigs.

TAKE a pound and a half of flour, and half a pint of milk made warm, mix thefe together, and cover it up, and let it lie by the fire half an hour; then take half a pound of fugar, and half a pound of butter, then work thefe in the pafte, and make it into wigs with as little flour as poffible; let the oven be pretty quick, and they will rife very much.

To make very good Wigs.

TAKE a quarter of a peck of the fineft flour, rub into it three quarters of a pound of frefh butter, till it is like grated bread,

bread, something more than half a pound of sugar, half a nutmeg, and half a race of grated ginger, three eggs, yolks and whites, beaten very well, and put to them half a pint of thick ale-yeast, and three or four spoonfuls of sack; make a hole in your flour, and pour in your yeast and eggs, and as much milk just warm as will make it into a light paste; let it stand before the fire to rise half an hour, then make it into a dozen and a half of wigs; wash them over with eggs just as they go into the oven; a quick oven and half an hour will bake them.

To make Buns.

TAKE two pounds of fine flour, a pint of ale-yeast, put a little sack in the yeast and three eggs beaten, knead all these together with a little warm milk, a little nutmeg, and a little salt; then lay it before the fire till it rise very light; then knead in a pound of fresh butter, and a pound of round carraway-comfits, and bake them in a quick oven on floured papers in what shape you please.

To make French Bread.

TAKE half a peck of fine flour, put to it six yolks of eggs, and four whites, a little salt, a pint of good ale yeast, and as much new milk, made a little warm, as will make it a thin light paste; stir it about with your hand, but by no means knead it: then have ready six wooden quart dishes, and fill them with dough; let them stand a quarter of an hour to heave, and then turn them out into the oven; and when they are baked, rasp them: the oven must be quick.

To make brown French Loaves.

TAKE a peck of coarse flour, and as much of the raspings of bread beaten and sifted as will make it look brown, then wet it with a pint of good yeast, and as much milk and warm water as will wet it pretty stiff; mix it well, and set it before the fire to rise; make it into six loaves; make it up as light as you can, and bake it well in a quick oven.

To make March-pane unboiled.

TAKE a pound of almonds, blanch them and beat them in rose-water; when they are finely beaten, put to them half a pound of sugar, beat and searced, and work it to a paste; spread some on wafers, and dry it in an oven; when it is cold, have ready the white of an egg beaten with rose-water, and double refined sugar. Let it be as thick as butter, then draw your march-pane through it, and put it in the oven: it will ice in a little time, then keep them for use.

The COMPLETE HOUSEWIFE. 151

If you have a mind to have your march-pane large, cut it when it is rolled out by a pewter-plate, and edge it about the top like a tart, and bottom with wafer-paper, and set it in the oven, and ice it as aforesaid: when the icing rises, take it out, and strew coloured comfits on it, or serve sweet-meats on it.

To make March-pane.

TAKE a pound of Jordan almonds, blanch and beat them in a marble mortar very fine; then put to them three quarters of a pound of double refined sugar, and beat them with a few drops of orange-flower-water; beat all together till it is a very good paste, then roll it into what shape you please; dust a little fine sugar under it as you roll it, to keep it from sticking. To ice it, searce double refined sugar as fine as flour, wet it with rose-water, and mix it well together, and with a brush or bunch of feathers spread it over your march-pane: bake them in an oven that is not too hot; put wafer-paper at the bottom, and white paper under that, so keep them for use.

To make a Jam of Raspberries.

To a quart of raspberries, and a pint of currant juice, you must have a pound and a half of sugar; bruise your raspberries well in a pan, put it over a charcoal fire, and let it boil enough; then put it into your pots.

To make a Jam of Cherries.

YOU must first of all stalk and stone your cherries, then bruise them in a pan with currants, and add sugar according to your quantity, and boil it till you think it is enough; then put it into your pots, and put paper over them.

To make a Jam of Gooseberries.

GATHER your gooseberries full ripe, of the green sort, top and tail them, and weigh them; put a pound of fruit to three quarters of a pound of double refined sugar, and half a pint of water; boil your water and sugar together; skim it, and put in your gooseberries, and boil them till they are clear and tender; then break them, and put them into your pots.

A Tansy.

BOIL a quart of cream or milk with a stick of cinnamon, a quartered nutmeg, and a large blade of mace; when half cold, mix it with twenty yolks of eggs, and ten whites; strain it, then put to it four grated biscuits, half a pound of butter, a pint

pint of spinach-juice, a little tanſy, ſack, orange-flower-water, ſugar, and a little ſalt; then gather it to a body over the fire, and pour it into your diſh, being well buttered: when it is baked turn it on a pye-plate; ſqueeze on it an orange, grate on ſugar, and garniſh it with ſliced orange and a little tanſy. Made in a diſh, cut as you pleaſe.

To make a Tanſy to bake.

TAKE twenty eggs, but eight whites, beat the eggs very well, and ſtrain them into a quart of thick cream, one nutmeg, and three Naples biſcuits grated, as much juice of ſpinach, with a ſprig or two of tanſy, as will make it as green as graſs; ſweeten it to your taſte; then butter your diſh very well, and ſet it into an oven, no hotter than for cuſtards; watch it, and as ſoon as it is done, take it out of the oven, and turn it on a pye-plate; ſcrape ſugar, and ſqueeze orange upon it. Garniſh the diſh with orange and lemon, and ſerve it up.

To make a Gooſberry Tanſy.

PUT ſome freſh butter in a frying-pan; when it is melted put into it a quart of gooſberries, fry them till they are tender, and break them all to maſh; then beat ſeven eggs, but four whites, a pound of ſugar, three ſpoonfuls of ſack, as much cream, a penny-loaf grated, and three ſpoonfuls of flour; mix all theſe together, then put the gooſberries out of the pan to them, and ſtir all well together, and put them into a ſaucepan to thicken; then put butter into the frying-pan, and fry them brown: ſtrew ſugar on the top.

To make an Apple Tanſy.

TAKE three pippins, ſlice them round in thin ſlices, and fry them in butter; then beat four eggs, with ſix ſpoonfuls of cream, a little roſe-water, nutmeg, and ſugar; ſtir them together, and pour it over the apples; let it fry a little, and turn it with a pye-plate. Garniſh with lemon, and ſugar ſtrewed over it.

Balls for Lent.

GRATE white bread, nutmeg, ſalt, ſhred parſley, a very little thyme, and a little orange or lemon-peel cut ſmall; make them up into balls with beaten eggs, or you may add a ſpoonful of cream; and roll them up in flour, and fry them.

CHAP.

CHAP. II.

Of TARTS.

To make different Sorts of Tarts.

IF you bake in tin patties, butter them, and you must put a little crust all over, because of the taking them out; if in china or glass, no crust but the top one. Lay fine sugar at the bottom, then your plumbs, cherries, or any other sort of fruit, and sugar at top; then put on your lid, and bake them in a slack oven. Mince pyes must be baked in tin patties, because of taking them out, and puff-paste is best for them. All sweet tarts the beaten crust is best; but as you fancy. Apple, pear, apricot, &c. make thus; apples and pears, pare them, cut them into quarters, and core them; cut the quarters across again, set them on in a saucepan with just as much water as will barely cover them, let them simmer on a slow fire just till the fruit is tender; put a good piece of lemon-peel in the water with the fruit, then have your patties ready. Lay fine sugar at the bottom, then your fruit, and a little sugar at top; that you must put in at your discretion. Pour over each tart a tea-spoonful of lemon-juice, and three tea-spoonfuls of the liquor they were boiled in; put on your lid, and bake them in a slack oven. Apricots do the same way, only do not use lemon.

As to preserved tarts, only lay in your preserved fruit, and put a very thin crust at top, and let them be baked as little as possible; but if you would make them very nice, have a large patty, the size you would have your tart. Make your sugar crust, roll it as thick as a halfpenny; then butter your patties, and cover it. Shape your upper crust on a hollow thing on purpose, the size of your patty, and mark it with a marking-iron for that purpose, in what shape you please, to be hollow and open to see the fruit through; then bake your crust in a very slack oven, not to discolour it, but to have it crisp. When the crust is cold, very carefully take it out, and fill it with what fruit you please, lay on the lid, and it is done; therefore if the tart is not eat, your sweetmeat is not the worse, and it looks genteel.

To make a Chervil or Spinach Tart.

SHRED a gallon of spinach or chervil very small; put to it half a pound of melted butter, the meat of three lemons picked from the skins and seeds; the rind of two lemons grated, a pound of sugar; put this in a dish or pattipan with puff-paste on the bottom and top, and so bake it; when it is baked, cut
off

off the lid, and put cream or custard over it, as you do codlin tarts; scrape sugar over it; serve it cold; this is good among other tarts in the winter for variety.

To make a Lemon Tart.

TAKE three clear lemons, and grate off the outside rinds; take the yolks of twelve eggs, and six whites; beat them very very well, squeeze in the juice of a lemon; then put in three quarters of a pound of fine powdered sugar, and three quarters of a pound of fresh butter melted; stir all well together, put a sheet of paste at the bottom, and sift sugar on the top; put it in a brisk oven, three quarters of an hour will bake it; so serve it to the table.

To make Orange or Lemon Tarts.

TAKE six large lemons, and rub them very well with salt, and put them in water for two days, with a handful of salt in it; then change them into fresh water without salt every other day for a fortnight: then boil them for two or three hours till they are tender; then cut them in half quarters, and cut them thus ⊂⊃ as thin as you can; then take pippins pared, cored and quartered, and a pint of fair water, let them boil till the pippins break; put the liquor to your orange or lemon, half the pippins well broken, and a pound of sugar; boil these together a quarter of an hour; then put it in a gallipot, and squeeze an orange in it if it be lemon, or a lemon if it is orange; two spoonfuls are enough for a tart; your pattipans must be small and shallow; put fine puff paste, and very thin; a little while will bake it. Just as your tarts are going into the oven, with a feather or brush do them over with melted butter, and then sift double refined sugar on them, and this is a pretty icing on them.

To make Puff-Paste for Tarts.

RUB a quarter of a pound of butter into a pound of fine flour; then whip the whites of two eggs to snow, and with cold water and one yolk make it into a paste; then roll it abroad, and put in by degrees a pound of butter, flouring it over the butter every time, roll it up, and roll it out again, and put in more butter: so do for six or seven times, till it has taken up all the pound of butter. This paste is good for tarts, or any small things.

Another

Another Paste for Tarts.

ONE pound of flour, three quarters of a pound of butter; mix up together, and beat well with a a rolling-pin.

Another.

HALF a pound of butter, half a pound of flour, and half a pound of sugar; mix it well together, and beat it with a rolling-pin well, then roll it out thin.

To Ice Tarts.

TAKE a little yolk of egg and melted butter, beat it very well together, and with a feather wash over your tarts, and sift sugar on them just as you put them into the oven.

CHAP. III.
Of PASTIES and PUFFS.

To make a Sweet-bread Pasty to fry or bake.

PARBOIL your sweet-breads, and shred them very fine, with an equal quantity of marrow; mix with them a little grated bread, some nutmeg, salt, the yolks of two hard eggs bruised small, and sugar; then mix up with a little cream and the yolk of an egg: make paste with half a pound of the finest flour, an ounce of double refined sugar beat and sifted, the yolks of two eggs, and white of one, and fair water; then roll in half a pound of butter, and roll it out in little pasties the breadth of your hand; put your meat in, close them up well, and fry or bake them; a very pretty side-dish.

To season and bake a Venison Pasty.

BONE your haunch or side of venison, and take out all the sinews and skin; and then proportion it for your pasty, by taking away from one part, and adding to another, till it is of an equal thickness; then season it with pepper and salt, about an ounce of pepper; save a little of it whole, and beat the rest; and mix with it twice as much salt, and rub it all over your venison, letting it lie till your paste is ready. Make your paste thus: a peck of fine flour, six pounds of butter, a dozen of eggs; rub your butter in your flour, beat your eggs, and with
them

them and cold water make up your paste pretty stiff: then drive it forth for your pasty; let it be the thickness of a man's thumb; put under it two or three sheets of cap-paper well floured: then have two pounds of beef suet, shred exceeding fine; proportion it on the bottom to the breadth of your venison, and leave a verge round your venison three fingers broad, wash that verge over with a bunch of feathers or brush dipped in an egg beaten, and then lay a border of your paste on the place you washed, and lay your venison on the suet; put a little of your seasoning on the top, a few corns of whole pepper, and two pounds of very good fresh butter; then turn over your other sheet of paste, so close your pasty. Garnish it on the top as you think fit; vent it in the middle, and set it in the oven. It will take five or six hours baking. Then break all the bones, wash them, and add to them more bones, or knuckles; season them with pepper and salt, and put them with a quart of water, and half a pound of butter, in a pan or earthen pot; cover it over with coarse paste, and set it in with your pasty; and when your pasty is drawn and dished, fill it up with the gravy that came from the bones.

A Venison Pasty.

BONE your venison, take out the gristles, skin and films; to a side of doe venison three ounces of salt, and three quarters of an ounce of pepper: or to seven pounds of lean venison, without the bones, put in two ounces and a half of salt, and half an ounce of pepper.

To make Marrow Pasties.

MAKE your little pasties the length of a finger, and as broad as two fingers, put in large pieces of marrow dipped in eggs, and seasoned with sugar, cloves, mace, and nutmeg; strew a few currants on the marrow; bake or fry them.

To make little Pasties to fry.

TAKE the kidney of a loin of veal or lamb, fat and all, shred it very small, season it with a little salt, cloves, mace, nutmeg, all beaten small, some sugar, and the yolks of two or three hard eggs minced very fine; mix all these together with a little sack or cream; put them in puff-paste and fry them; serve them hot.

Apple Pasties to fry.

PARE and quarter apples, and boil them in sugar and water, and a stick of cinnamon, and when tender, put in a little white

white wine, the juice of a lemon, a piece of fresh butter, and a little ambergreaſe or orange-flower-water; ſtir all together, and when it is cold put it in puff-paſte; and fry them.

Paſte for Paſties.

RUB ſix pounds of butter into fourteen pounds of flour, put to it eight eggs, whip the whites to ſnow, and make it into a pretty ſtiff paſte with cold water.

To make Sugar Puffs.

TAKE the whites of ten eggs, and beat them till they riſe to a high froth; put it in a ſtone mortar, or wooden bowl, and add as much double refined ſugar as will make it thick; put in ſome ambergreaſe to give it a taſte, and rub it round the mortar for half an hour; put in a few carraway-ſeeds, take a ſheet of wafers and lay it on as broad as ſix-pence and as high as you can; put them in a moderate hot oven half a quarter of an hour, and they will look as white as ſnow.

To make Seed Puffs.

TAKE gum-dragant and ſteep it in roſe-water; then take ſome double refined ſugar, ſearce and wet it with ſome gum as ſtiff as paſte; work it with a ſpoon till it becomes white, roll it out upon white paper very thin, and cut it out in ſhapes with a jigging-iron, and bake it in an oven, taking care not to ſcorch it.

To make Lemon Puffs.

TAKE a pound and a quarter of double refined ſugar beaten and ſifted, and grate the rind of two lemons, and mix well with the ſugar; then beat the whites of three new-laid eggs very well, and mix it well with your ſugar and lemon-peel; beat them together an hour and a quarter, then make it up in what form you pleaſe; be quick to ſet them in a moderate oven; do not take them off the papers till cold.

To make Almond Puffs.

TAKE half a pound of Jordan almonds, blanch and beat them very fine with three or four ſpoonfuls of roſe-water; then take half an ounce of the fineſt gum dragant ſteeped in roſe-water three or four days before you uſe it, then put it to the almonds, and beat it together; then take three quarters of a pound of double refined ſugar beaten and ſifted, and a little fine
flour,

flour, and put to it; roll it into what shape you please; lay them on white paper, and put them in an oven gently hot, and when they are baked enough, take them off the papers, and put them on a sieve to dry in the oven when it is almost cold.

To make Puff-Paste.

TO a peck of flour you must have three quarters the weight in butter; dry your flour well, and lay it on a table; make a hole, and put in it a dozen whites of eggs well beaten, but first break into it a third part of your butter; then with water make up your paste, then roll it out, and by degrees put in the rest of the butter.

CHAP. IV.
Of CUSTARDS.

To make Custards.

TAKE two quarts of thick sweet cream, boil it with some bits of cinnamon, and a quartered nutmeg, keep it stirring all the while, and when it has boiled a little time, pour it into a pan to cool, and stir it till it is cool, to keep it from creaming; then beat the yolks of sixteen eggs, the whites of but six, and mix your eggs with the cream when it is cool, and sweeten it with fine sugar to your taste, put in a very little salt, and some rose or orange-flower-water; then strain all through a hair sieve, and fill your cups or crust; it must be a pretty quick oven; when they boil up they are enough.

Rice Custards.

TAKE a quart of cream, and boil it with a blade of mace, and a quartered nutmeg; put into it boiled rice, well beat with your cream; mix them together, and stir them all the while it boils on the fire; when it is enough take it off, and sweeten to your taste; put in a little orange-flower-water, pour it in your dishes; when cold serve it.

To make Almond Tourt.

BLANCH and beat half a pound of Jordan almonds very fine; use orange-flower-water in the beating your almonds;

pare the yellow rind of a lemon pretty thick; boil it in water till it is very tender: beat it with half a pound of sugar, and mix it with the almonds, and eight eggs, but four whites, half a pound of butter melted, almost cold, and a little thick cream; mix all together, and bake it in a dish with paste at bottom. This may be made the day before it is used.

To make Hasty Puddings, to boil in Custard Dishes.

TAKE a large pint of milk, put to it four spoonfuls of flour; mix it well together, set it over the fire, and boil it into a smooth hasty pudding; sweeten it to your taste; grate nutmeg in it, and when it is almost cold, beat five eggs very well, and stir into it; then butter your custard-cups, put in your stuff, and tie them over with a cloth, put them in the pot when the water boils, and let them boil something more than half an hour; pour on them melted butter.

To make a Custard Pudding.

TAKE a pint of cream, and mix with it six eggs well beat, two spoonfuls of flour, half a nutmeg grated, a little salt, and sugar to your taste; butter a cloth, put it in when the pot boils; boil it just half an hour; melt butter for sauce.

Boiled Custards.

TAKE a pint of cream, and put into it two ounces of almonds, blanched and beaten very fine with rose or orange-flower-water, or a little cream; let them boil till the cream is a little thickened, then sweeten your eggs, and keep it stirring over the fire till it is as thick as you would have it; then put into it a little orange-flower-water, stir it well together, and put it into china cups.

N. B. You may make them without almonds.

CHAP. V.

All Sorts of CAKES.

To make a rich great Cake.

TAKE a peck of flour well dried, an ounce of cloves and mace, half an ounce of nutmegs, as much cinnamon; beat the spice well, and mix them with your flour, and a pound and a half of sugar, a little salt, thirteen pounds of currants well washed, picked and dried, and three pounds of raisins stoned and cut into small pieces; mix all these well together; then make five pints of cream almost scalding hot, and put into it four pounds of fresh butter; then beat the yolks of twenty eggs, three pints of good ale-yeast, a pint of sack, a quarter of a pint of orange-flower-water, three grains of musk, and six grains of ambergrease; mix these together, and stir them into your cream and butter, then mix all in the cake, and set it an hour before the fire to rise, before you put it into your hoop; mix your sweetmeats in it, two pounds of citron, and one pound of candied orange and lemon-peel, cut in small pieces; you must bake it in a deep hoop; butter the sides, put two papers at the bottom, flour it and put in your cake; it must have a quick oven, four hours will bake it; when it is drawn, ice it over the tops and sides; take two pounds of double refined sugar beat and sifted, and the whites of six eggs beaten to a froth, with three or four spoonfuls of orange-flower-water, and three grains of musk and ambergrease together; put all these in a stone mortar, and beat them with a wooden pestle till it is as white as snow, and with a brush or bunch of feathers spread it all over the cake, and put it in the oven to dry, but take care the oven does not discolour it; when it is cold paper it; it will keep good five or six weeks.

To make an ordinary Seed Cake.

TAKE six pounds of fine flour, rub it into a thimbleful of carraway-seeds finely beaten, and two nutmegs grated, and mace beaten; then heat a quart of cream hot enough to melt a pound of butter in it, and when it is no more than blood-warm, mix your cream and butter with a pint of good ale-yeast, and then wet your flour with it; make it pretty thin; just before it goes into the oven, put in a pound of rough carraways, and some citron sliced thin; three quarters of an hour in a quick oven will bake it.

To make the Marlborough Cake.

TAKE eight eggs, yolks and whites, beat and strain them, and put to them a pound of sugar beaten and sifted; beat it three quarters of an hour together, then put three quarters of a pound of flour well dried, and two ounces of carraway-seeds; beat it all well together, and bake it in a quick oven in broad tin pans.

Another.

Another Sort of little Cakes.

TAKE a pound of flour and a pound of butter, rub the butter into the flour, two spoonfuls of yeast and two eggs, make it up into a paste; slick white paper, roll your paste out the thickness of a crown, cut them out with the top of a tin canister, sift fine sugar over them, and lay them on the slicked paper; bake them after tarts an hour.

To make the white Cake.

TAKE three quarts of the finest flour, a pound and a half of butter, a pint of thick cream, half a pint of ale yeast, half a quarter of a pint of rose-water and sack together, a quarter of an ounce of mace, nine eggs, abating four whites, beat them well, five ounces of double refined sugar, mix the sugar and spice and a very little salt with your dry flour; and keep out half a pint of the flour to strew over the cake; when it is all mixed, melt the butter in the cream; when it is a little cool, strain the eggs into it, yeast, &c. make a hole in the midst of the flour, pour all the wetting in, stirring it round with your hand all one way till well mixed; strew on the flour that was saved out, and set it before the fire to rise, covered over with a cloth; let it stand so a quarter of an hour; you must have in readiness three pounds and a half of currants, washed and picked, and well dried in a cloth; mingle them in the paste without kneading; put it in a tin hoop; set it in a quick oven, or it will not rise; it must stand an hour and a half in the oven.

To make Orange Cakes.

PARE your oranges very thin, and take off the white rinds in quarters; boil the white rinds very tender, and when they are enough, take them up, scrape the black off, and squeeze them between two trenchers; beat them in a stone mortar to a fine pulp with a little sugar; pick the meat out of the oranges from the skins and seeds, and mix the pulp and meat together; and take the weight and half of sugar; boil the sugar to a candy height, and put in the oranges, stir them well together, and when it is cold drop them on a pye-plate, and set them in a stove. You may perfume them. To the rinds of six oranges put the meat of nine lemons. Cakes are made the same way, only as many rinds as meat, and twice the weight of sugar.

To make Shrewsbury Cakes.

TAKE to one pound of sugar three pounds of the finest flour, a nutmeg grated, some beaten cinnamon; the sugar and spice

spice must be sifted into the flour, and wet it with three eggs, and as much melted butter as will make it of a good thickness to roll into a paste; mould it well and roll it; cut it into what shape you please, perfume them, and prick them before they go into the oven.

To make Almond Cakes.

TAKE a pound of almonds, blanch and beat them exceeding fine with a little rose or orange-flower-water; then beat three eggs, but two whites, and put to them a pound of sugar sifted; then put in your almonds, and beat all together very well; put sheets of white paper, and lay the cakes in what form you please, and bake them; you may perfume them if you like it; bake them in a cool oven.

To make Whetstone Cakes.

TAKE half a pound of fine flour, and half a pound of loaf-sugar searced, a spoonful of carraway-seeds dried, the yolk of one egg, the whites of three, a little rose-water, with ambergrease dissolved in it; mix it together, and roll it out as thin as a wafer, cut them with a glass, lay them on floured paper, and bake them in a slow oven.

To make Portugal Cakes.

TAKE a pound and a quarter of fine flour well dried, and break a pound of butter into the flour, and rub it in, adding a pound of loaf-sugar beaten and sifted, a nutmeg grated, four perfumed plumbs, or some ambergrease; mix these well together, and beat seven eggs, but four whites, with three spoonfuls of orange-flower-water; mix all these together, and beat them up an hour; butter your little pans, just as they are going into the oven, fill them half full, and searce some fine sugar over them; little more than a quarter of an hour will bake them. You may put a handful of currants into some of them; take them out of the pans as soon as they are drawn, keep them dry; they will keep good three months.

To make Jumbals.

TAKE the whites of three eggs, beat them well, and take off the froth; then take a little milk, and a little flour, near a pound, as much sugar sifted, and a few carraway-seeds beaten very fine; work all these in a very stiff paste, and make them into what form you please: bake them on white paper.

To make a good Plumb Cake.

TAKE four pounds of flour, put to it half a pound of loaf sugar beaten and sifted, of mace and nutmegs half an ounce beaten fine, a little salt; beat the yolks of thirty eggs, the whites of fifteen, a pint and a half of ale-yeast, three quarters of a pint of sack, with two grains of ambergrease and two of musk steeped in it five or six hours; then take a large pint of thick cream, set it on the fire, and put in two pounds of butter to melt, but not boil; then put your flour in a bowl, make a hole in the midst, and pour in your yeast, sack, cream, and eggs; mix it well with your hands, make it up not too stiff, set it to the fire a quarter of an hour to rise; then put in seven pounds of currants picked and washed in warm water, then dried in a coarse cloth, and kept warm till you put them into your cake, which mix in as fast as you can, and put candied lemon, orange and citron in it; put it in your hoop, which must be ready buttered and fixed; set it in a quick oven, bake it two hours or more; when it is near cold, ice it.

Another Plumb Cake.

TAKE four pounds of flour, four pounds of currants, and twelve eggs, half the whites taken out, near a pint of yeast, a pound and a half of butter, a good half pint of cream, three quarters of a pound of loaf sugar, beaten mace, nutmegs and cinnamon, half an ounce, beaten fine; mingle the spices and sugar with the flour; beat the eggs well and put to them a quarter of a pint of rose-water, that had a little musk and ambergrease dissolved in it; put the butter and cream into a jug, and put it in a pot of boiling water to melt; when you have mixed the cake, strew a little flour over it; cover it with a very hot napkin, and set it before the fire to rise; butter and flour your hoop, and just as your oven is ready, put your currants into boiling water to plump; dry them in hot cloth, and mix them in your cake; you may put in half a pound of candied orange, lemon, and citron; let not your oven be too hot, two hours will bake it, three if it is double the quantity; mix it with a broad pudding-stick, not with your hands; when your cake is just drawn, pour all over it a gill of brandy or sack; then ice it.

Another Plumb Cake with Almonds.

TAKE four pounds of fine flour dried well, five pounds of currants well picked and rubbed, but not washed, five pounds of butter washed and beaten in orange-flower-water and sack, two pounds of almonds beaten very fine, four pounds of eggs weighed,

weighed, half the whites taken out, three pounds of double refined fugar, three nutmegs grated, a little ginger, a quarter of an ounce of mace, as much cloves finely beaten; a quarter of a pint of the beſt brandy; the butter muſt be beaten to cream, then put in your flour and all the reſt of the things, beating it till you put it in the oven; four hours will bake it, the oven muſt be very quick; put in orange, lemon-peel candied, and citron, as you like.

To make little Plumb Cakes.

TAKE two pounds of flour dried in the oven, half a pound of fugar finely powdered, four yolks of eggs, two whites, half a pound of butter waſhed with roſe-water, ſix ſpoonfuls of cream warmed, a pound and a half of currants unwaſhed, but picked and rubbed very clean in a cloth, mix all together, make them into cakes, and bake them up in an oven almoſt as hot as for manchet, let them ſtand half an hour till they be coloured on both ſides; then take down the oven lid, and let them ſtand a little to ſoak.

An ordinary Cake to eat with Butter.

TAKE two pounds of flour, and rub it into half a pound of butter; then putt o it ſome ſpice, a little ſalt, a quartern and a half of ſugar, half a pound of raiſins ſtoned, and half a pound of currants; make theſe into a cake, with half a pint of ale-yeaſt, four eggs, and as much warm milk as you ſee convenient; mix it well together; an hour and a half will bake it. This cake is good to eat with butter for breakfaſt.

A French Cake to eat hot.

TAKE a dozen of eggs, a quart of cream, and as much flour as will make it into a thick batter; put to it a pound of melted butter, half a pint of ſack, and one nutmeg grated; mix it well, and let it ſtand three or four hours; then bake it in a quick oven, and when you take it out, ſlit it in two, and pour a pound of butter on it melted with roſe-water; cover it with the other half, and ſerve it up hot.

A good Seed Cake.

TAKE five pounds of fine flour well dried, and four pounds of ſingle refined ſugar beaten and ſifted; mix the ſugar and flour together, and ſift them thro' a hair ſieve; then waſh four pounds of butter in roſe or orange-flower-water; you muſt work the butter with your hand till it is like cream, beat twenty eggs,

eggs, half the whites, and put to them six spoonfuls of sack; then put in your flour, a little at a time, keeping it stirring with your hand all the time; you must not begin mixing it till the oven is almost hot; you must let it lie a little while before you put the cake into the hoop; when you are ready to put it into the oven, put into it eight ounces of candied orange-peel sliced, as much citron, and a pound and a half of carraway-comfits; mix all well together, and put it in the hoop, which must be papered at the bottom, and buttered; the oven must be quick; it will take two or three hours baking; you may ice it if you please.

Another Seed Cake.

TAKE seven pounds of fine flour well dried, mix with it a pound of sugar beaten and sifted, and three nutmegs grated; rub three pounds of butter into the flour; then beat the yolks of eight eggs, the whites of but four, and mix with them a little rose-water, a quart of cream blood warm, a quart of ale-yeast, and a little salt; strain all into your flour, and put a pint of sack in with it, and make up your cake; put it into a buttered cloth, and lay it half an hour before the fire to rise; the mean while fit your paper, and butter your hoop; then take a pound and three quarters of biscuit-comfits, and a pound and a half of citron cut in small pieces, mix these in your cake, and put it into your hoop, run a knife cross down to the bottom; a quick oven, and near three hours will bake it.

Another.

DRY two pounds of flour, then put two pounds of butter into it; beat ten eggs, leave out half the whites; then put to them eight spoonfuls of cream, six of ale-yeast, run it through a sieve into the batter, and work them well together, and lay it a quarter of an hour before the fire; then work into it a pound of rough carraways. Less than an hour bakes it.

Another Seed Cake.

TAKE a pound of flour, dry it by the fire, add to it a pound of fine sugar beaten and sifted; then take a pound and a quarter of butter, and work it in your hand till it is like cream; beat the yolks of ten eggs, the whites of six; mix all these together with an ounce and a half of carraway-seeds, and a quarter of a pint of brandy; it must not stand to rise.

A rich Seed Cake, called the Nun's Cake.

TAKE four pounds of your finest flour, and three pounds of double refined sugar beaten and sifted, mix them together and dry them by the fire till you prepare your other materials. Take four pounds of butter, beat it in your hands till it is very soft like cream; then beat thirty-five eggs, leave out sixteen whites, and strain out the treddles of the rest, and beat them and the butter together till all appears like butter; put in four or five spoonfuls of rose or orange-flower-water, and beat it again; then take your flour and sugar, with six ounces of carraway-seeds, and strew it in by degrees, beating it up all the time for two hours together; you may put in as much tincture of cinnamon or ambergreafe as you please; butter your hoop, and let it stand three hours in a moderate oven.

To make Sugar Cakes.

TAKE three pounds of fine flour, dried well and sifted, and add two pounds of loaf-sugar beaten and sifted; put in the yolks of four eggs, a little mace, a quarter of a pint of rose-water, and if you please, you may dissolve musk or ambergreafe in your sugar; mix all together, make it up to roll out, then bake them in a quick oven, and sift some sugar on them.

To make clear Cakes of Goosberries.

TAKE your white Dutch goosberries when they are thorough ripe, break them with your fingers, and squeeze out all the pulp into a fine piece of cambric or thick muslin, to run through clear; then weigh the juice and sugar one against the other; then boil the juice a little while; then put in your sugar and let it dissolve, but not boil; skim it and put it into glasses, and stove it in a warm stove.

To Ice a great Cake.

TAKE two pounds of double refined sugar, beat and sift it very fine, and likewise beat and sift a little starch and mix with it; then beat six whites of eggs to a froth, and put to it some gum-water; the gum must be steeped in orange-flower-water; then mix and beat all these together two hours. and put it on your cake; when it is baked, set it in the oven a quarter of an hour.

To make Cheesecakes.

TAKE a pint of cream and warm it, and put to it five quarts of milk warm from the cow, then put renner to it, and when it is come, put the curd in a linen bag or cloth, and let it drain well from the whey, but do not squeeze it much; then put it in a mortar, and break the curd as fine as butter; then

put

The COMPLETE HOUSEWIFE. 167

put to your curd half a pound of almonds blanched, and beaten exceeding fine (or half a pound of dry mackaroons beat very fine) if you have almonds, grate in a Naples biscuit: but if you use mackaroons, you need not; then add to it the yolks of nine eggs beaten, a whole nutmeg grated, two perfumed plumbs dissolved in rose or orange-flower-water, half a pound of fine sugar, mix all well together; then melt a pound and a quarter of butter, and stir it well in, and half a pound of currants plumped; let it stand to cool till you use it. Then make your puff-paste thus: Take a pound of fine flour, and wet it with cold water, roll it out, and put into it by degrees a pound of fresh butter; use it just as it is made.

Another Way to make Cheesecakes.

TAKE a gallon of new milk, set it as for a cheese, and gently whey it; then break it in a mortar, sweeten it to your taste; put in a grated nutmeg, some rose-water and sack; mix these together, and set it over the fire, a quart of cream, and make it into a hasty pudding, mix that with it very well, and fill your pattipans just as they are going into the oven; your oven must be ready, that you may not stay for that; when they rise well up they are enough. Make your paste thus: Take about a pound of flour, and strew into it three spoonfuls of loaf sugar beaten and sifted, and rub into it a pound of butter, one egg, and a spoonful of rose-water, the rest cold fair water; make it into a paste, roll it very thin, and put it into your pans, and fill them almost full.

Another.

TAKE a pound of potatoes when they are boiled and peeled, beat them fine; put to them twelve eggs, six whites; then melt a pound of butter and stir it in; grate half a nutmeg; you must sweeten it to your palate with double refined sugar; then put a piece of puff-paste round the edges of the dish; it must not be over-baked; when the crust is enough draw it.

Another Method.

TAKE four quarts of new milk and rennet very cold, and when it is come to a curd and whey take half a pound of butter and rub it with the curd; then boil a point of cream with a blade of mace and cinnamon, and as much grated Naples biscuit as will make it of the thickness of pancake batter, and when it is almost cold put it to your curd; then put in a spoonful or two of sack, and as many currants as you like, and put them into a puff-paste.

M 4

To make Cheesecakes without Rennet.

TAKE a quart of thick cream, and set it over a clear fire, with some quartered nutmeg in it; just as it boils up, put in twelve eggs well beaten, and a quarter of a pound of fresh butter; stir it a little while on the fire, till it begins to curdle; then take it off, and gather the curd as for cheese; put it in a clean cloth, tie it together, and hang it up, that the whey may run from it; when it is pretty dry, put it in a stone mortar, with a pound of butter, a quarter of a pint of thick cream, some sack, orange-flower-water, and half a pound of fine sugar; then beat and grind all these very well together for an hour or more, till it is very fine; then pass it through a hair sieve, and fill your pattipans but half full; you may put currants in half the quantity if you please; a little more than a quarter of an hour will bake them; take the nutmeg out of the cream when it is boiled.

To make Orange Cakes.

CUT your oranges, pick out all their meat and juice free from the strings and seeds, and set it by; then boil it, and shift the water till your peels are tender; dry them in a cloth, mince them small, and put them to the juice; to a pound of that, weigh a pound and a half of double refined sugar; dip your lumps of sugar in water, and boil it to a candy height; take it off the fire, and put in your juice and peel; stir it well, and when it is almost cold put it in a bason, and set it in a stove; then lay it thin on earthen plates to dry, and as it candies fashion it with your knife; and as they dry lay them on glass; when your plate is empty, put more out of your bason.

To make Lemon Cakes.

GRATE off the yellow rind of your lemon, and squeeze your juice to that peel; take two apples to every lemon, pare and core them, and boil them clear, then put them to your lemon; to a pound of this put two pounds of double refined sugar, then order it as the orange.

Potatoe or Lemon Cheesecake.

TAKE six ounces of potatoes, four ounces of lemon-peel, four ounces of sugar, four ounces of butter; boil the lemon-peel tender, pare and scrape the potatoes, boil them tender and bruise them; beat the lemon-peel with the sugar, then beat all

together

together very well, and melt the butter in a little thick cream; mix all together very well, and let it lie till cold; put cruft in your pattipans, and fill them little more than half full. Bake them in a quick oven half an hour, sift some double refined sugar on them as they go into the oven; this quantity will make a dozen small pattipans.

To make Lemon Cheesecakes.

TAKE two large lemons, grate off the peel of both, and squeeze out the juice of one; add to it half a pound of fine sugar, twelve yolks of eggs, eight whites well beaten; then melt half a pound of butter in four or five spoonfuls of cream; then stir it all together and set it over the fire, stirring it till it begins to be pretty thick; take it off, and when it is cold fill your pattipans little more then half full: put a fine paste very thin at the bottom of the pattipans: half an hour with a quick oven will bake them.

Another Method.

TAKE the peel of two large lemons, boil it very tender, then pound it well in a mortar, with a quarter of a pound or more of loaf sugar, the yolks of six eggs, and half a pound of fresh butter; pound and mix all well together, and fill the pattipans but half full: orange cheesecakes are done the same way, only you must boil the peel in two or three waters, to take out the bitterness.

To make Cheesecakes without Curd.

BEAT two eggs very well, then put as much flour as will make them thick; then beat three eggs more very well, and put to the other, with a pint of cream, and half a pound of butter; set it over the fire, and when it boils put in your two eggs and flour; stir them well, and let them boil till they be pretty thick; then take it off the fire, and season it with sugar, a little salt and nutmeg; put in the currants, and bake them in pattipans, as you do others.

To make Almond Cheesecakes.

TAKE a good handful or more of almonds, blanch them in warm water, and throw them in cold; pound them fine, and in the pounding put a little sack, or orange-flower-water, to keep them from oiling; then put to your almonds the yolks of two hard eggs, and beat them together; beat the yolks of six eggs, the whites of three, and mix with your almonds, and half a pound of butter melted, and sugar to your taste; mix all well together, and use it as other cheesecake stuff.

CHAP. VI.
Of BISCUITS.

To make Drop Biscuits.

TAKE eight eggs, and one pound of double refined sugar beaten fine, and twelve ounces of fine flour well dried; beat your eggs very well, then put in your sugar and beat it, and then your flour by degrees, beating it all very well together for an hour without ceasing: your oven must be as hot as for half-penny bread; then flour some sheets of tin, and drop your biscuits what bigness you please, and put them into the oven as fast as you can; and when you see them rise, watch them; and if they begin to colour, take them out again, and put in more; and if the first are not enough, put them in again; if they are right done, they will have a white ice on them; you may put in carraway-seeds if you please; when they are all baked, put them all in the oven again till they are very dry, and keep them in your stove.

To make little Cracknels.

TAKE three pounds of flour finely dried, three ounces of lemon and orange-peel dried, and beaten to a powder, an ounce of coriander-seeds beaten and searced, and three pounds of double refined sugar, beaten fine and searced; mix these together with fifteen eggs, half of the whites taken out, a quarter of a pint of rose-water, as much orange-flower-water; beat the eggs and water well together, then put in your orange-peel and coriander-seeds, and beat it again very well with two spoons, one in each hand; then beat your sugar in by little and little, then your flour by a little at a time, so beat with both spoons an hour longer; then strew sugar on papers, and drop them the bigness of a walnut, and set them in the oven; the oven must be hotter than when pyes are drawn; do not touch them with your finger before they are baked; let the oven be ready for them against they are done; be careful the oven does not colour them.

To make the thin Dutch Biscuit.

TAKE five pounds of flour, two ounces of carraway-seeds, half a pound of sugar, and something more than a pint of milk; warm the milk, and put into it three quarters of a pound of butter; then make a hole in the middle of your flour, and put in a full pint of good ale-yeast; then pour in the butter and milk, and make these into a paste, letting it stand a quarter of an hour by the fire to rise; then mould it and roll it, into cakes pretty thin; prick them all over pretty much, or they will blister; bake them a quarter of an hour.

Another Biscuit.

TO a quart of flour take a quarter of a pound of butter, and a quarter of a pound of sugar, one egg, and what carraway-seeds you please; wet it with milk as stiff as you can, then roll them out very thin, cut them with a small glass, bake them on tin plates; your oven must be slack; prick them very well just as you set them in, and keep them dry when baked.

Another.

TAKE a pound of loaf-sugar beaten and sifted, and half a pound of almonds blanched and beat in a mortar, with the whites of five or six eggs; put your sugar in a bason, with the yolks of five eggs; when they are both mingled, strew in your almonds; then put in a quarter of a pound of flour, and fill your pans fast; butter them and put them into the oven; strew sugar over them, bake them quick, and then turn them on a paper, and put them again into the oven to harden.

To make little hollow Biscuits.

BEAT six eggs very well with a spoonful of rose-water, then put in a pound and two ounces of loaf-sugar beaten and sifted; stir it together till it is well mixed in the eggs, then put in as much flour as will make it thick enough to lay out in drops upon sheets of white paper; stir it well together till you are ready to drop it on your paper; then beat a little very fine sugar and put it into a lawn sieve, and sift some on them, the oven must not be too hot, and as soon as they are baked, whilst they are hot, pull off the papers from them, and put them in a sieve, and set them in an oven to dry; keep them in boxes with papers between.

To make Ratafia Biscuit.

TAKE four ounces of bitter almonds, blanch and beat them as fine as you can; in beating them put in the whites of four eggs, one at a time; then mix it up with sifted sugar to a light paste; roll them, and lay them on wafer paper, and on tin plates; make the paste so light that you may take it up with a spoon; bake them in a quick oven.

To make the hard Biscuit.

TAKE half a pound of fine flour, one ounce of carraway-seeds, the whites of two eggs, a quarter of a pint of ale-yeast, and as much warm water as will make it into a stiff paste; then make it into long rolls, bake it an hour; the next day pare it round, then slice it in thin slices, about half an inch thick; dry it in the oven; then draw it, turn it, and dry the other side; they will keep the whole year.

To make Lemon Biscuit.

TAKE six yellow rinds well beat, with a pound of double refined sugar, and whites of four eggs, till come to a paste; lay them on wafer paper, so bake them on tins.

CHAP. VII.
Of elegant ORNAMENTS for the TABLE.

WHEN a silver web, or a desert is to be spun, always take particular care that your fire is clear, and a pan of water upon the fire, to keep the heat from your face and stomach, for fear the heat should make you faint; you must not spin it before a kitchen fire, for the smaller the grate is, so that the fire be clear and hot, the better able you will be to sit a long time before it, for if you spin a whole desert, you will be several hours about it; be sure to have a tin box to put every basket in as you spin them, and cover them from the air; keep them warm, until you have done the whole as your receipt directs you.

If you spin a gold web, take care your chafing-dish is burnt clear, before you set it upon the table where your mould is, set your ladle on the fire, and keep stirring it with a wood skewer till it just boils, then let it cool a little, for it will not spin when it is boiling hot, and if it grows cold it is equally as bad, but as it cools on the sides of your ladle, dip the point of
your

your knife in, and begin to spin round your mould as long as it will draw, then heat it again. The only art is to keep it of a proper heat, and it will draw out like a fine thread, and of a gold colour. It is a great fault to put in too much sugar at a time; for often heating takes the moisture out of the sugar, and burns it, therefore the best way is to put in a little at a time, and clean out your ladle.

When you make a hen or bird-nest, let part of your jelly be set in your bowl, before you put on your flummery, or straw; for if your jelly is warm, they will settle to the bottom, and mix together.

If it be a fish-pond, or a transparent pudding, put in your jelly at three different times, to make your fish or fruit keep at a proper distance one from another, and be sure your jelly is very clear and stiff, or it will not shew the figures, nor keep whole; when you turn them out, dip your bason in warm water, as your receipt directs; then turn your dish or salver upon the top of your bason, and turn your bason upside down.

When you make flummery, always observe to have it pretty thick, and your moulds wet in cold water, before you put in your flummery, or your jelly will settle to the bottom, and the cream swim at the top, so that it will look to be two different colours.

If you make custards, do not let them boil after the yolks are in, but stir them all one way, and keep them of a good heat till they be thick enough, and the rawness of the eggs is gone off.

When you make whips or syllabubs, raise your froth with a chocolate mill, and lay it upon a sieve to drain, it will be much prettier, and will lie upon your glasses, without mixing with your wine, or running down the sides of your glasses; and whatever you make, keep them in a cool airy place, for a close place will give them a bad taste, and soon spoil them.

To spin a Silver Web for covering Sweetmeats.

TAKE a quarter of a pound of treble refined sugar, in one lump, and set it before a moderate fire on the middle of a silver salver, or pewter plate, set it a little aslant, and when it begins to run like clear water to the edge of the plate or salver, have ready a tin cover, or china bowl set on a stool, with the mouth downward, close to your sugar, that it may not cool by carrying too far; then take a clean knife, and take up as much of the syrup as the point of the knife will hold, and a fine thread will come from the point, which you must draw as quick as possible backwards and forwards, and also around the mould, as long as it will spin from the knife; be very careful you do not drop the syrup on the web, if you do, it will spoil it; then dip your knife into the syrup again, and take up more, and so keep
spinning

spinning till your sugar is done, or your web is thick enough; be sure you do not let the knife touch the lump on the plate that is not melted, as it will make it brittle, and not spin at all. If your sugar is spent before your web is done, put fresh sugar on a clean plate or salver, and not spin from the same plate again. If you do not want the web to cover the sweetmeats immediately, set it in a deep pewter dish, and cover it with a tin cover, and lay a cloth over it, to prevent the air from getting to it, and set it before the fire. It requires to be kept warm, or it will fall. When your dinner or supper is dished, have ready a plate or dish, of the size of your web, filled with different coloured sweetmeats, and set your web over it.

To spin a Gold Web for covering Sweetmeats.

TAKE four ounces of treble refined sugar, beat it in a marble mortar, and sift it through a hair sieve; then put it in a silver or brass ladle, but silver makes the colour better; set it over a chafing-dish of charcoal, that is burnt clear; set it on a table, and turn a tin cover or china bowl upside down upon the same table, and when your sugar is melted, it will be of a gold colour; take your ladle off the fire, and begin to spin it with a knife, the same way as the silver web; when the sugar begins to cool and set, put it over the fire to warm, and spin it as before, but do not warm it too often, as it will turn the sugar of a bad colour; if you have not enough sugar, clean the ladle before you put in more, and spin it till your web is thick enough; then take it off, and set it over the sweetmeats, as you did the silver web.

To make a Desert of Spun Sugar.

SPIN two large webs, turn one upon the other to form a globe, and put in the inside of them a few sprigs of small flowers and myrtle; spin a little more round to bind them together, and set them covered close up before the fire; then spin two more on a lesser bowl, and put in a sprig of myrtle, and a few small flowers; bind them as before, set them by, and spin two more less than the last; put in a few flowers, bind them and set them by; then spin twelve couple on tea-cups of three different sizes, in proportion to the globes, to represent baskets, and bind them two and two as the globes with spun sugar; set the globes on a silver salver, one upon another, the largest at the bottom, and smallest at the top; when you have fixed the globes, run two small wires through the middle of the largest globes, across each other; then take a large darning needle and silk, and run it through the middle of the largest baskets; cross it at the bottom, and bring it up to the top, and make a loop to hang them on the wire; do so with the rest of your baskets, hang the
largest

largest baskets on the wires, then put two more wires a little shorter across, through the middle of the second globes, and put the ends of the wires out betwixt the baskets, and hang on the four middle ones; then run two more wires shorter than the last thro' the middle of the top globe, and hang the baskets over the lowest; stick a sprig of myrtle on the top of your globes, and set it on the middle of the table.—Observe you do not put too much sugar down at a time for a silver web, because the sugar will lose its moisture, and run in lumps instead of drawing out; nor too much in the ladle, for the gold web will lose its colour by heating too oft.——You may make the baskets of a silver, and the globes of a gold colour, if you chuse them.

To make Flummery.

THOUGH the making of flummery may here appear as an article out of place, yet the reader will soon find, that she would be at a loss in the management of some of the following receipts, were not this article previously given.——Take one ounce of bitter, and one of sweet almonds into a bason, pour over them some boiling water. to make the skins come off, which is called blanching; strip off the skins, and throw the kernels into cold water; then take them out and beat them in a marble mortar, with a little rose-water to keep them from oiling, when they are beat, put them into a pint of calf's-foot stock; set it over the fire, and sweeten it to your taste with loaf sugar; as soon as it boils strain it through a piece of muslin or gauze, and when a little cold put it into a pot of thick cream, and keep stirring it often, till it grows thick and cold; wet your moulds in cold water, and pour in the flummery, and let it stand five or six hours at least before you turn them out; if you make the flummery stiff, and wet the moulds, it will turn out without putting it into warm water, for water takes off the figures of the mould, and makes the flummery look dull.——N. B. Be careful you keep stirring it till cold, or it will run in lumps when you turn it out of the mould.

To make a Fish-pond.

FILL four large fish-moulds with flummery, and six small ones; take a china bowl, and put in half a pint of stiff clear calf's-foot jelly; let it stand till cold, then lay two of the small fishes on the jelly, the right side down, and put in half a pint more jelly; let it stand till cold: then lay in the four small fishes across one another, that when you turn the bowl upside down, the heads and tails may be seen; then almost fill your bowl with jelly, and let it stand till cold; then lay in the jelly four large fishes, fill the bason quite full with jelly, and let it stand till the next day; when you want to use it, set your bowl to the brim in hot water for one minute; but take care that you do not let the water go into the bason; lay your plate on the top of the bason, and turn it upside down: if you want it for the middle, turn it out upon a salver. Be sure you make your jelly very stiff and clear.

To make a Hen's-nest.

TAKE three or five of the smallest pullet eggs you can get, fill them with flummery, and when they are stiff and cold, peel off the shells; pare off the rinds of two lemons very thin, and boil them in sugar and water to take off the bitterness; when they are cold, cut them in long shreds to imitate straw; then fill a bason one third full of stiff calf's-foot jelly, and let it stand till cold; then lay in the shreds of the lemons, in a ring about two inches high in the middle of your bason, strew a few corns of sagoe to look like barley, fill the bason to the height of the peel, and let it stand till cold; then lay your eggs of flummery in the middle of the ring that the straw may be seen round, fill the bason quite full of jelly, and let it stand. Turn it out the same way as directed for the fish-pond.

To make Blomange of Isinglass.

BOIL one ounce of isinglass in a quart of water till it is reduced to a pint, then put in the whites of four eggs, with two spoonfuls of rice water, to keep the eggs from poaching, and sugar to your taste; run it through a jelly bag, then put to it two ounces of sweet, and one ounce of bitter almonds; give them a scald in your jelly, put them through a hair sieve, and put it in a china bowl. The next day turn it out, and stick it all over with almonds blanched and cut lengthway. Garnish with green leaves or flowers.

Green Blomange of Isinglass.

DISSOLVE your isinglass, and put to it two ounces of sweet, and two ounces of bitter almonds, with as much juice of spinach as will make it green, and a spoonful of French brandy; set it over a stove fire till it be almost ready to boil, and then strain it thro' a gauze sieve; when it grows thick put it into a mellon mould, and the next day turn it out. Garnish it with red and white flowers.

Clear Blomange.

TAKE a quart of strong calf's-foot jelly, skim off the fat and strain it, beat the whites of four eggs, and put them to your jelly;

jelly; set it over the fire, and keep stirring it till it boils; then pour it into a jelly-bag, and run it through several times till it is clear: beat one ounce of sweet almonds, and one of bitter, to a paste, with a spoonful of rose water squeezed through a cloth; then mix it with your jelly, and three spoonfuls of very good cream; set it over the fire again, and keep stirring it till it is almost boiling; then pour it into a bowl, and stir it very often till it is almost cold; after which wet your moulds, and fill them.

Yellow Flummery.

TAKE two ounces of isinglass, beat it and open it, put it into a bowl, and pour a pint of boiling water upon it; cover it up till almost cold, then add a pint of white wine, the juice of two lemons with the rind of one, the yolks of eight eggs beat well, sweeten it to your taste, put it in a tossing-pan and keep stirring it; when it boils strain it through a fine sieve. When almost cold put it into cups or moulds.

A good Green.

LAY an ounce of gambouge in a quarter of a pint of water, and put an ounce and a half of good stone blue in a little water; when they are both dissolved, mix them together; add a quarter of a pint more water, and a quarter of a pound of fine sugar; boil it a little, then put it in a gally pot, cover it close and it will keep for years. Be careful not to make it too deep a green, for a very little will do at a time.

Gilded Fish in Jelly.

MAKE a little clear blomange as is directed in the preceding receipt; then fill two large fish moulds with it, and when it is cold turn it out, and gild them with gold leaf, or strew them over with gold and silver bran mixed; then lay them on a soup-dish, and fill it with clear thin calf's-foot jelly: it must be so thin that they will swim in it. If you have no jelly, Lisbon wine, or any kind of pale made wines, will do.

Hen and Chickens in Jelly.

MAKE some flummery, with a large quantity of sweet almonds in it; colour a little of it brown with chocolate, and put it in a mould the shape of a hen; then colour some more flummery with the yolk of a hard egg beat as fine as possible, but leave part of your flummery white; then fill the moulds of seven chickens, three with white flummery, and three with low, and one the colour of the hen; when they are cold turn them into a deep dish; put under and round them lemon-peel boiled tender and cut like straw, and a little clear calf's-foot jelly under them, to keep them in their places; let it stand till it is stiff, and then fill up your dish with more jelly.

To make a Desart Island.

TAKE a lump of paste, and form it into a rock three inches broad at the top; colour it, and set it in the middle of a deep china dish; set a cast figure on it, with a crown on its head, and a knot of rock-candy at the feet; then make a roll of paste an inch thick, and stick it on the inner edge of the dish, two parts round, and cut eight pieces of eringo-root, about three inches long, and fix them upright to the roll of paste on the edge; make gravel walks of shot comfits, from the middle to the edge of the dish, and set small figures in them; roll out some paste, and cut it open like Chinese rails; bake it, and fix it on either side of one of the gravel walks, with gum; have ready a web of spun sugar, and set it on the pillars of eringo-root, and cut part of the web off, to form an entrance where the Chinese rails are.

To make a Floating Island.

GRATE the yellow rind of a large lemon into a quart of cream, and put in a large glass of Madeira wine; make it pretty sweet with loaf-sugar, mill it with a chocolate-mill, to a strong froth, take it off as it rises, and lay it upon a sieve to drain all night; then take a deep glass dish, and lay in your froth, with a Naples biscuit in the middle of it; beat the white of an egg to a strong froth, and roll a sprig of myrtle in it to imitate snow; stick it in the Naples biscuit, and lay all over your froth currant jelly, cut in very thin slices; pour over it very fine strong calf's-foot jelly, and when it grows thick, lay it all over, till it looks like a glass. When your dish is full to the brim, let it stand till it is quite cold and stiff, then lay on rock candied sweetmeats upon the top of your jelly, and sheep and swans to pick at the myrtle; stick green sprigs in two or three places upon the top of your jelly, amongst your shapes.—You must not put the shapes on the jelly till you are going to send it to the table.

Another Method.

TAKE calf's-foot jelly that is set, break it a little, but not too much, for it will make it frothy, and prevent it from looking clear; have ready a middle-sized turnip, and rub it over

with

with gum-water, or the white of an egg; then strew it thick over with green shot comfits, and stick in the top of it a sprig of myrtle, or any other pretty green sprig; put your broken jelly round it, set sheep, or swans, upon your jelly, with either a green leaf, or a knot of apple-paste under them, to keep the jelly from dissolving. There are sheep and swans made for that purpose. You may put in snakes, or any wild animals of the same sort.

To make the Rocky Island.

MAKE a little stiff flummery, and put it into five fish moulds; wet them before you put it in: when it is stiff turn it out, and gild them with gold leaf; then take a deep china dish, fill it near half full of clear calf's-foot jelly, and let it stand till it is set; then lay on your fishes, and a few slices of red currant jelly, cut very thin round them; then rasp a small French roll, and rub it over with the white of an egg, and strew all over it silver bran, and glitter mixed together; stick a sprig of myrtle in it, and put it into the middle of your dish; beat the white of an egg to a very high froth, then hang it on your sprig of myrtle like snow, and fill your dish to the brim with clear jelly. When you send it to table, put lambs and ducks upon your jelly, with either green leaves, or moss under them, with their heads towards the myrtle.

To make Moonshine.

TAKE the shapes of a half-moon, and five or seven stars; wet them, and fill them with flummery; let them stand till they are cold, then turn them into a deep china dish, and pour lemon-cream round them, made thus: Take a pint of spring water, put to it the juice of three lemons, and the yellow rind of one lemon, the whites of five eggs well beaten, and four ounces of loaf sugar; then set it over a slow fire, and stir it one way till it looks white and thick. If you let it boil it will curdle. Then strain it through a hair sieve, and let it stand till it is cold; beat the yolks of five eggs, mix them with your whites, set them over the fire, and keep stirring it till it is almost ready to boil, when you must pour it into a bason; when it is cold pour it among your moon and stars. Garnish with flowers.

To make Moon and Stars in Jelly.

TAKE a deep china dish, turn the mould of a half-moon, and seven stars, with the bottom side upward in the dish; lay a weight upon every mould to keep them down; then make some flummery, and fill your dish with it; when it is cold and stiff, take your moulds carefully out, and fill the vacancy with clear calf's-foot jelly; you may colour your flummery with cochineal and chocolate, to make it look like the sky, and your moon and stars will shew more clear. Garnish with rock-candy sweetmeats.

To make Eggs and Bacon in Flummery.

TAKE a pint of stiff flummery, and make part of it a pretty pink colour, with the colouring for the flummery; dip a potting pot in cold-water, and pour in red flummery, the thickness of a crown-piece; then the same of white flummery, and another of red, and twice the thickness of white flummery at the top; one layer must be stiff and cold before you pour on another; then take five tea-cups, and put a large spoonful of white flummery into each tea-cup, and let them stand all night; then turn your flummery out of your potting-pots, on the back of a plate wet with cold water, cut your flummery into thin slices, and lay them on a china dish; then turn your flummery out of the cups on the dish, and take a bit out of the top of every one, and lay in half of a preserved apricot; it will confine the syrup from discolouring the flummery, and make it like the yolk of a poached egg. Garnish with flowers.

Solomon's Temple in Flummery.

MAKE a quart of stiff flummery, divide it into three parts, make one part a pretty pink colour, with a little cochineal bruised fine, and steeped in French brandy; scrape one ounce of chocolate very fine, dissolve it in a little strong coffee, and mix it with another part of your flummery, to make it a light stone colour: the last part must be white. Wet your temple mould, and fix it in a pot to stand even; then fill the top of the temple with red flummery to the steps, and the four points with white; then fill it up with chocolate flummery; let it stand till the next day, then loosen it round with a pin, and shake it loose very gently, but do not dip your mould in warm water, as it will take off the gloss, and spoil the colour; when you turn it out, stick a small sprig, or a flower-stalk, down from the top of every point, for it will strengthen them, and make it look pretty: lay round it rock-candy sweetmeats.

To make a Dish of Snow.

TAKE twelve large apples, put them in cold water, and set them over a very slow fire, and when they are soft, put them upon a hair sieve; take off the skin, and put the pulp into a bason; then beat the whites of twelve eggs to a very strong froth, beat and sift half a pound of double refined sugar, and strew it over the eggs; beat the pulp of your apples to a strong froth,

froth, then beat them all together till they are like a stiff snow, lay it upon a china dish, heap it up as high as you can, and set round it green knots of paste, in imitation of Chinese rails; stick a sprig of myrtle in the middle of the dish, and serve it up.

To make black Caps.

TAKE six large apples, and cut a slice of the blossom end; put them in a tin, and set them in a quick oven till they are brown; then wet them with rose-water, and grate a little sugar over them; set them in the oven again till they look bright, and very black; then take them out, and put them into a deep china dish or plate, and pour round them thick cream custard, or white wine and sugar.

To make Green Caps.

TAKE codlings just before they are ripe, green them as you would for preserving, then rub them over with a little oiled butter, grate double refined sugar over them, and set them in the oven till they look bright, and sparkle like frost; then take them out and put them into a deep china dish, make a very fine custard, and pour it round them; stick single flowers in every apple, and serve them up.

PART IV.

Of Preparing BACON, HAMS, *and* TONGUES, *and* Making BUTTER, CHEESE, &c.

CHAP. I.
Of Preparing BACON, &c.

To salt Bacon.

CUT your flitches of bacon very smooth, make no holes in it: to about threescore pounds of bacon, ten pounds of salt; dry your salt very well, and make it hot, then rub it hard over the outside, or skinny part, but on the inside lay it all over, without rubbing, only lightly on, about half an inch thick. Let it lie on a flat board, that the brine may run from it nine days; then mix with a quart of hot salt, two ounces of salt-petre, and strew it all over your bacon; then heat the rest of your salt, put over it, and let it lie nine days longer; then hang it up a day, and put it in a chimney where wood is burnt, and there let it hang three weeks or more, as you see occasion.

To make Westphalia Bacon.

MAKE a pickle as follows: Take a gallon of pump water, a quarter of a peck of bay salt, as much of white-salt, a pound of petre-salt, and a quarter of a pound of salt-petre, a pound of coarse sugar, and an ounce of socho tied up in a rag; boil all these together very well, and let it stand till it is cold; then put in the pork, and let it lie in this pickle a fortnight; then take it out, and dry it over saw dust; this pickle will do tongues, but you must first let the tongues lie six or eight hours in pump-water, to take out the sliminess: and when you have laid them in the pickle, dry them as your pork.

To salt and dry a Ham of Bacon.

TAKE bay-salt, and put it in a vessel of water suitable to the quantity of hams you do; make your pickle strong enough to bear an egg with your bay-salt; then boil and skim it very well; then let the pickle be thoroughly cold, and put into it so much red saunders as will make it out of the colour of claret; then let your pickle stand three days before you put your hams into it; the hams must lie in the pickle three weeks; then carefully dry them where wood is burnt.

To salt Hams, or Tongues, &c.

TAKE of bay-salt a peck, of salt-petre four ounces; three pounds of very brown sugar; put to all these water till it will but just bear an egg; after it is well stirred lay in the hams so that they are covered with the pickle; let them lie three weeks, if middling hams, if large, a month; when you take them out, dry them well in a cloth and rub them with bay-salt, then hang them up to dry, and smoke them with saw-dust every day for a fortnight together; the chimney you hang them in must be of a moderate heat; the pickle must be raw, and not boiled. This quantity is enough to salt six hams at a time. When you take them out, you may boil the pickle, and skim it clean, putting in some fresh salt. If you keep your hams till they are dry and old, lay them in hot grains, and let them lie till cold, then wrap them up in hay, and boil them tender; set them on in cold water when they are dry, the houghs being before stopped with salt, and tied up close in brown paper, to keep out the flies.

Neats hearts, tongues, or hogs cheeks, do well in the same pickle; the best way is to rub hams with bay-salt and sugar three or four days before you put them in this pickle.

Another Method.

TAKE three or four gallons of water, put to it four pounds of bay-salt, four pounds of white-salt, a pound of petre-salt, a quarter of a pound of salt-petre, two ounces of prunella-salt, a pound of brown sugar; let it boil a quarter of an hour; skim it well, and when it is cold sever it from the bottom into the vessel you keep it in.

Let hams lie in this pickle four or five weeks.
A clod of Dutch beef as long.
Tongues a fortnight.
Collared beef eight or ten days.
Dry them in a stove, or with wood in a chimney.

To dry Tongues.

TAKE to every two ounces of salt-petre, a pint of petre-salt, and rub it well, after it is finely beaten, strew it over your tongue, and then beat a pint of bay-salt, and rub that on over it, and every three days turn it: when it has lain nine or ten days, hang it in wood smoke to dry. Do a hog's-head this way. For a ham of pork or mutton, have a quart of bay-salt, half a pound of petre salt, a quarter of a pound of salt petre, a quarter of a pound of brown sugar, all beaten very fine, mixed together, and rubbed well over it; let it lie a fortnight; turn it often, and then hang it up a day to drain, and dry it in wood-smoke.

To dry a Leg of Mutton like Pork.

TAKE a large leg of mutton, and beat it down flattish with a cleaver, to make it like Westphalia ham; then take two ounces of salt-petre, beat it fine, rub it all over your mutton, and let it lie all night; then make a pickle with bay-salt and pump-water, strong enough to bear an egg, put you mutton into it, and let it lie ten days; then take it out and hang it in a chimney where wood is burnt, till it is thorough dry, which will be about three weeks. Boil it with hay, till it is very tender; do it in cold weather, or it will not keep well.

To make Sausages.

TAKE three pounds of fat, and three pounds of lean pork; cut the lean into thin slices, and scrape every slice, and throw away the skin; have the fat cut as small as can be; mix fat and lean together, shred and mix them well; two ounces and a half of salt, half an ounce of pepper, thirty cloves, and three or four large blades of mace, six spoonfuls of sage, two spoonfuls of rosemary cut exceeding fine, with three nutmegs grated; beat six eggs, and work them well together with a pint of water that has been boiled, and is perfectly cold: if you put in no herbs, slice a penny white loaf in cream, steep it all night, and work it in well with sausage-meat, with as much cream as will infuse the bread. If you put in raw water, the sausages are said not to keep so well as when it is boiled.

Very fine Sausages.

TAKE a leg of pork or veal; pick it clean from skin or fat, and to every pound of lean meat put two pounds of beef suet picked from the skins; shred the meat and suet severally very fine; then mix them well together, and add a large

handful

handful of green sage shred very small, season it with grated nutmeg, salt and pepper; mix it well, and press it down hard in an earthen pot, and keep it for use. When you use them, roll them up with as much egg as will make them roll smooth, but use no flour: in rolling them up, make them the length of your finger, and as thick as two fingers: fry them in clarified suet, which must be boiling hot before you put them in. Keep them rolling about in the pan; when they are fried through they are enough.

To make Dutch Beef.

TAKE the lean part of a buttock of beef raw; rub it well with brown sugar all over, and let it lie in a pan or tray two or three hours, turning it three or four times; then salt it well with common salt and salt-petre, and let it lie a fortnight, turning it every day; then roll it very strait in a coarse cloth, put it in a cheese press a day and a night, and hang it to dry in a chimney. When you boil it, you must put it in a cloth; when it is cold, it will cut out into shivers as Dutch beef.

To dry Mutton to cut out in Shivers as Dutch Beef.

TAKE a middling leg of mutton, then take half a pound of brown sugar, rub it hard all over your mutton, and let it lie twenty-four hours; then take an ounce and a half of salt petre, and mix it with a pound of common salt, and rub that all over the mutton every other day, till it is all on, and let it lie nine days longer; keep the place free from brine, and hang it up to dry three days; then smoke it in a chimney where wood is burnt; the fire must not be too hot; a fortnight will do it: boil it like other hams, and when it is cold cut it out in shivers like Dutch beef.

To prepare Hung Beef.

MAKE a strong brine with bay salt, petre-salt, and pump-water, and steep therein a rib of beef for nine days; then hang it up in a chimney where wood or saw dust is burnt; when it is a little dry, wash the outside with blood two or three times, to make it look black, and when it is dried enough, boil it for use.

Another Method.

TO a pound of beef, put a pound of bay-salt, two ounces of salt-petre, and a pound of sugar mixed with the common salt; let it lie six weeks in this brine, turning it every day, then dry it and boil it.

To

To prepare the fine hanged Beef.

THE piece that is fit to do, is the navel-piece, and let it hang in your cellar, as long as you dare for ſtinking, till it begins to be a little ſappy; take it down, and waſh it in ſugar and water; waſh it with a clean rag very well, one piece after another, for you may cut that piece in three; then take ſix penny-worth of ſalt-petre, and two pounds of bay-ſalt; dry it, and pound it ſmall, and mix with it two or three ſpoonfuls of brown ſugar, and rub your beef in every place very well with it; then take of common ſalt, and ſtrew all over it as much as you think will make it ſalt enough; let it lie cloſe, till the ſalt be diſſolved, which will be in ſix or ſeven days; then turn it every other day, the undermoſt uppermoſt, and ſo for a fortnight; then hang it where it may have a little warmth of the fire; not too hot to roaſt it. It may hang in the kitchen a fortnight; when you uſe it, boil it in hay and pump water, very tender: it will keep boiled two or three months, rubbing it with a greaſy cloth, or putting it two or three minutes into boiling water to take off the mouldineſs.

A Pickle for Pork which is to be eat ſoon.

YOU muſt take two gallons of pump-water, one pound of bay-ſalt, one pound of coarſe ſugar, ſix ounces of ſalt-petre; boil it all together, and ſkim it when cold. Cut the pork in what pieces you pleaſe, lay it down cloſe, and pour the liquor over it. Lay a weight on it to keep it cloſe, and cover it cloſe from the air, and it will be fit to uſe in a week. If you find the pickle begins to ſpoil, boil it again, and ſkim it; when it is cold, pour it on your pork again.

To make Veal Hams.

CUT the leg of veal like a ham, then take a pint of bay-ſalt, two ounces of ſalt-petre, and a pound of common ſalt; mix them together, with an ounce of juniper-berries beat; rub the ham well, and lay it in a hollow tray, with the ſkinny ſide downwards. Baſte it every day with the pickle for a fortnight, and then hang it in wood-ſmoke for a fortnight. You may boil it, or parboil it and roaſt it. In this pickle you may do two or three tongues, or a piece of pork.

To make Beef Hams.

YOU muſt take the leg of a fat, but ſmall beef, the fat Scotch or Welch cattle is beſt, and cut it ham-faſhion. Take an ounce of bay-ſalt, an ounce of ſalt-petre, a pound of common salt, and a pound of coarse sugar (this quantity for about fourteen or fifteen pounds weight, and so accordingly, if you pickle the whole quarter) rub it with the above ingredients, turn it every day, and baste it well with the pickle for a month: take it out and roll it in bran or saw-dust, then hang it in wood-smoke, where there is but little fire, and a constant smoke, for a month; then take it down, and hang it in a dry place, not hot, and keep it for use. You may cut a piece off as you have occasion, and either boil it or cut it in rashers, and broil it with poached eggs, or boil a piece, and it eats fine cold, and will shiver like Dutch beef. After this beef is done, you may do a thick brisket of beef in the same pickle. Let it lie a month, rubbing it every day with the pickle, then boil it till it is tender, hang it in a dry place, and it eats finely cold, cut in slices on a plate. It is a pretty thing for a side-dish, or for supper. A shoulder of mutton laid in this pickle for a week, hung in wood-smoke two or three days, and then boiled with cabbage, is very good.

To recover Venison when it stinks.

TAKE as much cold water in a tub as will cover it a handful over, and put in good store of salt, and let it lie three or four hours; then take your venison out, and let it lie in as much hot water and salt, and let it lie as long as before; then have your crust in readiness, and take it out, and dry it very well, and season it with pepper and salt pretty high, and put it in your pasty. Do not use the bones of your venison for gravy, but get fresh beef or other bones.

Another and better Method.

TAKE some lukewarm water and wash it clean; then take fresh milk and water lukewarm, and wash it again; then dry it in clean cloths very well, and rub it all over with beaten ginger, and hang it in an airy place. When you roast it, you need only wipe it with a clean cloth and paper it, as beforementioned. Never do any thing else to venison, for all other things spoil your venison, and take away the fine flavour, and this preserves it better than any thing you can do. A hare you may manage just the same way.

CHAP. II.
To make BUTTER, CHEESE, &c.

To make Butter.

AS soon as you have milked, strain your milk into a pot, and stir it often for half an hour, then put it in your pans or trays; when it is creamed, skim it exceeding clean from the milk,

milk, and put your cream into an earthen pot; if you do not churn immediately for butter, shift your cream once in twelve hours into another clean scalded pot, and if you find any milk at the bottom of the pot, put it away; when you have churned, wash your butter in three or four waters, and then salt it to your taste, and beat it well, but not wash it after it is salted: let it stand in a wedge, if it be to pot, till the next morning, and beat it again, and make your layers the thickness of three fingers, and then strew a little salt on it, and so do till your pot is full.

To make Lemon Butter.

TAKE three pints of cream, set it on the fire, and when it is ready to boil, crush the juice of a lemon into it; then stir it about, and hang it up in a cloth, that the whey may run from it; and when it is well drained, sweeten it to your taste; and, if you think fit, bruise some peel in the sugar you sweeten it with, and so serve it.

French Butter.

TAKE the yolks of four hard eggs, half a pound of loaf-sugar beat and sifted, and half a pound of sweet butter; bray them in a marble mortar, or some other convenient thing, with a spoonful or two of orange-flower-water; when it is well mixed, force it through the corner of a coarse cloth, in little heaps on a china plate, or through the top of a dredging-box.

To make a Summer Cream Cheese.

TAKE three pints of milk just from the cow, and five pints of good sweet cream, which you must boil free from smoke; then put it to your milk, cool it till it is but blood-warm, and then put in a spoonful of rennet: when it is well come, take a large strainer, lay it in a great cheese-fat, then put the curd in gently upon the strainer, and when all the curd is in, lay on the cheese board, and a weight of two pound; let it so drain three hours, till the whey be well drained from it: then lay a cheese cloth in your lesser cheese fat, and put in the curd, laying the cloth smooth over it as before, the board on the top of that, and a four pound weight on it; turn it every two hours into dry cloths before night, and be careful not to break it next morning; salt it, and keep it in the fat till next day; then put it into a wet cloth, which you must shift every day till it is ripe.

To make a Newmarket Cheese to cut at two years old.

ANY morning in September take twenty quarts of new milk warm from the cow, and colour it with marigolds;

when

when this is done, and the milk not cold, get ready a quart of cream, and a quart of fair water, which muſt be kept ſtirring over the fire till it is ſcalding hot, then ſtir it well into the milk and rennet, as you do other cheeſe; when it is come, lay cheeſe-cloths over it, and ſettle it with your hands; the more hands the better; as the whey riſes, take it away, and when it is clean gone, put your curd into your fat, breaking it as little as you can: then put it in the preſs, and preſs it gently an hour; take it out again, and cut it in thin ſlices, and lay them ſingly on a cloth, and wipe them dry; then put it in a tub, and break it with your hands as ſmall as you can, and mix it with a good handful of ſalt, and a quart of cold cream; put it in the fat, and lay a pound weight on it till next day; then preſs and order it as others.

To make Lady Huncks's freſh Cheeſe.

TAKE a quart of cream, and the whites of five eggs; beat and ſtir them into your cream, ſet them on the fire till they begin to curdle, put in a little glaſs full of white wine, and ſet it over the fire again till it be all curds and whey; then put it into a curd ſieve, and let the whey paſs from it; beat the curd with roſe-water and ſugar, and mingle it with ſome almonds finely beaten, and amber-ſugar, and put it into your freſh cheeſe-pans; then boil another quart of cream, and when it is cold ſeaſon it with roſe-water and ſugar, ſtirring it a while; then turn out your cheeſes into a diſh, pour your cream about them, and ſcrape on ſugar.

To make Mrs. Skynner's freſh Cheeſe.

TAKE a pint of milk, and a pint of cream; boil it, and ſkim it, with a nutmeg quartered in it; when it boils up again, put in the yolks of three or four eggs well beaten, one whie, and the juice of two lemons; ſtir it once about to mix it; keep it hot upon the fire, but not to boil; and when it is all curdled drain your whey from them through a cloth; then put a ſpoonful of cold cream to it, and mix the curd and that well together, with ſugar to your taſte; put it in your pan, and when it is thorough cold, turn it upon your diſh, and eat it with cold cream and ſugar.

To make a Chedder Cheeſe.

TAKE the new milk of twelve cows in the morning, and the evening cream of twelve cows, putting to it three ſpoonfuls of rennet: when it is come, break it and whey it; that being done, break it again, work into the curd three pounds of freſh butter, put it in your preſs; turn it very often for an hour or more, and change the cloths, washing them every time you change them; you may put wet cloths at first to them, but towards the last put two or three fine dry cloths; let it lie thirty or forty hours in the press, according to the thickness of the cheese; then take it out, wash it in whey, and lay it in a dry cloth till it is dry; then lay it on your shelf, and turn it often.

The Queen's Cheese.

TAKE six quarts of the best stroakings, and let them stand till they are cold, then set two quarts of cream on the fire till it is ready to boil, take it off, and boil a quart of fair water, and take the yolks of two eggs, one spoonful of sugar, and two spoonfuls of rennet; mingle all these together, and stir it till it is but blood warm; when the cheese is come, use it as other cheese; set it at night, and the third day lay the leaves of nettles under and over it; it must be turned and wiped, and the nettles shifted every day, and in three weeks it will be fit to eat. This cheese is made between Michaelmas and Allhallowtide.

To make a thick Cream Cheese.

TAKE the morning's milk from the cow, and the cream of the night's milk, and rennet, pretty cool together, and when it is come, make it pretty much in the cheese-fat, and put in a little salt, and make the cheese thick in a deep mould, or a melon mould, if you have one; keep it a year and a half, or two years before you cut it; it must be well salted on the outside.

To make Slip-Coat Cheese.

TAKE new milk and rennet, quite cold, and when it is come, break it as little as you can in putting it into the cheese-fat; let it stand and whey itself for some time; then cover it, and set about two pound weight on it; when it will hold together, turn it out of that cheese-fat, and keep it turning upon clean cheese-fats for two or three days, till it has done wetting, and then lay it on sharp-pointed dock-leaves till it is ripe; shift the leaves often.

A Cream Cheese.

TAKE six quarts of new milk warm from the cow, and put to it three quarts of good cream, and rennet it; when it comes, put a cloth in the cheese mould, and with your flitting dish take it out in thin slices, and lay on your mould by degrees till it is all in; then let it stand with a cheese-board upon it till it is enough to turn, which will be at night: then salt it on both
sides

sides a little, and let it stand with a two pound weight on it all night; then take it out and put it into a dry cloth, and so do till it is dry; ripen it with laying it on nettles; shift the nettles every day.

To make a fresh Cheese.

TAKE a quart of cream, and set it over the fire till it is ready to boil, then beat nine eggs, yolks and white, very well; when you are beating them, put to them as much salt as will lie on a small knife's point; put them to the cream, with some nutmeg quartered, and tied up in a rag; let them boil till the whey is clear; then take it off the fire, put it in a pan, and gather it as you do cheese; then put it in a cloth, and drain it between two; then put it in a stone mortar, grind it, and season it with a little sack, orange-flower-water and sugar; then put it in a little earthen colander, and let it stand two hours to drain out the whey, then put it in the middle of a china dish and pour thick cream about it. So serve it to table.

To make Cream Cheese with old Cheshire.

TAKE a pound and a half of old Cheshire cheese, shave it all very thin, then put it in a mortar, and add to it a quarter of an ounce of mace beaten fine and sifted, half a pound of fresh butter, and a glass of sack; mix and beat all these together till they are perfectly incorporated; then put it in a pot what thickness you please, and cut it out in slices for cream cheese, and serve it with the desert.

To make Rennet.

TAKE a calf's bag, skewer it up, and let it lie a night in cold water, then turn out the curd into fresh water, wash and pick it very clean, and scour the bag inside and outside; then put a handful of salt to the curd, put it into a bag, skewer it up, and let it lie in a clean pot a year; then put half a pint of sack into the bag, and as much into the pot, and prick the bag, then bruise one nutmeg, four cloves, a little mace, and tie them up in a bit of thin cloth; put it into the pot, and now and then squeeze the spice cloth; in a few days you may use it; put a spoonful, or at most a spoonful and a half, to twenty quarts of milk.

To make a Rennet-Bag.

LET the calf suck as much as he will before he is killed, then take the bag out of the calf, and let it lie twelve hours, covered over in stinging nettles till it is very red; then take out your curd, wash your bag clean, salt it within-side and without,

out, letting it lie sprinkled with salt twenty-four hours; then wash your curd in warm new milk, pick it, and put away all that is yellow and hollow, keep what is white and close; then wash it well, and sprinkle it with salt; when the bag has lain twenty-four hours, put it into the bag again, and put to it three spoonfuls of the stroakings of a cow, beat up with the yolk of an egg or two, twelve cloves, and two blades of mace; put a skewer through it, and hang it in a pot; then make the rennet water thus:

Take half a pint of fair water, a little salt, and six tops of the red buds of black-thorn, as many sprigs of burnet, and two of sweet marjoram; boil these in the water, and strain it out, when it is cold put one half in the bag, and let the bag lie in the other half, taking it out as you use it; when you want, make more rennet, which you may do six or seven times; three spoonfuls of this will make a large Cheshire or Chedder cheese, and half as much to a common cheese.

PART

PART V.

Of FOREIGN DISHES.

CHAP. I.
Of FRENCH DISHES.

As the French are esteemed to be very elegant in their dishes, or, however, as their cookery is much in vogue with persons in high life, we shall give three of their dishes, communicated by a noted cook.

To prepare Bouillion, or Broth.

INSTEAD of the leg or shin of beef (which are the common pieces in your two-penny cut shops) take eight or ten pounds of the lean part, which, in London, is called the mouse-buttock, with a little knuckle of veal, neatly trimmed, that it may serve to send up in your soup. A pot that holds three or four gallons will do. When you have washed your meat, put it over the stove full of water; take care that it is well skimmed before it boils, or you will lose the whole beauty of your soups and sauces; sprinkle in a little salt now and then, and it will cause the scum to rise; let it but just boil upon the stove, but take it off, and to simmer sideways, then all the soil will sink to the bottom; to season it take ten or twelve large sound onions, eight or ten whole carrots, three or four turneps, a parsnip, two or three leeks, and a little bundle of celery tied up, a few cloves, a blade or two of mace, and some whole white pepper; let it boil no longer than the meat is thoroughly boiled to eat; (for to boil it to rags, as is the common practice) it makes the broth thick and grouty, and spoils the pleasing aspect of all your dinner, and hurts the meat that thousands of families would leap mast-high at; strain it through a lawn sieve into a clean earthen pan, skim the fat off.

Beef A-la-mode.

TAKE a piece of the buttock of beef, and some fat bacon cut into little long bits, then take two tea-spoonfuls of salt, one tea spoonful of beaten pepper, one of beaten mace, and one of nutmeg; mix all together, have your larding-pins ready, first dip the bacon in vinegar, then roll it in your spice, and lard your beef very thick and nice; put the meat into a pot with two or three large onions, a good piece of lemon-peel, a bundle of herbs, and three or four spoonfuls of vinegar; cover it down close, and put a wet cloth round the edge of the cover, that no steam can get out, and set it over a very slow fire : when you think one side is done enough, turn the other, and cover it with the rind of the bacon; cover the pot close again as before, and when it is enough (which it will be when quite tender) take it up and lay it in your dish; take off all the fat from the gravy, and pour the gravy over the meat. If you chuse your beef to be red, you may rub it with salt-petre over night.

Note, You must take great care in doing your beef this way that your fire is very slow; it will at least take six hours doing, if the piece be any thing large. If you would have the sauce very rich, boil half an ounce of truffles and morels in half a pint of good gravy till they are very tender, and add a gill of pickled mushrooms, but fresh ones are best; mix all together with the gravy of the meat, and pour it over your beef. You must mind and beat all your spices very fine; and if you have not enough, mix some more, according to the bigness of your beef.

Another Method.

TAKE a good buttock of beef interlarded with great lard, rolled up in savoury spice and sweet-herbs; put it in a great saucepan, and cover it close, and set in the oven all night. This is fit to eat cold. The common beef a-la-mode is made of the mouse buttock.

Beef A-la-mode in Pieces.

CUT a buttock of beef into two-pound pieces, lard them with bacon, fry them brown, put them into a pot that will just hold them, put in two quarts of broth or gravy, a few sweet-herbs, an onion, some mace, cloves, nutmeg, pepper and salt; when that is done, cover it close, and stew it till it is tender; skim off all the fat, lay the meat in the dish, and strain the sauce over it. Serve it up hot or cold.

Beef Escarlot.

A BRISKET of beef, half a pound of coarse sugar, two ounces of bay salt, a pound of common salt; mix all together, and rub the beef, lay it in an earthen pan, and turn it every day. It may lie a fortnight in the pickle; then boil it, and serve it up either with savoys, or pease pudding.

Note, It eats much finer cold, cut into slices, and sent to table.

Beef A-la-daub.

LARD a buttock or rump, fry it brown in some sweet butter, then put it into a pot that will just hold it; put in some broth or gravy hot, some pepper, cloves, mace, and a bundle of sweet-herbs; stew it four hours, till it is tender, and season it with salt; take half a pint of gravy, two sweet-breads cut into eight pieces, some truffles and morels, palates, artichoke-bottoms, and mushrooms, boil all together, lay your beef into the dish; strain the liquor into the sauce, and boil all together. If it is not thick enough, roll a piece of butter in flour, and boil in it; pour this all over the beef. Take forcemeat rolled in pieces half as long as one's finger; dip them into batter made with eggs, and fry them brown; fry some sippets dipped into batter cut three corner-ways, stick them into the meat, and garnish with forcemeat.

A Piece of Beef trembling.

A RUMP of beef is the best piece for this; but it must be vastly cut and trimmed; cut the edge of the ache-bone off quite close to the meat, that it may lay flat in your dish, and if it is large, cut it at the chump-end so as to make it square; hang it up for three or four days, or more, without salt; prepare a marinade as before, and leave it all night in soak, fillet it two or three times across, and put it into a pot, the fat uppermost; put in as much water as will a little more than cover it, take care to skim it well, and season as you would for a good broth, adding about a pint of white wine; let it simmer for as long a time as it will hang together; there are many sauces for this piece of meat, but the two favourites with * Clouet were, sauce aux carrots, and sauce hachée; sauce with carrots, and a sauce of herbs, &c. minced. Your carrots should be cut an inch long, and boiled a little in water, and afterwards stewed in some cullis proportionate to your meat; when they are done tender, dash in a glass of white wine, a little minced eschalot and parsley, and the juice of a lemon; take your beef out upon a cloth, clean it neatly from its fat and liquor; place it hot and whole in your dish, and pour your sauce hot over it, and serve it up.

* Late cook to the Duke of Newcastle.

To boil a Rump of Beef the French fashion.

TAKE a rump of beef, boil it half an hour, take it up, lay it into a large deep pewter dish or stew-pan, cut three or four gashes in it all along the side, rub the gashes with pepper and salt, and pour into the dish a pint of red wine, as much hot water, two or three large onions cut small, the hearts of eight or ten lettuces cut small, and a good piece of butter rolled in a little flour; lay the fleshy part of the meat downwards, cover it close, let it stew an hour and a half over a charcoal fire, or a very slow coal fire. Observe that the butcher chops the bone so close, that the meat may lie as flat as you can in the dish. When it is enough, take the beef, lay it in the dish, and pour the sauce over it.

Note, When you do it in a pewter dish, it is best done over a chaffing-dish of hot coals, with a bit or two of charcoal to keep it alive.

Sweet-breads A-la-daub.

TAKE three of the largest and finest sweet-breads you can get, and put them in a saucepan of boiling water for five minutes; then take them out, and when they are cold, lard them with a row down the middle, with very little pieces of bacon; then a row on each side with lemon-peel cut the size of wheat straw, and then a row on each side of pickled cucumbers, cut very fine; put them in a tossing-pan, with good veal gravy, a little juice of lemon, a spoonful of browning; stew them gently a quarter of an hour; a little before they are ready thicken them with flour and butter; dish them up, and pour the gravy over; lay round them bunches of boiled celery or oyster patties. Garnish with stewed spinach, green-coloured parsley, and stick a bunch of barberries in the middle of each sweet-bread. —It is a pretty corner-dish for either dinner or supper.

A Leg of Mutton A-la-royal.

LARD your mutton and slices of veal with bacon rolled in spice and sweet-herbs; bring them to a brown with melted lard; boil the leg of mutton in strong broth, with all sorts of sweet-herbs, and an onion stuck with cloves; when it is ready lay it on the dish, lay round the collops, then pour on it a ragoo. Garnish with lemon and orange.

A Goose, Turkey, or Leg of Mutton A-la-daube.

LARD it with bacon, and half roast it; take it off the spit, and put it in as small a pot as will boil it; put to it a quart of of white wine, strong broth, a pint of vinegar, whole spice, bay-leaves, sweet-marjoram, winter-savoury, and green onions. When it is ready, lay it in the dish, make sauce with some of the liquor, mushrooms, diced lemon, two or three anchovies; thicken it with brown butter, and garnish it with sliced lemon.

Ducks A-la-mode.

TAKE two fine ducks, cut them into quarters, fry them in butter a little brown, then pour out all the fat, and throw a little flour over them; and half a pint of good gravy, a quarter of a pint of red wine, two eschalots, an anchovy, and a bundle of sweet-herbs; cover them close, and let them stew a quarter of an hour; take out the herbs, skim off the fat, and let your sauce be as thick as cream; send it to table, and garnish with lemon.

To boil Ducks the French Way.

LET your ducks be larded, and half roasted, then take them off the spit, put them into a large earthen pipkin, with half a pint of red wine, and a pint of good gravy, some chesnuts, first roasted and peeled, half a pint of large oysters, the liquor strained, and the beards taken off, two or three little onions minced small, a very little stripped thyme, mace, pepper, and a little ginger beat fine; cover it close, and let them stew half an hour over a slow fire, and the crust of a French roll grated when you put in your gravy and wine; when they are enough take them up, and pour the sauce over them.

To stew a Hare.

TAKE a young hare (a leveret is another thing) and cut into ten pieces, the two legs, two wings or shoulders, the chine in four, and the stomach and skirts in two, do not blanch them, but skim your wine, &c. well; put it into your stew-pan, with about three half-pints of port wine, two or three onions, a carrot or two, some sweet-basil, thyme, and parsley, and a ladle of gravy, a little salt and pepper, a clove or two, and a bit of mace, and let it stew gently for two hours; take out your hare clean into another stew-pan, and strain your sauce to it, adding a ladle of cullis, and if not thick enough, put in a bit of butter and flour, and boil it a minute, and keep it hot till your dinner is ready; fling in a spoonful or two of capers, some minced parsley, and the juice of a lemon or orange, and serve it up with some fried bits of bread in the dish and round it.

To dress a Pig the French Way.

SPIT your pig, lay it down to the fire, let it roast till it is thoroughly warm, then cut it off the spit, and divide it in twenty pieces. Set them to stew in half a pint of white wine, and a pint of strong broth, seasoned with grated nutmeg, pepper, two onions cut small, and some stripped thyme. Let it stew an hour, then put to it half a pint of strong gravy, a piece of butter rolled in flour, some anchovies, and a spoonful of vinegar, or mushroom pickle: when it is enough, lay it in your dish, and pour the gravy over it, then garnish with orange and lemon.

The best Method of dissecting, preparing, and dressing a Turtle.

TO dissect it, let its head be chopped off close to the shell, set it on that part that all the blood may run away, have plenty of water in several pails or tubs, lay your fish upon the back, or callepash, cut off the under-shell or callepee, in the first line or partition from the edge of the callepash, take that off, and immediately put it into water; next cut off the four fins in the shoulder and ache-bone joints, and put into water too, and with a cleaver chop out the bones from the shoulders and hinder parts, and put to the rest; take out your guts and tripe clean, and the other entrails, and lay your callepash in water while you prepare your callepee, which should be done as follows: Cut off all superfluous bits for your soup, and trim it neatly; cut little holes in the thick flesh, with the point of your knife, lay it in a dish, and soak it well in Madeira wine, and season with Cayan pepper (but not too much) a little salt, plenty of eschalot and parsley minced and strewed upon it; next take the callepash, and order in the same manner, first cutting off the shell to the crease on the other side of the edge, and put a neat rim of paste quite round, and adorn it well; pour a little cullis round, and squeeze the juice of some lemons or oranges and they are ready for your oven: the common way is to put some of the flesh into the callepash, but in my opinion it is best to put none. The next to be made ready is your fins and head; blanch them till you can take off the outer skin, trim them, and put them into a stew-pan with the head, pour in some Madeira, a ladle of broth, a pinch of Cayan, a small bunch of onions, herbs, and eschalots, and stew them tender with a little salt, and it is ready; the two biggest fins for one dish, and the head and two smallest for another; now cut the side shells in pieces, and blanch them so that you may take the gristles or

jelly-

jelly-part out whole; while this is doing prepare the tripe or guts with a sharp knife, flit them from end to end; and care muſt be taken that all is waſhed and ſcraped clean, cut them into pieces about two inches in length, and blanch them; when your broth is made of the fleſh, to the tripe in a ſtew-pan put as much as will cover it, put in a bunch of herbs, with an onion or two, a couple of whole eſchalots, ſome mace, and a little ſalt; ſtew all till pretty tender; take out the herbs, &c. and put butter and flour to thicken it; provide a liaiſon as for a fricaſey of chickens, and at your dinner-time toſs it up with the juice of lemon or orange, and it is ready. Next take the jellies of your ſide ſhells, and prepare for a diſh done in the ſame manner as the fins and head; ſqueeze in ſome juice of orange or lemon, and it is ready. And now for the ſoup; moſt of which that I have ſeen or taſted has been poor inſipid ſtuff: to ſay why it was is ſaying leſs than nothing. The whole matter is, to ſhew how it may be made good: thus, they cut all the fleſh from the bones into ſmall pieces, and to about a pound of meat put a quart of water, and to five or ſix quarts a pint of Madeira: take care that it is well ſkimmed; tie up in a bit of lnen three or four onions, ſome bits of carrot, a leek, ſome herbs and parſley, with two or three pinches of Cayan; and let it boil with the meat; add ſalt according to your taſte; let it ſimmer an hour or a little more, and ſend it up in a terrine or ſoup-diſh only the meat and broth.

Theſe ſeven diſhes make a pretty firſt courſe, the callepaſh and callepee at the top and bottom, ſoup in the middle, and the other four the corners.

The Queen's Soup.

TO make a proper ſtock for this, to about three quarts of broth put about a pound of lean veal and ſome bits of ham, two or three whole onions, carrots, parſley, and a blade of mace; boil it all together as you do gravy, for an hour; take all from your broth, and ſtir in the white part of a roaſted fowl or chicken, and about two ounces of ſweet almonds blanched, and both well pounded, the yolks of three or four hard eggs maſhed, with the ſoft of a manchet boiled in good milk or cream; rub it well through an etamine*, and pour it into your ſoup pot; take care to keep it boiling hot, but never let it boil a moment over your ſtove, but keep it moving; provide ſome cruſts well ſoaked, and a chicken in your diſh, and ſerve it up, with a little of your beſt gravy poured in circles and patches. This is the moſt modern way.

* Etamine, mentioned above, is a ſtuff uſed for a ſtrainer.

To make Nantile Soup.

NANTILES are a sort of grain that come from abroad, and are sold at most of the oil-shops in London, in shape like a vetch or tare, but much less. Take about a quart of them, and boil in water only till very tender, for your stock. You must be so extravagant as to have a roasted partridge; pick off the flesh, and I will presently shew the use of it; the bones you may crush to pieces, and put to them some bits of ham, with about three quarts of broth and gravy mixed: add to it as before, onions, carrots, and parsley; boil this as the last; take all from it; see that your partridge meat is well pounded, and your nantiles, and stir them into your broth, and let them boil a few minutes; strain it through your etamine, and serve it with a partridge in the middle, and some thin morsels of bacon for garnish, which may be both boiled in your broth, being well blanched: have some crusts soaked as before, and serve it up.

To make Water Souchy.

TO make this in perfection you should have several sorts of small fish, flounders, gudgeons, eels, perch, and a pike or two; but it is often with perch only; they ought to be very fresh; take care all is very clean, for what they are boiled in is the soup: cut little notches in all, and put them a little while in fresh spring water; (this is what is called crimping of fish in London); put them into a stew-pan with as much water as you think will fill your dish, half a pint of white wine, a spoonful or two of vinegar, and as much salt as you would for broth. Put them over your fire in cold water, and take particular care you skim it well in boiling; provide some parsley-roots cut in slices, and boiled very tender, and a large quantity of leaves of parsley boiled nice and green. When your fish have boiled gently for a quarter of an hour take them from the fire, and put in your roots, and when you serve it to table strew your leaves over it; take care not to break your fish, and pour your liquor on softly and hot; some plates of bread and butter are generally served up with this, so be sure to have them ready.

To make Herb Soup without Meat.

FOR the summer season three or four carrots, a little bunch of green onions, a few beet-leaves, and a handful of spinach and sorrel, a little purslane and chervil, and two or three lettuces, and some spice and pepper, strip all into small bits, and fry them in a large stew pan, with a bit of fresh butter: pour in about two quarts of water, and let it boil gently for an hour at least, strain it off to the soft of a French roll well soaked, and

and pass it through your etamine; prepare a heart or two of nice light savoys or cabbage, a couple of lettuce, and a handful or two of young pease, stew them well, and drain them upon a sieve; when it draws towards your dinner-time have ready the yolks of half a dozen eggs, mixed well with half a pint of cream; put your pease, &c. into the soup, and boil it for a few minutes, a few slices of white bread, then your cream and eggs; stir it well together, cover it down very close till you are ready for it; just shew it to the fire, and send it up. This soup is frequently done with cucumbers quartered, and the seed cut out, instead of the things before mentioned. For the winter, celery and endives, white beet-roots, sliced thin, or the bottoms of artichokes, which in some families are preserved for such uses, and in most of the oil shops in and about London.

A Matelotte of Chickens with Mushrooms.

CUT your chickens as for a fricasey, the legs and wings, pinions, breast and back in two, blanch them in water for two or three minutes, put them into a stew-pan, with a bit or two of ham, a ladle of gravy and cullis mixed, seasoned with a bunch of onions and parsley, a little sweet-basil, a morsel of eschalot, pepper, salt, a blade of mace; stew all together gently for an hour.

N. B. This sauce may serve for several good uses; but for your matelotte prepare it with a ladle or two of your cullis, with a few nice button mushrooms, put in your chickens, and stew all together, with a little pepper, salt, and nutmeg, add the juice of a lemon or orange and serve it up. The reason of changing the sauce is, that your dish may have a decent appearance: your mushrooms would be broke, and your herbs, &c. by so long stewing, be crumbled, and spoil the beauty of the most favourite dish of all.

This is often done with pease or tops of asparagus.

Rabbets collared with Sauce a l'Ivernoise.

TWO couple of rabbets for this dish I think is not too many: take care to take the bones out quite up to the wings or shoulders, but leave them on with the head; prepare a nice hot forcemeat of some bits of the rabbets that may be spared, a bit of veal or lamb fat, a little scraped bacon, a morsel of green onion, a mushroom, pepper, salt, and a little parsley, fry all together for a few minutes; put it into a mortar with some soft of a French roll soaked in cream or milk, a little nutmeg; pound all well together with the yolks of two or three eggs; spread your rabbets in a dish, and lay your forcemeat on, roll them up to the wings, and bind it with a bit of packthread; stew them in a braize about an hour and a half, and prepare your
sauce

sauce thus: It is a sort of sauce hachée, as you have seen before, only to this you cannot put too many sorts of strong herbs, such as tarragon, pimpernel, thyme, marjoram, and savoury, a green onion or two, mushrooms, and a bit of eschalot, all minced very fine and separate; to a ladle or two of gravy and cullis mixt, put in just as much of each as will make palatable in boiling a quarter of an hour with pepper, salt, and nutmeg, and a spoonful or two of good oil; throw in a handful of capers, clean your rabbets well from grease, add the juice of a couple of lemons or oranges, and dish up, with your sauce over.

Hodge-podge of Beef, with Savoys.

PROVIDE a piece of the middlemost part of brisket-beef about six pounds, cut it in square pieces so as to make ten or twelve of it; do not put it into too big a pot, but such a one as will be full with a gallon of water to it; take care to skim it well, and season it well with onions, carrots, turneps, leeks and celery, and a little bundle of parsley, and some pepper; when your meat is boiled very tender, strain your broth from it, and put it into a soup-pot or stew-pan; take another with an ounce or little more of butter; melt it, and put in a large spoonful of flour, stir it over the fire till it becomes brown, take the fat off your broth, and put to it, boil it a few minutes, and strain to your beef; your savoys should be well blanched, and tied up separate, put them into your meat, and let it stew very gently till your dinner is called; take it off and clean all from the fat, place your meat in neat order in your dish or soup-dish, lay your savoys between, pour you soup or sauce over it, and serve it up with a little parsley sprinkled genteely over it. This dish is frequently sent to table with turneps or carrots instead of savoys, cut in neat bits and boiled, before you put them to your soup.—It is but to say, des tendrons aux carrots, i. e. with carrots; or aux navets, with turneps.

Hodge-podge of veal or mutton is done after the same manner, with this difference only, instead of making your soup brown, stir your flour no longer than while it retains its whiteness, and pour your broth in, and strain to your meat.

To make Pease Soup without Meat.

FOR this soup a great quantity of garden things is used, five or six large onions, as many carrots, and a turnep or two, three or four leeks, celery, plenty of spinach, sorrel, parsley, and mint; cut and slice all these into a large stew-pan, and fry as before, pour in about three quarts of water, (for some will be lost amongst so many roots and herbs), and boil about an hour and an half very softly, strain into a pan with some soft bread, and pass it through your etamine; prepare some blue or white pease, which is best liked or handiest, well pounded, and stir it from the lumps and strain it again, rubbing the pease well though; have some celery and endive, well boiled, a little spinach and sorrel cut and boiled with your soup; provide some white bread fried in small dice in a bit of good butter; strew it in your soup when it is dished up, and serve it to table.

Take care it does not burn, for it is very apt to do so when your pease are to it, so keep it stirring.

Pease Françoise.

TAKE a quart of shelled pease, cut a large Spanish onion or two middling ones small, and two cabbage or Silesia lettuces, cut small, put them into a saucepan, with half a pint of water, season them with a little salt, a little beaten pepper, and a little beaten mace and nutmeg. Cover them close, and let them stew a quarter of an hour, then put in a quarter of a pound of fresh butter rolled in a little flour, a spoonful of catchup, a little piece of burnt butter as big as a nutmeg; cover them close, and let it simmer softly an hour, often shaking the pan. When it is enough, serve it up for a side-dish.

For an alteration, you may stew the ingredients as above: then take a small cabbage lettuce, and half boil it, then drain it, cut the stalks flat at the bottom, so that it will stand firm in the dish, and with a knife very carefully cut out the middle, leaving the outside leaves whole. Put what you cut out into a saucepan, chop it, and put a piece of butter, a little pepper, salt, and nutmeg, the yolk of an hard egg chopped, a few crumbs of bread, mix all together, and when it is hot fill your cabbage; put some butter into a stew-pan, tie your cabbage, and fry it till you think it is enough; then take it up, untie it, and first pour the ingredients of pease into your dish, set the forced cabbage in the middle, and have ready four artichoke-bottoms fried, and cut in two, and laid round the dish. This will do for a top-dish.

To make a French Pye.

TO two pounds of flour, put three quarters of a pound of butter; make it into a paste, and raise the walls of the pye; then roll out some paste thin as for a lid, cut it into vine leaves, or the figures of any moulds you have; if you have no moulds, you may make use of a crocran, and pick out pretty shapes; beat the yolks of two eggs, rub the outside of the walls of the pye with it, lay the vine leaves or shapes round the walls, and rub them over with the eggs; fill the pye with the bones of the meat, to keep the pye in shape, and lay a thin lid on to keep the steam in, that the crust may be well soaked; it is to go to table without a lid.

Take

Take a calf's-head, wash and clean it well, boil it half an hour, when it is cold cut it in thin slices, and put it in a tossing-pan, with three pints of veal gravy, and three sweet-breads cut thin, and let it stew one hour, with half an ounce of morels, and half an ounce of truffles; then have ready two calves feet boiled and boned, cut them in small pieces, and put them into your tossing-pan, with a spoonful of lemon-pickle, and one of browning, Cayan pepper, and a little salt; when the meat is tender, thicken the gravy a little with flour and butter, strain it, and put in a few pickled mushrooms, but fresh ones, if you can get them; put the meat into the pye you took the bones out of, and lay the nicest part at the top, have ready a quarter of a hundred of asparagus heads, strew them over the top of the pye, and serve it up.

Receipt to make French Bread.

BEAT two eggs with a little salt, lay to them half a pint of ale-yeast, or more; then put to it three pounds of fine flour, and put into it as much blood-warm milk as will make it soft and light; then make it into loaves or rolls, and, when baked and cold, rasp or grate all the outside off, and then it is fit to set at table.

CHAP. II.
Of JEWISH, SPANISH, DUTCH, GERMAN, and ITALIAN DISHES.

Other nations and people have their peculiar ways of cooking, and do not eat such quantities of solid food as the English do; two or three of their dishes may, perhaps, now and then suit a British appetite, and afford a greater variety of dishes for the Complete Housewife.

To stew green Pease the Jews way.

TO two full quarts of pease put in a full quarter of a pint of oil and water, not so much water as oil; a little different sort of spices, as mace, clove, pepper, and nutmeg, all beat fine; a little Cayan pepper, a little salt; let all this stew in a broad flat pipkin; when they are half done, with a spoon make two or three holes; into each of these holes break an egg, yolk and white; take one egg and beat it, and throw over the whole when enough, which you will know by tasting them; and the egg being quite hard, send them to table.

If

The COMPLETE HOUSEWIFE. 205

If they are not done in a very broad open thing, it will be a great difficulty to get them out to lie in a dish.

They would be better done in a silver or tin dish, on a stew-hole, and go to table in the same dish: it is much better than putting them out into another dish.

Marmalade of Eggs the Jews way.

TAKE the yolks of twenty-four eggs, beat them for an hour; clarify one pound of the best moist sugar, four spoonfuls of orange-flower-water, one ounce of blanched and pounded almonds; stir all together over a very slow charcoal fire, keeping stirring it all the while one way, till it comes to a consistence; then put it into coffee-cups, and throw a little beaten cinnamon on the top of the cups.

This marmalade, mixed with pounded almonds, with orange-peel, and citron, are made in cakes of all shapes, such as birds, fish, and fruit.

English Jews Puddings; an excellent dish for six or seven people, for the expence of six-pence.

TAKE a calf's-lights, boil them, chop them fine, and the crumb of a two-penny loaf softened in the liquor the lights were boiled in; mix them well together in a pan; take about half a pound of kidney fat of a loin of veal or mutton that is roasted, or beef; if you have none, take suet; if you can get none, melt a little butter and mix in; fry four or five onions, cut small and fried in dripping, not brown, only soft; a very little winter-savoury and thyme, a little lemon-peel shred fine; season with all-spice, pepper, and salt to your palate, break in two eggs; mix it all well together, and have ready some sheep's guts nicely cleaned, and fill them and fry them in dripping. This is a very good dish, and a fine thing for poor people; because all sort of lights are good, and will do, as hog's, sheep's, and bullock's, but calf's are best; a handful of parsley boiled and chopped fine, is very good, mixed with the meat. Poor people may, instead of the fat above, mix the fat the onions were fried in, and they will be very good.

To dress Haddocks the Jews Way.

TAKE two large fine haddocks, wash them very clean, cut them in slices about three inches thick, and dry them in a cloth; take a gill either of oil or butter in a stew-pan, a middling onion cut small, a handful of parsley washed and cut small; let it just boil up in either butter or oil, then put in the fish; season it with beaten mace, pepper, and salt, half a pint of soft water;

let

let it stew softly, till it is thoroughly done: then take the yolks of two eggs, beat up with the juice of a lemon, and just as it is done enough, throw it over, and send it to table.

Artichoke-Suckers dressed the Spanish Way.

CLEAN and wash them, and cut them in half; then boil them in water, drain them from the water, and put them into a stew-pan, with a little oil, a little water, and a little vinegar; season them with pepper and salt; stew them a little while, and then thicken them with the yolks of eggs.

They make a pretty garnish done thus; clean them and half boil them; then dry them, flour them, and dip them in yolks of eggs, and fry them brown.

Artichokes preserved the Spanish Way.

TAKE the largest you can get, cut the tops of the leaves off, wash them well and drain them; to every artichoke pour in a large spoonful of oil, seasoned with pepper and salt. Send them to the oven, and bake them, they will keep a year.

N. B. The Italians, French, Portuguese, and Spaniards, have variety of ways of dressing fish, which we have not, viz.

As making fish soups, ragoos, pyes, &c.

For their soups they use no gravy, nor in their sauces, thinking it improper to mix flesh and fish together; but make their fish soups with fish, viz. either of cray-fish, lobsters, &c. taking only the juice of them.

For Example.

TAKE your cray fish, tie them up in a muslin rag, and boil them; then press out their juice for the abovesaid use.

For their Pyes.

THEY make some of carp, others of different fish: and some they make like our minced pyes, viz. They take a carp, and cut the flesh from the bones, and mince it, adding currants, &c.

Asparagus dressed the Spanish Way.

TAKE the asparagus, break them in pieces, then boil them soft, and drain the water from them: take a little oil, water and vinegar, let it boil, season it with pepper and salt, throw in the asparagus, and thicken with yolks of eggs.

Endive done this way is good; the Spaniards add sugar, but that spoils them. Green peafe done as above, are very good; only add a lettuce cut small, and two or three onions, and leave out the eggs.

A Spanish

A Spanish Pease Soup.

TAKE one pound of spanish pease, and lay them in water the night before you use them; then take a gallon of water, one quart of fine sweet oil, a head of garlic; cover the pot close, and let it boil till the pease are soft; then season with pepper and salt: then beat up the yolk of an egg, and vinegar to your palate; poach some eggs, lay in the dish on sippets, and pour the soup on them. Send it to table.

To make Onion Soup the Spanish Way.

TAKE two large Spanish onions, peel and slice them; let them boil very softly in half a pint of sweet oil till the onions are very soft; then pour on them three pints of boiling water; season with beaten pepper, salt, a little beaten clove and mace, two spoonfuls of vinegar, a handful of parsley washed clean, and chopped fine; let it boil fast a quarter of an hour; in the mean time, get some sippets to cover the bottom of the dish, fried quick, not hard; lay them in the dish, and cover each sippet with a poached egg; beat up the yolks of two eggs, and throw over them; pour in your soup, and send it to table.

Garlic and sorrel, done the same way, eats well.

Cauliflowers dressed the Spanish Way.

BOIL them, but not too much; then drain them, and put them into a stew-pan; to a large cauliflower put a quarter of a pint of sweet oil, and two or three cloves of garlic; let them fry till brown; then season them with pepper and salt, two or three spoonfuls of vinegar; cover the pan very close, and let them simmer over a very slow fire an hour.

To dress Haddocks after the Spanish Way.

TAKE a haddock, washed very clean and dried, and broil it nicely; then take a quarter of a pint of oil in a stew-pan, season it with mace, cloves, and nutmeg, pepper and salt, two cloves of garlic, some love-apples, when in season, a little vinegar; put in the fish, cover it close, and let it stew half an hour over a slow fire.

Flounders done the same way, are very good.

A Cake the Spanish Way.

TAKE twelve eggs, three quarters of a pound of the best moist sugar, mill them in a chocolate-mill till they are all of a lather; then mix in one pound of flour, half a pound of pounded almonds, two ounces of candied orange-peel, two ounces of citron,

citron, four large spoonfuls of orange-water, half an ounce of cinnamon, and a glass of sack. It is better when baked in a slow oven.

Milk Soup the Dutch Way.

TAKE a quart of milk, boil it with cinnamon and moist sugar; put sippets in the dish, pour the milk over it, and let it over a charcoal fire to simmer, till the bread is soft. Take the yolks of two eggs, beat them up, and mix with a little of the milk, and throw it in; mix it all together, and send it up to table.

Carrots and French Beans dressed the Dutch Way.

SLICE the carrots very thin, and just cover them with water; season them with pepper and salt, cut a good many onions and parsley small, a piece of butter; let them simmer over a slow fire till done. Do French beans the same way.

Red Cabbage dressed after the Dutch Way.

TAKE the cabbage, cut it small, and boil it soft, then drain it, and put in a stew pan, with a sufficient quantity of oil and butter, a little water and vinegar, and an onion cut small; season it with pepper and salt, and let it simmer on a slow fire till all the liquor is wasted.

Minced Haddocks after the Dutch Way.

BOIL them, and take out all the bones, mince them very fine with parsley and onions; season with nutmeg, pepper and salt, and stew them in butter, just enough to keep moist: squeeze the juice of a lemon, and when cold, mix them up with eggs, and put into a puff-paste.

Beans dressed the German Way.

TAKE a large bunch of onions, peel and slice them, a great quantity of parsley washed and cut small, throw them into a stew-pan, with a pound of butter; season them well with pepper and salt, put in two quarts of beans; cover them close, and let them do till the beans are brown, shaking the pan often. Do pease the same way.

Fish Pasties the Italian Way.

TAKE some flour, and knead it with oil; take a slice of salmon; season it with pepper and salt, and dip into sweet oil, chop onion and parsley fine, and strew over it; lay it in the paste,

paste, and double it up in the shape of a slice of salmon: take a piece of white paper, oil it, and lay under the pasty, and bake it; it is best cold, and will keep a month.

Mackarel done the same way; head and tail together folded in a pasty, eats fine.

To dress Mutton the Turkish Way.

FIRST cut your meat into thin slices, then wash it in vinegar, and put it into a pot or saucepan that has a close cover to it, put in some rice, whole pepper, and three or four whole onions; let all these stew together, skimming it frequently: when it is enough, take out the onions, and season it with salt to your palate, lay the mutton in the dish, and pour the rice and liquor over it.

Note, The neck or leg are the best joints to dress this way. Put in to a leg four quarts of water, and a quarter of a pound of rice; to a neck two quarts of water, and two ounces of rice. To every pound of meat allow a quarter of an hour, being close covered. If you put in a blade or two of mace, and a bundle of sweet-herbs, it will be a great addition. When it is just enough put in a piece of butter, and take care the rice don't burn to the pot. In all these things you should lay skewers at the bottom of the pot to lay your meat on, that it may not stick.

To make a fricasey of Calves-feet and Chaldron, after the Italian way.

TAKE the crumb of a three-penny loaf, one pound of suet, a large onion, two or three handfuls of parsley, mince it very small, season it with salt and pepper, three or four cloves of garlick, mix with eight or ten eggs; then stuff the chaldron; take the feet and put them in a deep stew-pan: it must stew upon a slow fire till the bones are loose; then take two quarts of green pease, and put in the liquor; and when done, you must thicken it with the yolks of two eggs and the juice of a lemon. It must be seasoned with pepper, salt, mace, and onion, some parsley and garlick. You must serve it up with the abovesaid pudding in the middle of the dish, and garnish the dish with fried suckers, and sliced onion.

To fricasey Pigeons the Italian Way.

QUARTER them, and fry them in oil; take some green pease, and let them fry in the oil till they are almost ready to burst; then put some boiling water to them; season it with salt, pepper, onions, garlick, parsley and vinegar. Veal and lamb do the same way, and thicken with yolks of eggs.

Terms of Art for Carving.

Barbel, to tusk
Bittern, to disjoint
Brawn, to leach
Bream, to splay
Brew, to untach
Bustard, to cut up
Capon, to souce
Chevin, to fin
Chicken, to frush
Coney, to unlace
Crab, to tame
Crane, to display
Curlew, to untach
Deer, to break
Eel, to transon
Egg, to tire
Egript, to break
Flounder, to sauce
Goose, to rear
Haddock, to side
Hen, to spoil
Hern, to dismember
Lamprey, to string
Lobster, to barb
Mullard, to unbrace
Partridge, to wing
Pasty, to border
Peacock, to disfigure
Pheasant, to allay
Pigeon, to thigh
Pike, to splat
Plover, to mince
Quail, to wring
Salmon, to chine
Small Birds, to thigh
Sturgeon, to tranch
Swan, to lift
Tench, to sauce
Trout, to culpon
Turkey, to cut up
Woodcock, to thigh.

Instructions for Carving according to these Terms of Art.

To unjoint a Bittern.

RAISE his wings and legs as a hern, and no other sauce but salt.

To cut up a Bustard.

See Turkey.

To souce a Capon.

TAKE a capon, and lift up the right leg, and so array forth, and lay in the platter; serve your chicken in the same manner, and sauce them with green sauce, or verjuice.

To unlace a Coney.

TURN the back downward, and cut the flaps or apron from the belly or kidney; then put in your knife between the kidneys, and loosen the flesh from the bone, on each side; then turn the belly downward, and cut the back cross between the wings, drawing your knife down on each side the back-bone, dividing the legs and sides from the back; pull not the leg too hard,

hard, when you open the side from the bone; but with your hand and knife neatly lay open both sides from the scut to the shoulder; then lay the legs close together.

To display a Crane.

UNFOLD his legs; then cut off his wings by the joints; after this take up his legs and wings, and sauce them with vinegar, salt, mustard, and powdered ginger.

To unbrace a Duck.

RAISE up the pinions and legs, but take them not off, and raise the merry-thought from the breast; then lace it down each side of the breast with your knife, wriggling your knife to and fro, that the furrows may lie in and out; after the same manner unbrace the mallard.

To rear a Goose.

TAKE off both legs fair, like shoulders of lamb; then cut off the belly-piece round close to the end of the breast; then lace your goose down on both sides of the breast half an inch from the sharp bone; then take off the pinion on each side, and the flesh you first laced with your knife; raise it up clean from the bone, and take it off with the pinion from the body; then cut up the merry-thought; then cut from the breast-bone another slice of flesh quite through; then turn up your carcase, and cut it asunder, the back bone above the loin-bones; then take the rump-end of the back bone and lay it in a dish, with the skinny side upwards; lay at the fore-end of it the merry-thought, with the skinny side upwards, and before that the apron of the goose; then lay the pinions on each side contrary, set the legs on each side contrary behind them, that the bone-ends of the legs may stand up cross in the middle of the dish, and the wing-pinions may come on the outside of them; put the long slice which you cut from the breast-bone, under the wing-pinions on each side, and let the ends meet under the leg-bones, and let the other ends lie cut in the dish betwixt the leg and the pinion; then pour in your sauce under the meat; throw on salt, and serve it to table again.

To dismember a Hern.

TAKE off both the legs, and lace it down the breast on both sides with your knife, and open the breast-pinion, but take it not off; then raise up the merry-thought between the breast-bone and the top of it; then raise up the brawn; then turn it outward

outward upon both sides, but break it not, nor cut it off; then cut off the wing-pinions at the joint next the body, and stick in each side the pinion in the place you turned the brawn out; but cut off the sharp end of the pinion, and take the middle piece, and that will just fit in the place. You may cut up a capon or pheasant the same way.

To unbrace a Mullard.

THIS is done the same way as to unbrace a duck; which see.

To wing a Partridge.

RAISE his legs and wings, and sauce him with wine, powdered ginger, and a little salt.

To allay a Pheasant.

DO this as you do a partridge, but use no other sauce but salt.

To wing a Quail.

DO this the same way as you do a partridge.

To lift a Swan.

SLIT the swan down in the middle of the breast, and so clean through the back, from the neck to the rump; then part it in two halves, but do not break or tear the flesh; then lay the two halves in a charger, with the slit sides downwards; throw salt upon it; set it again on the table; let the sauce be chaldron, and serve it in saucers.

To break a Teal.

DO this the same way as you do a pheasant.

To cut up a Turkey.

RAISE up the leg fairly, and open the joint with the point of your knife, but take not off the leg; then with your knife lace down both sides of the breast, and open the breast-pinion, but do not take it off; then raise the merry-thought betwixt the breast-bone and the top of it; then raise up the brawn; then turn it outward upon both sides, but not break it, nor cut it off; then cut off the wing-pinions at the joint next the body, and stick each pinion in the place you turned the brawn out, but cut off the sharp end of the pinion, and take the middle piece, and that will just fit in the place. You may cut up a bustard, a capon, or pheasant, the same way.

To thigh a Woodcock.

RAISE the wings and legs as you do a hern, only lay the head open for the brains; and as you thigh a hern, so you must a curlew, plover, or snipe, excepting that you have no other sauce but salt.

General Directions to be observed before the cutting up a pickled Herring, which Way soever it is to be eat.

LAY the fish in a pewter plate, or trencher. Beat it on each side, with the flat of the knife, to loosen the skin. Cut a thin strip off the belly, and slit the back, to divide the skin; which then must be stripped off, on each side (with the knife and fingers) beginning at the neck. Take out the roe; and rub the inside, and the whole herring, with the corner of a towel, dipped in vinegar.

First way.] The fish being prepared, as above, cut off the head and tail. Then divide the herring into pieces of about an inch long. Afterwards put the pieces together, as though the fish were entire. Then eat it with, or without, oil and vinegar, new bread and butter, &c.

Second way.] The herring lying skinned, &c. in the plate, (as observed in the general directions) shave it very thin; and, when cut to the bone, turn it, and shave it in like manner, on the other side. A herring may thus be cut so thin, that the pieces of it will quite cover a plate.

Third way.] The herring being prepared (pursuant to the general directions) take it by the tail, in the middle of which cut a slit, half an inch long, or more. Pull each tip of the tail, opposite ways; by which means the herring will be split into two parts. In one of these parts no bone will be left; and the bone left in the other part may easily be taken out (from a new pickled herring) by loosening the bone at the neck, and drawing it along. The two divided parts of the herring may then be laid together, cut it into slices, and eat between bread and butter; or minced and mixed with a sallad of any kind; or else made into a salamongundy, with chicken, rabbet or veal. They eat very well with green pease, Windsor beans, kidney beans, or potatoes; if, after these are drained off, when boiled, a pickled herring, or more, be thrown into the same water, and then taken out, after the water hath bubbled up a minute or two. Herring-pickle may be used for that of an anchovy; and a little of this pickle thrown into the butter, made as sauce for eels, takes off from their lusciousness.—In many countries, pickled herrings are made to serve all the purposes of ham, or bacon.

PART VII.

Of POTTING, COLLARING, and PICKLING.

CHAP. I.
Of POTTING.

To pot Beef.

TAKE a good buttock of beef, cut out the bone, lay it flat, and flash it in several places; salt it well, and let it lie in the salt three days; then take it out, and let it lie in running water with a handful of salt three days longer; then take it out, dry it with a cloth, and season it with pepper, salt, nutmeg, cloves, mace, and two ounces of salt-petre finely beaten; then shred two or three pounds of beef suet, and one pound in lumps, and three pound of butter, put some in the bottom of the pot you bake it in; then put in your beef and the rest of the butter and suet on the top; cover your pot over with coarse paste, and set it in all night with houshold-bread; in the morning draw it, and pour off all the fat into a pot, and drain out all the gravy; pull the meat all to pieces, fat and lean, and work it into your pots that you keep it in while it is hot, or it will not close so well; then cover it with the clear fat you poured off; paper it when it is cold; it will keep good a month or six weeks.

Another Method.

TAKE six pounds of the buttock of beef, cut it in pieces as big as your fist, season it with a large spoonful of mace, a spoonful of pepper, with twenty-five or thirty cloves, and a good race of ginger; beat them all very fine, mix them with salt, and put them to the beef; lay it in a pot, and upon it two pounds of butter:

butter: bake it three or four hours, well covered up with paste; before it is cold take out the beef, beat it fine, putting in the warm butter as you do it, and put it down close in pots; if you keep it long, keep back the gravy, and if it wants seasoning, add some in the beating; pour on clarified butter.

A fine Way to pot a Tongue.

TAKE a dried tongue, boil it till it is tender, then peel it; take a large fowl, bone it; a goose, and bone it; take a quarter of an ounce of mace, a quarter of an ounce of cloves, a large nutmeg, a quarter of an ounce of black pepper, beat all well together; a spoonful of salt; rub the inside of the fowl well, and the tongue. Put the tongue into the fowl; then season the goose, and fill the goose with the fowl and tongue, and the goose will look as if it was whole. Lay it in a pan that will just hold it, melt fresh butter enough to cover it, send it to the oven, and bake it an hour and a half; then uncover the pot, and take out the meat. Carefully drain it from the butter, lay it on a coarse cloth till it is cold; and when the butter is cold, take off the hard fat from the gravy, and lay it before the fire to melt, put your meat into the pot again, and pour the butter over. If there is not enough, clarify more, and let the butter be an inch above the meat; and this will keep a great while, eats fine, and looks beautiful. When you cut it, it must be cut cross-ways down through, and looks very pretty. It makes a pretty corner-dish at table, or side-dish for supper. If you cut a slice down the middle quite through, lay it in a plate, and garnish with green parsley and nasturtium flowers. If you will be at the expence, bone a turkey, and put over the goose. Observe, when you pot it, to save a little of the spice to throw over it, before the last butter is put on, or the meat will not be seasoned enough.

To pot Neats-Tongues.

TAKE neats-tongues, and rub them very well with salt and water (bay-salt is best;) then take pump-water, with a good deal of salt-petre, some white salt, and some cloves and mace; boil it well and skim it; when it is cold put your tongues in, and let them lie in it six days; then wash them out of the liquor, put them in a pot, and bake them with bread till they are very tender; when they are taken out of the oven, pull off their skins, put them in the pot you intend to keep them in, and cover them over with clarified butter: they will keep four or five months.

To pot Ducks or any Fowls, or small Birds.

BREAK all the bones of your ducks with a rolling-pin, take out the thigh-bones, and as many others as you can, keeping the ducks whole; feafon it with pepper, falt, nutmeg, and cloves; lay them clofe in a pot with their breaft down, put in a little red wine, a good deal of butter, and lay a fmall weight upon them; when they are baked, let them ftand in the pot till they are near cold, to fuck up the feafoning the better; then put them in another pot, and pour clarified butter on them; if they are to keep long, put away the gravy; if to fpend foon, put it in; take care to feafon them well.

To pot a Swan.

BONE and fkin your fwan, and beat the flefh in a mortar, taking out the ftrings as you beat it; then take fome clear fat bacon, and beat with the fwan, and when it is of a light flefh-colour there is bacon enough in it: when it is beaten till it is like dough, it is enough; then feafon it with pepper, falt, cloves, mace, and nutmeg, all beaten fine; mix it well with your flefh, and give it a beat or two all together; then put it in an earthen pot, with a little claret and fair water, and at the top two pounds of frefh butter fpread over it; cover it with coarfe pafte, and bake it with bread; then turn it out into a difh; fqueeze it gently to get out the moifture; then put it in a pot fit for it; and when it is cold, cover it with clarified butter, and next day paper it up; in this manner you may do goofe, duck, beef, or hare's flefh.

To pot Goofe and Turkey.

TAKE a fat goofe and a fat turkey; cut them down the rump, and take out all the bones; lay them flat open, and feafon them very well with white pepper, nutmeg, and falt, allowing three nutmegs, with the like proportion of pepper, and as much falt as both the fpices; when you have feafoned them all over, let your turkey be within the goofe, and keep them in feafon two nights and a day; then roll them up as collared beef, very tight, and as fhort as you can, and bind it very faft with ftrong tape. Bake it in a long pot, with good ftore of butter, till it is very tender, as you may feel by the end; let it lie in the hot liquor an hour, then take it out, and let it ftand till next day; then unbind it, place it in your pot, and melt butter, and pour over it. Keep it for ufe, and flice it out thin.

To pot Venifon.

TAKE a piece of venifon, fat and lean together, lay it in a difh, and ftick pieces of butter all over: tie brown paper over it, and bake it. When it comes out of the oven, take it out of the liquor hot, drain it, and lay it in a difh; when cold, take off all the fkin, and beat it in a marble mortar, fat and lean together;

together; seaso[n] [it with] [cl]oves, nutmeg, black pepper, and salt to your [taste]; [when the b]utter is cold that it was baked in, take it [off], and beat in with it to moisten it; th[en p]ut it [in a pot] [wh]ole, and cover it with clarified butter.

You m[u]st be sure to beat it till it is like a paste.

To pot a Hare.

TAKE three pounds of the pure flesh of a hare, and a pound and a half of the clear fat of pork or bacon, and beat them in a mortar, till you cannot diftinguifh each from the other; then feafon it with pepper, falt, a large nutmeg, a large handful of fweet-herbs, fweet-marjoram, thyme, and a double quantity of parfley; fhred all very fine, mix it with the feafoning, and beat it all together, till all is very well mingled; then put it into a pot, laying it lower in the middle than the fides, and pafte it up; two hours will bake it: when it comes out of the oven, have clarified butter ready; fill the pot an inch above the meat while it is hot; when it is cold, paper it up, and keep it; which you may do three or four months before it is cut: the fat of pork is much better than the fat of bacon.

To pot Mufhrooms.

TAKE of the beft mufhrooms, and rub them with a woollen cloth; thofe that will not rub, peel, and take out the gills, and throw them into water, as you do them; when they are all done, wipe them dry, and put them in a faucepan, with a handful of falt and a piece of butter; then ftew them till they are enough, fhaking them often for fear of burning; then drain them from their liquor, and when they are cold wipe them dry, and lay them in a pot one by one as clofe as you can, till your pot be full; then clarify butter; let it ftand till it is almoft cold, and pour it into your mufhrooms; when cold, cover them clofe in your pot; when you ufe them, wipe them clean from the butter, and ftew them in gravy thickened, as when frefh.

To pot Salmon.

LET your falmon be quite frefh, fcale and wafh it well, and dry it with a cloth, fplit it up the back and take out the bone, feafon it well with white pepper and falt, a little nutmeg and mace; let it lie two or three hours, then put it in your pot, with half a pound of butter, tie it down, put it in the oven and bake it an hour, when it comes out, lay it on a flat difh that the oil may run from it, cut it to the fize of your pots, lay it in layers till you fill the pot, with the fkin upward, put a board over it, lay on a weight to prefs it till cold, then pour over it clarified butter; when you cut it, the skin makes you ribbed, you may send it to the table either cut in slices, or [in the] pot.

Another Method.

SCALE and chine your salmon down the back, and dry it well; cut it as near the shape of your pot as you can; take two nutmegs, near an ounce of cloves and mace, half an ounce of white pepper, about an ounce of salt, take out all the bones, and cut off the joll below the fins; cut off the tail; season the scaly side first, and lay that at the bottom of the pot; then rub the seasoning on the other side; cover it with a dish, and let it stand all night. It must be put double, and the scaly side top and bottom. Put butter on the bottom and top; cover the pot with some stiff coarse paste; three hours if it is a large fish, if not, two hours will bake it. When it comes out of the oven, let it stand half an hour; then uncover it, and raise it up at one end that the gravy may run out; then put a trencher and a weight on it, to press out the gravy, melt the butter that came from it, but let no gravy be in it; let the butter boil up, and add more butter to it, if there be occasion. Skim it, and fill the pot with the clear butter; when it is cold, paper it up.

Salmon or Mackarel to pot.

AFTER you have washed and cleansed them, dry them in a cloth, cut off the heads, tails and fins, cut them down the bellies, take out the roes, and wipe the black that lies under the roes; take out the bones as clean as you can; season twelve or thirteen with four ounces of salt, half an ounce of nutmegs, as much pepper, a quarter of an ounce of cloves, as much ginger beat very fine; mix with the salt and season them; lay them into a long pot with a few bay-leaves and lemon peel on the top. a good quantity of fresh butter, and bake them with houshold bread at least three hours: lay on a double brown paper, wetted and tied close. When they are baked, take them out of the pot while hot, and pull them in small pieces with you fingers; place them close in your potting-pots, and pour clarified butter on the top.

Mackarel to caveack.

CUT your mackarel in pieces; season them as for potting, and rub it in well; fry them in oil or clarified butter, then lay them on straw by the fire to drain; when cold put them in vinegar, and cover them with oil, dry them before you season them; they will keep, and are extremely good.

To pot Lobsters.

TAKE a dozen of large lobsters; take out all the meat of their tails and claws after they are boiled; then season them with beaten pepper, salt, cloves, mace, and nutmeg, all finely beaten and mixed together; then take a pot, put therein a layer of fresh butter, upon which put a layer of lobsters, and then strew over some seasoning, and repeat the same till your pot is full, and your lobster all in; bake it about an hour and a half, then set it by two or three days, and it will be fit to eat. It will keep a month or more, if you pour from it the liquor when it comes out of the oven, and fill it up with clarified butter. Eat it with vinegar.

To pot Eels.

CASE your eels and gut them, wash them, and dry them, slit them down the back, and take out the bones; cut them in pieces to fit your pot; then rub every piece on both sides with pepper, salt, and grated nutmeg; then lay them close in the pot till it is full; cover the pot with close paste, and bake them. A pot that holds eight pounds weight must have two hours baking; when they come out of the oven, open the pot and pour out all the liquor, then cover them with clarified butter.

To pot Herrings.

CUT off their heads, and put them in an earthen pot, lay them close, and between every layer of herrings strew some salt, not too much; put in cloves, mace, whole pepper, and nutmeg cut in bits; fill up the pot with vinegar, water, and a quarter of a pint of white wine; cover it with brown paper, tie it down, and bake it with brown bread. When cold it is fit to eat.

CHAP. II.
Of COLLARING.

To collar Beef.

TAKE a flank and cut the skin off, lay it in pump-water, with three handfuls of bay-salt and an ounce of salt-petre; let it lie in the brine three days; then take some pepper, two nutmegs, and a good handful of green sweet marjoram, half a handful of sage, some rosemary and thyme, all green, with a
good

good handful of parsley; chop the herbs small, then lay the beef on the table; cut the lean piece, and put in the thick fat part, strew it all over with the herbs and spice; roll it up as close as you can, tie it very well with tape bound about it; then put it into a long pot, and fill it up with the brine it was laid in, tie a wet paper over it, put it in an oven when your bread is drawn, let it stand all night: next day heat your oven hot, and let your beef stand four hours, then draw it out, and let it stand in the liquor till it is half cold, then take it out, and strain your tape and bind it up closer: you must put two middling handfuls of salt into the herbs when you roll it up, besides the brine; the rosemary ought to be chopped fine by itself, and then with the rest of the herbs.

Another Method.

LAY your flank of beef in ham-brine eight or ten days, then dry it in a cloth, and take out all the leather and the skin; scotch it cross and cross, season it with savoury spice, two or three anchovies, an handful or two of thyme, sweet-marjoram, winter-savoury, and onions; strew it on the meat, and roll it in a hard collar in a cloth; sew it close, and tie it at both ends; put it in a long pan with a pint of claret and cochineal, and two quarts of pump-water, and bake it all night; then take it out hot, and tie it up close at both ends; then set it upon one end, put a weight upon it, and let it stand till it is cold; then take it out of the cloth, and keep it dry.

To keep collared Beef.

YOU may keep a collar of beef two months in a liquor made of one quart of cyder and two of stale small beer, boiled with a handful of salt; if it mothers, take it off, and boil it again, and when cold put in your beef; first keep it as long as you can dry, which is to be done by rolling it up in a cloth when it is first baked, tying it up at both ends, hanging it up to dry till cold, and taking off the cloths, wrap it up in white paper and keep it in a dry place, but not near the fire; when you have kept it dry as long as you can, put it into the pickle as before.

To collar Flat Ribs of Beef.

BONE your beef, lay it flat upon a table, and beat it half an hour with a wooden mallet till it is quite soft; then rub it with six ounces of brown sugar, four ounces of common salt, and one ounce of salt-petre beat fine; let it lie then for ten days, and turn it once every day; take it out, then put it in warm

warm water for eight or ten hours; then lay it flat upon a table, with the outward skin down, and cut it in rows, and a-cross about the breadth of your finger, but take care you do not cut the outside skin; then fill one nick with chopped parsley, the second with fat pork, the third with crumbs of bread, mace, nutmeg, pepper, and salt, then parsley, and so on till you have filled all your nicks; then roll it up tight, and bind it round with coarse broad tape; wrap it in a cloth, and boil it four or five hours; then take it up, and hang it up by one end of the string to keep it round; save the liquor it was boiled in, and the next day skim it, and add to it half the quantity of allegar as you have liquor, and a little mace, long pepper, and salt; then put in your beef and keep it for use. When you send it to the table, cut a little off both ends, and it will be in diamonds of different colours, and look very pretty; set it upon a dish as you do brawn; if you make a fresh pickle every week, it will keep a long time.

Collared Mutton to eat hot.

TAKE two loins of mutton, or a neck and breast, bone them and take off all the skin; then take some of the fat off from the loins, and make savoury forcemeat to spread on them, and clap the two insides together, and where the flesh is thick, cut it, and put in some of the forcemeat, (first beating it with a rolling-pin) and season it well with pepper and salt, besides the spice that is in the forcemeat; roll this up as close as you can, and then bind a cloth over it, and sew it up close: boil it in broth, or salt and water; and when it is more than half boiled, straiten the cloth; when enough, cut the collar into three pieces, lay upon them heaps of boiled spinach, sliced lemon, and pickled barberries: before you divide your collar, cut a little slice off from each end, that they may stand well in the dish; make sauce with the bones of the mutton boiled in some of the broth, an onion, some whole spice, a piece of bacon, a bay-leaf, an anchovy, a little piece of lemon-peel, and some red wine; beat it up with butter, and some oysters, if you have them; this will require near four hours boiling; your collar may be made over night; you may boil a little brown toast in your sauce with walnut-pickle; you ought to make forcemeat enough for balls, to fry and put into the sauce.

To collar a Breast of Mutton.

TAKE a large breast of mutton, cut off the red skin, the bones and gristles, then grate white bread, a little cloves, mace, salt, and pepper, the yolks of three hard eggs bruised small, and a little lemon-peel shred fine; make your meat even and flat, and strew your seasoning over it, with four or five anchovies washed and boned; then roll your meat like a collar, and bind it with coarse tape, and bake, boil, or roast it; cut it into three or four pieces, and dish it with strong gravy sauce thickened with butter; you may fry oysters and forcemeat balls on it if you please; it is very good cold: cut it in slices like collared beef.

To collar a Breast of Veal.

TAKE a breast of veal, bone it, wash it, and dry it in a clean cloth; then shred thyme, winter-savoury, and parsley, very small, and mix it with salt, pepper, cloves, mace, and nutmeg; then strew it on the inside of your meat, and roll it up hard, beginning at the neck end; tie it up with tape, and put it in a pot fit to boil it in, standing upright: you must boil it in water and salt, and a bunch of sweet-herbs; when it is boiled enough take it off the fire, put it in an earthen pot, and when the liquor is cold, pour it over, or else boil salt and water strong enough to bear an egg; and when that is cold, pour it on your veal: when you serve it to the table, cut it in round slices. Garnish with laurel and fennel.

Another Method.

TAKE the finest breast of veal, bone it, and rub it over with the yolks of two eggs, and strew over it some crumbs of bread, a little grated lemon, a little pepper and salt, and a handful of chopped parsley, roll it up tight, and bind it hard with twine; wrap it in a cloth, and boil it one hour and a half; then take it up to cool, and, when a little cold, take off the cloth, and clip off the twine carefully, lest you open the veal; cut it in five slices, lay them on a dish with the sweet-bread boiled and cut in thin slices and laid round them, with ten or twelve forcemeat balls; pour over your white sauce, and garnish with barberries, or green pickles.

The white sauce must be made thus:—Take a pint of good veal gravy, put to it a spoonful of lemon-pickle, half an anchovy, a tea-spoonful of mushroom-powder, or a few pickled mushrooms; give it a gentle boil, and then put in half a pint of cream, the yolks of two eggs beat fine, shake it over the fire after the eggs and cream is in, but do not let it boil, for it will curdle the cream: it is proper for a top-dish at night, or a side-dish for dinner.

To collar a Calf's-Head.

TAKE a calf's-head with the skin and hair upon it; scald it to fetch off the hair; parboil it, but not too much; then get it
clean

clean from the bones while it is hot; you must slit it in the forepart; season it with pepper, salt, cloves, mace, nutmeg, and sweet-herbs, shred small, and mixed together with the yolks of three or four eggs; spread it over the head, and roll it up hard. Boil it gently for three hours, in just as much water as will cover it; when it is tender it is boiled enough. If you do the tongue, first boil it and peel it, and slice it in thin slices, and likewise the palate, putting them and the eyes in the inside of the head before you roll it up. When the head is taken out, season the pickle with salt, pepper, and spice, and give it a boil, adding to it a pint of white wine, and as much vinegar. When it is cold, put in the collar; and when you use it, cut it in slices.

To grill a Calf's-Head.

WASH your calf's-head clean, and boil it almost enough, then take it up and hash one half, the other half rub over with the yolk of an egg, a little pepper and salt, strew over it bread crumbs, parsley chopped small, and a little grated lemon-peel; set it before the fire, and keep basting it all the time to make the froth rise; when it is a fine light brown, dish up your hash, and lay the grilled side upon it.

Blanch your tongue, slit it down the middle, and lay it on a soup-plate; skin the brains, boil them with a little sage and parsley; chop them fine, and mix them with some melted butter, and a spoonful of cream; make them hot, and pour them over the tongue; serve them up, and they are sauce for the head.

To collar Cow-heels.

TAKE five or six cow-heels or feet, and bone them while they are hot; lay them one upon another, strewing some salt between; then roll them up in a coarse cloth, and squeeze in both ends, and tie them up very hard; boil it an hour and an half; then take it out, and when it is cold, put it in common souce drink for brawn. Cut off a little at each end, it looks better. Serve it in slices, or in the collar, as you please.

To collar a Pig.

CUT off the head of your pig, and the body asunder; bone it, and cut two collars off each side; lay it in water to take out the blood; then take sage and parsley, shred them very small, mix them with pepper, salt, and nutmeg, strewing some on every side, or collar, and roll it up, and tie it with coarse tape; boil them in fair water and salt, till they are very tender: put two or three blades of mace in the kettle, and when they are enough, take them up and lay them in something to cool; then put some of the liquor, and add to it some vinegar and salt, a

little

little white wine, and three or four bay-leaves; give it a boil up, and when it is cold put it to the collars, and keep them for use.

Another Method.

KILL your pig, dress off the hair, draw out the entrails, and wash it clean; take a sharp knife, rip it open, and take out all the bones; then rub it all over with pepper and salt beaten fine, a few sage leaves, and sweet-herbs chopped small; then roll up your pig tight, and bind it with a fillet; then fill your boiler with soft water, one pint of vinegar, and a handful of salt, eight or ten cloves, a blade or two of mace, a few pepper-corns, and a bunch of sweet-herbs; when it boils put in your pig, and boil it till it is tender, then take it up, and when it is almost cold, bind it over again, and put it into an earthen pot, and pour the liquor your pig was boiled in upon it: keep it covered, and it is fit for use.

To collar Venison.

TAKE a side of venison, bone it, and take away all the sinews, and cut it into square collars of what bigness you please; it will make two or three collars; lard it with fat clear bacon, cut your lards as big as the top of your finger, and as long as your little finger, then season your venison with pepper, salt, cloves, mace, and nutmeg; roll up your collars, and tie them close with coarse tape; then put them into deep pots; put seasoning at the bottom of the pot, with fresh butter, and three or four bay-leaves; then put in your venison, some seasoning, and butter on the top, and over that some beef suet finely shred and beaten; then cover up your pot with coarse paste; they will take four or five hours baking; then take them out of the oven, and let it stand a little; then take out your venison, and let it drain well from the gravy: take off all the fat from the gravy, and add more butter to that fat, and set it over a gentle fire to clarify; then take it off, and let it stand a little, and skim it well; then make your pots clean, or have pots fit for each collar; put a little seasoning at the bottom, and some of your clarified butter; then put in your venison, and fill up your pots with clarified butter; and be sure your butter be an inch above the meat; and when it is thorough cold, tie it down with double paper, and lay a tile on the top; they will keep six or eight months; you may, if you please, when you use a pot, put it in boiling water a minute, and it will come whole out. Let it stand till it is cold, and stick it round with bay-leaves, and one sprig on the top.

To collar Salmon.

TAKE a side of salmon, and cut off about a handful of the tail; wash your large piece very well, and dry it with a cloth; wash it over with the yolks of eggs; then make some forcemeat with that you cut off the tail; but take off the skin, and put to it a handful of parboiled oysters, a tail or two of lobsters, the yolks of three or four eggs boiled hard, six anchovies, a good handful of sweet-herbs chopped small, a little salt, cloves, mace, nutmeg, pepper, and grated bread; work all these together into a body with the yolks of eggs, and lay it all over the fleshy part, and a little more pepper and salt over the salmon; so roll it up in a collar, and bind it with broad tape; then boil it in water and salt, and vinegar; but let the liquor boil first; then put in your collars, and a bunch of sweet-herbs, sliced ginger and nutmeg; let it boil, but not too fast; it will require near two hours boiling; when it is near enough, take it up; put it in your sousing-pan, and when the pickle is cold, put it to your salmon, and let it stand in it till used; otherwise you may pot it after it is boiled, and fill it up with clarified butter, as you pot fowls; that way will keep longest and best.

To collar Eels.

TAKE your eel, and cut it open; take out the bones, cut off the head and tail, and lay the eel flat on a dresser; shred sage as fine as possible, and mix it with black pepper beat, nutmeg grated, and salt, and lay it all over the eel, and roll it up hard in little cloths, and tie it up tight at each end: then set over some water with pepper and salt, five or six cloves, three or four blades of mace, a bay-leaf or two; boil it and the bones and head and tail together; then take out the head and tail, and put it away, and put in your eels, and let them boil till they are tender; then take them out of the liquor, and boil the liquor longer; then take it off, and when it is cold put it to your eels, but do not take off the little cloths till you use them.

To collar Mackarel.

GUT and slit your mackarel down the belly, cut off the head, take out the bones, take care you do not cut it in holes; then lay it flat upon its back, season it with mace, nutmeg, pepper and salt, and a handful of parsley shred fine; strew it over them, roll them tight, and tie them well separately in cloths; boil them gently twenty minutes in vinegar, salt and water; then take them out, put them into a pot, pour the liquor on them, or the cloth will stick to the fish; the next day take the cloth off your fish, put a little more vinegar to the pickle, and keep them for use; when you send them to the table, garnish with fennel, or parsley, and put some of the liquor under them.

CHAP. III.
All SORTS of PICKLES.

To pickle Hams or Ribs of Beef.

TAKE six gallons of your bloody beef-rine, or from pork, and put to it two pounds of brown sugar, and a pound of salt-petre; boil them together, and skim it well; when it is cold, put it into the thing you design to pickle in, and put in your hams; large ones must lie in the pickle three weeks; small ones but a fortnight, sometimes turning them; the pickle must be strong enough to bear an egg; this way is only for great families, that kill or use a great deal of beef.

To pickle a Buttock of Beef.

TAKE a large fine buttock of well fed ox-beef, and with a long narrow knife make holes through, through which you must run square pieces of fat bacon, about as thick as your finger, in about a dozen or fourteen places, and have ready a great deal of parsley clean washed and picked fine, but not chopped; and in every hole where the bacon is, stuff in as much of the parsley as you can get in, with a long round stick; then take half an ounce of mace, cloves and nutmegs, an equal quantity of each, dried before the fire, and pounded fine, and a quarter of an ounce of black pepper beat fine; a quarter of an ounce of cardamum-seeds beat fine, and half an ounce of juniper-berries beat fine, a quarter of a pound of loaf-sugar beat fine, two large spoonfuls of fine salt, two tea-spoonfuls of India pepper; mix all together, and rub the beef well with it; let it lie in this pickle two days, turning and rubbing it twice a day; then throw into the pan two bay leaves; six eschalots peeled and cut fine, and pour a pint of fine white wine vinegar over it, keeping it turned and rubbed as above; let it lie thus another day; then pour over it a bottle of red port or Madeira wine; let it lie thus in this pickle a week or ten days; and when you dress it, stew it in the pickle it lies in, with another bottle of red wine; it is an excellent dish, and eats best cold, and will keep a month or six weeks good.

To pickle Ox-Palates.

TAKE your palates and wash them well with salt in the water, and put them in a pipkin, with water and some salt, and when they are ready to boil skim them very well, and put into them whole pepper, cloves and mace, as much as will give them a quick taste: when they are boiled tender (which will require four or five hours) peel them and cut them into small pieces, and let them cool; then make the pickle of white wine vinegar, and as much white wine; boil the pickle, and put in the spice as was boiled in the palates, adding a little fresh spice: put in six or seven bay-leaves, and let both pickle and palates be cold before you put them together; then keep them for use.

To pickle Pigeons.

TAKE your pigeons and bone them, beginning at the rump; take cloves, mace, nutmegs, pepper, salt, thyme, and lemon-peel; beat the spice, shred the herbs and lemon-peel very small, and season the inside of your pigeons; then sew them up, and place the legs and wings in order; then season the outside, and make a pickle for them: to a dozen of pigeons two quarts of water, one quart of white wine, a few blades of mace, some salt, some whole pepper; and when it boils put in your pigeons, and let them boil till they are tender; then take them out, and strain out the liquor, and put your pigeons in a pot, and when the liquor is cold pour it on them; when you serve them to table, dry them out of the pickle, and garnish the dish with fennel or flowers; eat them with vinegar and oil.

To pickle Sparrows, or Squab-Pigeons.

TAKE your sparrows, pigeons, or larks, draw them, and cut off their legs; then make a pickle of water, a quarter of a pint of white wine, a bunch of sweet-herbs, salt, pepper, cloves, and mace; when it boils put in your sparrows, and when they are enough take them up, and when they are cold, put them in the pot you keep them in; then make a strong pickle of Rhenish wine, and white wine vinegar; put in an onion, a sprig of thyme and savoury, some lemon-peel, some cloves, mace, and whole pepper; season it pretty high with salt; boil all these together very well; then set it by till it is cold, and put it to your sparrows; once in a month new boil the pickle, and when the bones are dissolved they are fit to eat; put them in china saucers and mix with your pickles.

To pickle Mushrooms.

GATHER your mushrooms in the morning, as soon as possible after they are out of the ground; for one of them that are round and unopened, is worth five that are open; if you gather any that are open, let them be such as are reddish in the gills, for those that have white gills are not good: having gathered them, peel them into water; when they are all done, take them out and put them into a saucepan; then put to them a good quantity of salt, whole pepper, cloves, mace and nutmeg quartered; let them boil in their own liquor a quarter of an hour with a quick fire; then take them off the fire, and drain them through a colander, and let them stand till they are cold; then put all the spice that was used in the boiling them, to one half white wine, and the other half white wine vinegar, some salt, and a few bay-leaves; then give them a boil or two; there must be liquor enough to cover them; when they are cold, put a spoonful or two of oil on the top to keep them; you must change the liquor once a month.

Another Method.

TAKE only the buttons, wash them in milk and water with a flannel; put milk on the fire, and when it boils put in your mushrooms, and give them four or five boils; have in readiness a brine made with milk and salt, and take them out of the boiling brine, and put them into the milk brine, covering them up all night; then have a brine with water and salt; boil it, and let it stand to be cold, and put in your buttons, and wash them in it. When you first boil your mushrooms, you must put with them an onion and spice; then have in readiness a pickle made with half white wine, and half white wine vinegar; boil in it ginger, mace, nutmegs, and whole white pepper; when it is quite cold put your mushrooms into the bottle, and some bay-leaves on the sides, and strew between some of your boiled spice; then put in the liquor, and a little oil on the top; cork and rosin the top; set them cool and dry, and the bottom upwards.

Another excellent Method.

PUT your mushrooms into water, and wash them clean with a spunge, throw them into water as you do them; then put in water and a little salt, and when it boils put in your mushrooms; and when they boil up skim them clean, and put them into cold water, and a little salt: let them stand twenty-four hours, and put them into white wine vinegar, and let them stand a week; then take your pickle from them, and boil it very well with pepper, cloves, mace, and a little all-spice; when your pickle is cold, put it to your mushrooms in the glass or pot you keep them in; keep them close tied down with a bladder, the air will hurt them: if you pickle mothers, boil it again: you may make your pickle half white wine, and half white wine vinegar.

Another Method.

AFTER your mushrooms are well cleansed with a woollen cloth in salt and water, boil milk and water and put them in; let them boil eight or ten minutes; drain them in a sieve; put them immediately into cold water that has been boiled and made cold; take them out of it, and put them into boiled vinegar that is cold also; let them stand twenty-four hours, and in that time get ready a pickle with white wine vinegar, a few large blades of mace, a good quantity of whole pepper and ginger sliced; boil this, and when cold put in your mushrooms from the other vinegar. Put them into wide-mouth glasses, and oil upon them; they will keep a great while, if you put them thus in two pickles.

To pickle Walnuts.

IN July gather the largest walnuts, and let them lie nine days in salt and water, shifting them every third day; let the salt and water be strong enough to bear an egg, then put two pots of water on the fire; when the water is hot put in your walnuts; shift them out of one pot into the other, for the more clean water they have the better; when some of them begin to rise in the water they are enough; then pour them into a colander, and with a woollen cloth wipe them clean, and put them in the jar you keep them in; then boil as much vinegar as will cover them, with beaten pepper, cloves, mace, and nutmeg, just bruised, and put some cloves of garlic into the pot to them, with whole spice and Jamaica pepper; when they are cold put into every half hundred of nuts three spoonfuls of mustard-seed. Tie a bladder over them, and cover that with leather.

Another Method.

TAKE walnuts about Midsummer, when a pin will pass through them, and put them in a deep pot, and cover them over with ordinary vinegar: change them into fresh vinegar once in fourteen days, repeat this fourteen times; then take six quarts of the best vinegar, and put into it an ounce of dill seeds grosly bruised; ginger sliced, three ounces; mace whole, one ounce; nutmegs quartered, two ounces; whole pepper, two ounces; give all a boil or two over the fire: then put your nuts into a crock, and pour your pickle boiling hot over them; cover them up close till it is cold, to keep in the steam; then have gallipots ready, and place your nuts in them till your pots are full; put in the middle of each pot a large clove of garlic stuck full of cloves; strew over the tops of the pots mustard-seed finely beaten, a spoonful, more or less, according to the bigness of your pot; then put the spice on, lay vine-leaves, and pour on the liquor, laying a slate on the top to keep them under the liquor. Be careful not to touch them with your fingers, lest they turn black, but take them out with a wooden spoon; put a handful of salt in with the spice. When you first boil the pickle, you must likewise remember to keep them under the pickle they are first steeped in, or they will lose their colour. Tie down the pots with leather. A spoonful of this liquor will relish sauce for fish, fowl, or fricasey.

Another Method.

TAKE your nuts fit to preserve, prick them full of holes, and cut the slit in the crease half through; put them as you do them into brine; let them lie three weeks, changing the brine every four days; take them out with a cloth, and wipe them dry; put them in a pot, with a good deal of bruised mustard-seed; then have your pickle ready, which must be wine vinegar, as much as will cover them: put in cloves, mace, ginger, pepper, salt, three or four cloves of garlic stuck with cloves, and pour the liquor boiling hot upon them, and keep them close tied for a fortnight; boil the pickle again, so do three times; put oil on the top.

To pickle Cucumbers.

WIPE your cucumbers very clean with a cloth, then get so many quarts of vinegar as you have hundreds of cucumbers, and take dill and fennel; cut it small, put to it vinegar, set it over the fire in a copper kettle, and let it boil; then put in your cucumbers till they are warm through, but not boil while they are in; when they are warm thro', pour all out into a deep earthen pot, and cover it up very close till the next day; then do the same again; but the third day season the liquor before you set it over the fire; put in salt till it is brackish, some sliced ginger, whole pepper, and whole mace; then set it over the fire again, and when it boils put in your cucumbers; when they are hot through, pour them into the pot, cover it close; when they are cold, put them in glasses, and strain the liquor over them; pick out the spice, and put to them; cover them with leather.

To pickle Cucumbers in Slices.

TAKE your cucumbers at the full bigness, but not yellow, and slice them half an inch thick; cut an onion or two with them, and strew a pretty deal of salt on them, and let them stand to drain all night; then pour the liquor clear from them; dry them in a coarse cloth, and boil as much vinegar as will cover them, with whole pepper, mace, and a quartered nutmeg; pour it scalding hot on your cucumbers, keeping them very close stopped; in two or three days heat your liquor again, and pour over them; so do two or three times more; then tie them up with leather.

To mango Cucumbers.

CUT a little slip out of the side of the cucumber and take out the seeds, but as little of the meat as you can; then fill the inside with mustard-seed bruised, a clove of garlic, some slices of ginger, and some bits of horse-radish; tie the piece in again, and make a pickle of vinegar, salt, whole pepper, cloves, mace, and boil it, and pour it on the mangoes, and do so for nine days together; when cold, cover them with leather.

To pickle Barberries.

TAKE of white wine vinegar and fair water an equal quantity, and to every pint of this liquor put a pound of six-penny sugar; set it over the fire, and bruise some of the barberries and put in it a little salt; let it boil near half an hour; then take it off the fire and strain it, and when it is pretty cold pour it into a glass over your barberries; boil a piece of flannel in the liquor and put over them, and cover the glass with leather.

Another Method.

TAKE water, and colour it red with some of the worst of your barberries, and put salt to it, and make it strong enough to bear an egg; then set it over the fire, and let it boil half an hour; skim it, and when it is cold strain it over your barberries; lay something on them to keep them in the liquor, and cover the pot or glass with leather.

To pickle Grapes.

GET grapes at the full growth, but not ripe; cut them in small bunches fit for garnishing, put them in a stone-jar, with vine-leaves between every layer of grapes; then take as much spring-water as you think will cover them, put in a pound of

bay-

bay-falt and as much white falt as will make it bear an egg. Dry your bay-falt and pound it, it will melt the fooner, put it into a bell-metal, or copper-pot, boil it and fkim it very well; as it boils, take all the black fcum off, but not the white fcum. When it has boiled a quarter of an hour, let it ftand to cool and fettle; when it is almoft cold, pour the clear liquor on the grapes, lay vine-leaves on the top, tie them down clofe with a linen cloth, and cover them with a difh. Let them ftand twenty-four hours; then take them out, and lay them on a cloth, cover them over with another, let them be dried between the cloths, then take two quarts of vinegar, one quart of fpring-water, and one pound of coarfe fugar. Let it boil a little while, fkim it as it boils very clean, let it ftand till it is quite cold, dry your jar with a cloth, put frefh vine-leaves at the bottom, and between every bunch of grapes, and on the top; then pour the clear off the pickle on the grapes, fill your jar that the pickle may be above the grapes, tie a thin bit of board in a piece of flannel, lay it on the top of the jar, to keep the grapes under the pickle, tie them down with a bladder, and then a leather; take them out with a wooden fpoon. Be fure to make pickle enough to cover them.

To pickle Gerkins.

TAKE what quantity of cucumbers you think fit, and put them in a ftone jar, then take as much fpring-water as you think will cover them: to every gallon of water put as much falt as will make it bear an egg; fet it on the fire, and let it boil two or three minutes, then pour it on the cucumbers and cover them with a woollen cloth, and over that a pewter difh; tie them down clofe, and let them ftand twenty-four hours; then take them out, lay them in a cloth, and another over them to dry them. When they are pretty dry, wipe your jar out with a dry cloth, put your cucumbers, and with them a little dill and fennel, a very fmall quantity. For the pickle, to every three quarts of vinegar one quart of fpring-water, till you think you have enough to cover them; put in a little bay-falt and a little white, but not too much. To every gallon of pickle put one nutmeg cut in quarters, a quarter of an ounce of cloves, a quarter of an ounce of mace, a quarter of an ounce of whole pepper, and a large race of ginger fliced; boil all thefe together in a bell-metal or copper-pot, pour it boiling hot on your cucumbers, and cover them as before. Let them ftand two days, then boil your pickle again, and pour it on as before; do fo a third time; when they are cold cover them with a bladder and then a leather. Mind always to keep your pickles clofe covered, and never take them out with any thing but a wooden fpoon, or one for the purpofe. This pickle will do the next year, only boiling it up again.

The COMPLETE HOUSEWIFE. 233

You are to observe to put the spice in the jar with the cucumbers, and only boil the vinegar, water, and salt, and pour over them. The boiling of your spice in all pickles spoils them, and loses the fine flavour of the spice.

To pickle Currants for present Use.

TAKE either red or white, being not thorough ripe; give them a warm in white wine vinegar, with as much sugar as will indifferently sweeten them; keep them well covered with liquor.

To pickle Nasturtium-Buds.

GATHER your little knobs quickly after your blossoms are off; put them in cold water and salt for three days, shifting them once a day; then make a pickle (but do not boil it at all) of some white wine, some white wine vinegar, eschalot, horse-radish, pepper, salt, cloves and mace whole, and nutmeg quartered; then put in your seeds and stop them close; they are to be eaten as capers.

To keep Quinces in Pickle.

CUT five or six quinces all to pieces, and put them in an earthen pot or pan, with a gallon of water, and two pounds of honey; mix all these together well, and then put them in a kettle to boil leisurely half an hour, and then strain your liquor into an earthen pot; and when it is cold, wipe your quinces clean, and put them into it: they must be covered very close, and they will keep all the year.

To pickle Asparagus.

GATHER your asparagus, and lay them in an earthen pot; make a brine of water and salt strong enough to bear an egg, pour it hot on them, and keep it close covered: when you use them hot, lay them in cold water for two hours, then boil and butter them for the table; if you use them as a pickle, boil them and lay them in vinegar.

Cabbage Lettuce to keep.

ABOUT the latter end of the season take very dry sand, and cover the bottom of a well seasoned barrel; then set your lettuce in so as not to touch one another: you must not lay above two rows one upon another; cover them well with sand, and set them in a dry place, and be careful that the frost come not at them. The lettuce must not be cut, but be pulled up by the roots.

To

To pickle Red Cabbage.

TAKE your close-leaved red cabbage, and cut it in quarters; when your liquor boils put in your cabbage, and give it a dozen walms; then make the pickle of white wine vinegar and claret; you may put to it beet-root, boil them first, and turneps half boiled; it is very good for the garnishing of dishes, or to garnish a sallad.

To pickle Pods of Radishes.

GATHER the youngest pods, and put them in water and salt twenty-four hours; then make a pickle for them of vinegar, cloves, mace, and whole pepper; boil this, drain the pods from the salt and water, and pour the liquor on them boiling hot: put to them a clove of garlic a little bruised.

To pickle Ashen-keys.

TAKE ashen-keys as young as you can get them, and put them in a pot with salt and water; then take green whey, when it is hot, and pour over them; let them stand till they are cold before you cover them; when you use them, boil them in fair water till they are tender; then take them out, and put them in salt and water.

To pickle French Beans.

TAKE young slender French beans, cut off top and tail; then make a brine with cold water and salt, strong enough to bear an egg; put your beans into that brine, and let them lie fourteen days; then take them out, wash them in fair water, set them over the fire in cold water without salt, and let them boil till they are so tender as to eat; when they are cold, drain them from their water, and make a pickle for them: to a peck of French beans, you must have a gallon of white wine vinegar; boil it with some cloves, mace, whole pepper, and sliced ginger; when it is cold put it and your beans into a glass, and keep them for use.

Another Method.

PICK the small slender beans from the stalks, and let them lie fourteen days in salt and water, then wash them clean from the brine, and put them in a kettle of water over a slow fire, cover-ed over with vine-leaves; let them stew, but not boil, till they are almost as tender as for eating; then strain them off, laying

laying them on a coarse cloth to dry; then put them in your pots: boil alegar, skim it and pour it over them, covering them close; boil it so three or four days together, till they be green: put spice, as to other pickles; and when cold cover with leather.

French Beans to keep.

TAKE a peck of French beans, break them every one in the middle; to them put two pounds of beaten salt; ram them well together, and when the brine arises, put them in a narrow-mouthed jar; press them down close, and lay somewhat that will keep them down with a weight, and tie them up close, that no air comes to them; the night before you use them, lay them in water.

To make Melon Mangoes.

TAKE small melons not quite ripe, cut a slip down the side, and take out the inside very clean; beat mustard-seed, and shred garlic, which mix with the seeds, and put in your mangoes; put the pieces you cut out into their places again, tie them up, and put them into your pot; then boil some vinegar (as much as you think will cover them) with whole pepper, some salt, and Jamaica pepper, which pour in scalding hot over your mangoes, and cover them close to keep in the steam; repeat this nine days, and when they are cold cover them with leather.

To pickle Samphire.

PICK your samphire from dead or withered branches; lay it in a bell-metal or brass-pot; then put in a pint of water and a pint of vinegar; so do till your pickle is an inch above your samphire; have a lid for the pot, and paste it close down, that no steam may go out; keep it boiling an hour, take it off, and cover the pot close with old sacks, &c. when it is cold, put it up in tubs or pots, the best by itself; the great stalks lay uppermost in boiling, it will keep the cooler and better. The vinegar you use must be the best.

To pickle Asparagus.

TAKE of the largest asparagus, cut off the white at the ends, and scrape them lightly to the head, till they look green; wipe them with a cloth, and lay them in a broad gallipot very even; throw over them whole cloves, mace, and a little salt; put over them as much white wine vinegar as will cover them very

very well: let them lie in cold pickle nine days; then pour the pickle out into a brass-kettle, and let them boil; then put them in, stove them down close, and set them by a little; then set them over again, till they are very green; but take care they don't boil to be soft; then put them in a large gallipot, place them even, and pour the liquor over them; when cold tie them down with leather: it is a good pickle, and looks well in a savoury made dish or pye.

To pickle Broom-Buds.

PUT your broom-buds into little linen bags, tie them up; make a pickle of bay-salt and water boiled, and strong enough to bear an egg; put your bags in a pot, and when your pickle is cold, put it to them; keep them close, and let them lie till they turn black: then shift them two or three times, till they change green; then take them out, and boil them as you have occasion for them: when they are boiled, put them out of the bag; in vinegar they will keep a month after they are boiled.

To pickle Purslane-Stalks.

WASH your stalks, and cut them in pieces six inches long; give them in water and salt a dozen walms; take them up, drain them, and when they cool make a pickle of stale beer, white wine vinegar, and salt; put them in, and cover them close.

Another Method.

TAKE the largest and greenest purslane-stalks, gather them dry, and strip off all the leaves; lay the stalks close in an earthen pot; you may lay kidney-beans among them, for you may do them the same way; then lay a stick or two across to keep them under the pickle, which must be made thus: Take whey, and set it on the fire, with as much salt as will make it almost as salt as brine; skim off all the curd, and let it boil a quarter of an hour longer, with Jamaica pepper in it; next day, when it is cold, pour the clear through a clean cloth upon the pickles, and tie it down close, and set it in a cool cellar; in winter, take a few out as you use them, wash them till the water runs clean; then put your beans or stalks into cold water, and set them over the fire, very close covered, and let them scald two hours; and though they be as black as ink, or stink before you put them in, they will be very green and good when done; then boil vinegar, salt, pepper, Jamaica pepper, and ginger, for half a quarter of an hour; and when your stalks are

well

The COMPLETE HOUSEWIFE. 237

well drained from the water through a colander, then put your pickle to them, and when these are used, green more, but do not do many at a time.

To pickle Lemons.

TAKE twelve lemons, scrape them with a piece of broken glass, then cut them cross into four parts downright, but not quite through, but that they will hang together; then put in as much salt as they will hold, rub them well, and strew them over with salt: let them lie in an earthen dish, and turn them every day for three days; then slice an ounce of ginger very thin, and salted for three days, twelve cloves of garlic parboiled and salted three days, a small handful of mustard-seed bruised, and searced through a hair sieve, some red Indian pepper, one to every lemon; take your lemons out of the salt, and squeeze them gently, and put them into a jar with the spice, and cover them with the best white wine vinegar; stop them up very close, and in a month's time they will be fit to eat.

To pickle small Onions.

TAKE young white unset onions, as big as the tip of your finger; lay them in water and salt two days; shift them once, then drain them in a cloth; boil the best vinegar with spice according to your taste, and when it is cold, keep them in it, covered with a wet bladder.

To make Vinegar.

TO every gallon of water put a pound of coarse Lisbon sugar, let it boil, and keep skimming of it as long as the scum rises; then pour it into tubs, and when it is as cold as beer to work, toast a good toast, and rub it over with yeast. Let it work twenty-four hours; then have ready a vessel iron-hooped, and well painted, fixed in a place where the sun has full power, and fix it so as not to have any occasion to move it. When you draw it off, then fill your vessels, lay a tile on the bung to keep the dust out. Make it in March, and it will be fit to use in June or July. Draw it off into little stone bottles the latter end of June or beginning of July, let it stand till you want to use it, and it will never foul any more: but when you go to draw it off, and you find it is not four enough, let it stand a month longer before you draw it off. For pickles to go abroad, use this vinegar alone; but in England you will be obliged, when you pickle, to put one half cold spring-water to it, and then it will be full four with this vinegar. You need not boil, unless you please, for almost any sort of pickles, it will keep them quite good.

good. It will keep walnuts very fine without boiling, even to go to the Indies; but then don't put water to it. For green pickles, you may pour it fcalding hot on two or three times. All other forts of pickles you need not boil it. Mushrooms only wash them clean, dry them, put them into little bottles, with a nutmeg juft fcalded in vinegar, and fliced (whilft it is hot) very thin, and a few blades of mace; then fill up the bottle with the cold vinegar and fpring-water, pour the mutton fat tried over it, and tie a bladder and leather over the top. Thefe mushrooms won't be fo white, but as finely tafted as if they were juft gathered; and a fpoonful of this pickle will give fauce a very fine flavour.

White walnuts, fuckers, and onions, and all white pickles, do in the fame manner, after they are ready for the pickle.

To make Goofberry Vinegar.

TAKE goofberries full ripe, bruife them in a mortar, then meafure them, and to every quart of goofberries put three quarts of water, firft boiled, and let it ftand till cold; let it ftand twenty-four hours; then ftrain it through a canvas, then a flannel; and to every gallon of this liquor put one pound of feeding brown fugar; ftir it well, and barrel it up; at three quarters of a year old it is fit for ufe; but if it ftands longer it is the better: this vinegar is likewife good for pickles.

To keep Artichokes in Pickle, to boil all Winter.

THROW your artichokes into falt and water half a day, then make a pot of water boil, and put in your artichokes, and let them boil till you can juft draw off the leaves from the bottom; then cut off the bottom very fmooth and clean, and put them into a pot with pepper, falt, cloves, mace, two bay-leaves, and as much vinegar as will cover them; then pour as much melted butter over them as will cover them an inch thick; tie it down clofe, and keep them for ufe; when you ufe them, put them into boiling water, with a piece of butter in the water to plump them; then ufe them for what you pleafe.

The Lemon Sallad.

TAKE lemons and cut them into halves, and when you have taken out the meat, lay the rinds in water twelve hours; then take them out, and cut the rinds thus ☙; boil them in water till they are tender; take them out and dry them; then take a pound of loaf fugar, putting to it a quarter of a pint of white wine, and twice as much white wine vinegar, and boil it a little; then take it off, and when it is cold put it in the pot to your peels; they will be ready to eat in five or six days; it is a pretty fallad.

To make English Catchup.

TAKE a wide-mouthed bottle, put therein a pint of the best white wine vinegar, putting in ten or twelve cloves of eschalot peeled and just bruised; then take a quarter of a pint of the best langoon white wine, boil it a little, and put to it twelve or fourteen anchovies washed and shred, and dissolve them in the wine, and when cold, put them in the bottle; then take a quarter of a pint more of white wine, and put in it mace, ginger sliced, a few cloves, a spoonful of whole pepper just bruised, and let them boil all a little; when near cold, slice in almost a whole nutmeg, and some lemon-peel, and likewise put in two or three spoonfuls of horse-radish; then stop it close, and for a week shake it once or twice a day; then use it; it is good to put into fish-sauce, or any savoury dish of meat; you may add to it the clear liquor that comes from mushrooms.

Another Way.

TAKE the large flaps of mushrooms, pick nothing but the straws and dirt from it, then lay them in a broad earthen pan, strew a good deal of salt over them, let them lie till next morning, then with your hand break them, put them into a stewpan, let them boil a minute or two, then strain them through a coarse cloth, and wring it hard. Take out all the juice, let it stand to settle, then pour it off clear, run it through a thick flannel bag, (some filter it through brown paper, but that is a very tedious way) then boil it; to a quart of the liquor put a quarter of an ounce of whole ginger, and half a quarter of an ounce of whole pepper. Boil it briskly a quarter of an hour, then strain it, and when it is cold, put it into pint bottles. In each bottle put four or five blades of mace, and six cloves, cork it tight, and it will keep two years. This gives the best flavour of the mushrooms to any sauce. If you put to a pint of this catchup, a pint of mum, it will taste like foreign catchup.

Another Way.

TAKE the large flaps, and salt them as above; boil the liquor, strain it through a thick flannel bag: to a quart of that liquor put a quart of stale beer, a large stick of horse-radish cut in little slips, five or six bay-leaves, an onion stuck with twenty or thirty cloves, a quarter of an ounce of mace, a quarter of an ounce of nutmegs beat, a quarter of an ounce of black and white pepper,

pepper, a quarter of an ounce of all-ſpice, and four or five races of ginger. Cover it cloſe, and let it ſimmer very ſoftly till about one third is waſted; then ſtrain it through a flannel bag, when it is cold bottle it in pint bottles, cork it cloſe, and it will keep a great while: you may put red wine in the room of beer; ſome put in a head of garlic, but I think that ſpoils it. The other receipt you have in the Chapter for the Sea.

To make Catchup to keep Twenty Years.

TAKE a gallon of ſtrong ſtale beer, one pound of anchovies waſhed from the pickle, a pound of eſchalots, peeled, half an ounce of mace, half an ounce of cloves, a quarter of an ounce of whole pepper, three or four large races of ginger, two quarts of the large muſhroom-flaps rubbed to pieces. Cover all this cloſe, and let it ſimmer till it is half waſted, then ſtrain it through a flannel bag; let it ſtand till it is quite cold, then bottle it. You may carry it to the Indies. A ſpoonful of this to a pound of freſh butter melted, makes a fine fiſh-ſauce; or in the room of gravy-ſauce. The ſtronger and ſtaler the beer is, the better the catchup will be.

A Pickle in imitation of Indian Bamboe.

TAKE the young ſhoots of elder, about the beginning or middle of May; take the middle of the ſtalk, for the top is not worth doing; peel off the out rind, and lay them in a ſtrong brine of ſalt and beer, one night; dry them in a cloth ſingle, and in the mean time, make a pickle of half gooſberry vinegar, and half ale allegar; to every quart of pickle put one ounce of long pepper, one ounce of ſliced ginger, a few corns of Jamaica pepper, and a little mace; boil it, and pour it hot upon the ſhoots, ſtop the jar cloſe, and ſet it cloſe by the fire twenty-four hours, ſtirring it very often.

To diſtil Verjuice for Pickles.

TAKE three quarts of the ſharpeſt verjuice, and put in a cold ſtill, and diſtil it off very ſoftly; the ſooner it is diſtilled in the ſpring, the better for uſe.

To pickle Salmon.

TAKE two quarts of good vinegar, half an ounce of black pepper, and as much Jamaica pepper, cloves and mace, of each a quarter of an ounce, near a pound of ſalt; bruiſe the ſpice groſly,

grosly, and put all these to a small quantity of water, put just enough to cover your fish; cut the fish round, three or four pieces, according to the size of the salmon, and when the liquor boils put in your fish, boil it well; then take the fish out of the pickle, and let it cool; and when it is cold put your fish into the barrel or stein you keep it in, strewing some spice and bay-leaves between every piece of fish; let the pickle cool, and skim off the fat, and when the pickle is quite cold pour it on your fish, and cover it very close.

To pickle Oysters.

TAKE a hundred and a half of large oysters, wash them and scald them in their own liquor; then take them out, and lay them on a clean cloth to cool; strain their liquor, and boil and skim it clean, adding to it one pint of white wine, half a pint of white wine vinegar, one nutmeg beat grosly, one onion slit, an ounce of white pepper, half whole, the other half just bruised, six or eight blades of mace, a quarter of an ounce of cloves, and five or six bay-leaves; boil up this pickle till it is of a good taste, then cool it in broad dishes, and put your oysters in a deep pot or barrel, and when the pickle is cold put it to them; in five or six days they will be ready to eat, and will keep three weeks or a month, if you take them out with a spoon, and not touch them with your fingers.

Another Method.

WASH your oysters in their own liquor, squeezing them between your fingers, that there be no gravel in them; strain the liquor, and wash the oysters in it again; put as much water as the liquor, set it on the fire, and as it boils skim it clean; then put a pretty deal of whole pepper, boil it a little, then put in some blades of mace, and your oysters, stirring them apace, and when they are firm in the middle part, take them off, pour them quick into an earthen pot, and cover them very close; put in a few bay-leaves; be sure your oysters are all under the liquor; the next day put them up for use, cover them very close; when you dish them to eat, put a little white wine or vinegar on the plate with them.

To pickle Lobsters.

BOIL your lobsters in salt and water, till they will easily slip out of the shell; take the tails out whole, just crack the claws, and take the meat out as whole as possible; then make the pickle half white wine and half water; put in whole cloves, whole pepper, whole mace, two or three bay-leaves; then put in the lobsters, and let them have a boil or two in the pickle; then take them out, and set them by to be cold, boil the pickle longer, and when both are cold put them together, and keep them for use. Tie the pot down close; eat them with oil, vinegar, and lemon.

Tench to pickle.

WHEN your tench are cleansed, have a pickle ready boiled, half white wine and half vinegar, a few blades of mace, some sliced ginger, whole pepper, and a bay-leaf, with a piece of lemon-peel and some salt; boil your tench in it, and when it is enough, lay them out to cool; and when the liquor is cold, put them in; it will keep but few days.

To pickle Mackarel.

SLIT your mackarel in halves, take out the roes, gut and clean them, strew salt over them, and lay one on another, the back of one to the inside of the other; let them lie two or three hours, then wipe every piece clean from the salt, and strew them over with pepper beaten and grated nutmeg; let them lie two or three hours longer; then fry them well, take them out of the pan, and lay them on coarse cloths to drain; when cold, put them in a pan, and cover them over with a pickle of vinegar boiled with spice, when it is cold.

To pickle Sprats for Anchovies.

TAKE an anchovy-barrel, or a deep glazed pot, put a few bay-leaves at the bottom, a layer of bay-salt, and some petre-salt mixed together; then a layer of sprats, crouded close, then bay-leaves, and the same salt and sprats, and so till your barrel or pot be full; then put in the head of your barrel close, and once a week turn the other end upwards; in three months they will be fit to eat as anchovies raw, but they will not dissolve.

To marinate Smelts.

TAKE your smelts, gut them neatly, wash and dry them, and fry them in oil; lay them to drain and cool, and have in readiness a pickle made with vinegar, salt, pepper, cloves, mace, onion, horse-radish; let it boil together half an hour; when it is cold put in your smelts.

To pickle Muscles or Cockles.

TAKE your fresh muscles or cockles; wash them very clean, and put them in a pot over the fire till they open; then take them out of their shells, pick them clean, and lay them to cool; then put their liquor to some vinegar, whole pepper, ginger sliced thin, and mace, setting it over the fire: when it is scalding hot, put in your muscles, and let them stew a little; then pour out the pickle from them, and when both are cold put them in an earthen jug, and cork it up close: in two or three days they will be fit to eat.

PART VIII.

PRESERVES, CONSERVES, SYRUPS, CREAMS, and JELLIES.

CHAP. I.
Of PRESERVES.

To preserve Oranges whole.

AKE the beſt Bermudas oranges, pare them with a penknife very thin, and lay your oranges in water three or four days ſhifting them every day; then put them in a kettle with fair water, putting a board on them, to keep them down in the water; have a ſkillet on the fire with water, that may be in readineſs to ſupply the kettle with boiling water: as it waſtes it muſt be filled up three or four times while the oranges are doing, for they will take up ſeven or eight hours in boiling, for they muſt be ſo tender that a wheat-ſtraw may be thruſt through them; then take them up, and ſcoop the ſeeds out of them, making a little hole on the top; then weigh them, and to every pound of orange take a pound and three quarters of double refined ſugar, finely beaten and ſifted; fill up your oranges with ſugar, and ſtrew ſome on them, and let them lie a little; then make your jelly for them thus; take two dozen of pippins, and ſlice them into water, and when they are boiled tender, ſtrain the liquor from the pulp, and to every pound of orange you muſt have a pint and a half of this liquor, and put to it three quarters of the ſugar left in filling the oranges; ſet it on the fire, and let it boil, and ſkim it well, and put it in a clean earthen pan till it is cold; then put it in your ſkillet, and put in your oranges, and with a ſmall bodkin jobb the oranges as they are boiling, to let the ſyrup into them; ſtrew on the reſt of your ſugar while they are boiling; and when they look clear, take them up and put them in your glaſſes, but one in a glaſs juſt fit for them, and boil the ſyrup till it is almoſt a jelly; then fill up your oranges and glaſſes, and when they are cold paper them up, and put them in your ſtove.

Another Way.

TAKE the best and largest Seville oranges, water them three days, shifting them twice a day, boiling them in a copper with a great deal of water till they are tender; they must be tied in a cloth, and kept under water, the water must boil before you put them in; then take to every pound of orange, a pound and a half of double refined sugar, beaten and sifted; then have in readiness apple-water made of john-apples; take to every pint of that water a pound of sugar; then take a third part of the sugar and put to the water; boil it a while, and set it by to cool; then cut a little hole in the bottom of your orange, pick out all the seeds, and fill them up with what sugar is left; prick your oranges all over with a bodkin, then put them into your syrup, boiling them so fast that the syrup may cover them, then put in your sugar that is left: when the syrup will jelly, and the oranges look clear, they are enough; then glass them with the holes uppermost, and pour the syrup upon them.

Another Way to preserve Oranges.

TAKE right Seville oranges, the thickest rind you can get, lay them in water, changing the water twice a day for two days, then rub them well with salt, wash them well afterwards, and put them in water, changing the water twice a day for two days more; then put them in a large pot of water to boil, having another pot of boiling water ready to throw them into, as the other grows bitter; change them often till they are tender; then take them up in a linen cloth, and a woollen over it, to keep them hot; take out one at a time, and make a little hole at the top, and pick out the seeds, but do not break the meat; pare them as thin as you can with a sharp penknife; take to a pound of oranges before they are opened, a pound of double refined sugar and a pint of fair water, boil it and skim it, and let it be ready when you pare them, to throw them into; when they are all pared, set them on the fire, cover them close, and keep them boiling as fast as they can boil, till they look clear; then take them up into a deep gallipot, with the holes upward, fill them with syrup, and when they are almost cold, pour the rest of the syrup over them; let them stand a fortnight or three weeks in that syrup; then make a jelly of pippins, and when it is almost ready, take your oranges out of the gallipot, pour all the syrup out of them, put them into the jelly, and let them have a boil or two; then put them into your glasses, and when they are near cold fill them with jelly; the next day paper them.

The Dutchess of Cleveland's Receipts to preserve Lemons, Citrons and Oranges.

TAKE good lemons, fair and well coloured, and scrape a little of the uppermost rind; take out the seeds, and the juice; lay them in spring water, shifting them twice a day for a day or two; then boil them, to be tender, with a pound and a quarter of double refined sugar, and a pint and three quarters of spring-water; take the scum off, and put in your lemons; have ready a pint of pippin-water; boil it first with half a pound of sugar, and put it to them; then boil it to a jelly, and put in the juice of your lemons; then let them boil but a little after, and put them into your glasses, but be sure to cover them with syrup.

How to take out the Seeds.

YOU must cut a hole in the top, but it must be a little one, and take them out with a scoop; dry them, before you put them into your syrup, with a clean cloth.

To preserve whole Quinces white.

TAKE the largest quinces of the greenest colour, and scald them till they are pretty soft, then pare them, and core them with a scoop; then weigh your quinces against so much double refined sugar, and make a syrup of one half, and put in your quinces and boil them as fast as you can; then you must have in readiness pippin-liquor, let it be very strong of the pippins; and when it is strained out, put in the other half of your sugar, and make it a jelly; and when your quinces are clear put them into the jelly, and let them simmer a little, they will be very white: so glass them up, and when they are cold paper them, and keep them in a stove.

To preserve Gooseberries.

TAKE of the best Dutch gooseberries before they are too ripe, stone them, and put them in a skillet with so much fair water as will cover them; set them on a fire to scald, and when they are tender take them out of the liquor, and peel off the outer skin as you do codlins, and throw them into some double refined sugar, powdered and sifted; put a handful of more gooseberries into that water, and let them boil a little, then run the liquor through a sieve; take the weight of your peeled gooseberries in double refined sugar, break the sugar in lumps, and wet the lumps in the liquor that the gooseberries were scalded in, in, and put your ſugar in a preſerving-pan over a clear fire, let it boil up, and ſkim it well; then put in your gooſberries, and let them boil till they look clear; then place them in your glaſſes, and boil the liquor a little longer, and pour it on your gooſberries in the glaſſes; when they are cold paper them.

To preſerve Gooſberries in Hops.

TAKE the largeſt Dutch gooſberries, and with a knife cut them acroſs at the head and half way down, picking out the ſeeds clean with a bodkin, but do not break them; then take fine long thorns, ſcrape them, and put them on your gooſberries, putting the leaf of the one to the cut of the other, and ſo till your thorn is full, then put them into a new pipkin with a cloſe lid, cover them with water, and let them ſtand ſcalding till they are green; then take them up, and lay them upon a ſieve to drain from the water; be ſure they boil not in the greening; for if they have but one walm they are ſpoiled; and while they are greening make a ſyrup for them. Take whole green gooſberries and boil them in water till they all break, then ſtrain the water through a ſieve, and weigh your hops, and to a pound of hops put a pound and a half of double refined ſugar; put the ſugar and hops into the liquor, and boil them open till they are clear and green, then take them up and lay them upon pye plates, and boil your ſyrup longer; lay your hops in a pretty deep gallipot, and when the ſyrup is cold pour it on them; cover them with paper, and keep them in a ſtove.

To preſerve Gooſberries whole without ſtoning.

TAKE the largeſt preſerving gooſberries, and pick off the black eye, but not the ſtalk, then ſet them over the fire in a pot of water to ſcald, cover them very cloſe, and let them ſcald, but not boil or break, and when they are tender take them up into cold water; then take a pound and a half of double refined ſugar to a pound of gooſberries, clarify the ſugar with water, a pint to a pound of ſugar; when the ſyrup is cold, put your gooſberries ſingle into your preſerving-pan, put the ſyrup to them, ſet them on a gentle fire, and let them boil, but not too faſt, leſt they break; when they are boiled, and you perceive the ſugar has entered them, take them off, cover them with white paper, and ſet them by till the next day; then take them out of the ſyrup, and boil the ſyrup till it begins to be ropy, ſkim it and put it to them again, and ſet them on a gentle fire, and let them preſerve gently till you perceive the ſyrup will rope; then take them off, and ſet them by till they are co covering them with paper; then boil ſome gooſberries in Id, water, and when the liquor is ſtrong enough ſtrain it out, let it ſtand

stand to settle, and to every pint take a pound of double refined sugar, make a jelly of it, and put the goosberries in glasses; when they are cold cover them with the jelly; the next day paper them; wet, and then half dry the paper that goes in the inside, it closes down better; and then put on the other papers, and put them in your stove.

To preserve Apricots.

TAKE your apricots, stone and pare them; take their weight in double refined sugar beaten and sifted, and put your apricots in a silver cup or tankard, and cover them over with the sugar, letting them stand so all night; the next day put them in a preserving-pan, set them on a gentle fire, and let them simmer up a little while; then let them boil till they are tender and clear, taking them off sometimes to turn and skim; keep them under the liquor as they are doing, and with a small clean bodkin or great needle jobb them sometimes, that the syrup may penetrate into them; when they are enough take them and put them in glasses, boil and skim the syrup, and when it is cold put it on your apricots.

To preserve Apricots ripe.

GATHER your apricots of a fine colour, but not too ripe; weigh them, and to every pound of apricots put a pound of double refined sugar beaten and sifted; stone and pare your apricots; as you pare them put them into the pan you do them in, with sugar strewed over and under them; let them not touch one another, but put sugar between; cover them up and let them lie till the next day, then stir them gently till the sugar is melted; then put them on a quick fire and let them boil half an hour, skimming exceeding well all the while; then take it off, and cover it till it is quite cold, or till the next day; then boil it again, skimming it very well till it is enough; so put it in pots.

To preserve green Apricots.

TAKE green apricots, about the middle of June, or when the stone is hard, put them on the fire in cold water three or four hours, cover them close, but first take their weight in double refined sugar; then pare them nicely; dip your sugar in water, and boil the water and sugar very well; then put in your apricots, and let them boil till they begin to open; then take out the stone, and close it up again, and put them in the syrup, and let them boil till they are enough, skimming all the while; then put them in pots.

Another

Another Method.

BEFORE the stones are hard, wet them and lay them in a coarse cloth, and put to them two or three handfuls of salt, rubbing them till the roughness is off; then put them in scalding water, and set them over the fire till almost boiled; then set them off till almost cold; do this two or three times; after this let them be close covered, and when they look green, let them boil till they begin to be tender; weigh them, and take their weight of double refined sugar, to a pound of sugar half a pint of water; make the syrup, and when almost cold put in your apricots, boil them well till clear; warm the syrup two or three times till thick, or put them in cold jelly, or dry them as you use them.

To preserve Plumbs green.

THE plumbs that will be greenest are the white plumbs that are ripe in wheat harvest; gather them about the middle of July whilst they are green; when gathered, lay them in water twelve hours; then scald them in two several waters, let not the first be too hot, but the second must boil before you put the plumbs in; when they begin to shrivel, peel off the skin as you do codlins, keep them whole, and let a third water be made hot, and when it boils, put in your plumbs, and give them two or three walms; then take them off the fire, and cover them close for half a quarter of an hour, till you perceive them to look greenish and tender; then take them out and weigh them with double refined sugar, equal weight; wet a quarter of a pound of your sugar in four spoonfuls of water, set it on the fire, and when it begins to boil, take it off, and put in your plumbs one by one, and strew the rest of your sugar upon them, only saving a little to put in with your perfume, musk or ambergrease, which must be put in a little before they are done: let them boil softly on a moderate fire half an hour or more, till they are green and the syrup thickish, put your plumbs in a pot or glasses; let the syrup have two or three walms more, and put it to them; when they are cold paper them up.

Another Method.

TAKE green plumbs grown to their full bigness, but before they begin to ripen; let them be carefully gathered with their stalks and leaves, put them into cold spring-water over a fire, and let them boil very gently; when they will peel, take off the skins; then put the plumbs into other cold water, and let them stand over a very gentle fire till they are soft; put two pounds of double refined sugar to every pound of plumbs, and

make

make the sugar with some water into a thick syrup before the plumbs are put in: the stones of the plumbs are not to be grown so hard, but that you may thrust a pin through them. After the same manner do green apricots.

To preserve black Pear-Plumbs, or any black Plumb.

TAKE a pound of plumbs, give them a little slit in the seam; then take some of your worst plumbs, and put them in a gallipot close covered, and set them in a pot of boiling water, and as they yield liquor still pour it out. To a pint of this liquor, take a pound and a quarter of sugar; put them together, and give them a boil and a skim, after which take it off to cool a little; then take your pound of plumbs, and as you put them in, give every one of them a prick or two with a needle, so set them again on a soft fire a pretty while; then take them off, and let them stand till the next day, that they may drink up the syrup without breaking the skin; the next day warm them again once or twice, till you see the syrup grows thick, and the plumbs look of the right black, still skimming them, and when they will endure a boil, give them two or three walms, and skim them well, and put them in your glasses. Be sure you keep some of the syrup in a glass, that when your plumbs are settled and cold, you may cover them with it. The next day paper them up, and keep them for use.

To preserve the great white Plumb.

TO a pound of plumbs take three quarters of a pound of double refined sugar in lumps; dip your sugar in water, and boil and skim very well; slit your plumbs down the seam, and put them into the syrup with the slit downward; let them stew over the fire a quarter of an hour; skim very well, and take them off; and when cold turn them, and cover them up, and turn them in the syrup, every day, two or three times a day for five days; then put them in pots.

To preserve white Pear-Plumbs.

TAKE pear-plumbs when they are yellow, before they are too ripe, give them a slit in the seam, and prick them behind; make your water almost scalding hot, and put a little sugar to it to sweeten it; and put in your plumbs, and cover them close; set them on the fire to coddle, and take them off sometimes a little, and set them on again; take care they do not break; have in readiness as much double refined sugar boiled to a height as will cover them, and when they are coddled pretty tender, take them out of the liquor, and put them into your preserving-pan to your syrup, which must be but blood warm when your

plumbs

plumbs go in; let them boil till they are clear, skim them, take them off, and let them stand two hours; then set them on again, and boil them, and when they are thoroughly preserved, take them up, and lay them in glasses; boil your syrup till it is thick, and when it is cold put in your plumbs; a month after, if your syrup grows thin, you must boil it again, or make a fine jelly of pippins, and put on them. This way you may do the Primordian-plumb, or any white plumb; and when they are cold paper them up.

To preserve Damsons whole.

TAKE some damsons, cut them in pieces, and put them in a skillet over the fire, with as much water as will cover them; when they are boiled, and the liquor pretty strong, strain it out; and for every pound of your whole damsons wiped clean, a pound of single refined sugar, put the third part of the sugar in the liquor, and set it over the fire, and when it simmers put in your damsons; let them have one good boil, and take them off for half an hour, covered up close; then set them on again, and let them simmer over the fire, often turning them; then take them out, put them into a bason, and strew all the sugar that was left on them, and pour the hot liquor over them; cover them up, and let them stand till the next day; then boil them up again till they are enough; take them up, and put them in pots; boil the liquor till it jellies, and pour it on them when it is almost cold, so paper them up.

To preserve Cherries.

PRICK and stone your cherries; weigh them, and take their weight of single refined sugar beaten fine; mix three parts of the sugar with juice of currants, put in your preserving-pan, giving it a boil and a skim, and then put in your cherries; let them boil very fast, now and then strewing in some of the sugar that was left till all is in; skim it well, and when they are enough, which you may know by trying some in a spoon, and when it jellies, take it off, and fill your glasses, and when they are cold paper them up.

Another Method.

GATHER your cherries of a bright red, not too ripe, weigh them, and to every pound of cherries put three quarters of a pound of double refined sugar beaten fine; stone them, and strew some sugar on them as you stone them; to keep their colour, wet your sugar with fair water, near half a pint, and boil and skim it, then put in three small spoonfuls of the juice of currants that was infused with a little water; give it another boil and skim, and put in your cherries; boil them till they are tender, then pour them into a china bason; cover them with paper,

paper, and set them by twenty-four hours; then put them in your preserving-pan, and boil them till they look clear; put them in your glass clear from the syrup, and put the syrup on them strained through muslin.

To preserve Barberries.

TAKE the largest barberries you can get, and stone them; to every pound of barberries take three pounds of sugar, and boil it till it is candy high; then put in the barberries, and let them boil till the sugar boils over them all; then take them off, skim them, set them on again, and give them another boil, and put them in an earthen pan, cover them with paper, and set them by till the next day; then put them in pots, and pour the syrup over them; cover them with paper, and keep them in a stove. If the syrup grows thin you may make a little jelly of pippins, and put them in when it is ready, and give them one walm, and pour them again into glasses.

Another Method.

TAKE a pound of barberries picked from the stalks, put them into two quart pans, set them in a brass-pot full of hot water, to stew them; after this, strain them, add a pound of sugar, and a pint of rose-water, boil them together a liittle, take half a pound of the best clusters of barberries you can get, dip them into the syrup while it is boiling, take out the barberries, and let the syrup boil till it is thick; when they are cold, put them into glasses or gallipots with the syrup.

To dry Barberries.

STONE the barberries and use them in bunches; weigh them, and to every pound of berries clarify two pounds of sugar; make the syrup with half a pint of water to a pound of sugar, put your barrberries into the syrup when it is scalding hot, let them boil a little, and set them by with a paper close to them; the next day make them scalding hot, repeat this two days, but do not boil it after the first time, and when they are cold lay them on earthen plates, strew sugar well over them, the next day turn them on a sieve, and sift them again with sugar; turn them daily till they are dry, taking care your stove is not too hot.

A fine Way to preserve Raspberries.

TAKE the juice of red and white raspberries and codlin jelly; to a pint and a half, two pounds of double refined sugar; boil and skim it, and then put in three quarters of a pound of large picked raspberries; let them boil very fast, till they jelly and are clear; do not take them off the fire, that will make them

... hour will do them when they begin
... raspberries in the glass first, and strain
... jelly, and put it to them; and when they
... them gently, that they may not all lie on
... glass; and when cold, lay papers close on them;
... papers, and dry them in a cloth.

To preserve Raspberries whole.

TAKE the full weight of your raspberries in double refined sugar, beaten and sifted; lay your raspberries single in the bottom of your preserving-pan, and put all your sugar over them; set them on a slow fire, till there is some syrup in the bottom of the pan; then set them on a quick fire, till all the sugar be thoroughly melted; give them two or three walms, skim them, take them up, and put them in glasses.

To preserve Raspberries in Jelly.

TAKE of the largest and best raspberries, and to a pound take a pound and a quarter of sugar made into a syrup, and boiled candy high; then put in the raspberries, set them over a gentle fire, and as they boil shake them; when the sugar boils over them, take them off the fire, skim them, and set them by a little; then set them on again, and have half a pint of juice of currants by you, and at several times put in a little as it boils; shake them often as they grow nearer to be enough, which you may know by setting some in a spoon to try if it will jelly, for when they jelly they are enough; then lay them in your glasses, and keep the jelly to cover them; but before you put it to them pick out all the seeds, and let the jelly cover them well.

To preserve Currants in Jelly.

TAKE your currants, strip them, and put them in an earthen pot; tie them close down, set them in a kettle of boiling water, and let them stand three hours, keeping the water boiling; then take a clean flaxen cloth, and strain out the juice; when it has settled, take a pound of double refined sugar, beaten and sifted, and put to a pint of the clear juice; have in readiness some whole currants stoned, and when the juice boils, put in your currants, and boil them till your syrup jellies, which you may know by taking up some in a spoon; then put it in your glasses. This way make jelly of currants, only leaving out the whole currants; when cold, paper them up.

To

To dry Currants in Bunches.

STONE your currants, and tie them up in bunches; to every pound of currants boil two pounds of sugar, till it blows very strong; dip in the currants, let them boil very fast till the sugar flies all over them, let them settle a quarter of an hour, and boil them again till the sugar rises almost to the top of the pan; let them settle, skim them, and set them by till next day; then drain them and lay them out, taking care to spread the sprigs that they may not dry clogged together; dust them very much and dry them in a hot stove.

To preserve small Cucumbers green.

TAKE small cucumbers, boil them, but not very tender; when you take them out of the water, make a hole thro' every one with a large needle; then pare and weigh them, and to every pound allow a pound of sugar, which make into syrup, with a pint of water to every pound of sugar; you must green them before you put them into the sugar; then let them boil, keeping them close covered; then put them by, and for three or four days boil them a little every day; put into the syrup the peel of a fresh lemon; then make a fresh syrup with double refined sugar, you must have three quarters of a pound to a pound of cucumbers, and a quarter of a pint of fair water, the juice of a lemon, and a little ambergrease boiled in it; so do them for use; paper them when cold.

To preserve green Cucumbers.

TAKE gerkins, rub them clean, and green them in hot water; then take their weight in double refined sugar, boil it to a thick syrup with a quarter of a pint of spring-water to every pound of sugar; then put in your cucumbers and set them over the fire, but not to boil fast, so do two or three days; the last day boil them till they are tender and clear, so glass them up.

To preserve whole Pippins.

TAKE Kentish pippins or apple-johns, pare them, and slice them into fair water; set them on a clear fire, and when they are boiled to mash, let the liquor run through a hair sieve. Boil as many apples thus, till you have the quantity of liquor you would have. To a pint of this liquor you must have a pound of double refined sugar in great lumps, wet the lumps of sugar with the pippin-liquor, set it over a gentle fire, let it boil, and skim it it well, and while you are making the jelly, you muſt have your whole pippins boiling at the ſame time; they muſt be the faireſt and beſt pippins you can get; ſcoop out the cores, and pare them neatly, and put them into fair water as you do them; you muſt likewiſe make a ſyrup ready to put them into, the quantity as you think will boil them in clear; you muſt make that ſyrup with double refined ſugar and water; tie up your whole pippins in a piece of fine muſlin ſeverally, and when your ſugar and water boils put them in; let them boil very faſt, ſo faſt that the ſyrup always boils over them; ſometimes take them off, and then ſet them on again; let them boil till they are clear and tender; then take off the tiffany or muſlin they were tied up in, and put them into glaſſes that will hold but one in a glaſs; then ſee if your jelly of apple johns be boiled to jelly enough; if it be, ſqueeze in the juice of two lemons, and put muſk and ambergreaſe in a rag, and let it have a boil, then ſtrain it through a jelly-bag into the glaſſes your pippins were in; you muſt be ſure to drain your pippins well from the ſyrup they were boiled in; before you put them in your glaſſes, you may if you pleaſe boil lemon-peel in little pieces in water till they are tender, and then boil them in the ſyrup your pippins were boiled in; then take them out, and lay them about the pippins before the jelly is put in; when they are cold, paper them up.

To preſerve Mulberries whole.

SET ſome mulberries over the fire in a ſkillet, and draw from them a pint of juice, when it is ſtrained; then take three pounds of ſugar beaten very fine, wet the ſugar with the pint of juice; boil up your ſugar and ſkim it, and put in two pounds of ripe mulberries, letting them ſtand in the ſyrup till they are thoroughly warm; then ſet them on the fire, and let them boil very gently; do them but half enough, ſo put them by in the ſyrup till next day; then boil them gently again, and when the ſyrup is pretty thick, and will ſtand in a round drop when it is cold, they are enough; put all together in a gallipot for uſe.

To preſerve green Grapes.

TAKE the largeſt and beſt grapes before they are thorough ripe; ſtone them, ſcald them, and let them lie two days in the water they are ſcalded in; then drain them, and put them into a thin ſyrup, and give them a heat over a ſlow fire; the next day turn the grapes in the pan, and heat them again the day after; then drain them, put them into a clarified ſugar, give them a good boil, ſkim them, and ſet them by: the following day, boil more ſugar to blow, put it to the grapes, give all a good boil,

boil, skim them, and set them in a warm stove all night; the day after drain the grapes, and lay them out to dry, first dusting them very well.

To preserve or dry Samphire.

TAKE it in bunches as it grows, put on the fire a large deep stew-pan filled with water; when it boils throw in a little salt, put in your samphire, and when you see it look of a fine beautiful green, take off the pan directly, and with a fork take up the samphire, lay it on sieves to drain, and when cold, either preserve it, or dry it as the barberries; if you frost them they will be very pretty.

To keep green Pease till Christmas.

SHELL what quantity you please of young pease, put them in the pot when the water boils, let them have four or five walms; then first pour them into a colander, and then spread a cloth on a table, and put them on that, and dry them well in it; have bottles ready dried, and fill them to the necks, and pour over them melted mutton fat, and cork them down very close, that no air come to them; set them in your cellar, and when you use them, put them into boiling water, with a spoonful of fine sugar, and a good piece of butter; and when they are enough, drain and butter them.

To keep Artichokes all the Year.

IN the latter end of the season boil them till they be half enough, and then dry them on a hair-cloth upon a kiln the space of fifty hours, till they are very dry; lay them in a dry place; when you use them, soak them a night in water, and boil them till they are tender.

To keep Walnuts all the Year.

ALMOST in the latter end of the season, take off the green shell of your nuts, and dry them on a hair-cloth on the kiln forty hours; when they are dry, keep them for use; when you would use them, soak them three days in water, shifting them three times a day.

CHAP.

… *The* COMPLETE HOUSEWIFE. 257

CHAP. II.
Of CONSERVES and SYRUPS.

To make Conserve of red Roses, or any other Flowers.

TAKE rose-buds, pick them, and cut off the white part from the red; put the red flowers into a sieve and sift them to take out the seeds; then weigh them, and to every pound of flowers take two pounds and an half of loaf sugar; beat the flowers pretty fine in a stone mortar, then by degrees put the sugar to them, and beat it very well till it is well incorporated together; then put it into gallipots, and tie it over with paper, and over that leather; it will keep for seven years.

To stew Apples.

TAKE to a quart of water a pound of double refined sugar beaten fine, boil and skim it, and put into it a pound of the largest and clearest pippins, pared, cut in halves, and cored; let them boil, covered with a continual froth, till they be as tender and clear as you would have them; then put in the juice of two lemons, and a little peel cut like threads; let them have five or six walms after the lemon is in, then put them in a china dish or salver you serve them in; they should be done two hours before used.

To dry Plumbs or Apricots.

TAKE your plumbs or apricots and weigh them, and to every pound of fruit allow a pound of double refined sugar; then scald your plumbs, stone them, and take off the skins, laying your plumbs on a dry cloth; then just wet your sugar, set it over the fire, and keep it stirring all one way till it boils to sugar again; take that sugar, laying some at the bottom of your preserving-pan, and your plumbs on it; strew the rest of the sugar on the plumbs, and let it stand till it is melted; then heat it scalding hot twice a day, but let it not boil; when the syrup is very thick, and candies about the pan, then take them out of the syrup, lay them on glasses to dry, and keep them continually warm, sifting a little sugar over them till they are almost dry; wet the stones in the syrup, and dry them with sugar, and put them at one end of the plumb, and when they are thorough dry, keep them in boxes, with papers between.

S T

To dry Apricots like Prunello's.

TAKE a pound of apricots, being cut in halves or quarters, let them boil till they be very tender in a thin syrup; let them stand a day or two in the stove; then take them out of the syrup, and lay them drying till they be as dry as prunello's, then box them; you may make your syrup red with the juice of red plumbs; if you please you may pare them.

To dry Apricots.

TAKE to a pound of apricots, a pound of double refined sugar; stone them, pare them, and put them into cold water; when they are all ready, put them into a skillet of hot water, and scald them till they are tender; then drain them very well from the water, and put them into a silver bason; have in readiness your sugar boiled to sugar again, and pour that sugar over your apricots; cover them with a silver plate, and let them stand all night; the next day set them over a gentle fire, and let them be scalding hot, turning them often; you must do them twice a day, till you see them begin to be candy; then take them out, and set them in your stove or glasses to dry, heating your stove every day till they are dry.

To make Apricot Chips.

PARE your apricots, and part them in the middle; take out the stone, and cut them crofs-ways pretty thin; as you cut them strew a very little sugar over them beaten and sifted; then set them on the fire, and let them stew gently a quarter of an hour; then take them off, cover them up, and set them by till the next day; then set them on the fire as long as before; take them out one by one and lay them on a sieve; strew sugar on the sieve, and over them; dry them in the sun or cool oven, turn them often; when dry put them in boxes.

To make Marmalade of Apricots.

GATHER your apricots just turned from the green, of a very pale yellow, pare them thin and weigh them, three quarters of a pound of double refined sugar to a pound of apricots; then cut them in halves, take out the stones, and slice them thin; beat your sugar, and put it in your preserving-pan with your sliced apricots, and three or four spoonfuls of water; boil and skim them, and when they are tender put them in glasses.

To make white Marmalade.

TAKE your quinces, scald them, pare them, and scrape the pulp clean from the cores, adding to every pound of pulp a pound of double refined sugar; put a little water to your sugar to dissolve it, and boil it candy high; then put in the quince pulp, and set it on the fire till it comes to a body; let it boil very fast; when it is enough put it in gallipots.

To make white Quince Marmalade.

SCALD your quinces tender, take off the skin, and pulp them from the core very fine, and to every pound of quince have a pound and a half of double refined sugar in lumps, and half a pint of water; dip your sugar in the water, and boil and skim it till it is a thick syrup; then put in your quince, boil and skim it on a quick fire a quarter of an hour, so put it in your pots.

To make red Quince Marmalade.

PARE, core, and quarter your quinces, then weigh them, and to a pound of quince allow a pound of single refined sugar beaten small, and to every pound of quince a pint of liquor; make your liquor thus; put your parings and cores, and three or four quinces cut in pieces, into a large skillet, with water proportionable to the quantity of quinces you do; cover it and set it over the fire, and let it boil two or three hours; then put in a quart of barberries, and let them boil an hour, and strain all out; then put your quince, and liquor, and a quarter of your sugar, into a skillet or large preserving-pan, and let them boil together over a gentle fire; cover it close, and take care it does not burn; strew in the rest of your sugar by degrees, and stir it often from the bottom, but do not break the quince till it is near enough; then break it in lumps as small as you like it; when it is of a good colour and very tender, try some in a spoon; if it jellies it is enough, then take it off, and put it in gallipots; when it is cold paper it up.

To make red Quince Marmalade another Way.

PARE and core a pound of quince, beat the parings and cores and some of your worst quinces, and strain out the juice; to every pound of quince take ten or twelve spoonfuls of that juice and three quarters of a pound of loaf sugar; put all into your preserving pan, cover it close, and let it stew over a gentle fire two hours; when it is of an orange red, uncover, and boil it up as fast as you can; when of a good colour, break it as you like it; give it a boil and pot it up.

To make Orange Marmalade.

TAKE a pound of the best Seville oranges, pare off all the yellow rind very thin, quarter the peel, put them in water, cover them down close, and shift the water six or seven times as it boils, to take the bitterness out, and that they may look clear and be tender; then take them out, dry them in a cloth, take out all the strings, and cut them thin as palates; then take a pound of double refined sugar beaten, and boil it with a little water to a candy height; skim it clean and put in your peels; let them boil near half an hour; have in readiness your orange-meat all picked from the skins and seeds, and the juice of two large lemons, and put it into the peels, boiling all together a quarter of an hour longer; so glass it up, and paper it when cold.

Another Way to make Orange Marmalade.

RASP your oranges, cut out all the meat, boil the rinds very tender, and cut them very fine; then take three pounds of double refined sugar, and a pint of water, boil and skim it, and then put in a pound of rind; boil very fast till the sugar is very thick, then put in the meat of your oranges, the seeds and skins being picked out, and a pint of very strong pippin-jelly; boil all together very fast half an hour, then put it in flat pots or glasses; when it is cold paper it up.

To make Marmalade of Cherries.

TAKE four pounds of cherries, stone them and put them in a preserving-pan, with a quart of juice or currants; set them on a charcoal fire, and let the fire draw away most of the juice; break or mash them, and boil three pounds of sugar candy high, and put the cherries to it, and set it on the fire again, and boil it till it comes to a body; so put it in glasses, and when it is cold paper up.

To make Syrup of Orange-Peel.

TO every pint of the water, in which the orange-peels were steeped, put a pound of sugar; boil it, and when it has boiled a little squeeze in some juice of lemon, making it more or less sharp to your taste; filter the lemon juice through cap-paper; as it boils skim it clear; when boiled enough to keep, take it off the fire, and when cold bottle it; when your orange-peels are dried on one side, turn the other, and so do till they

are

are crisp; brush the sugar from them, then take a cloth dipped in warm water and wipe off all that remains of sugar on the rind side; then lay them on the sieve again, and in an hour they will be dry enough to put into your boxes to keep.

To keep Orange-Flowers in Syrup.

PICK off the leaves, and throw them in water boiling on the fire, and squeeze into it the juice of two or three lemons; let them boil half a quarter of an hour, and then throw them into cold water; then lay them on cloths to drain well; then beat and sift some double refined sugar, lay some on the bottom of a gallipot, and then a layer of flowers, and then more sugar, till all is in; when the sugar melts put in more, till there is a pretty deal of syrup, so paper them up for use; you may put them in jelly, or what you please.

To keep Fruit in Syrup to candy.

IF you candy orange or lemon-peels, you must first rub them with salt, then cut in what fashion you please, and keep them in water two days, then boil them tender, shifting the water you boil them in two or three times; you must have a syrup ready, a pint of water to a pound of sugar, scald your peels in it till they look clear. Fruit is done the same way, but not boiled till you put them in your syrup; you must heat your syrup once a week, taking out your fruit, and put them in again while the syrup is hot; the syrup will keep all the year.

To make Syrup of any Flowers.

CLIP your flowers, and take their weight in sugar; then take a gallipot, and put a row of flowers and a strewing of sugar, till the pot is full; then put in two or three spoonfuls of the same syrup or stilled water; tie a cloth on the top of the pot, put a tile on that, set your gallipot in a kettle of water over a gentle fire, and let it infuse till the strength is out of the flowers, which will be in four or five hours; then strain it thro' a flannel, and when it is cold bottle it up.

To candy Orange-Flowers.

TAKE orange-flowers that are stiff and fresh picked; boil them in a good quantity of spring-water in a preserving-pan; when they are tender, take them out, drain them in a sieve, and lay them between two napkins till they be very dry; take the weight of your flowers in double refined sugar, if you have a pound, take half a pint of water and boil with the sugar till it will stand in a drop, then take it of the fire, and when it is
almost

almost cold put it to the flowers, which must be in a silver bason; shake them very well together, and set them in a stove or in the sun, and as they begin to candy, take them out, and put them on glasses to dry, keeping them turning till they are dry.

Another Method.

TAKE half a pound of double refined sugar, finely beaten, wet it with orange-flower-water, and boil it candy high; then put in a handful of orange-flowers, keeping it stirring, but let it not boil; when the sugar candies about them, take it off the fire; drop it on a plate, and set it by till it is cold.

Another Way.

FIRST pick your orange-flowers, and boil them quick in fair water till they are very tender; then drain them thro' a hair sieve very clean from the water; to a pound of double refined sugar take half a pint of fair water, and as much orange-flower-water, and boil it up to a thick syrup; then pour it out into broad flat glasses, and let the syrup stand in the glasses about an inch thick; when it is near cold, drop in your flowers, as many as you think convenient, and set your glasses in a stove with a moderate heat, for the slower they candy, the finer the rock will be; when you see it is well candied top and bottom, and that it glitters, break the candy at top in as great flakes as you can, and lay the biggest piece at the bottom on glass plates, and pick out the rest, piling it up with the flowers to what size you please; after that it will presently be dry in a stove.

To candy Orange Chips.

PARE your oranges, and soak the peelings in water two days, shifting the water twice; but if you love them bitter, soak them not; tie your peels up in a cloth, and when your water boils put them in, and let them boil till they are tender; then take what double refined sugar will do, break it small, wet it with a little water, and let it boil till it is near candy high; then cut your peels of what lengths you please and put them into the syrup; set them on the fire, and let them heat well through; then let them stand a while; heat them twice a day, but not boil; let them be so done till they begin to candy; then take them out, and put them on plates to dry, and when dry keep them near the fire.

To candy Angelica.

TAKE angelica that is young, cut it in fit lengths, and boil it till it is pretty tender, keeping it close covered; then take it up and

and peel off the ſtrings, then put it in again, and let it ſimmer and ſcald till it is very green; then take it up, dry it in a cloth, and weigh it, putting to every pound of angelica a pound of double refined ſugar beaten and ſifted; put your angelica in an earthen pan, ſtrew the ſugar over it, and let it ſtand two days, then boil it till it looks very clear; put it in a colander to dry the ſyrup from it, and take a little double refined ſugar and boil it to ſugar again; then throw in your angelica, and take it out in a little time, and put it on glaſs plates; it will dry in a ſtove, or in an oven after pyes are drawn.

To candy any Sort of Fruit.

AFTER you have preſerved your fruit, dip them ſuddenly into warm water, to take off the ſyrup; then ſift on them double refined ſugar till they look white; then ſet them on a ſieve in a warm oven, taking them out to turn two or three times; let them not be cold till they be dry, and they will look clear as diamonds; ſo keep them dry.

To candy Flowers.

GATHER your flowers when dry, cut off the leaves as far as the colour is good; according to your quantity, take of double refined ſugar, and wet it with fair water, and boil it to a candy height; then put in your flowers, of what ſort you pleaſe, as primroſes, violets, cowſlips, or borage with a ſpoon; take them out as quick as you can, with as little of the ſyrup as may be, and lay them in a diſh over a gentle fire, and with a knife ſpread them, that the ſyrup may run from them; then change them upon another warm diſh, and when they are dry from the ſyrup, have ready ſome double refined ſugar beaten and ſifted, and ſtrew ſome on your flowers; then take the flowers in your hand, and rub them gently in the hollow of your hand, and that will open the leaves, a ſtander-by ſtrewing more ſugar into your hand, as you ſee convenient; ſo do till they are thoroughly opened and dry; then put your flowers into a dry ſieve, and ſift all the ſugar clean from them; they muſt be kept in a dry place; roſemary-flowers muſt be put whole into your ſyrup; young mint-leaves you muſt open with your fingers, but all bloſſoms rub with your hand as directed.

To make Cakes of Flowers.

BOIL double refined ſugar candy high, and then ſtrew in your flowers, and let them boil once up, then with your hand lightly ſtrew in a little double refined ſugar ſifted, and then as quick as may be put it into your little pans, made of card, and pricked full of holes at bottom; you may ſet the pans on a pillow, or cuſhion; when they are cold, take them out.

To make Wormwood Cakes.

TAKE one pound of double refined sugar sifted, mix it with the whites of three or four eggs well beat; into this drop as much chymical oil of wormwood as you please, so drop them on paper, you may have some white and some marble, with specks of colours with the point of a pin; keep your colours severally in little gallipots; for red, take a drachm of cochineal, a little cream of tartar, as much of allum, tie them up severally in little bits of fine cloth, and put them to steep in one glass of water two or three hours; when you use the colour, press the bags in the water, and mix some of it with a little of the white of egg and sugar. Saffron colours yellow, and must be ti-d in a cloth, as the red, and put in water. Powder blue mixed with the saffron-water, makes a green: for blue, mix some dry powder blue with some water.

To scald Fruit for present Use.

PUT your fruit into boiling water, as much as will almost cover them, set them over a slow fire, keep it in a scald till tender, turning the fruit where the water does not cover; when tender, lay paper close on it, let it stand till cold; to a pound of fruit put half a pound of sugar; let it boil, but not fast, till it looks clear; all fruit are done whole but pippins, and they in halves, with orange or lemon-peel, and juice of lemon; cut your peel very thin, like threads, and strew them on your pippins.

To make Pastils.

TAKE double refined sugar beaten and sifted as fine as flour; perfume it with musk and ambergrease; then have ready steeped, some gum-arabick in orange-flower-water, and with that make the sugar into a stiff paste; drop into some of it three or four drops of oil of mint, oil of cloves, oil of cinnamon, or what oil you like, and let some only have the perfume; then roll them up in your hand like little pellets, and squeeze them flat with a seal. Dry them in the sun.

To fricasey Almonds.

TAKE a pound of Jordan almonds, do not blanch them, or but one half of them: beat the white of an egg very well, and pour it on your almonds, and wet them all over; then take half a pound of double refined sugar, and boil it to sugar again; put your almonds in, and stir them till as much sugar hangs on them as will; then set them on plates, and put them into the oven to dry after bread is drawn, and let them stay in all night.

They

They will keep the year round if you keep them dry, and are a pretty sweet-meat.

To dry Pears or Pippins without Sugar.

TAKE your pears or apples, wipe them clean, and take a bodkin and run it in at the head and out at the ftalk; put them in a flat earthen pot and bake them, but not too much; you muft put a quart of ftrong new ale to half a peck of pears, tie white paper over the pot, that they may not be fcorched in baking; and when they are baked let them ftand to be cold, and take them out to drain; fqueeze the pears flat, and the apples the eye to the ftalk; lay them on fieves with wide holes to dry, either in a ftove or an oven that is not too hot.

To make Rofe Drops.

THE rofes and fugar muft be beat feparately into a very fine powder, and both fifted; to a pound of fugar an ounce of red rofes; they muft be mixed together, and then wet with as much juice of lemon as will make it into a ftiff pafte; fet it on a flow fire in a filver porringer, and ftir it well, and when it is fcalding hot quite through, take it off, and drop it on a paper; fet them near the fire, the next day they will come off.

To make a Pafte of green Pippins.

TAKE pippins, fcald them, and peel them till they are green; when you have peeled them, have frefh warm water ready to put them into, and cover them clofe, and keep them warm till they are very green; then take the pulp of them, but none of the core, and beat it in a mortar, and pafs it through a colander, and to a pound of the pulp put a pound and an ounce of double refined fugar; boil your fugar till it will ball between your fingers, put in your pulp, and take it off the fire to mix it well together; fet it on the fire again, and boil it till it is enough, which you may know by dropping a little on a plate, and then put it in what form you pleafe; duft it with fugar, and fet it in the ftove to dry; turn it, and duft the other fide.

To make white Quince Pafte.

SCALD the quinces tender to the core, pare them, and fcrape the pulp clean from the core; beat it in a mortar, and pulp it through a colander; take to a pound of pulp a pound and two ounces of fugar; boil the fugar till it is candy high, then put in your pulp; ftir it about conftantly till you fee it come clear from the bottom of the preferving-pan, then take it off and lay it on plates pretty thin; you may cut it in what fhape you

you please, or make quince chips of it; you must dust it with sugar when you put it into the stove, and turn it on papers in a sieve, and dust the other side; when they are dry put them in boxes, with papers between; you may make red quince paste the same way as this, only colour the quince with cochineal.

To dry Pears or Apples.

TAKE poppering pears, and thrust a picked stick into the head of them beyond the core; then scald them, but not too tender, and pare them the long way; put them in water, and take the weight of them in sugar; clarify it with water, a pint of water to a pound of sugar; strain the syrup, and put in the pears; set them on the fire and boil them pretty fast for half an hour; cover them with paper, and set them by till the next day; then boil them again, and set them by till the next day; then take them out of the syrup, and boil it till it is thick and roapy; then put the syrup to them; if it will not cover them, add some sugar to them; set them over the fire and let them boil up, then cover them with paper and set them in a stove twenty-four hours; then lay them on plates, dust them with sugar, and set them in your stove to dry; when one side is dry, lay them on papers, turn them, and dust the other side with sugar; squeeze the pears flat by degrees; if it is apples, squeeze the eye to the stalk; when then they are quite dry put them in boxes, with papers between.

To make clear Candy.

TAKE six ounces of water, and four ounces of fine sugar searced; set it on a slow fire to melt without stirring, let it boil till it comes to a strong candy: then have ready your peel or fruit scalded hot in the syrup they were kept in, drain them very well from it, and put them into your candy, which you must rub on the sides of your bason with the back of your spoon, till you see the candy pretty white; take out the fruit with a fork, touch it not with your fingers; if right, the candy will shine on your fruit, and dry in three or four hours in an indifferent hot stove; lay your fruit on sieves.

To make Sugar Plates.

TAKE a pound of double refined sugar beaten and searced; blanch and beat some almonds and mix with it, and beat them together in a mortar, with gum-dragant dissolved in rose-water, till it is a paste; roll it out, and strew sugar on the papers or plate, and bake it after manchet; gild it if you please, and serve sweet-meats on it.

To clear Sugar.

TAKE two or three whites of eggs, and put them into a bason of water, and with a very clean hand lather that as you do soap; take nothing but the froth, and when your syrup boils, with a ladle cover it with it; do this till your syrup is clear, making still more froth, and covering the syrup with it; it will make the worst sugar as clear as any, and fit to preserve any fruit.

To make brown Sugar.

TAKE gum-arabick, and dissolve it in water till it is pretty thick; then take as much double refined sugar finely sifted and perfumed as will make the gum into a stiff paste; roll it out like jumbals, and set it in an oven exactly heated, that it may raise them and not boil, for if it boils it is spoiled; you may colour some of them.

To make Sugar of Roses.

CLIP off all the whites from the red rose-buds, and dry the red in the sun; to an ounce of that finely powdered, you must have one pound of loaf sugar; wet the sugar with rose-water (but if in the season, juice of roses) boil it to a candy height; then put in your powder of roses, and the juice of a lemon; mix it well together; then pour it on a pye-plate, and cut it into lozenges, or what form you please.

To parch Almonds.

TAKE a pound of sugar, make it into a syrup, and boil it candy high, then put in three quarters of a pound of Jordan almonds blanched; keep them stirring all the while till they are dry and crisp, then put them in a box, and keep them dry.

CHAP. III.
Of CREAMS.

Lemon Cream.

TAKE five large lemons, and squeeze out the juice, and the whites of six eggs well beaten, ten ounces of double refined sugar beaten very fine, and twenty spoonfuls of spring-water; mix all together and strain it through a jelly-bag; set it over a gentle

gentle fire, skim it very well; when it is as hot as you can bear your finger in it, take it off, and pour it into glasses; put shreds of lemon-peel into some of the glasses.

Another Lemon Cream.

TAKE the juice of four large lemons, half a pint of water, a pound of double refined sugar, beaten fine, the whites of seven eggs, and the yolk of one beaten very well; mix all together, strain it, set it on a gentle fire, stirring it all the while, and skim it clean; put into it the peel of one lemon when it is very hot, but not boil; take out the lemon-peel, and pour it into china dishes.

To make White Lemon Cream.

TAKE four large lemons, chip them very thin, shred the chips very small, put them into a porringer, and squeeze the juice of the lemons into them, and let them stand two or three hours, or more; then put to them the whites of eight eggs well beaten, a porringer of spring-water, and a fourth part of rose-water; stir all well together, and strain it through a cotton cloth; season it pretty sweet, and add to it a little musk, or amber, if you please; then set it on a chafing-dish of coals, let it scald, but not boil, stirring it continually, till it is as thick as cream; then take it off, and eat it when cold.

If you would have it yellow, put in one yolk of an egg, and, instead of chipping, grate the lemon-peel.

To make Orange Cream.

TAKE a pint of the juice of Seville oranges, put to it the yolks of six eggs, the whites of four; beat the eggs very well, and strain them and the juice together; add to it a pound of double refined sugar beaten and sifted; set all these together on a soft fire, and put the peel of half an orange into it, keep it stirring all the while, and when it is almost ready to boil, take out the orange-peel, and pour out the cream into glasses or china dishes.

Another Method.

TAKE the juice of six oranges, set it on the fire, let it be scalding hot, but not boil; beat three yolks of eggs with as much sugar as will make it sweet enough to your taste; beat them up together, and let them have one boil up, keep it stirring, skim it, and put it into glasses, and serve it up cold.

To make Goosberry Cream.

TAKE two quarts of goosberries, put to them as much water as will cover them; let them boil all to mash, and run them through a sieve with a spoon; to a quart of the pulp, you must have six eggs well beaten, and when the pulp is hot, put in an ounce of fresh butter, sweeten it to your taste, put in your eggs, and stir them over a gentle fire till they grow thick; then set it by, and when it is almost cold, put into it two spoonfuls of the juice of spinach, and a spoonful of orange flower-water or sack, stir it well together, and put it in your basons; when it is cold serve it to the table.

Some love the goosberries only mashed, not pulped through a sieve, and put the butter, and eggs, and sugar as the other, but no juice of spinach.

To make Barley Cream.

TAKE a small quantity of pearl barley, and boil it in milk and water till it is tender: then strain the liquor from it, and put your barley into a quart of cream, and let it boil a little; then take the whites of five eggs, and the yolk of one beaten with a spoonful of fine flour, and two spoonfuls of orange-flower-water, then take the cream off the fire, and mix the eggs in by degrees, and set it over the fire again to thicken; sweeten it to your taste; pour it into basons, and when it is cold serve it up.

To make Steeple Cream.

TAKE five ounces of hart's-horn, and two ounces of ivory; put them into a stone-bottle, fill it up with fair water to the neck, and put in a small quantity of gum-arabick, and gum-dragant; then tie up the bottle very close, and set it into a pot of water with hay at the bottom, let it boil six hours, then take it out, and let it stand an hour before you open it, left it fly in your face; then strain it in, and it will be a strong jelly; then take a pound of blanched almonds, beat them very fine, and mix it with a pint of thick cream, letting it stand a little; then strain it out and mix it with a pound of jelly; set it over the fire till it is scalding hot, sweeten it to your taste with double refined sugar; take it off, and put in a little amber, and pour it out into small thin high gallipots like a sugar-loaf at top, when it is cold turn it out, and lay whipped cream about them in heaps.

To make whipped Cream.

TAKE a quart of thick cream, and the whites of eight eggs beaten with half a pint of sack; mix it together, and sweeten

sweeten it to your taste with double refined sugar; you may perfume it if you please with some musk or ambergrease tied in a rag, and steeped a little in the cream; whip it up with a whisk, and a bit of lemon-peel tied in the middle of the whisk; take the froth with a spoon, and lay it in your glasses or basons.

To make white Wine Cream.

TAKE a quart of cream, set it on the fire, and stir it till it is blood-warm; then boil a pint of white wine with sugar till it is syrup, so mingle the wine and cream together; put it in a china bason, and when it is cold serve it up.

To make Sack Cream.

TAKE a quart of thick cream, and set it over the fire, and when it boils take it off; put a piece of lemon-peel in it, and sweeten it very well; then take the china bason you serve it in, and put into the bason the juice of half a lemon, and nine spoonfuls of sack; then stir in the cream into the bason by a spoonful at at a time, till all the cream is in; when it is little more than blood-warm, set it by till next day; serve it with wafers round it.

To make Blanched Cream.

TAKE a quart of the thickest sweet cream you can get, season with fine sugar and orange-flower-water; then boil it; then beat the whites of twenty eggs with a little cold cream, take out the treddles, and when the cream is on the fire and boils, pour in your eggs, stirring it very well till it comes to a thick curd; then take it up and pass it through a hair sieve; then beat it very well with a spoon till it is cold, and put it in dishes for use.

To make Cream of any preserved Fruit.

TAKE half a pound of the pulp of any preserved fruit, put it in a large pan, put to it the whites of two or three eggs; beat them together exceeding well for an hour; then with a spoon take it off, and lay it heaped up high on the dish or salver with other creams, or put it in the middle bason: raspberries will not do this way.

Lady Huncks's Spanish Cream.

SCALD your milk from the cow, and set it in earthen pans; take off your cream without milk, and churn it in a glass churn, or beat it with a spoon till it comes near to butter; then lay it in a dish, and scrape on sugar.

The COMPLETE HOUSEWIFE. 271

To make plain raw Cream thicker than usual.

FIRST scald the bowl you intend to file your milk into from the cow, then wipe it clean, and file your milk into it; then put a very little into it between your thumb and finger, stir it well together, and so let it stand till next morning; then take off your cream with as little milk as you can, and it will be extremely thick, and as sweet as you can desire. The bowl, or pan, must be just popped into scalding water, and then taken out again. The best way is to milk the cow into your bowl through a hair sieve.

To make Crisp Cream.

TAKE a bottle of stroakings from the cow, as much sweet cream, boil them together with four cloves, and a little stick of cinnamon. When it boils, put a lighted fire in the oven, that it may be as hot as when you draw a batch of bread, and boil it about half an hour; then take out the spice, and put your cream into a pan or bason brim-full, and froth it up with as high a froth as you can, all alike, till it will be warmer than from the cow; then put it into your oven all night close stopped; the next morning set it on the cold stones uncovered for a day and a night, or longer, if you think fit, before you use it.

To make Sack Cream.

TAKE the yolks of two eggs, three spoonfuls of fine sugar, and a quarter of a pint of sack; mix them together, and stir them into a pint of cream; then set them over the fire till it is scalding hot, but let it not boil. You may toast some thin slices of white bread, and dip them in sack or orange-flower-water, and pour your cream over them.

To make Rice Cream.

TAKE three spoonfuls of the flour of rice, as much sugar, the yolks of two eggs, two spoonfuls of sack, or rose or orange-flower-water; mix all these, and put them to a pint of cream, stir it over the fire till it is thick, then pour it into china dishes.

To make Pistachia Cream.

PEEL your pistachias, beat them very fine, and boil them in cream; if it is not green enough, add a little juice of spinach; thicken it with eggs, and sweeten to your taste; pour it in basons, and set it by till it is cold.

To

To make Quince Cream.

TAKE quinces, scald them till they are soft; pare them, mash the clear part of them, and pulp it through a sieve; take an equal weight of quince, and double refined sugar beaten and sifted, and the whites of eggs, and beat it till it is as white as snow, then put it in dishes.

To make Almond Cream.

TAKE a quart of cream, boil it with nutmeg, mace, and a bit of lemon-peel, and sweeten it to your taste; then blanch some almonds, and beat them very fine; then take nine whites of eggs well beaten, and strain them to your almonds, and rub them very well through a thin strainer; so thicken your cream; just give it one boil, and pour it into china dishes, and when it is cold serve it up.

To make Ratafia Cream.

TAKE six large laurel leaves, and boil them in a quart of thick cream; when it is boiled, throw away the leaves, and beat the yolks of five eggs with a little cold cream, and sugar to your taste; then thicken your cream with your eggs, and set it over the fire again, but let it not boil; keeping it stirring all the while, and pouring it into china dishes; when it is cold it is fit for use.

CHAP. IV.
Of JELLIES, SYLLABUBS, &c.

To make Pippin Jelly.

TAKE fifteen pippins pared, cored and sliced, and put them into a pint and a half of water, let them boil till they are tender, then put them into a strainer, and let the thin run from them as much as it will; to a pint of liquor take a pound of double refined sugar, wet your sugar and boil it to sugar again; then cut some chips of candied orange or lemon-peel, cut it as fine as threads, and put it into your sugar, and then your liquor, and let it boil till it is a jelly, which will be quickly; you may perfume it with ambergrease if you please; pour the jelly into shallow glasses; when it is cold paper it up, and keep it in your stove.

To make white Jelly of Quinces.

PARE your quinces, and cut them in halves; then core and parboil them; when they are soft, take them up and crush them through a strainer, but not too hard, only the clear juice. Take the weight of the juice in fine sugar; boil the sugar-candy high, and put in your juice and let it scald a while, but not boil; if any froth arise, skim it off, and when you take it up, have ready a white preserved quince cut in small slices, laying them in the bottom of your glasses, and pour your jelly to them; it will candy on the top, and keep moist on the bottom a long time.

To make Jelly of Currants.

STRIP your currants, put them in a jug, and infuse in water; strain out the juice upon sugar; sweeten to your taste; boil it a great while till it jellies; skimming all the while, and then put it in your glasses.

To make Jelly of white Currants.

TAKE your largest currants, strip them into a bason; bruise and strain them, and to every pint of juice a pound of double refined sugar; just wet your sugar with a little fair water, and set it on a slow fire till it melts; then make it boil, and at the same time let your juice boil in another thing; skim them both very well, and when they have boiled a pretty while, take off your sugar, and strain the juice into it through a muslin; then set it on the fire and let it boil; if you please you may stone some white currants and put them in, and let them boil till they are clear; have a care you do not boil them too high; let them stand a while, then put them in glasses.

If you would make clear cakes of white currants, boil the juice just as this is; but this observe, that when you put your juice and sugar together, they must stand but so long on the fire till they are warm and well mixed, they must boil together; and when it is cold put it in flat glasses, and into your stove to dry them; turn them often.

To make Jelly of Cherries.

TAKE an ale-quart of running water, a pound of green pippins, and a pound of cherries well coloured, and free from spots; pull off the stalks, and break them between your fingers into the liquor with three ounces of fine sugar, and boil them till they come to a pint of liquor; then strain it into a gallipot, and when it is cold set it on the fire, and put to it six ounces of

T   double

double refined fugar; then put in a pound of fair chofen cherries, keeping the pan boiling fo quick, that you cannot fee one cherry; it muft boil when you put in the cherries, and during the boiling you muft now and then fhake the pan; when it has boiled fome time, put in as much fugar as will make your nine ounces a good pound; never take it off, but whilft it is boiling, put this laft fugar in, and when it is boiled to a jelly take it off, and put it up in glaffes.

To make Jelly of Apricots.

PARE your apricots, and fet them to ftew in a filver fkillet, with a very little water, and have at the fame time a flagon full of white pear-plumbs ftewing in a kettle of water, which fo order, that both may be enough together; and when the apricots are diffolved, pour the juice through tiffany into a meafure-glafs, and the juice of your pear-plumbs into another, but take only one part of pear-plumbs to two parts of apricots; then take the weight of thefe (fo mixed) in double refined fugar, wet it in fair water, and boil it to a candy; then by degrees put in the mixed jelly, give it one boil, and let it be kept ftirring till it grows thick enough; then glafs it, and keep it in a warm place.

To make a ftrong Apple Jelly.

LET your water boil in the pan you make it in, and when the apples are pared and quartered, put them into your boiling water; let there be no more water than will juft cover them, and let them boil as faft as poffible; and when the apples are all to pieces, put in about a quart of water more, and let it boil half an hour longer; then run it through a jelly-bag, and ufe it as occafion for any fort of fweet-meat; in the fummer codlins are beft, in the winter golden rennets or winter pippins.

To make Ribbon Jelly.

TAKE out the great bones of four calves-feet, and put the feet into a pot with ten quarts of water, three ounces of hart's-horn, three ounces of ifinglafs, a nutmeg quartered, four blades of mace; then boil this till it comes to two quarts, and ftrain it through a fine flannel bag; let it ftand twenty-four hours; then fcrape off all the fat from the top very clean; then heat it, and put to it the whites of fix eggs beaten to a froth; boil it a little, and ftrain it again through a fine flannel bag; then run the jelly into little high glaffes; run every colour as thick as your finger; one colour muft be thorough cold before you put another on, and that you run on muft not be blood-warm for fear it mixes together; you muft colour red with cochineal, green with fpinach, yellow with faffron, blue with fyrup of violets, white with thick cream, and fometimes the jelly by itfelf.

To make Hart's-horn or Calves-feet Jelly without Lemons.

TAKE a pair of calves-feet, boil them with six quarts of fair water to mash; it will make three quarts of jelly; then strain it off, and let it stand still till it is cold, take off the top, and save the middle, and melt it again and skim it; then take six whites of eggs beaten to a froth, half a pint of Rhenish wine, and one lemon juiced, and half a pound of fine powdered sugar; stir all together, and let it boil, then take it off, and put to it as much spirit of vitriol as will sharpen it to your palate, about one penny-worth will do; let it not boil after the vitriol is in; let your jelly-bag be made of thick flannel, then run it through till it is very clear; you may put the whites of the eggs that swim at the top into the bag first, and that will thicken the bag.

To make Hart's-horn Jelly.

TAKE a large gallipot, and fill it with hart's-horn, and then fill it full with spring-water, and tie a double paper over the gallipot, and set it in a baker's oven with houshold bread; in the morning take it out, run it through a jelly-bag, season with juice of lemons, double refined sugar, and the whites of eight eggs well beaten; let it have a boil, and run it through the jelly-bag again into your jelly-glasses; put a bit of lemon-peel in the bag.

To make Calves-feet Jelly.

TO four calves-feet, take a gallon of fair water, cut them in pieces, put them in a pipkin close covered, and boil them softly till almost half be consumed; and run it through a sieve, and let it stand till it is cold; then with a knife take off the fat, and top and bottom, and the fine part of the jelly melt in a preserving-pan or skillet, and put in a pint of Rhenish wine, the juice of four or five lemons, double refined sugar to your taste, the whites of eight eggs beaten to a froth; stir and boil all these together near half an hour; then strain it through a sieve into a jelly-bag; put into your jelly-bag a sprig of rosemary, and a piece of lemon-peel; pass it through the bag till it is as clear as water. You may cut some lemon peel like threads, and put in half the glasses.

To make very fine Syllabubs.

TAKE a quart and half a pint of cream, a pint of Rhenish, half a pint of sack, three lemons, and near a pound of double refined sugar; beat and sift the sugar, and put it to your cream; grate off the yellow rind of your three lemons, and put that in; squeeze the juice of the three lemons into your wine, and put that to your cream, then beat all together with a whisk just half an hour; then take it up all together with a spoon, and fill your glasses; it will keep good nine or ten days, and is best three or four days old; these are called The Everlasting Syllabubs.

To make Lemon Syllabubs.

TAKE a quart of cream, half a pound of sugar, a pint of white wine, the juice of two or three lemons, the peel of one grated; mix all these, and put them in an earthen pot, and milk it up as fast as you can till it is thick, then pour it in your glasses, and let them stand five or six hours; you may make them over night.

To make whipped Syllabubs.

TAKE a quart of cream, not too thick, a pint of sack, and the juice of two lemons; sweeten it to your palate, put it into a broad earthen pan, and with a whisk whip it; as the froth rises, take it off with a spoon, and lay it in your syllabub-glasses; but first you must sweeten some claret, sack, or white wine, and strain it, and put seven or eight spoonfuls of the wine into your glasses, and then gently lay in your froth. Set them by. Do not make them long before you use them.

King William's Posset.

TAKE a quart of cream, and mix it with a pint of ale, then beat the yolks of ten eggs, and the whites of four; when they are well beaten, put them to the cream and ale; sweeten it to your taste, and slice some nutmeg in it; set it over the fire, and keep it stirring all the while; when it is thick, and before it boils, take it off, and pour it into the bason you serve it in to the table.

Lord Carlisle's Amber Posset.

TAKE three pints of cream to ten eggs, take away five of the whites, beat them very well, and when your cream boils put in as much sugar as will season it; let it dissolve, then take it off the fire, and take out some of your cream, hot as it is, and beat with your eggs; then stir them together all the while they are upon the fire, and when they grow thick, take them off a little. While this is doing, you must have a quarter of a pint of sack on the fire, with a little amber sugar, which must be very hot; then pour in your cream, stirring it as you pour it, and cover it with a hot dish for a little while; then take it off the fire, and strew on amber sugar.

A Sack

A Sack Posset without Eggs.

TAKE a quart of cream, or new milk, and grate three Naples biscuits in it, and let them boil in the cream; grate some nutmeg in it, and sweeten it to your taste; let it stand a little to cool, and then put half a pint of sack a little warm in your bason, and pour your cream to it, holding it up high in the pouring; let it stand a little, and serve it.

A Sack Posset without Cream or Eggs.

TAKE half a pound of Jordan almonds, lay them all night in water, blanch, and beat them in a stone mortar very fine, with a pint of orange-flower-water, or fair water a quart, and half a pound of sugar, a two-penny loaf of bread grated; let it boil till it is thick, continually stirring it; then warm half a pint of sack, and put to it; stir it well together, and put a little nutmeg and cinnamon in it.

To make the Pope's Posset.

BLANCH and beat three quarters of a pound of almonds so fine, that they will spread between your fingers like butter; put in water as you beat them, to keep them from oiling; then take a pint of sack or sherry, and sweeten it very well with double refined sugar; make it boiling hot, and at the same time put half a pint of water to your almonds, and make them boil; then take both off the fire, and mix them very well together with a spoon; serve it in a china dish.

To make a Snow Posset.

TAKE a quart of new milk, and boil it with a stick of cinnamon and quartered nutmeg; when the milk is boiled, take out the spice, and beat the yolks of sixteen eggs very well, and by degrees mix them in the milk till it is thick; then beat the whites of the sixteen eggs with a little sack and sugar into a snow; then take the bason you design to serve it up in, and put in it a pint of sack; sweeten it to your taste; set it over the fire, and let one take the milk, and another the whites of eggs, and so pour them together into the sack in the bason; keep it stirring all the while it is over the fire; when it is thorough warm take it off, cover it up, and let it stand a little before you use it.

To make a Jelly Poffet.

TAKE twenty eggs, leave out half the whites, and beat them very well; put them into the bafon you ferve it in, with near a pint of fack, and a little ftrong ale; fweeten it to your tafte, and fet it over a charcoal fire, keep it ftirring all the while; then have in readinefs a quart of milk or cream boiled with a little nutmeg and cinnamon, and when your fack and eggs are hot enough to fcald your lips, put the milk to it boiling hot; then take it off the fire, and cover it up half an hour; ftrew fugar on the brim of the difh, and ferve it to the table.

To make an Oatmeal Sack Poffet.

TAKE a pint of milk, and mix it in two fpoonfuls of flour of oatmeal, and one of fugar; put in a blade of mace, and let it boil till the rawnefs of the oatmeal is gone off; in the mean time have in readinefs three fpoonfuls of fack, three of ale, and two of fugar; fet them over the fire till fcalding hot, then put them to your milk; give one ftir, and let it ftand on the fire a minute or two, and pour it in your bafon; cover your bafon with a pye-plate, and let it ftand a little to fettle.

To make Oatmeal Caudle.

TAKE two quarts of ale, one of ftale beer, and two quarts of water; mix them all together, and add to it two fpoonfuls of pot oatmeal, twelve cloves, five or fix blades of mace, and a nutmeg quartered or bruifed; fet it over the fire, and let it boil half an hour, ftirring it all the while; then ftrain it out thro' a fieve, and put in near a pound of fine fugar, and a bit of lemon-peel; pour it into a pan and cover it clofe; that it may not fcum; warm it as you ufe it.

To make Flummery Caudle.

TAKE a pint of oatmeal, and put to it two quarts of fair water; let it ftand all night, in the morning ftir it, and ftrain it into a fkillet, with three or four blades of mace, and a nutmeg quartered; fet it on the fire, and keep it ftirring, and let it boil a quarter of an hour; if it is too thick, put in more water, and let it boil longer; then add a pint of Rhenifh white wine, three fpoonfuls of orange flower-water, the juice of two lemons, and one orange, a bit of butter, and as much fine fugar as will fweeten it; let all thefe have a walm, and thicken it with the yolks of two or three eggs. Drink it hot for a breakfaft.

To make Tea Caudle.

MAKE a quart of strong green tea, pour it out into a skillet, and set it over the fire; then beat the yolks of four eggs, and mix them with a pint of white wine, a grated nutmeg, sugar to your taste, and put all together; stir it over the fire till it is very hot, then drink it in china dishes as caudle.

A fine Caudle.

TAKE a pint of milk, and turn it with sack; then strain it, and when it is cold, put it in a skillet with mace, nutmeg, and some white bread sliced; let all these boil, and then beat the yolks of four or five eggs, the whites of two, and thicken your caudle, stirring it all one way, for fear it curdles; let it warm together, then take it off, and sweeten it to your taste.

To make Spanish Pap.

TAKE some cream, boil a blade of mace in it, and when it has boiled four or five walms, take your mace out, and scarce in as much flour of rice as will make it pretty thick, stirring it all the while; then make it boil, and never cease stirring till you think it is enough; then sweeten it with sugar to your taste, put it into dishes, and eat it cold. You may put in two or three yolks of eggs, and a little rose-water and saffron.

Buttered Oranges.

TAKE eight eggs, and the whites of four; beat them well together, squeeze into them the juice of seven good oranges, and three or four spoonfuls of rose-water, and let them run through a hair sieve into a silver bason: then put to it half a pound of sugar beaten, set it over a gentle fire, and when it begins to thicken, put in a bit of butter, about the bigness of a large nutmeg, and when it is somewhat thicker, pour it into a broad flat china dish, and eat it cold. It will not keep well above two days, but it is very wholesome and pleasant to the taste.

To make white Leach.

TAKE half a pound of almonds, blanch and beat them with rose-water, and a little milk; then strain it out, and put to it a piece of isinglass, and let it boil on a chafing-dish of coals half an hour; then strain it into a bason, sweeten it, and put a grain of musk into it; let it boil a little longer, and put to it two or three drops of oil of mace or cinnamon, and keep it till it is cold; eat it with wine or cream.

To make Strawberry or Raspberry Fool.

TAKE a pint of raspberries, squeeze and strain the juice with orange-flower-water; put to the juice five ounces of fine sugar; then set a pint of cream over the fire, and let it boil up; then put in the juice; give it one stir round, and then put it into your bason; stir it a little in the bason, and when it is cold use it.

To make Hart's-horn Flummery.

TAKE three ounces of hart's-horn, and boil it with two quarts of spring-water; let it simmer over the fire six or seven hours, till half the water is consumed; or else put it in a jug, and set it in the oven with houshold bread; then strain it thro' a sieve, and beat half a pound of almonds very fine, with some orange-flower-water in the beating; when they are beat mix a little of your jelly with it, and some fine sugar; strain it out and mix it with your other jelly; stir it together till it is little more than blood-warm, then pour it into half-pint basons, fill them about half full; when you use them, turn them out of the dish as you do flummery; if it does not come out clean, hold the bason a minute or two in warm water; eat it with wine and sugar.

Put six ounces of hart's-horn in a glazed jug with a long neck, and put in three pints of soft water; cover the top of the jug close, and put a weight on it to keep it steady; set it in a pot or kettle of water twenty-four hours; let it not boil, but be scalding hot; then strain it out, and make your jelly.

To make Almond Butter.

TAKE a pound of the best Jordan almonds, blanched in cold water, and as you blanch them throw them into fair water; then beat them in a marble mortar very fine, with some rose or orange-flower-water, to keep them from oiling; then take a pound of butter out of the churn before it is salted, but it must be very well washed; and mix it with your almonds, with near a pound of double refined sugar beaten and sifted; when it is very well mixed, set it up to cool; when you are going to use it, put it into a colander, and pass it through with the back of a spoon into the dish you serve it in. Hold your hand high and let it be heaped up.

To make Salop.

TAKE a quart of water, and let it boil a quarter of an hour, then put in a quarter of an ounce of salop finely powdered,

dered, and let it boil half an hour longer, stirring it all the while; then season it with white wine and juice of lemons, and sweeten it to your taste; drink it in china cups, as chocolate; it is a great sweetener of the blood.

Boil sago till it is tender and jellies, a spoonful and a half to a quart of water; then season it as you do salop, and drink it in chocolate dishes; or if you please leave out the wine and lemon, and put in a pint of thick cream and a stick of cinnamon, and thicken it up with two or three eggs.

PART IX.

All Sorts of MADE WINES, and CORDIAL WATERS.

CHAP. I.
Of MADE WINES, &c.

To make Apricot Wine.

TAKE three pounds of sugar, and three quarts of water, let them boil together, and skim it well; then put in six pounds of apricots pared and stoned, and let them boil till they are tender; then take them up, and when the liquor is cold bottle it up; you may, if you please, after you have taken out the apricots, let the liquor have one boil with a sprig of flowered clary in it: the apricots make marmalade, and are very good for present spending.

To make Damson Wine.

GATHER your damsons dry, weigh them, and bruise them with your hand; put them into an earthen stein that has a faucet, put a wreath of straw before the faucet; to every eight pounds of fruit a gallon of water; boil the water, skim it, and put to it your fruit scalding hot; let it stand two whole days; then draw it off, and put it into a vessel fit for it, and to every gallon of liquor put two pounds and a half of fine sugar; let the vessel be full, and stop it close; the longer it stands the better; it will keep a year in the vessel; bottle it out; the small damson is the best: you may put a very small lump of double refined sugar in every bottle.

To make Gooseberry Wine.

TAKE to every four pounds of gooseberries a pound and a quarter of sugar, and a quart of fair water; bruise the berries,

and

and steep them twenty-four hours in the water, stirring them often; then press the liquor from them, and put your sugar to the liquor; then put it in a vessel fit for it, and when it has done working stop it up, and let it stand a month; then rack it off into another vessel, and let it stand five or six weeks longer; then bottle it out, putting a small lump of sugar into every bottle; cork your bottles well, and at three months end it will be fit to drink. In the same manner is currant and raspberry wine made; but cherry wine differs, for the cherries are not to be bruised, but stoned, and put the sugar and water together, and give it a boil and a skim, and then put in your fruit, letting it stew with a gentle fire a quarter of an hour; then let it run thro' a sieve without pressing, and when it is cold put it in a vessel, and order it as your gooseberry or currant wine. The only cherries for wine are, the great bearers, murrey cherries, morelloes, black Flanders, or the John Tredufkin cherries.

Another Method.

TAKE twenty-four quarts of gooseberries full ripe, and twelve quarts of water, after it has boiled two hours; pick and bruise your gooseberries one by one in a platter with a rolling-pin, as little as you can, so they be all bruised; then put the water, when it is cold, on your mashed gooseberries, and let them stand together twelve hours; when you drain it off, be sure to take none but the clear; then measure the liquor, and to every quart of that liquor put three quarters of a pound of fine sugar, the one half loaf-sugar; let it stand to dissolve six or eight hours, stirring it two or three times; then put it in your vessels, with two or three spoonfuls of the best new yeast; stop it easy at first, that it may work if it will; when you see it has done working, or will not work, stop it close, and bottle it in frosty weather.

Another.

BOIL eight gallons of water, and one pound of sugar an hour; skim it well, and let it stand till it is cold; then to every quart of that water allow three pounds of gooseberries, first beaten or bruised very well; let it stand twenty-four hours; then strain it out, and to every gallon of this liquor put three pounds of seven-penny sugar; let it stand in the vat twelve hours; then take the thick scum off, and put the clear into a vessel fit for it, and let it stand a month; then draw it off, and rinse the vessel with some of the liquor; put it in again, and let it stand four months, and bottle it.

Pearl

Pearl Gooseberry Wine.

TAKE as many as you please of the best pearl gooseberries, bruise them, and let them stand all night; the next morning press or squeeze them out, and let the liquor stand to settle seven or eight hours; then pour off the clear from the settling, and measure it as you put it into your vessel, adding to every three pints of liquor a pound of double refined sugar; break your sugar in small lumps, and put it in the vessel, with a bit of isinglass; stop it up, and at three months end bottle it out, putting into every bottle a lump of double refined sugar. This is the fine gooseberry wine.

To make Raisin Wine.

TAKE the best Malaga raisins, and pick the large stalks out, and have your water ready boiled and cold; measure as many gallons as you design to make, and put it into a great tub, that it may have room to stir: to every gallon of water put six pounds of raisins, and let it stand fourteen days, stirring it twice a day; when you strain it off, or press it, you must do nothing to it, but leave enough to fill up your cask, which you must do as it wastes; it will be two months or more before it has done working: you must not stop it while you hear it hiss.

Another Method.

TAKE two gallons of spring-water, and let it boil half an hour; then put into a stein-pot two pounds of raisins stoned, two pounds of sugar, the rind of two lemons, and the juice of four; then pour the boiling water on the things in the stein, and let it stand covered four or five days; strain it out and bottle it up: in fifteen or sixteen days it will be fit to drink; it is a very cool and pleasant drink in hot weather.

To make Orange Wine with Raisins.

TAKE thirty pounds of new Malaga raisins, pick them clean, and chop them small; you must have twenty large Seville oranges, ten of them you must pare as thin as for preserving. Boil about eight gallons of soft water, till a third part be consumed; let it cool a little; then put five gallons of it hot upon your raisins and orange-peel; stir it well together, cover it up, and when it is cold, let it stand five days, stirring it up once or twice a day; then pass it through a hair sieve, and with a spoon press it as dry as you can, and put it in a rundlet fit for it, and put to it the rinds of the other ten oranges, cut as thin as the first; then make a syrup of the juice of twenty oranges with a

pound

pound of white sugar. It must be made the day before you turn it up; stir it well together, and stop it close; let it stand two months to clear, then bottle it up; it will keep three years, and is better for keeping.

To make Cherry Wine.

PULL off the stalks of the cherries, and mash them without breaking the stones; then press them hard through a hair bag, and to every gallon of liquor put two pounds of eight-penny sugar. The vessel must be full, and let it work as long as it makes a noise in the vessel, then stop it up close for a month or more, and when it is fine, draw it into dry bottles, and put a lump of sugar into every bottle. If it makes them fly, open them all for a moment, and stop them up again; it will be fit to drink in a quarter of a year.

To make Morella Cherry Wine.

LET your cherries be very ripe, pick off the stalks, and bruise your fruit without breaking the stones; put them in an open vessel together; let them stand twenty-four hours; then press them, and to every gallon put two pounds of fine sugar; then put it up in your cask, and when it has done working stop it close; let it stand three or four months and bottle it; it will be fit to drink in two months.

To make Raspberry Wine.

TAKE your quantity of raspberries and bruise them, put them in an open pot twenty-four hours, then squeeze out the juice, and to every gallon put three pounds of fine sugar and two quarts of canary; put it into a stein or vessel, and when it hath done working stop it close; when it is fine bottle it. It must stand two months before you drink it.

To make Raspberry Wine another Way.

POUND your fruit and strain them through a cloth, then boil as much water as juice of raspberries, and when it is cold put it to your squeezings; let it stand together five hours, then strain it and mix it with the juice, adding to every gallon of this liquor two pounds and a half of fine sugar; let it stand in an earthen vessel close covered a week, then put it in a vessel fit for it, and let it stand a month, or till it is fine: bottle it off.

Another Sort of Raspberry Wine.

TAKE four gallons of raspberries, and put them in an earthen pot; then take four gallons of water, boil it two hours,

let

let it stand till it is blood-warm, put it to the raspberries, and stir them well together; let it stand twelve hours; then strain it off, and to every gallon of liquor put three pounds of loaf sugar, set it over a clear fire, and let it boil till all the scum is taken off; when it is cold, put it into bottles, and open the corks every day for a fortnight, and then stop them close.

To make Lemon Wine.

TAKE six large lemons, pare off the rind, cut them, and squeeze out the juice; steep the rind in the juice, and put to it a quart of brandy; let it stand in an earthen pot close stopt three days; then squeeze six more, and mix with two quarts of spring-water, and as much sugar as will sweeten the whole; boil the water, lemons and sugar together, letting it stand till it is cool; then add a quart of white wine, and the other lemon and brandy, and mix them together, and run it through a flannel bag into some vessel; let it stand three months and bottle it off; cork your bottles very well, and keep it cool; it will be fit to drink in a month or six weeks.

To make Elder Wine.

TAKE twenty-five pounds of Malaga raisins, rub them and shred them small; then take five gallons of fair water; boil it an hour, and let it stand till it is but blood-warm; then put in it an earthen crock or tub, with your raisins; let them sleep ten days, stirring them once or twice a day; then pass the liquor through a hair sieve, and have in readiness five pints of the juice of elder-berries drawn off as you do for jelly of currants; then mix it cold with the liquor, stir it well together, put it into a vessel, and let it stand in a warm place; when it has done working stop it close: bottle it about Candlemas.

To make Clary Wine.

TAKE twenty-four pounds of Malaga raisins, pick them and chop them very small, put them in a tub, and to each pound a quart of water; let them steep ten or eleven days, stirring it twice every day; you must keep it covered close all the while; then strain it off, and put it into a vessel, and about half a peck of the tops of clary, when it is in blossom; stop it close for six weeks, and then bottle it off; in two or three months it is fit to drink. It is apt to have a great settlement at bottom; therefore is best to draw it off by plugs, or tap it pretty high.

To make Quince Wine.

TAKE your quinces when they are thorough ripe, wipe off the fur very clean; then take out the cores, bruise them as you do apples for cyder, and press them, adding to every gallon of juice two pounds and a half of fine sugar; stir it together till it is dissolved; then put it in your cask, and when it has done working, stop it close; let it stand till March before you bottle it. You may keep it two or three years, it will be the better.

Another Method.

GATHER the quinces when pretty ripe, in a dry day, rub off the down with a clean linen cloth, then lay them in hay or straw, for ten days, to sweat; so cut them in quarters, and take out the core, and bruise them well in a mashing-tub with a wooden beetle, and squeeze out the liquid part, by pressing them in a hair bag by degrees in a cyder press; strain this liquor through a fine sieve, then warm it gently over a fire, and scum it, but suffer it not to boil; sprinkle into it loaf-sugar reduced to powder, then in a gallon of water, and a quart of white wine, boil a dozen or fourteen large quinces thinly sliced; add two pounds of fine sugar, and then strain out the liquid part, and mingle it with the natural juice of the quinces, put it into a cask not to fill it, and jumble them well together; then let it stand to settle; put in juice of clary half a pint to five or six gallons, and mix it with a little flour and white of eggs, then draw it off, and if it be not sweet enough, add more sugar, and a quart of the best malmsey: you may, to make it the better, boil a quarter of a pound of stoned raisins of the sun, and a quarter of an ounce of cinnamon, in a quart of the liquor, to the consumption of a third part, and straining the liquor, put it into the cask when the wine is upon the ferment.

To make Barley Wine.

TAKE half a pound of French barley and boil it in three waters, and save three pints of the last water, and mix it with a quart of white wine, half a pint of borage-water, as much clary-water, a little red rose-water, the juice of five or six lemons, three quarters of a pound of fine sugar, and the thin yellow rind of a lemon; brew all these quick together, run it through a strainer and bottle it up; it is pleasant in hot weather, and very good in fevers.

To make Plumb Wine.

TAKE twenty pounds of Malaga raisins, pick, rub, and shred them, and put them into a tub; then take four gallons of fair water, boil it an hour, and let it stand till it is blood-warm; then put it to your raisins; let it stand nine or ten days, stirring it once or twice a day; strain out your liquor, and mix with it two quarts of damson-juice; put it in a vessel, and when it has done working stop it close; at four or five months bottle it.

To make Orange Wine.

PUT twelve pounds of fine sugar and the whites of eight eggs well beaten, into six gallons of spring-water; let it boil an hour, skimming it all the time; take it off, and when it is pretty cool put in the juice and rind of fifty Seville oranges, and six spoonfuls of good ale-yeast, and let it stand two days; then put it into your vessel, with two quarts of Rhenish wine, and the juice of twelve lemons; you must let the juice of lemons and wine, and two pounds of double refined sugar, stand close covered ten or twelve hours before you put it in the vessel to your orange wine, and skim off the seeds before you put it in; the lemon-peels must be put in with the oranges, half the rinds must be put into the vessel; it must stand ten or twelve days before it is fit to bottle.

To make Currant Wine.

GATHER your currants full ripe, strip them and bruise them in a mortar, and to every gallon of the pulp put two quarts of water, first boiled, and cold; you may put in some rasps, if you please; let it stand in a tub twenty-four hours to ferment; then let it run through a hair sieve; let no hand touch it; let it take its time to run; and to every gallon of this liquor put two pounds and a half of white sugar; stir it well, and put it in your vessel, and to every six gallons put in a quart of the best rectified spirit of wine; let it stand six weeks, and bottle it; if it is not very fine, empty it into other bottles, or at first draw it into large bottles; and then, after it has stood a fortnight, rack it off into smaller.

To make the fine Clary Wine.

TO ten gallons of water put twenty-five pounds of sugar, and the whites of twelve eggs well beaten; set it over the fire, and let it boil gently near an hour; skim it clean, and put it in a tub; and when it is near cold, then put into the vessel you keep it in, about half a strike of clary in the blossom, stript from the stalks, flowers and little leaves together, and a pint of new ale-yeast; then put in the liquor, and stir it two or three times a day for three days; when it has done working, stop it up; and bottle it at three or four months old, if it is clear.

To make Wine of English Figs.

TO do this, take the large blue figs, pretty ripe; steep them in white wine, having made some slits in them, that they may swell and gather in the substance of the wine, then slice some other figs, and let them simmer over a fire in fair water till they are reduced to a kind of pulp, strain out the water, pressing the pulp hard, and pour it as hot as may be to those figs that are imbused in the wine, let the quantities be near equal, the water somewhat more than the wine and figs; then having infused twenty-four hours, mash them well together, and draw off what will run voluntarily, then press the rest, and if it prove not pretty sweet, add loaf-sugar to render it so; let it ferment, and add a little honey and sugar-candy to it, then fine it with whites of eggs and a little isinglass, and so draw it off, and keep it for use.

To make Wine of Roses.

TO do this, fit a glass bason, or body, or for want of it, a well glazed earthen vessel, and put into it three gallons of rose-water, drawn with a cold still; put into it a convenient quantity of rose leaves; cover it close, and put it for an hour in a kettle or cauldron of water, heating it over the fire to take out the whole strength and tincture of the roses, and when cold, press the rose-leaves hard into the liquor, and steep fresh ones in, repeating it till the liquor has got a full strength of the roses; and then to every gallon of liquor add three pounds of loaf-sugar; stir it well, that it may melt and disperse in every part, then put it up into a cask, or other convenient vessel, to ferment; and to make it do so the better, add a little fixed nitre and flour, and two or three whites of eggs; let it stand to cool about thirty days, and it will be ripe, and have a curious flavour, having the whole strength and scent of the roses in it; and you may add, to meliorate it, some wine and spices, as your taste or inclination leads you.

By this way of infusion, wine of carnations, clove-gilly-flowers, violets, primroses, or any flower having a curious scent, may be made; to which, to prevent repetition, I refer you.

To make Wine of Mulberries.

TAKE mulberries, when they are just changed from their redness to a shining black, gather them in a dry day, when the sun has taken off the dew, spread them thinly on a fine cloth on a floor or table for twenty-four hours, boil up a gallon of water to each gallon of juice you get out of them; scum the water well, and add a little cinnamon slightly bruised; put to every gallon six ounces of white sugar-candy finely beaten, scum and strain the water when it is taken off and settled, and put to it the juice of mulberries, and to every gallon the mixture of a pint of white or Rhenish wine; let them stand in a cask to purge or settle five or six days, then draw off the wine, and keep it cool.

To make Wine of Apples and Pears.

AS for apples, make them first into good cyder, by beating and pressing, and other orderings, as I shall direct, when I come to treat of those sort of liquors, after I have ended this of wines; and to good cyder, when you have procured it, put the herb scurlea, the quintessence of wine, and a little fixed nitre, and to a barrel of this cyder, a pound of the syrup of honey; let it work and ferment at spurge-holes in the cask ten days, or till you find it clear and well settled, then draw it off, and it will not be much inferior to Rhenish in clearness, colour, and taste.

To make wine of pears, procure the tartest perry, but by no means that which is tart by sowering, or given that way, but such as is naturally so; put into a barrel about five ounces of the juice of the herb clary, and the quintessence of wine, and to every barrel a pound, or pint of the syrup of blackberries, and, after fermentation and refining, it will be of a curious wine taste, like sherry, and not well distinguishable, but by such as have very good palates, or those who deal in it.

To make Wines of Blackberries, Strawberries, or Dewberries.

TAKE of these berries, in their proper season, moderately ripe, what quantity you please: press them as other berries; boil up water and honey, or water and fine sugar, as your palate best relishes, to a considerable sweetness; and when it is well scummed, put the juice in and let it simmer to incorporate it well with the water; and when it is done so, take it off, let it cool, scum it again, and put it up in a barrel, or rather a close-glazed earthen vessel, to ferment and settle; to every gallon put half a pint of Malaga, draw it off as clear as possible; bottle it up, and keep it cool for use.

To make Sage Wine.

TAKE four handfuls of red sage, beat it in a stone mortar like green sauce, put it into a quart of red wine, and let it stand three or four days close stopped, shaking it twice or thrice, then let it stand and settle, and the next day in the morning take of the sage wine three spoonfuls, and of running water one spoonful, fasting after it one hour or better; use this from Michaelmas to the end of March: it will cure any aches or humours in the joints, dry rheums, keep from all diseases to the fourth degree; it helps the dead palsy, and convulsions in the sinews, sharpens the memory, and from the beginning of taking it will keep the body mild, strengthen nature, till the fulness of your days be finished; nothing will be changed in your strength, except the change of your hair; it will keep your teeth sound that were not corrupted before; it will keep you from the gout, the dropsy, or any swellings of the joints or body.

Sage Wine another Way.

TAKE thirty pounds of Malaga raisins picked clean and shred small, and one bushel of green sage shred small; then boil five gallons of water, let the water stand till it is lukewarm, then put it in a tub to your sage and raisins; let it stand five or six days, stirring it twice or thrice a day; then strain and press the liquor from the ingredients; put it in a cask; and let it stand six months, then draw it clean off into another vessel; bottle it in two days; in a month or six weeks it will be fit to drink, but best when it is a year old.

Another Method.

TO three gallons of water put six pounds of sugar; boil these together, and as the scum rises, take it off, and when it is well boiled, put it in a tub, boiling hot, in which there is already a gallon of red sage leaves clean picked and washed; when the liquor is near cold, put in the juice of four large lemons beaten well, with a little ale-yeast; mix these all well together, cover it very close from the air, and let it stand forty-eight hours; then strain all through a fine hair sieve, and put it into a vessel that will but just hold it, and when it has done working stop it down close, and let it stand three weeks or a month before you bottle it, putting a lump of loaf-sugar into every bottle. This wine is best when it is three months old. After this manner you may make wine of any other herb or flower.

To make Sugar Wine.

BOIL twenty-six quarts of spring-water a quarter of an hour, and when it is blood-warm put twenty-five pounds of Malaga raisins picked, rubbed, and shred into it, with half a bushel of red sage shred, and a porringer of ale-yeast; stir all well together, and let it stand in a tub covered warm six or seven days, stirring it once a day; then strain it out and put it in a rundlet; let it work three or four days, and stop it up; when it has stood six or seven days put in a quart or two of Malaga sack, and when it is fine bottle it.

To make Cowslip Wine.

TO six gallons of water put fourteen pounds of sugar, stir it well together, and beat the whites of twenty eggs very well, and mix it with the liquor, and make it boil as fast as possible; skim it well, and let it continue boiling two hours; then strain it through a hair sieve, and set it a cooling; and when it is as cold as wort should be, put a small quantity of yeast to it on a toast, or in a dish; let it stand all night working; then bruise a peck of cowslips, put them into your vessel, and your liquor upon them, adding six ounces of syrup of lemons; cut a turf of grass and lay on the bung; let it stand a fortnight, and then bottle it; put your tap into your vessel before you put your wine in, that you may not shake it.

Cyprus Wine imitated.

YOU must to nine gallons of water, put nine quarts of the juice of the white elder-berries, which has been pressed gently from the berries with the hand, and passed through a sieve, without bruising the kernels of the berries: add to every gallon of liquor three pounds of Lisbon sugar, and to the whole quantity put an ounce and a half of ginger sliced, and three quarters of an ounce of cloves; then boil this near an hour, taking off the scum as it rises, and pour the whole to cool in an open tub, and work it with ale-yeast, spread upon a toast of white bread for three days, and then turn it into a vessel that will just hold it, adding about a pound and a half of raisins of the sun split, to lie in liquor till we draw it off, which should not be till the wine is fine, which you will find in January.

Mountain Wine.

PICK out the big stalks of your Malaga raisins; then chop them very small, five pounds to every gallon of cold spring-water; let them steep a fortnight or more, squeeze out the liquor, and barrel it in a vessel fit for it; first fume the vessel with brimstone; don't stop it up till the hissing is over.

Lemon Wine, or what may pass for Citron Water.

TAKE two quarts of brandy, one quart of spring-water, half a pound of double refined sugar, and the rinds of sixteen lemons; put them together into an earthen pot, pour into it
twelve

twelve spoonfuls of milk boiling hot; stir it together, and let it stand three days; then take off the top, and pass the other two or three times through a jelly-bag; bottle it; it is fit to drink, or will keep a year or two.

To make Turnep Wine.

TAKE a good many turneps, pare them, slice them, put them into a cyder press, and press out all the juice very well; to every gallon of juice put three pounds of lump sugar; have a vessel ready just big enough to hold the juice, and put your sugar into a vessel; and also to every gallon of juice half a pint of brandy; pour in the juice, and lay something over the bung for a week to see if it works; if it does, you must not bung it down till it has done working; then stop it close for three months, and draw it off into another vessel, and when it is fine, bottle it off.

To make Dr. Radcliffe's Stomach Wine.

TAKE the roots of Virginia snake-weed and gentian, of each three ounces; of galangal, cloves, cubebs, mace, nutmeg, and saffron, of each one drachm; infuse these cold, in three pints of Canary.

To make Frontiniac Wine.

TAKE six gallons of water, twelve pounds of white sugar, and six pounds of raisins of the sun cut small; boil these together an hour; then take of the flowers of elder, when they are falling, and will shake off, the quantity of half a peck; put them in the liquor when it is almost cold; the next day put in six spoonfuls of syrup of lemons, and four spoonfuls of ale-yeast, and two days after put it in a vessel that is fit for it; and when it has stood two months, bottle it off.

To make English Champaign, or the fine Currant Wine.

TAKE to three gallons of water nine pounds of Lisbon sugar; boil the water and sugar half an hour, skim it clean, then have one gallon of currants picked, but not bruised; pour the liquor boiling hot over them; and when cold, work it with half a pint of baum two days; then pour it through a flannel or sieve; then put it into a barrel fit for it, with half an ounce of isinglass well bruised; when it has done working, stop it close for a month; then bottle it, and in every bottle put a very small lump of double refined sugar; this is excellent wine, and has a beautiful colour.

To make Saragosa Wine, or English Sack.

TO every quart of water put a sprig of rue, and to every gallon a handful of fennel-roots; boil these half an hour, then strain it out, and to every gallon of this liquor put three pounds of honey, boil it two hours, and skim it well; when it is cold, pour it off, and turn it into the vessel, or such cask as is fit for it; keep it a year in the vessel, and then bottle it; it is a very good sack.

To fine Wine the Lisbon Way.

TO every twenty gallons of wine, take the whites of ten eggs, and a small handful of salt; beat it together to a froth, and mix it well with a quart or more of the wine; then pour it into the vessel, and in a few days it will be fine.

To make Palermo Wine.

TAKE to every quart of water a pound of Malaga raisins, rub and cut the raisins small, and put them to the water, and let them stand ten days, stirring once or twice a day; you may boil the water an hour before you put it to the raisins, and let it stand to cool; at ten days end strain out your liquor, and put a little yeast to it; and at three days end put it in the vessel, with one sprig of dried wormwood; let it be close stopt, and at three months end bottle it off.

To make Birch Wine.

IN March bore a hole in a birch-tree, and put in a faucet, and it will run two or three days together without hurting the tree; then put in a pin to stop it, and the next year you may draw as much from the same hole; put to every gallon of the liquor a quart of good honey, and stir it well together; boil it an hour, skim it well, and put in a few cloves and a piece of lemon-peel; when it is almost cold put to it so much ale-yeast as will make it work like new ale; and when the yeast begins to settle, put it in a rundlet that will just hold it; so let it stand six weeks, or longer if you please; then bottle it, and in a month you may drink it, it will keep a year or two; you may make it with sugar, two pounds to a gallon, or something more, if you keep it long; this is admirably wholesome as well as pleasant, an opener of obstructions, good against the phthisic, the spleen and scurvy, a remedy for the stone; it will abate heat in a fever or thrush, and has been given with good success.

To make Mead.

TO thirteen gallons of water put thirty-two pounds of honey, boil and skim it well, then take rosemary, thyme, bay-leaves, and sweet-briar, one handful all together; boil it an hour, then put it into a tub with two or three good handfuls of the flour of malt; stir it till it is but blood-warm, then strain it through a cloth and put it into a tub again; then cut a toast round a quartern loaf, spread it over with good ale-yeast, and put it into your tub; when the liquor has done fermenting put it up in your vessel; then take cloves, mace, nutmegs, an ounce and a half, ginger an ounce, sliced; bruise the spice, and tie all up in a rag, and hang it in the vessel; stop it up close for use.

To make strong Mead.

TAKE of spring-water what quantity you please, make it more than blood-warm, and dissolve honey in it till it is strong enough to bear an egg, the breadth of a shilling, then boil it gently near an hour, taking off the scum as it rises; then put to about nine or ten gallons, seven or eight large blades of mace, three nutmegs quartered, twenty cloves, three or four sticks of cinnamon, two or three roots of ginger, and a quarter of an ounce of Jamaica pepper; put these spices into the kettle to the honey and water, a whole lemon, with a sprig of sweet-briar, and a sprig of rosemary; tie the briar and rosemary together, and when they have boiled a little while, take them out, and throw them away; but let your liquor stand on the spice in a clean earthen pot, till the next day; then strain it into a vessel that is fit for it, put the spice in a bag, hang it in the vessel, stop it, and at three months draw it into bottles: be sure that it is fine when it is bottled; after it is bottled six weeks, it is fit to drink.

To make small white Mead.

TAKE three gallons of spring-water, make it hot, and dissolve in it three quarts of honey, and a pound of loaf-sugar; let it boil about half an hour, and skim it as long as any rises; then pour it out into a tub, and squeeze in the juice of four lemons, put in the rinds but of two, twenty cloves, two races of ginger, a top of sweet-briar, and a top of rosemary; let it stand in a tub till it is but blood-warm; then make a brown toast, and spread it with two or three spoonfuls of ale-yeast; put it into a vessel fit for it; let it stand four or five days, then bottle it out.

How to make Cyder.

AFTER all your apples are bruised, take half of your quantity and squeeze them, and the juice you press from them pour upon the others half bruised, but not squeezed, in a tub for the purpose, having a tap at the bottom; let the juice remain upon the apples three or four days, then pull out your tap, and let your juice run into some other vessel set under the tub to receive it; and if it runs thick, as at the first it will, pour it upon the apples again, till you see it run clear; and as you have a quantity, put it into your vessel, but do not force the cyder, but let it drop as long as it will of its own accord: having done this, after you perceive that the sides begin to work, take a quantity of isinglass, an ounce will serve forty gallons, infuse this into some of the cyder till it be dissolved; put to an ounce of isinglass a quart of cyder, and when it is so dissolved, pour it into the vessel, and stop it close for two days, or something more; then draw off the cyder into another vessel: this do so often till you perceive your cyder to be free from all manner of sediment, that may make it ferment and fret itself: after Christmas you may boil it. You may, by pouring water on the apples, and pressing them, make a pretty small cyder: if it be thick and muddy, by using isinglass, you may make it as clear as the rest; you must dissolve the isinglass over the fire, till it be jelly.

For fining Cyder.

TAKE two quarts of skim-milk, four ounces of isinglass, cut the isinglass in pieces, and work it lukewarm in the milk over the fire; and when it is dissolved, then put it in cold into the hogshead of cyder, and take a long stick, and stir it well from top to bottom, for half a quarter of an hour.

To make Turkish Sherbet.

TAKE nine Seville oranges, and three lemons, and grate the outside rinds just to the white: then take three pounds of double refined sugar, and a gill of water, and boil it to a candy height; then take it from the fire, put in the peel, and mix it well together; then strain in the juice, and keep it stirring till it is almost cold, and then put it into a pot for use.

To make Cock Ale.

TAKE ten gallons of ale and a large cock, the older the better; parboil the cock, flay him and stamp him in a stone mortar till his bones are broken (you must craw and gut him when you flay him) then put the cock into two quarts of sack,

and

and put to it three pounds of raisins of the sun stoned, some blades of mace, and a few cloves; put all these into a canvas bag, and a little before you find the ale has done working, put the ale and bag together in a vessel; in a week or nine days time bottle it up; fill the bottle but just above the neck, and give it the same time to ripen as other ale.

To make Ebulum.

TO a hogshead of strong ale take a heaped bushel of elder-berries, and half a pound of juniper-berries beaten; put in all berries when you put in the hops, and let them boil together till the berries break in pieces, then work it up as you do ale; when it has done working, add to it half a pound of ginger, half an ounce of cloves, as much mace, an ounce of nutmegs, as much cinnamon, grosly beaten, half a pound of citron, as much eringo-root, and likewise of candied orange-peel; let the sweet-meats be cut in pieces very thin, and put with the spice into a bag, and hang it in the vessel when you stop it up; so let it stand till it is fine, then bottle it up, and drink it with lumps of double refined sugar in the glass.

To make Shrub.

TAKE two quarts of brandy, and put it in a large bottle, adding to it the juice of five lemons, the peels of two, and half a nutmeg; stop it up and let it stand three days, and add to it three pints of white wine, a pound and a half of sugar; mix it, strain it twice through a flannel, and bottle it up; it is a pretty wine, and a cordial.

To make Cherry Brandy.

TAKE six dozen pounds of cherries, half red and half black, mash or squeeze them with your hands to pieces, and put to them three gallons of brandy, letting them stand steeping twenty-four hours; then put the mashed cherries and liquor a little at a time, into a canvas bag, and press it as long as any juice will run; sweeten it to your taste, put it into a vessel fit for it, let it stand a month, and bottle it out; put a lump of loaf-sugar into every bottle.

To make Usquebaugh.

TO three gallons of brandy, put four ounces of aniseeds bruised, the next day distil it in a cold still pasted up, then scrape four ounces of liquorice and pound it in a mortar, dry it in an iron pan, do not burn it, put it in the bottle to your distilled water, and let it stand ten days, then take out the liquorice, and to

every

every six quarts of the spirits, put in cloves, mace, nutmegs, cinnamon and ginger, of each a quarter of an ounce, dates stoned and sliced four ounces, raisins stoned half a pound; let these infuse ten days, then strain it out, tincture it with saffron, and bottle it and cork it well.

To make Elder Ale.

TAKE ten bushels of malt to a hogshead; then put two bushels of elder-berries, picked from the stalks, into a pot or earthen pan, and set it in a pot of boiling water till the berries swell; then strain it out, and put the juice into the guile vat, and beat it often in; and so order it as the common way of brewing.

To make Elder-flower Water.

TAKE two large handfuls of dried elder-flowers, and ten gallons of spring-water; boil the water, and pour it scalding hot upon the flowers; the next day put to every gallon of water five pounds of Malaga raisins, the stalks being first picked off, but not washed; chop them grosly with a chopping-knife, then put them into your boiled water, and stir the water, raisins and flowers well together; and so do twice a day for twelve days; then press out the juice clear, as long as you can get any liquor out; then put it in your barrel fit for it, and stop it up two or three days till it works; and in a few days stop it up close, and let it stand two or three months, till it is clear; then bottle it.

To recover the lost Colour of White Wine, or Rhenish Wine.

TO do this effectually, rack the wine from the lees, and if the colour of the wine be faint and tawny, put in coniac-lees, and pour the wine upon them, rolling and jumbling them together a considerable time in the cask; in ten or twelve days rack off the wine, and it will be of a proper colour, and drink brisk and fine.

To prevent the Decay of lowering Wine.

TAKE roach-allum powdered, an ounce, draw out four gallons of the wine, and strew the powder in it; beat it well for the space of half an hour, then fill up the cask, and set it on broach, being careful to let it take vent; by this means, in three or four days, you will find it a curious brisk wine.

Of Racking Wine.

THIS is is done with such instruments as are useful, and appropriated to the manner of doing it, and cannot be so well described by words as by seeing it done; however, this observe in doing it: Let it be when the wind sets full north, and the weather is temperate and clear, that the air may the better agree with the constitution of the wine, and make it take more kindly. It is moreover most proper to be done in the increase of the moon, when she is under the earth, and not in full height, &c.

To make Wines scent well, and give them a curious Flavour.

TAKE powder of sulphur, two ounces, half an ounce of calamus, incorporate them well together, and put them into a pint and a half of orange-water; let them steep in it a considerable time, and then, drawing off the water, melt the sulphur and calamus in an iron-pan, and dip in it as many rags as will soak it up, which put into the cask; then rack your wine, and put in a pint of rose-water, and stopping the hogshead, roll it up and down half an hour, after which let it continue still two days, and by so ordering any Gascoigne, or red wine, it will have a pleasant scent and gust.

To mend Wines that rope.

WHEN you have set your cask abroach, place a coarse linen cloth before the bore, then put in the linen, and rock it in a dry cask; add five or six ounces of the powder of allum, roll and jumble them sufficiently together, and upon settling it will be fined down, and prove a very fluid pleasant wine, both in taste and scent.

To mend White, or Rhenish Wines.

IF these wines have an unpleasant taste, the best way is speedily to draw either of them half off, and to either of the halves put two gallons of new milk, a handful of bay-salt, and as much rice; mix and beat them well together for half an hour, with a staff, or paddler, then fill up the cask, and when you have well rolled it, turn it over in the lees, and two or three days after you may broach it, and it will drink very fine and brisk.

CHAP.

CHAP. II.
All Sorts of CORDIAL WATERS.

BEFORE we proceed to particularife Cordial Waters, it may not be amifs to give fome general Directions concerning Diftilling. If your ftill be an alembic, when you fet it on, fill the top with cold water, and make a little pafte of flour and water, and clofe the bottom of your ftill well with it. Take great care that your fire is not too hot to make it boil over, for that will weaken the ftrength of your water; you muft change the water on the top of your ftill often, and never let it be fcalding hot, and your ftill will drop gradually off; if you ufe a hot ftill, when you put on the top, dip a cloth in white lead and oil, and lay it well over the edges of your ftill, and a coarfe wet cloth over the top. It requires a little fire under it; but you muft take care that you keep it very clear; when your cloth is dry, dip it in cold water, and lay it on again; and if your ftill be very hot, wet another cloth, and lay it round the very top, and keep it of a moderate heat, fo that your water is cold when it comes off the ftill.—If you ufe a worm-ftill, keep your water in the tub full to the top, and change the water often, to prevent it from growing hot. Obferve to let all fimple waters ftand two or three days before you work it, to take off the fiery tafte of the ftill.

To diftil Caudle Water.

TAKE wormwood, hore-hound, feverfew, and lavender-cotton, of each three handfuls, rue, pepper-mint, and Seville orange-peel, of each a handful; fteep them in red wine, or the bottoms of ftrong beer all night; then diftil them in a hot ftill pretty quick, and it will be a fine caudle to take as bitters.

To diftil Milk Water.

TAKE two handfuls of fpear or pepper-mint, the fame of balm, one handful of cardus, the fame of wormwood, and one of angelica; cut them into lengths a quarter long, and fteep them in three quarts of fkimmed milk twelve hours; then diftil it in a cold ftill, with a flow fire under it; keep a cloth always wet over the top of your ftill, to keep the liquor from boiling over. The next day bottle it, cork it well, and keep it for ufe.

To make Hephnatick Water for the Gravel.

GATHER your thorn flowers in May, when they are in full bloom, and pick them from the stems and leaves, and to every half peck of flowers, take three quarts of Lisbon wine, and put into it a quarter of a pound of nutmegs sliced, and let them steep in it all night; then put it into your still with the peeps, and keep a moderate even fire under it, for if you let it boil over, it will lose its strength.

To distil Pepper-Mint Water.

GET your pepper-mint when it is full grown, and before it seeds, cut it in short lengths; fill your still with it, and put it half full of water, then make a good fire under it, and when it is nigh boiling, and the still begins to drop, if your fire be too hot, draw a little out from under it, as you see it requires, to keep it from boiling over, or your water will be muddy: the slower your still drops, the water will be clearer and stronger, but do not spend it too far; the next day bottle it, and let it stand three or four days, to take the fire off the still, then cork it well, and it will keep a long time.

To distil Elder-Flower Water.

GET your elder-flowers, when they are in full bloom; shake the blossoms off, and to every peck of flowers, put one quart of water, and let them steep in it all night; then put them in a cold still, and take care that your water comes cold off the still, and it will be very clear, and draw it no longer than your liquor is is good; then put it into bottles, and cork it in two or three days, and it will keep a year.

To distil Rose Water.

GATHER your red roses when they are dry and full blown, pick off the leaves, and to every peck put one quart of water; then put them into a cold still, and make a slow fire under it; the slower you distil it the better it is: then bottle it, and cork it in two or three days time, and keep it for use. You may distil bean-flowers the same way.

To distil Penny-Royal Water.

GET your penny-royal when it is full grown, and before it is in blossom; then fill your cold still with it, and put it half full of water; make a moderate fire under it, and distil it off cold; then put it into bottles, and cork it in two or three days time, and keep it for use.

To

To diftil Lavender Water.

TO every twelve pounds of lavender-neps, put one quart of water; put them into a cold ftill, and make a flow fire under it; diftil it off very flow, and put it into a pot till you have diftilled all your water; then clean your ftill well out, and put your lavender water into it, and diftil it off as flow as before; then put it into bottles, and cork it well.

To diftil Spirits of Wine.

TAKE the bottoms of ftrong beer, and any kind of wines; put them into a hot ftill about three parts full, and make a very flow fire under under it. If you do not take great care to keep it moderate, it will boil over, for the body is fo ftrong, that it will rife to the top of the ftill; the flower you diftil it the ftronger your fpirit will be. Put it into an earthen pot till you have done diftilling, then clean your ftill well out, and put the fpirit into it, and diftil it as flow as before, and make it as ftrong as to burn in your lamp; then bottle it, cork it well, and keep it for ufe.

The great Palfey Water.

TAKE of fage, rofemary, and betony-flowers, of each a handful; and borage, buglofs-flowers, of each a handful; of lily of the valley and cowflip-flowers, of each four or five handfuls; fteep them in the beft fack; then put to them balm, fpike-flowers, mother-wort, bay-leaves, leaves of orange-tree, with the flowers, of each one ounce; citron-peel, piony-feeds, and cinnamon, of each half an ounce; nutmegs, cardamums, mace, cubebs, yellow fanders, of each half an ounce; lignum aloes, one drachm; make all thefe into powder; then add jujubes, the ftones taken out, and cut in pieces, half a pound; pearl prepared, fmaragdes, mufk and faffron, of each ten grains; ambergreafe one fcruple, red rofes dried one ounce; as many lavender-flowers as will fill a gallon glafs; fteep all thefe a month, and diftil them in an alembic very carefully; then take peal prepared, fmaragdes, mufk and faffron, of each ten grains; ambergreafe, one fcruple; red rofes dried, red and yellow fanders, of each one ounce; hang thefe in a white farcenet bag in the water; ftop it clofe. This water is of excellent ufe in all fwoonings, in weaknefs of heart and decay of fpirits; it reftores fpeech in apoplexies and palfies; it helps all pains in the joints from cold or bruifes, bathing the place outwardly, and dipping cloths and laying on it; it ftrengthens and comforts the vital fpirits, and helps the memory; reftoreth loft appetite, helpeth all weakness of the stomach; taken inwardly, or bathed outwardly, it taketh away giddiness of the head, and helpeth hearing; it makes a pleasant breath, it is good in the beginning of dropsies; none can sufficiently express the virtues of this water: when it is taken inwardly, drop ten or twelve drops on a lump of sugar, a bit of bread, or in a dish of tea; but in a fit of the palsey give so much every hour to restore speech. Add to the rest of the flowers single wall-flowers, and the roots and flowers of single pionies, and misleto of the oak, of each a good handful.

To make Aqua Mirabilis.

TAKE cubebs, cardamums, galingal, cloves, mace, nutmegs, cinnamon, of each two drachms, bruised small; then take of the juice of celandine a pint, the juice of spear-mint half a pint, the juice of balm half a pint; the flowers of melilot, cowslip, rosemary, borage, bugloss, and marigolds, of each three drachms; seeds of fennel, coriander, and carraway, of each two drachms; two quarts of the best sack, a quart of white wine, of brandy, the strongest angelica-water, and red rose-water, of each one pint; bruise the spices and seeds, and steep them with the herbs and flowers in the juices, waters, sack, white wine and brandy all night; in the morning distil it in a common still pasted up; from this quantity draw off a gallon at least; sweeten it to your taste with sugar-candy; bottle it up and keep it in sand, or very cool.

To make Orange-Flower Brandy.

TAKE a gallon of French brandy, and boil a pound of orange-flowers a little while, and put them to it; save the water, and with that make a syrup to sweeten it.

A Cordial Water that may be made in Winter.

TAKE three quarts of brandy or sack, put two handfuls of rosemary and two handfuls of balm to it chopped pretty small, one ounce of cloves, two ounces of nutmegs, three ounces of cinnamon; beat all the spices grosly, and steep them with the herbs in the wine; then put it in a still pasted up close; save near a quart of the first running, and so of the second, and of the third; when it is distilled mix it all together, and dissolve about a pound of double refined sugar in it, and when it is settled bottle it up.

A Tincture of Ambergreafe.

TAKE ambergreafe and musk, of each an ounce, and put to them a quarter of a pint of spirit of wine; stop it close, tie it down with leather, and set it in horse-dung ten or twelve days.

To make Orange or Lemon Water.

TO the outer rind of an hundred oranges or lemons, put three gallons of brandy and two quarts of sack, and let them steep in it one night; the next day diſtil them in a cold ſtill; a gallon, with the proportion of peels, is enough for one ſtill; and of that you may draw off between three and four quarts; draw it off till you taſte it begins to be ſouriſh; ſweeten it to your taſte with double refined ſugar; mix the firſt, ſecond and third running together; if it is lemon-water, it ſhould be perfumed; put two grains of ambergreaſe and one of muſk, ground fine, tie it in a rag, and let it hang five or ſix days in a bottle, and then put it in another, and ſo for a great many if you pleaſe, or elſe you may put three or four drops of tincture of ambergreaſe in it; cork it very well: the orange is an excellent water for the ſtomach, and the lemon is a fine entertaining water.

King Charles II's Surfeit Water.

TAKE a gallon of the beſt aqua-vitæ, a quart of brandy, a quart of aniſeed-water, a pint of poppy-water, and a pint of damaſk roſe-water: put theſe in a large glaſs jar, adding to it a pound of fine powdered ſugar, a pound and a half of raiſins ſtoned, a quarter of a pound of dates ſtoned and ſliced, one ounce of cinnamon bruiſed, cloves one ounce, four nutmegs bruiſed, one ſtick of liquorice ſcraped and ſliced; let all theſe ſtand nine days cloſe covered, ſtirring it three or four times a day; then add to it three pounds of freſh poppies, or three handfuls of dried poppies, a ſprig of angelica, two or three of balm; ſo let it ſtand a week longer, then ſtrain it out and bottle it.

The Fever Water.

TAKE of Virginia ſnake-root ſix ounces, carduus-ſeeds and marigold-flowers, of each four ounces, twenty green walnuts, carduus-water, poppy-water, of each two quarts, two ounces of hart's horn; ſlice the walnuts, and ſteep all in the waters a fortnight; then add to it an ounce of London treacle, and diſtil it all in an alembic paſted up; three drops of ſpirit of amber in three ſpoonfuls of this water, will deliver a woman of a dead child.

Black Cherry Water for Children.

TAKE ſix pounds of black cherries, and bruiſe them ſmall, then put to them the tops of roſemary, ſweet-marjoram, ſpearmint, angelica, balm, marigold-flowers, of each a handful, dried violets an ounce; aniſeeds and ſweet fennel-ſeeds, of each half

half an ounce bruised; cut the herbs small, mix them together, and distil them off in a cold still. This water is excellent for children, giving them two or three spoonfuls at a time.

To make Gripe Water.

TAKE of penny-royal ten handfuls, coriander-seeds, anise-seeds, sweet fennel-seeds, carraway-seeds, of each one ounce; bruise them and put them to the herbs in an earthen pot; sprinkle on them a pint of brandy; let them stand all night, the next day distil it off, and take six, seven, or eight spoonfuls of this water, sweetened with syrup of gilliflowers warm, and go to bed; cover very warm to sweat if you can, and drink some of it as long as the gripes continue.

Lily of the Valley Water.

TAKE the flowers of lily of the valley, distil them in sack, and drink a spoonful or two as there is occasion; it restores speech to those who have the dumb palsey or apoplexy, it is good against the gout, it comforts the heart, and strengthens the memory; it helps the inflammation of the eyes, being dropped into them. Take the flowers, put them into a glass close stopped, and set it into a hill of ants for a month; then take it out, and you will find a liquor that comes from the flowers, which keep in a phial; it easeth the pains of the gout; the place affected being anointed therewith.

To make Vertigo Water.

TAKE the leaves of red sage, cinquefoil, and wood betony, of each a good handful, boil them in a gallon of spring-water till it comes to a quart; when it is cold put into it a pennyworth of roch-allum, and bottle it up; when you use it put a little of it in a spoon, or in the palm of your hand, and snuff it up, go not into the air presently.

Dr. Burgess's Antidote against the Plague.

TAKE three pints of muscandine, and boil therein one handful of sage, as much rue, angelica-roots one ounce, zedoary-roots one ounce, Virginia snake-root half an ounce, saffron twenty grains; let all these boil till a pint be consumed, then strain it and set it over the fire again, and put therein two pennyworth of long pepper, half an ounce of ginger, as much nutmegs; beat all the spice, and let them boil together a little, and put thereto a quarter of an ounce of mithridate, as much Venice treacle, and a quarter of a pint of the best angelica-water; take it warm both morning and evening, two spoonfuls if already infected;

infected; if not infected, one spoonful is enough for a day, half a spoonful in the morning, and as much at night. This had great success, under God, in the plague; it is good likewise against the small-pox, or any other pestilential disease.

To make Lime Water.

TAKE a pound of unslacked lime, put it into an earthen jug well glazed, adding to it a gallon of spring-water boiling hot; cover it close till it is cold, then skim it clean, let it stand two days, pour it clear off into glass bottles, and keep it for use; the older the better. The virtues are as follow.

For a sore, warm some of the water and wash the sore well with it for half an hour, then lay a plaister on the sore of some gentle thing, and lay a cloth over the plaister four or five double, wet with this water, and as it dries wet it again, and it will heal it.

For a flux or looseness, take two spoonfuls of it cold in the morning, and two at night as you go to bed; do this seven or eight days together for a man or woman; but if for a child, one spoonful at a time is enough; and if very young, half a spoonful at a time; it will keep twenty years, and no one who has not experienced it knows the virtues of it.

Cock Water for a Consumption.

TAKE an old cock, kill him and quarter him, and with clean cloths wipe the blood from him; then put the quarters into a cold still, part of a leg of veal, two quarts of old Malaga sack, a handful of thyme, as much sweet-marjoram and rosemary, two handfuls of pimpernel, four dates stoned and sliced, a pound of currants, as many raisins of the sun stoned, a pound of sugar-candy finely beaten; when all is in, paste up the still, let it stand all night, the next morning distil it, mix the water together, and sweeten it to your taste with white sugar-candy; drink three or four spoonfuls an hour before dinner and supper.

Another Water against a Consumption.

TAKE a pound of currants, and of hart's-tongue, liverwort and speedwell, of each a large handful; then take a peck of snails, lay them all night in hyssop, the next morning rub and bruise them, and distil all in a gallon of new milk; sweeten it with white sugar-candy, and drink of this water two or three times a day, a quarter of a pint at a time; it has done great good.

Another.

TAKE three pints of the best Canary and a pint of mint-water, of candied eryngo-roots, dates, China-roots, and raisins

stoned,

stoned, of each three ounces; of mace a quarter of an ounce; infuse these twelve hours in an earthen pot close covered, over a gentle fire; when it is cold strain it out, and keep it in a clean pan or glass jar for use; then make about a quart of plain jelly of hart's-horn, and drink a quarter of a pint of this liquor with a large spoonful of jelly night and morning, for two or three months together.

Rue Water, good for Fits of the Mother.

TAKE of rue, and green walnuts, of each a pound, figs a pound and a half; bruise the rue and walnuts, slice the figs, lay them between the rue and walnuts, and distil it off; bottle it up and keep it for use: take a spoonful or two when there is any appearance of a fit.

An opening Drink.

TAKE penny-royal, red sage, liverwort, hore-hound, maiden-hair, hyssop, of each two handfuls, figs and raisins stoned, of each a pound, blue currants half a pound, liquorice, aniseeds, coriander-seeds, of each two ounces; put all these in two gallons of spring-water, and let it boil away two or three quarts; then strain it, and when it is cold put it in bottles: drink half a pint in the morning, and as much in the afternoon; keep warm and eat little.

PART X.

MEDICINES, SALVES, &c.

Reduced to Alphabetical Order, as nearly as the Nature of the Subject would admit of.

CHAP. I.
Of MEDICINES and SALVES.

An excellent Remedy for Agues, which has been often tried with very great Succefs.

AKE of black foap, gunpowder, tobacco and brandy, of each an equal quantity; mix them well together, and three hours before the fit comes, apply to the patient's wrift; let this be kept on for a fortnight.

Another.

GIVE as much Virginia fnake-root, dried and powdered, as will lie upon a fhilling, in a glafs of fherry or fack, juft before the cold fit begins; ufe this two or three times till the ague is gone.

Another.

TAKE an ounce and a half of the beft refined aloes, and fteep it in a quart of brandy; infufe it forty-eight hours, and take four fpoonfuls juft before the fit comes.

Another.

TAKE a pint of red rofe-water, and put to it an ounce of white fugar-candy, and the juice of three Seville oranges; mix all together, and drink it off an hour before you expect the fit; it cures at once or twice taking.

Another.

Another.

TAKE small packthread, as much as will go five times about the neck, wrists, and ancles; dip them in oil of amber twice a day for nine days together; keep them on a fortnight after the ague is gone.

Another.

TAKE tobacco-dust and soot, an equal quantity, and nine cloves of garlic; beat it well together, and mix it with soap into a pretty stiff paste, and make two cakes something broader than a five shilling piece, and something thicker; lay it on the inside of each wrist, and bind it on with rags; put it on an hour before the fit is expected: if it does not do the first time, in three or four days repeat it with fresh.

Another.

TAKE smallage, ribwort, rue, plantain, and olibanum, equal parts; beat all these well together with a little bay salt, and put them in a thin bag, and lay it to the wrist a little before the cold fit comes.

Another.

TAKE a quart of strong beer, and a good quantity of the youngest artichoke-leaves; shred them, and boil them very well together; when you think it almost enough, put a spoonful of mustard-seed bruised, and give it one boil; then strain it, and bottle it; take half a pint as hot as you can, half an hour before the fit comes.

For a Tertian Ague, a never-failing Remedy.

TAKE stone brimstone finely powdered, as much as will lie upon half a crown, in a glass of white wine, about an hour before the fit comes; it cures at twice taking. This I had from one that had cured scores with it, and it never failed once.

For an Asthma.

TAKE of virgins honey one spoonful, mix in it as much rosin as will lie upon a half-crown finely powdered; let the patient take it in the morning, an hour before breakfast, and again at night, an hour after supper; this must be continued a month.

For an old Ach or Strain.

TAKE an ounce of Lucatellus's balſam, and mix it with two drachms of oil of turpentine; gently heat it; anoint the place, and put new flannel on it.

For the Biting of a mad Dog.

PRIMROSE-ROOTS ſtamped in white wine, and ſtrained; let the patient drink a good draught of it.

Another Cure.

TAKE two quarts of ſtrong ale, two pennyworth of treacle, two garlic-heads, a handful of cinquefoil, ſage and rue; boil them all together to a quart; ſtrain it, and give the patient three or four ſpoonfuls twice a day: take dittany, agrimony, and ruſty bacon, beaten well together, and apply to the ſore, to keep it from feſtering.

An infallible Cure for the Bite of a mad Dog.

OF all the diſeaſes incident to mankind, there is none ſo ſhocking to our nature as the bite of a mad dog: and yet as terrible as it is, we have known inſtances, of thoſe who choſe rather to hazard the worſt effects of it, and to die the worſt of deaths, than to follow the advice of their phyſicians, by making uſe of the known ſpecific of dipping in the ſea, or ſalt water. It is for the ſake of people of this unhappy temper, who may have the misfortune to be bit, and of thoſe who may have cattle that are ſo, that we publiſh the following receipt, which has been frequently made uſe of in a neighbouring country, and (as the gentleman who communicated it ſays) was never known to fail.

Take the leaves of rue, picked from the ſtalks and bruiſed, ſix ounces; four ounces of garlic picked from the ſtalks and bruiſed, four ounces of Venice treacle, and four ounces of filed pewter, or ſcraped tin. Boil theſe in two quarts of the beſt ale, in a pan covered cloſe over a gentle fire, for the ſpace of an hour, then ſtrain the ingredients from the liquor. Give eight or nine ſpoonfuls of it warm to a man, or a woman, three mornings faſting. Eight or nine ſpoonfuls is ſufficient for the ſtrongeſt; a leſſer quantity to thoſe younger, or of a weaker conſtitution, as you may judge of their ſtrength. Ten or twelve ſpoonfuls for a horſe or a bullock; three, four, or five to a ſheep, hog, or dog. This muſt be given within nine days after the bite; it ſeldom fails in man or beaſt. If you bind ſome of the ingredients on the wound, it will be ſo much the better.

Another for the Bite of a mad Dog, which has cured when the Person was disordered, and the salt Water failed.

TAKE of tormentil-roots an ounce, assa-fœtida as much as a bean, castor four pennyworth, lignum aloes two pennyworth; steep these in milk twelve hours; boil the milk, and drink it fasting, before the change or full moon, or as oft as occasion.

Dr. Mead's Receipt for the Bite of a Mad Dog.

LET the patient bleed at the arm nine or ten ounces: take of the herb called in Latin, lichen cinerus terrestris, in English, ash-coloured ground liverwort, cleaned, dried and powdered, half an ounce; of black pepper powdered, two drachms: mix these well together, and divide the powder into four doses, one of which must be taken every morning fasting, for four mornings successively, in half a pint of cow's milk warm; after these four doses are taken, the patient must go into the cold-bath, or a cold spring or river, every morning fasting, for a month; he must be dipt all over, but not stay in (with head above water) longer than half a minute, if the water be very cold; after this he must go in three times a week for a fortnight longer. The lichen is a very common herb, and grows generally in sandy and barren soils all over England; the right time to gather it is in the months of October and November.

Cæsar's Cure for the Bite of a Rattle-Snake.

TAKE of the roots of plantain or horehound, (in the summer, roots and branches together) a sufficient quantity, bruise them in a mortar, and squeeze out the juice, of which give, as soon as possible, one large spoonful; if he is swelled, you must force it down his throat: this generally will cure; but if the patient finds no relief in an hour after, you may give another spoonful, which never fails.

If the roots are dried, they must be moistened with a little water.

To the wound may be applied a leaf of good tobacco moistened with rum.

An approved Remedy against spitting of Blood.

TAKE of the tops of stinging nettles, and plantain-leaves, of each a like quantity; bruise them, strain the juice out, and keep it close stopt in a bottle; take three or four spoonfuls every morning and evening, sweetened with sugar of roses; the juice of comfrey-roots drank with wine is also very good; let the patient be blooded at first, and sometimes gently purged; but if there happens to be any inward soreness, occasioned by straining, this electuary will be very convenient; viz. Take an ounce of Lucatellus's balsam, of conserve of roses two ounces, twelve drops of spirit of sulphur, to be made into a soft electuary with syrup of white poppies; the dose is the quantity of a nutmeg every morning and evening.

A Receipt that cured a Gentleman, who had a long Time spit Blood in a great Quantity, and was wasted with a Consumption.

TAKE of hyssop-water, and of the purest honey, of each a pint; of agrimony and colt's-foot of each a handful; a sprig of rue, brown sugar-candy, liquorice sliced, shavings of hart's-horn, of each two ounces, aniseeds bruised one ounce; of figs sliced, and raisins of the sun stoned, of each four ounces: put them all into a pipkin with a gallon of water, and boil it gently over a moderate fire, till half is consumed; then strain it, and when it is cold, put it into bottles, keep it close stopped, and take four or five spoonfuls every morning, at four in the afternoon, and at night the last thing: if you add fresh water to the ingredients, after the first liquor is strained off, you will have a pleasant drink, to be used at any time when you are dry.

A specific Cure for stopping Blood.

TAKE two ounces of clarified roche-allum, finely powdered, and melt it in a ladle, adding to it half an ounce of dragon's-blood in powder, and mix them well together; then take it off the fire; keeping it stirring till it comes to the consistence of a soft paste, fit for making up into pills; make your pills of the bigness of a large pea, and as the paste cools, warm it again to such a degree as the whole quantity may be made into pills; this medicine is proper in all cases of violent bleedings, without exception; the ordinary or usual dose is half a grain, to be taken once in four hours till the bleeding stops, taking a glass of water or ptisan after it, and after every dose, and another of the same liquor a quarter of an hour after; in violent cases give half a drachm for a dose.

For a violent Bleeding at the Nose.

LET the party put their feet in warm water; and if that does not do, let them sit higher in it.

To stop Bleeding at the Nose, or elsewhere.

TAKE an ounce-bottle, fill it half full of water, put into it as much Roman vitriol as will lie upon the point of a knife; let the part bleed into it, it will stop it in an instant.

To stop Bleeding inwardly.

TAKE two drachms of henbane-seed, and the like of white poppy-seed; beat them up with conserve of roses, and give the quantity of a nutmeg at a time; or take twelve handfuls of plantain-leaves, and six ounces of fresh comfrey-roots; beat these, and strain out the juice; adding to it some fine sugar, and drink it off.

To stop Bleeding in the Stomach.

TAKE oil of spike, natural balsam, bole-armoniac, rhubarb, and turpentine; mix these together, and take as much as a large nutmeg three times a day.

To stop Bleeding.

TAKE a pint of plantain-water, put to it two ounces of isinglass, and let it stand twenty-four hours to dissolve; pour it from the dregs, and put in a pint of red port wine, and add to it three or four sticks of cinnamon, and two ounces of double refined sugar; give it a boil or two, and pour it off: let the party take two or three spoonfuls two or three times a day.

For spitting Blood.

TAKE of cinnabar of antimony one ounce, and mix it with two ounces of conserve of red roses; take as much as a nutmeg night and morning.

To stop Bleeding at Mouth, Nose, or Ears.

IN the month of May take a clean cloth, and wet it in the spawn of frogs, nine days, drying it every day in the wind; lay up that cloth, and when you have need, hold it to the place where the blood runs, and it will stop.

Another to stop Bleeding.

TAKE two handfuls of the tops of bramble-wood and boil it in a quart of old claret till it comes to a pint; give six spoonfuls once in half an hour: in the winter the roots will do.

Lucatellus's

Lucatellus's Balsam.

TAKE of yellow wax one pound, melt it in a little Canary wine, then add to it oil of olives and Venice turpentine of each one pound and a half; boil them till the wine is evaporated, and when it is almost cold, stir in of red sanders two ounces, and keep it for use.

To make Lucatellus's Balsam to take inwardly

TAKE a quart of the purest oil, half a pound of yellow bees-wax, four ounces of Venice turpentine, six ounces of liquid storax, two ounces of oil-hypericon, two ounces of natural balsam, red rose-water half a pint, and as much plantain-water, red sanders six pennyworth, dragon's-blood six pennyworth, mummy six pennyworth, rosemary and bays, of each a handful, and sweet-marjoram half a handful; put the herbs and dragon's blood, the wax and mummy, into a pipkin; then put the oil, the turpentine, the oil hypericon, the storax, the rose-water, and plantain-water, and a quart of spring-water, and, if you please, some Irish slate, some balm of Gilead, and some sperma-ceti, into another pipkin; set both the pipkins over a soft fire, and let them boil a quarter of an hour; then take it off the fire, and put in the natural balsam and red sanders; give them a boil, and strain all in both pipkins together into an earthen pan; let it stand till it is cold, then pour the water from it, and melt it again; stir it off the fire till it is almost cold; then put it into gallipots, and cover it with paper and leather.

To take off Blackness by a Fall.

RUB it well with a cold tallow candle, as soon as it is bruised, and this will take off the blackness.

To break a Bile.

TAKE the yolk of a new-laid egg, some honey and wheat-flour; mix them well together, spread it on a rag, and lay it on cold.

A bitter Draught.

TAKE of the leaves of Roman wormwood, tops of centaury, and St. John's-wort, of each a small handful, roots of gentian sliced two drachms, carraway-seeds half an ounce; infuse these in half a pint of Rhenish and three pints of white wine, for four or five days; take a quarter of a pint in the morning,

morning, filling up the bottle, and it will serve two or three months.

Another.

TAKE of gentian-root three drachms, of camomile-flowers one ounce, of rosemary-flowers one ounce, tops of centaury, tops of Roman wormwood, tops of carduus, of each one handful; boil all these in two quarts of spring-water till it comes to a quart; you may add a pint of white wine to it; strain it out, and when it is cold, bottle it; drink a quarter of a pint in the morning, and as much at four o'clock in the afternoon.

To cure Blindness, when the Cause proceeds from within the Eye.

TAKE a double handful of the top leaves of celery, and a spoonful of salt; pound them together, and when it is pounded make it into a poultice, and put it on the party's contrary handwrist (that is, if the right eye is bad, put it to the left wrist) and repeat it for about three or four times, but put on fresh once in twenty-four hours.

If the eye is very bad, use bay-salt.

To raise a Blister.

THE seeds of clematitas peregrina, being bound hard on any place, will, in an hour or two, raise a blister, which you must cut and dress with melilot plaister, or colewort-leaves, as other blisters.

Likewise leaven mixed with a little verjuice, and about half a pennyworth of cantharides, and spread on leather the bigness you please, will, in nine or ten hours, raise a blister; which dress as usual.

Excellent for a Burn or Scald.

TAKE of oil-olive three ounces, white wax two ounces, sheep suet an ounce and an half, minium and Castile soap, of each half an ounce; dragon's-blood and camphire, of each three drachms; make them into a salve by melting them together: anoint with oil to take out the fire; then put the plaister on; dress it every day.

For a Burn.

TAKE common allum, beat and sift it, and beat it up with whites of eggs to a curd; then with a feather anoint the place; it will cure without any other thing.

Another

Another Remedy.

MIX lime-water with linseed-oil; beat it together, and with a feather anoint the place, and put on a plaister to defend it.

For a Cold, Dr. Radcliffe's Receipt.

MAKE some sack-whey with rosemary boiled in it; mix a little of it in a spoon with twenty grains of Gascoign's powder; then drink half a pint of your sack-whey, with twelve drops of spirit of hart's-horn in it; go to bed, and keep warm; do this two or three nights together.

A Method to cure a Cold.

SHEWING, 1. What the catching of cold is, and how dangerous. 2. A present and easy remedy against it. 3. The danger of delaying the cure of it. Taken from the celebrated Dr. Cheyne's Essay on Health and long Life, where he says, that Dr. Keill had made it out, beyond all possibility of doubting, that catching cold is nothing but sucking in, by the passages of perspiration, large quantities of moist air, and nitrous salts, which, by thickening the blood (as is evident from bleeding after catching cold) and thereby obstructing, not only the perspiration, but also all the other finer secretions, raises immediately a small fever, and a tumult in the whole animal œconomy, and, neglected, lays a foundation for consumptions, obstructions of the great viscera, and universal cachexies; the tender, therefore, and valetudinary, ought cautiously to avoid all occasions of catching cold; and if they have been so unfortunate as to get one, to set about its cure immediately, before it has taken too deep root in the habit. From the nature of the disorder thus described, the remedy is obvious; to wit, lying much a-bed, drinking plentifully of small warm sack-whey, with a few drops of spirits of hart's-horn, posset-drink, water-gruel, or any other warm small liquors, a scruple of Gascoign's powder morning and night, living low upon spoon-meats, pudding, and chicken, and drinking every thing warm; in a word, treating it at first as a small fever, with gentle diaphoretics; and afterwards, if any cough or spitting should remain, (which this method generally prevents) by softening the breast with a little sugar-candy, and oil of sweet almonds, or a solution of gum-armoniac, an ounce to a quart of barley-water, to make the expectoration easy, and going cautiously and well clothed into the air afterwards: this is a much more natural, easy, and effectual method than the practice by balsams, linctuses, pectorals, and the like trumpery in common use, which serve only to spoil the stomach, oppress the spirits, and hurt the constitution.

For a Cold.

TAKE rosemary and sliced liquorice, and boil it in small ale, and sweeten it with treacle, and drink it going to bed four or five nights together.

For a Hoarseness with a Cold.

TAKE a quarter of a pint of hyssop-water; make it very sweet with sugar-candy; set it over the fire; and when it is thorough hot, beat the yolk of an egg, brew it in it, and drink it morning and night.

An excellent Recipe to cure a Cold.

TAKE of Venice treacle half a drachm, powder of snake-root twelve grains, powder of saffron six grains, volatile salt of hart's-horn four grains, syrup of cloves a sufficient quantity to make it into a bolus, to be taken going to rest, drinking a large draught of mountain whey after it; those who cannot afford mountain whey, may drink treacle posset.

To such constitutions as cannot be provoked to sweat, open a vein, or a gentle purge will be of great service.

An Ointment for a Cold on the Stomach.

TAKE an ounce and a half of the oil of Valentia scabiosa, oil of sweet almonds a quarter of an ounce, a quarter of an ounce of man's fat, and four scruples of the oil of mace; mix these together, and warm a little in the spoon, and night and morning anoint the stomach; lay a piece of black or lawn-paper on it.

A Syrup for a Cough, or Asthma.

TAKE of hyssop and pennyroyal-water, of each a quarter of a pint, slice into it a small stick of liquorice, and a few raisins of the sun stoned: let it simmer together a quarter of an hour, and then make it into a syrup with brown sugar-candy; boil it a little, and then put in four or five spoonfuls of snail-water; give it a walm, and when it is cold, bottle it; take one spoonful morning and night, with three drops of balsam of sulphur in it; you may take a little of the syrup without the drops once or twice a day; if the party is short-breathed, a blister is very good.

To make Syrup of Balsam for a Cough.

TAKE one ounce of balsam of Tolu, and put to it a quart of spring-water, let them boil together two hours; then put in a pound of white sugar-candy finely beaten, and let it boil half an hour longer; take out the balsam, and strain the syrup through a flannel-bag twice; when it is cold, put it in a bottle. This syrup is excellent for a cough; take a spoonful of it as you lie down in your bed, and a little at any time when your cough troubles you; you may add to it two ounces of syrup of red poppies, and as much of raspberry syrup.

A Syrup for a Cough.

TAKE of oak-lungs, French moss, and maidenhair, of each a handful; boil all these in three pints of spring-water, till it comes to a quart; then strain it out, and put to it six penny-worth of saffron tied up in a rag, and two pounds of brown sugar-candy; boil it up to a syrup, and when it is cold bottle it; take a spoonful of it as often as your cough troubles you.

Another.

TAKE of unset hyssop, colt's-foot-flowers, and black maidenhair, of each an handful; of white horehound two handfuls; boil these herbs together in three quarts of water till it come to three pints; then take it off, and let the herbs stand in it till it is cold; then squeeze them out very dry, and strain the liquor, and let it boil a quarter of an hour, skim it well; to every pint put in half a pound of white sugar, and let it boil, and skim it, till it comes to a syrup; when it is cold bottle it; take two spoonfuls night and morning, and at any time when the cough is troublesome take one spoonful; don't cork the bottles, but tie them down with a paper.

For a Cough.

TAKE three quarts of spring-water, and put it in a large pipkin, with a calf's-foot, and four spoonfuls of barley, and a handful of dried poppies; boil it together till one quart be consumed; then strain it out, and add a little cinnamon, and a pint of milk, and sweeten it to your taste with loaf-sugar; warm it a little, and drink half a pint as often as you please.

Another.

TAKE two ounces of raisins of the sun stoned, one ounce of brown sugar-candy, one ounce of conserve of roses, add to
these

these a little flour of brimstone, mix all well together in a mortar, and take the quantity of a nutmeg night and morning.

Another Remedy for the same.

TAKE conserve of roses two ounces, diascordium half an ounce, powder of olibanum half a drachm, syrup of jubebs half an ounce; mix these, and take the quantity of a nutmeg three times a day; in the morning, at four, and at night.

For an inveterate Cough.

TAKE of sperma-ceti one scruple; put it into the yolk of a new-laid egg raw, sup it up in the morning fasting; it cures at once taking. Approved by several of my acquaintance, whom I knew it to cure. S. C.

For a Cough settled on the Stomach.

TAKE half a pound of figs sliced, raisins of the sun stoned as many, and a stick of liquorice scraped and sliced, a few aniseeds, and some hyssop washed clean; put all these into a quart of spring-water, boil it till it comes to a pint; then strain it, and sweeten it with white sugar-candy; take two or three spoonfuls morning and night, and when the cough troubles you.

The Tar-pills for a Cough.

TAKE tar, and drop it on powder of liquorice, and make it up into pills: take two every night going to bed, and in a morning drink a glass of water, that liquorice has been three or four days steeped in; do this for nine or ten days together, as you find good.

For a Chin-cough.

TAKE a spoonful of wood-lice, bruise them, mix them with breast-milk, and take them three or four mornings according as you find benefit. It will cure; but some must take it longer than others.

For the same.

TAKE a spoonful of the juice of pennyroyal, mixed with sugar-candy beaten to powder; take this for nine mornings together.

A Receipt for a Consumptive Cough.

TAKE of the syrup of white and red poppies, of each three ounces, of barley, cinnamon-water, and red poppy-water of each

each two ounces, of tincture of saffron one ounce, liquid laudanum forty drops, and as much spirit of sulphur as will make it acid: take three or four spoonfuls of it every night going to bed; increase or diminish the dose, according as you find it agrees with you.

Excellent Lozenges for a Cough.

TAKE a pound of brown sugar-candy and as much loaf-sugar, beat and searce them through a fine sieve; take an ounce of the juice of liquorice, and dissolve it in three or four spoonfuls of hyssop-water over a gentle fire; then mix your sugar and sugar-candy with one drachm of orrice-powder, one drachm of the powder of elecampane, of gum-dragant powdered half a drachm; add one drachm of the oil of aniseeds, and one grain of musk; mix all these together, and work it into a paste, and roll them into lozenges the bigness of a barley-corn, or something larger.

An Electuary for a Cough.

TAKE conserve of red roses two ounces, conserve of hips one ounce, Lucatellus's balsam half an ounce, species of diatragacanth frigid one drachm, syrup of balsam three drachms; mix all together well; take the quantity of a small bean three times a day.

Another Remedy for a Cough.

TAKE the yolk of a new-laid egg, and six spoonfuls of red rose-water; beat them well together, and make it very sweet with white sugar-candy; drink it six nights, going to bed.

An excellent Remedy for Whooping Coughs.

TAKE dried colt's-foot-leaves a good handful, cut them small, and boil them in a pint of spring-water till half a pint is boiled away; then take it off the fire, and when it is almost cold, strain it through a cloth, squeezing the herb as dry as you can, and then throw it away; dissolve in the liquor an ounce of brown sugar-candy finely powdered, and give the child (if it be about three or four years old, and so in proportion) one spoonful of it, cold or warm, as the season proves, three or four times a day (or oftener, if the fits of coughing come frequently) till well, which will be in two or three days; but it will presently almost abate the fits of coughing.

The herb seems to be a specific for those sorts of coughs, and indeed for all others, in old as well as young; the Latin name tussilago, from tussis, the cough, denotes as much; as does also the Latin word bechium, from the Greek word Βήχιον, a cough; and are the names given it by the antients, perhaps some thousand years ago; it has wonderfully eased them, when nothing else would do it, and greatly helps in shortness of breath: and in the asthma and phthisic I have not known any thing to exceed it; likewise in wastings or consumptions of the lungs it has been found of excellent use, by its smooth, softning, healing qualities, even where there has been spitting of blood, rawness and soreness of the passages, with hoarseness, &c. in blunting the acrimonious humours, which, in such cases, are almost continually dripping upon them; it is to be questioned, whether for those purposes, there is to be had, in the whole Materia Medica, a medicine so innocent, so safe, and yet so pleasant and effectual, or that can afford relief so soon as this will; grown people may take it stronger than for children. Get the herb of the same year's growth, and drying that you use; and the larger the leaves, as being the fuller grown, the better; it is best to be made fresh and fresh, as you want it, and not too much at a time, especially in warm weather.

Water in a Consumption, or in Weakness after Sickness.

TAKE a calf's-pluck fresh killed, but do not wash it; cut it in pieces, and put it in a cold still; but first put at the bottom of your still a sheet of white paper well buttered; then put in your pluck, with mint, balm, borage, hyssop, and oak-lungs, of each about two handfuls; wipe and cut the herbs, but do not wash them; put in a gallon of new milk warm from the cow, paste up the still, and let it drop on white sugar-candy; it will draw off about seven pints; mix it together, and bottle it for use: drink a quarter of a pint in the morning, and as much at four in the afternoon.

An infallible Cure for the galloping Consumption.

TAKE half a pound of raisins of the sun stoned, of figs and honey, of each a quarter of a pound; of Lucatellus's balsam, powder of steel, and flour of elecampane, of each half an ounce; a grated nutmeg, one pound of double refined sugar pounded: shred and pound all these together in a stone mortar, pour on it a pint of sallad-oil by degrees; eat a bit of it four times a day the bigness of a nutmeg; every morning drink a glass of old Malaga sack, with the yolk of a new-laid egg, and as much flour of brimstone as will lie upon a six-pence; the next morning as much flour of elecampane, alternately.

For the Cramp.

TAKE spirit of castor, and oil of worms, of each two drachms; oil of amber one drachm; shake them well together; warm a little in a spoon, and anoint the nape of the neck, chafe it in very well, and cover warm, anoint when in bed.

Another Method.

TAKE of rosemary-leaves, chop them very small, sew them in fine linen, make them into garters, and wear them night and day; lay a down pillow on your legs in the night.

For Costiveness.

TAKE virgin honey a quarter of a pound, and mix it with as much cream of tartar as will bring it to a pretty thick electuary, of which take the bigness of a walnut when you please; and for your breakfast eat water-gruel with common mallows boiled in it, and a good piece of butter; the mallows must be chopped small, and eaten with the gruel.

For a Canker in the Mouth.

TAKE celandine, columbine, sage and fennel, of each one handful; stamp and strain them, and to the juice put a spoonful of honey, half a spoonful of burnt allum, and as much bole-armoniac beaten fine; mix and beat all these together very well, and wrap a little flax about a stick, and rub the canker with it; if it bleeds it is the better.

An approved Remedy for a Cancer in the Breast.

TAKE off the hard knobs or warts which grow on the legs of a stone-horse; dry them carefully, and powder them; give from a scruple to half a drachm every morning and evening in a glass of sack; you must continue taking them for a month or six weeks, or longer, if the cancer is far gone.

To keep a Cancer in the Breast from increasing.

TAKE of lapis calaminaris four ounces, all in one piece; and having made it red hot in a crucible nine times, quench it every time in a pint of white wine; then take two ounces of lapis tutty, and having burnt that red hot in a crucible three times, quench that every time in a pint of red rose-water; then beat the tutty and the calaminaris stone together in a mortar very fine,

fine, and put in a glaſs bottle, with the roſe-water and white wine; ſhake it three or four times a day for nine days, before you begin to uſe it: you muſt keep the wine and the roſe-water cloſe covered when you quench the ſtone, that the ſteam does not go out; when you uſe it, ſhake it well, dip rags in it, and lay them to the breaſt; let the rags remain on till it is dreſſed again; it muſt be dreſſed twice a day, night and morning: the clear water is excellent for weak or ſore eyes.

To cure a Cancer.

TAKE a drachm of the powder of crab's-claws finely ſearced, and made into a paſte with damaſk roſe-water, and dried with pellets of lozenges; powder the lozenges as you uſe them, and drink the powder in whey every morning faſting: if there be a ſore, and it is raw, anoint it with a ſalve made of dock-roots and freſh butter; make a ſeaton or iſſue in the neck; keep a low diet, and abſtain from any thing that is ſalt, ſour or ſtrong.

A Medicine for the Cholic.

TAKE of camomile-flowers and mallow-leaves, of each a handful; juniper-berries and fenugreek-ſeeds, of each half an ounce; let the ſeeds and berries be bruiſed; boil them in a pint of water; add to it ſtrained, of turpentine diſſolved, with the yolk of an egg, and oil of camomile, of each an ounce; diacatholicon ſix drachms, hiera-picra two drachms; mix, and give it. After the operation of the clyſter, give the patient the following mixture: take of rue and camomile-water, of each an ounce; cinnamon-water an ounce, liquid laudanum twenty drops, ſyrup of white poppies an ounce.

Another.

TAKE of the beſt manna, and oil of ſweet almonds, of each an ounce and a half, of camomile-flowers boiled in poſſet-drink an handful; let the poſſet-drink be ſtrained from the flowers, and mingled very well with the oil of almonds and manna; let the patient take it three days ſucceſſively, and afterwards every third day for a fortnight. This not only gives eaſe in the moſt violent fits, but alſo, being often uſed, prevents their returning.

Another.

TAKE half a pint of Dr. Stephens's water, as much plague-water, as much juniper-berry-water, and an ounce of powder of rhubarb; ſhake the bottle, and take four or five ſpoonfuls at a time, when the fit is on you, or likely to come.

Another.

TAKE a drachm and a half of Dr. Holland's powder, mix it with a little fack, and take it, drinking a glafs of fack after it; it gives prefent eafe.

Another.

LET the patient, when they find any fymptoms of a fit, take a pint of milk warm, put into it four fpoonfuls of brandy, and eat it up, and fo let them take it any other time; if they are fubject to that diftemper, it will prevent the fit. This cured Mr. Blundel at Hampftead, after he had the advice of feveral other phyficians, and had been at the Bath without fuccefs.

A prefent Help for the Cholic.

MIX a drachm of mithridate in a fpoonful of dragon-water, and give it the party to drink in bed, laying a little fuet on the navel.

A Plaifter for the Cholic.

SPREAD the whites of four or five eggs well beaten on fome leather, and over that ftrew on a fpoonful of pepper, and as much ginger finely beaten and fifted; then put this plaifter on the navel; it often gives fpeedy eafe.

For Corns on the Feet.

TAKE the yeaft of beer (not of ale) and fpread it on a linen rag, and apply it to the part affected; renew it once a day for three or four weeks; it will cure.

For Chilblains.

ROAST a turnep foft; beat it to mafh, and apply it as hot as can be endured to the part affected; let it lie on two or three days, and repeat it two or three times.

To procure a good Colour.

TAKE germander, rue, fumitory, of each a good handful, one pennyworth of faffron tied up in a rag, half a pound of blue currants bruifed; ftamp the herbs, and infufe all the ingredients in three pints of fack over a gentle fire till half be confumed; drink a quarter of a pint morning and evening, and walk after it; repeat this quantity once or twice.

You may add a spoonful of the following syrup to every draught: Take three ounces of the filings of steel, and put it in a glass bottle with a drachm of mace, and as much cinnamon; pour on them a quart of the best white wine; stop it up close, and let it stand fourteen days, shaking the bottle every day; then strain it out into another bottle, and put two pounds of fine loaf sugar to it finely beaten; let it stand till the sugar is dissolved, without stirring it; then clear it into another bottle, and keep it for use.

A Cere-cloth.

TAKE three pounds of oil-olive, of red lead, and white lead, of each half a pound, both powdered and sifted; then take three ounces of virgin wax, two ounces of Spanish soap, and as much deer's suet; put all these into a brass kettle, setting it over the fire, stirring it continually till it comes to the height of a salve, which you may know by dropping a little on a trencher; and if it neither hangs to the trencher, nor your fingers, it is enough; then dip your cloths in, and when you take them out, throw them into a pail of water; as they cool, take them out, lay them on a table, and clap them; when you have done, roll them up with papers between, and keep them for use; they must be kept pretty cool. This cere-cloth is good for any pain, swelling, or bruise.

To make Conserve of Hips.

GATHER the hips before they grow soft, cut off the heads and stalks, slit them in halves, and take out all the seed and white that is in them very clean; then put them in an earthen pan, and stir them every day, else they will grow mouldy; let them stand till they are soft enough to rub through a coarse hair sieve; as the pulp comes take it off the sieve; then add its weight in sugar, and mix it well together without boiling, keeping it in deep gallipots for use.

To cure a Dropsy.

TAKE of horse-radish-roots sliced two ounces, sweet fennel-roots sliced two ounces, sweet fennel-seeds beaten two ounces, the tops of thyme, winter-savoury, sweet-marjoram, water-cresses and nettle-tops, of each one handful, wiped and shred small; boil these in three pints of spring-water, a quart of sack, and a pint of white wine; cover it close, and let it boil till half be consumed; then take it off the fire, and let it stand to settle three hours; then strain it out, and to every draught put in an ounce of the syrup of the five opening roots. Take this in the morning fasting, and at three o'clock in the afternoon, fasting three hours after it. If the party have the scurvy (which usually goes with the dropsy) then add a spoonful of the juice of scurvy-grass to each draught.

Another Method.

TAKE a good quantity of black snails, stamp them well with bay salt, and lay to the hollow of the feet, putting fresh twice a day; take likewise a handful of spearmint and wormwood, bruise them, and put them in a quart of cream, which boil till it comes to an oil; then strain and anoint those parts which are swelled. Take of the tops of green broom, which after you have dried in an oven, burn upon a clean hearth to ashes, which mingle very well with a quart of white wine, let it stand all night to settle, and in a morning drink half a pint of the clearest; at four in the afternoon, and at night going to bed, do the same. Continue laying the poultice to your feet, and drinking the white wine for three weeks together: this method has been often used with success.

A certain Cure for the Dropsy, if taken at the Beginning of the Distemper.

TAKE the stems that grow from the stick or root of the artichoke, pluck off the leaves, and bruise only the stems in a marble mortar; to a quart of juice put a quart of Madeira or mountain wine, straining the juice through a piece of muslin: let the patient take a wine glass of it fasting, and another just before going to bed, continuing till the cure is completed.

N. B. This cured a son of Dr. Moore, late Bishop of Ely (who had the advice of several physicians to no effect) and from whom I had the receipt.

Another Remedy for the same.

TAKE of horse-radish roots sliced thin, and sweet fennel-seeds bruised, of each two ounces; smallage and fennel-roots sliced, of each an ounce; of the tops of thyme, winter-savoury, sweet-marjoram, water-cresses, and nettles, of each a handful; bruise the herbs, and boil them in three pints of sack, and three of water, to the consumption of half; let it stand close covered for three hours; then strain it, and drink a draught of it twice a day, sweetened with syrup of fennel, fasting two hours after it.

An excellent Medicine for the Dropsy.

TAKE of the leaves that grow upon the stem or stalk of the artichoke, bruise them in a stone mortar, then strain them through a fine cloth, and put to each pint of the juice a pint of

Madeira

Madeira wine; take four or five spoonfuls the first thing in the morning, and the same quantity going to bed, shaking the bottle well every time you use it.

Another.

TAKE about three spoonfuls of the best mustard-seed, and about half a handful of bay-berries, the like quantity of juniper-berries, an ounce of horse-radish, and about half a handful of sage of vertue, as much wormwood-sage, half a handful of scurvy-grass, a quarter of a handful of stinking orach, a little sprig of wormwood, a sprig of green broom, and half an ounce of gentian-root; scrape, wipe, and cut all these, and put them into a bottle that will hold a gallon; then fill the bottle with the best strong beer you can get, stop it close; let it stand three or four days, and drink every morning fasting half a pint.

Another.

BRUISE a pint of mustard-seed; scrape and slice a large horse-radish-root, scrape a handful of the inner rind of elder, and a root of elecampane sliced; put all these into a large bottle, and put to it a quart of good stale beer; let it steep forty-eight hours; drink half a pint every morning fasting, and fast two hours after it; you may fill it up once or twice.

Another.

TAKE six gallons of ale pretty strong, but little hopt; alexander, red sage, scurvy-grass, ground-ivy, and the long green leaves of flowers-de-luce, of each two handfuls; bruise these well, and boil them well in ale; then strain it out, and when it is cool work it as other ale; put it in your vessel, and when it is clear, drink of it in a morning fasting; use no other drink except white wine; sometimes drink good draughts of it at a time.

For the Dropsy and Scurvy.

TAKE a quart of white wine, six sprigs of wormwood, as much rosemary, half a quarter of an ounce of aloes, the same quantity of myrrh, rhubarb, cinnamon, and saffron: bruise the drugs, pull the saffron, and put all into a three-pint stone bottle; tie the cork down close, set it in a kettle of water and hay, and let it boil three hours; then let it stand a day or two to settle; let the patient take four spoonfuls every morning fasting, and fast three hours after it, and walk abroad; if it is too long to fast, and the constitution will not bear it, they may drink a draught of water-gruel two hours after it; take this till the quantity is out.

An experienced Eye Water to strengthen the Sight, and prevent Cataracts.

TAKE of eye-bright tops, two handfuls, of celandine, vervain, betony, dill, ground-pine, clary, avens, pimpernel, and rosemary-flowers, of each a handful; of capon's gall and aloes bruised, of each half an ounce; of long pepper, a drachm; infuse twenty-four hours in two quarts of white wine: then draw it off in a glass still: drop the water with a feather into the eye often.

To draw a Rheum from the Eyes.

ROAST an egg hard; then cut out the yolk, and take a spoonful of cummin-seed, and a handful of bear's-foot; bruise them, and put them into the white of the egg; lay it on the nape of the neck, bind it on with a cloth, and let it lie twenty-four hours, and then renew it: it will cure in a little time.

To clear the Eyes.

TAKE the white of hen's-dung, dry it very well, and beat it to powder; sift, and blow it into the eyes when the party goes to bed.

For a Pin or Web in the Eye.

TAKE the gall of a hare, and honey, of each a like quantity; mix them together, take a feather, and put a little into the eye; it will cure in two or three days.

If a hair or fish-bone stick in the throat, immediately swallow the yolk of a raw egg: it is a very good thing.

A Water for sore or weak Eyes.

TAKE ground-ivy, celandine and daisies, of each a like quantity, stamped and strained; add to the juice a little sugar and white rose-water, shake this together, and with a feather drop it into the eyes; this takes away all manner of inflammations, spots, itching, smarting or web, and is an excellent thing for the eyes.

For Dimness of Sight and sore Eyes.

TAKE eye-bright, sweet-marjoram and betony dried, of each a like quantity, the same quantity of tobacco as of all the rest, take it in a pipe as you do tobacco for some time; and take of the right Portugal snuff, put it into the corner of your eyes morning and night, and take it likewise as snuff. This cured

Judge Ayres, Sir Edward Seymour, and Sir John Houblon, that they could read without spectacles, after they had used them many years. S. C.

A Powder that has restored Sight when almost lost.

TAKE of betony, celandine, saxifrage, eye-bright, pennyroyal, and ligusticum, of each a handful; of aniseeds and cinnamon, of each half an ounce; grains of paradise, ginger, hyssop, parsley, origany, osier of the mountain, of each a drachm; galangal and sugar, of each an ounce; make all into a fine powder, and eat of it every day with your meat such a quantity as you used to eat of salt, and instead of it: the osier you must have at the physic-garden.

An Electuary for a Pain in the Stomach.

TAKE conserve of wood-sorrel and mithridate an equal quantity; mix it well together, and take night and morning the quantity of a nutmeg; so do for fifteen days together.

An Electuary for a cold or windy Stomach.

TAKE gum-guaiacum one ounce, cubebs and cardamums, of each a quarter of an ounce; beat and sift all these, and mix it with syrup of gilliflowers into an electuary. Take night and morning the quantity of a nutmeg; drink a little warm ale after it.

To make Stoughton's Elixir.

PARE off the rinds of six Seville oranges very thin, and put them in a quart bottle, with an ounce of gentian scraped and sliced, and six pennyworth of cochineal; put to it a pint of the best brandy; shake it together two or three times the first day, and then let it stand to settle two days, and clear it off into bottles for use; take a large tea-spoonful in a glass of wine in the morning, and at four in the afternoon; or you may take it in a dish of tea.

To make Daffey's Elixir.

TAKE elecampane-roots sliced, and liquorice sliced, aniseeds, coriander-seeds, and carraway-seeds, oriental sena, guaiacum bruised, of each two ounces; rhubarb an ounce, saffron a drachm; raisins of the sun stoned a pound; put all these into a glass bottle of a gallon, adding to it three quarts of white aniseed-water; stop the bottle, and let it stand infusing four days, stirring it stongly three or four times a day; then strain it off, and put it into bottles corked very well; you must take it morning

ing and night, three spoonfuls going to bed, and as much in the morning, according as you find it work; it requires not much care in diet, nor keeping within; but you must keep warm, and drink something hot in the morning after it has worked. This elixir is excellent good for the cholic, the gravel in the kidneys, the dropsy, griping of the guts, or any obstructions in the bowels; it purgeth two or three times a day.

To make the true Daffey's Elixir.

TAKE five ounces of aniseeds, three ounces of fennel-seeds, four ounces of parsley-seeds, six ounces of Spanish liquorice, five ounces of sena, one ounce of rhubarb, three ounces of elecampane, seven ounces of jalap, twenty-one drachms of saffron, six ounces of manna, two pounds of raisins, a quarter of an ounce of cochineal, two gallons of brandy; stone the raisins, slice the roots, bruise the jalap; put them all together, keep them close covered fifteen days; then strain it out.

To cure the Joint Evil.

TAKE good store of elder-leaves, and distil them in a cold still; let the person drink every morning and evening half a pint of this water, and wash the sores with it morning and evening, first warming it a little; lay fresh elder-leaves on the sores, and in a little time you will find they will dry up; but be sure to follow it exactly. It has cured, when all other remedies have failed.

For a Drought in a Fever.

MAKE barley-water, sweeten it with syrup of violets, and tincture it with spirit of vitriol; let them drink sometimes of this; put sal prunella in beer or posset-drink, and sometimes drink of that; and if they are sick and faint, give a spoonful of cordial in a dish of tea.

To cure an intermitting Ague and Fever, without returning.

TAKE jesuits bark in fine powder one ounce, salt of steel and Jamaica pepper, of each a quarter of an ounce; treacle or melasses, four ounces; mix these together, and take the quantity of a nutmeg three times a day when the fit is off, and a draught of warm ale, or white wine after it.

An excellent Medicine for the spotted, and all other malignant Fevers.

TAKE of the best Virginia snakeweed, root of contrayerva finely powdered and Goa stone, of each half a scruple, castor

and

and camphire, of each five grains, make them into a bolus with a scruple of Venice treacle and as much syrup of piony as is sufficient; repeat the bolus every six hours, drinking a draught of the following julep after it.

Take scorzonera-roots two ounces, butter-bur-roots half an ounce, of balm and scordium, of each a handful, of coriander-seeds three drachms, of liquorice, figs, and raisins, of each an ounce; let them boil in three pints of spring-water to a quart, then strain it, and add to it compound piony-water three ounces, syrup of raspberries an ounce and a half: let the patients drink of it plentifully.

A very good Drink to be used in all Sorts of Fevers.

TAKE two ounces of burnt hart's-horn; boil it with a crust of bread in three pints of water to a quart; strain, and put to it of barley and cinnamon-water, two ounces, cochineal half a drachm; sweeten it with fine sugar, and let the patient, as often as he is thirsty, drink plentifully of it; rub the cochineal in a mortar, together with the sugar.

For a Drought in a Fever.

TAKE of sal-prunella one ounce, dissolve it in spring-water, and put as much sugar to it as will sweeten it; simmer it over the fire till it is a syrup; put some into posset-drink, and take it two or three times a day, or when very thirsty.

Sometimes an inward Fever attends such as are poisoned, for which the following is a good Remedy.

TAKE a pint of wood-ashes and three pints of water; stir and mix them well together, let them stand all night, and strain or decant the lye off in the morning, of which ten ounces may be taken six mornings following, warmed or cold, according to the weather.

These medicines have no sensible operation, tho' sometimes they work in the bowels, and give a gentle stool.

The Symptoms attending such as are poisoned, are as follows:

A PAIN of the breast, difficulty of breathing, a load at the pit of the stomach, an irregular pulse, burning and violent pains of the viscera above and below the navel, very restless at night, sometimes wandering pains over the whole body, a reaching and inclination to vomit, profuse sweats (which prove always serviceable) slimy stools, both when costive and loose, the face of a pale and yellow colour, sometimes a pain and inflammation of

the

the throat, the appetite is generally weak, and some cannot eat any thing; those who have been long poisoned, are generally very feeble and weak in their limbs, sometimes spit a great deal, the whole skin peels, and likewise the hair falls off.

A Drink for a Fever.

TAKE a quart of spring-water, an ounce of burnt hart's-horn, a nutmeg quartered, and a stick of cinnamon; let it boil a quarter of an hour; when it is cold sweeten it to your taste with syrup of lemons, or fine sugar, with as many drops of spirit of vitriol as will just sharpen it. Drink of this when you please.

For the Dysentery or bloody Flux.

TAKE an iron-ladle; anoint it with fine wax; put into it glass of antimony, what you please; set it on a slow fire without flame half an hour, still stirring it with a spatula; then pour it on a clean linen cloth, and rub off all the wax. Grind it to powder.

This is the receipt as I had it; but I kept it three quarters of an hour on the fire, and could not rub off any wax. The dose of a boy of seven or eight years is three grains; for a weak adult five grains; for a strong woman twelve or fourteen grains; for a very strong man eighteen or twenty grains.

N. B. I never gave above fourteen grains; and in the making of it put about a drachm of wax to an ounce of the glass. It sometimes vomits, always purges, and seldom fails of success. I always intermit one day at least betwixt every dose.

For the Bloody-Flux.

TAKE some garlic, press out a spoonful or two, warm it pretty hot, then dip a double rag in it, lay it upon the navel, let it lie till it is cold; then repeat it two or three times, it cures immediately. By this I cured a gentlemen, who had tried several other things without success. S. C.

For a Flux.

TAKE a pint of new milk, and dissolve in it half a quarter of a pound of loaf sugar, and two drachms of mithridate; give this for a clyster moderately warm; repeat it once or twice, if there be occasion.

To prevent Fits in Children.

TAKE saxifrage, bean-pods, black cherry, groundsel and parsley-waters: mix them together with syrup of single piony; give

give a spoonful very often, especially observe to give it at the change of the moon.

Another for the same.

TAKE assa-fœtida and wood-soot, of each one ounce, infuse them in a pint of French brandy; give a child in the month three or four drops in breast-milk, or black cherry-water, soon after it is born, and continue it two or three times a day for a week.

Another.

TAKE ten grains of coral finely powdered, give it in breast-milk or black cherry-water, it prevents their having any convulsion fits.

Another.

TAKE a quart of ale, and as much small beer: put into it a handful of southernwood, as much sage, and as much penny-royal; let it boil half an hour, strain it out, and let the child drink no other drink.

For Fits from Wind or Cold.

TAKE three drops of oil of amber in some burnt wine, or mace-ale. If it is given in black cherry-water, it is good to forward labour in child-bed.

A Powder for Convulsion Fits.

TAKE a drachm and a half of single piony-seed, of misletoe of the oak one drachm, pearl, white amber and coral, all finely powdered, of each half a drachm; bezoar two drachms, and five leaves of gold; make all these up in a fine powder, and give it in a spoonful of black cherry-water, or, if you please, hysteric-water: you may give to a child new-born, to prevent fits, as much as will lie on a three-pence, and likewise at each change of the moon; and to older people as much as they have strength and occasion.

To cure a pimpled Face.

TAKE an ounce of live brimstone, as much roche-allum, as much common salt; white sugar-candy, and sperma-ceti, of each two drachms; pound and sift all these into a fine powder, and put it in a quart bottle; then put to it half a pint of brandy, three ounces of white lily-water, and three ounces of spring-water; shake all these well together, and keep it for use. When you use it, shake the bottle, and bathe the face well; and when
you

you go to bed, dip rags in it, and lay it all over the face; in ten or twelve days it will be perfectly cured.

To cure a pimpled Face, and sweeten the Blood.

TAKE sena one ounce, put it in a small stone pot, and pour a quart or more of boiling water on it, then fill it up with prunes; cover with paper, and set it in the oven with houshold-bread; take every day, one, two, three, or more, of the prunes and liquor, according as it operates; continue this always, or at least half a year.

For a Swelling in the Face.

TAKE a handful of damask rose-leaves; boil them in running water till they are tender; stamp them to a pulp, and boil white bread and milk till it is soft; then put in your pulp, with a little hog's-lard, and thicken with the yolk of an egg, and apply it warm.

To take off Freckles.

TAKE either bean-flower-water, elder-flower-water, or May-dew gathered from corn, four spoonfuls, and add to it one spoonful of oil of tartar per deliquium; mix it well together, and often wash the face with it; let it dry on.

For the Gripes.

TAKE a glass of sack warmed, and dissolve in it one drachm of Venice treacle, or Diascordium; drink it off going to bed; cover warm.

A Receipt for the Gravel.

PUT two spoonfuls of linseed just bruised into a quart of water, and a little stick of liquorice; boil it a quarter of an hour; then strain it through a sieve, and sweeten it to your taste with syrup of marshmallows.

For the Gout in the Stomach, Dr. Lower's constant Remedy.

TAKE of Venice treacle one drachm, Gascoign's powder half a drachm, syrup of poppies as much as is sufficient to make it into a bolus; let the patient take it going to bed.

For the Gout.

TAKE a pound of bees-wax, and half a pound of rosin, of oilbanum four ounces, of litharge of gold finely powdered,

and

The COMPLETE HOUSEWIFE.   335

and white lead, of each twelve ounces; of neat's-foot oil a pint. Set the oil, together with the bees-wax and rosin, over the fire, as soon as they are melted put in the powders, keeping it continually stirring with a stick; as soon as it is boiled enough, take it off the fire, and pour it on a board anointed with neat's-foot oil, and make it into rolls; apply this plaister, spread on sheep's leather, to the part affected; once a week take of caryocostinum four drachms dissolved in white wine, keeping yourself warm after it; by applying this plaister, and taking the caryocostinum, there are many which have found very great benefit.

Another for the same.

TAKE as much Venice treacle as a hazel-nut, mixed up with a scruple of Gascoign's powder, three or four nights together, when the fit is either on you, or coming on.

For Pains of the Gout.

MIX Barbadoes tar and palm-oil, an equal quantity; just melt them together, and gently anoint the part affected.

For the Hemorrhoids inflamed.

LET the party dip their finger in balsam of sulphur, made with oil of turpentine, and anoint the place two or three times a day.

For the Piles, a present Remedy.

ANOINT the part with the ointment of tobacco. This cuured an acquaintance of mine, who told it me himself. S. C.

For the Piles.

TAKE the duck-meat that lies upon ponds and ditches, let it lie till it be dry, then lay it to the part; it cures presently.

For an inveterate Head-ach.

TAKE juice of ground-ivy, and snuff it up the nose, it not only easeth the most violent head-ach for the present, but taketh it quite away. Thus cured one that had been afflicted with it many years, and by the use of it, it immediately cured him, and it never returned.

For the Hiccup.

TAKE three or four preserved damsons in your mouth at a time, and swallow them by degrees.

For

For the Jaundice.

TAKE the juice of the leaves of artichoke-plants, put it into a quart of white wine; take three or four spoonfuls in the morning fasting, and at four in the afternoon.

Another.

TAKE three bottles of ale, half a pint of the juice of celandine, a quarter of a pint of feverfew, a good handful of the inner rind of a barberry-tree, and two pennyworth of saffron; divide all into three parts, and put a part into every one of the bottles of ale, and drink a bottle in three mornings: you must stir after it.

Another.

TAKE some tares, dry them in an oven, and beat them to powder; sift them and take a spoonful of that powder in a morning fasting, and drink half a pint of white wine after it; do this for three mornings together, and it will cure though very far gone.

Another.

TAKE half an ounce of rhubarb powdered, and beat it well, with two handfuls of good currants well cleansed; and of this electuary take every morning a piece as big as a nutmeg, for fourteen or fifteen mornings together, or longer, if need require.

For the Yellow Jaundice.

TAKE a handful of burdock-roots, cut them in slices to the cores, and dry them; half a handful of the inner rind of barberries, three races of turmeric beat very fine, three or four tabes of the whitest goose-dung; put all in a quart of strong beer; cover it close, and let it infuse in the embers all night; in the morning strain it off; add to it a groat's-worth of saffron; take half a pint at a time first and last.

To cure the Yellow or Black Jaundice.

TAKE a quart of white wine, a large red dock-root, a bur-root, that which bears the small bur, two pennyworth of turmeric, a little saffron; a little of the white goose-dung; boil all these together a little while; then let it run through a strainer; drink it morning and evening three days.

To cure the Itch without Sulphur.

TAKE a handful of elecampane-root, and as much sharp-pointed dock, shred them small, and boil them in two quarts of spring-water till it comes to a pint; strain the liquor, and with it let the party wash his hands and face two or three times a day.

Another for the Itch.

TAKE of camomile and velvet-leaves, scurvy-grass and capon's feathers, of each one handful; boil these in half a pound of butter out of the churn, till it is an ointment; then strain it out, and mix it with half an ounce of black pepper beaten fine; stir it in till it is cold, and anoint the party with it all over; keep on the same linen for a week; then wash with warm water and sweet-herbs, and put on clean linen: before you begin to use this, you must take brimstone and milk for three mornings; keep warm, and purge well after it is over.

To stay a Looseness.

TAKE a very good nutmeg, prick it full of holes, and toast it on the point of a knife; then boil it in milk till half be consumed; then eat the milk with the nutmeg powdered in it: in a few times it will stop.

For a Looseness.

TAKE sage, and heat it very hot between two dishes; put it in a linen rag, and sit on it.

For an inveterate Looseness.

TAKE a piece of bread of the bigness of a crown-piece, toast it hard on both sides, then put it into a quarter of a pint of French brandy; let it soak till it is soft, then eat the bread and drink the brandy at night going to bed; this must be taken thrice. This cured a near relation of mine who had tried several other things before to no purpose. S. C.

Another.

TAKE frankincense and pitch, and put it on some coals, and sit over it.

Another.

BOIL a good handful of bramble-leaves in milk, sweetened with loaf-sugar; drink it night and morning.

For Stuffing in the Lungs.

TAKE white sugar-candy powdered and sifted, two ounces; China-roots powdered and sifted, one ounce; flour of brimstone one ounce: mix these with conserve of roses, or the pap of an apple; and take the bigness of a walnut in the morning, fasting an hour after it; and the last at night, an hour after you have eaten or drank.

To make Brimstone Lozenges for a short Breath.

TAKE flour of brimstone and double refined sugar, beaten and sifted, an equal quantity; make it into lozenges with gum-dragant steeped in rose-water; dry them in the sun, and take three or four a day.

To make Lozenges for the Heart-burn.

TAKE of white sugar-candy a pound, chalk three ounces, bole-armoniac five scruples, crab's-eyes one ounce, red coral four scruples, nutmegs one scruple, pearl two scruples; let all these be beaten and sifted, and made all into a paste with a little spring-water; roll it out, and cut your lozenges out with a thimble; lay them to dry, eat four or five at a time, as often as you please.

To make Cashew Lozenges.

TAKE half an ounce of balsam of Tolu, put it in a silver tankard, and put to it three quarters of a pint of fair water; cover it very close, and let it simmer over a gentle fire twenty-four hours; then take ten ounces of loaf-sugar, and half an ounce of Japan earth, both finely powdered and sifted; and wet it with two parts of Tolu-water, and one part orange-flower-water, and boil it together, almost to a candy-height; then drop it on pye-plates, but first rub the plates over with an almond, or wash them over with orange-flower-water; it is best to do but five ounces at a time, because it will cool before you can drop it; after you have dropped them, set the plates a little before the fire; they will slip off the easier; if you would have them perfumed, put in ambergrease.

For a sore Mouth in Children.

TAKE half a pint of verjuice, strain into it four spoonfuls of the juice of sage; boil this with fine sugar to a syrup, and with a feather anoint the mouth often; touch it not with a cloth, or rub it; the child may lick it down, it will not hurt it.

To increase Milk in Nurses.

MAKE gruel with lentils, and let the party drink freely of it; or else boil them in posset-drink, which they like best.

To take away Morphew.

TAKE briony-roots, and wake-robin; stamp them with brimstone, and make it up in a lump; wrap it in a fine linen rag, dip it in vinegar, and rub the place pretty hard with it; it will take away the morphew spots.

The Bruise Ointment.

TAKE of rosemary, brown sage, fennel, camomile, hyssop, balm, woodbine-leaves, southernwood, parsley, wormwood, self-heal, rue, elder-leaves, clown's-all-heal, burdock-leaves, of each a handful; put them into a pot with very strong beer, or spirits enough to cover them well, and two pounds of fresh butter from the churn; cover it up with paste, and bake it with bread; and when it is baked, strain it out; when it is cold, skim off the butter, melt it, and put it into a gallipot for use; the liquor is very good to dip flannels into, and bathe any green bruise or ache, as hot as can be borne.

An Ointment for a scald Head.

TAKE a pound of May butter, without salt, out of the churn, a pint of ale, not too stale, a good handful of green wormwood, let the ale be hot, and put the butter to melt; shred the wormwood, and let them boil together till it turns green; strain it, and when it is cold, take the ointment from the dregs.

An Ointment to cause Hair to grow.

TAKE of boar's-grease two ounces, ashes of burnt bees, ashes of southernwood, juice of white lily-root, oil of sweet almonds, of each one drachm; six drachms of pure musk; and according to art make an ointment of these; and the day before the full moon shave the place, anointing it every day with this ointment; it will cause hair to grow where you will have it. Oil of sweet almonds, or spirit of vinegar, is very good to rub the head with, if the hair grows thin.

An extraordinary Ointment for Burns or Scalds.

TAKE of red dock-leaves and mallow-leaves, of each a large handful, two heads of housleek, of green elder, the bark being scraped from it, a small handful; wash the herbs, and the elder; which being cut small, boil in it a pint and a half of cream; boil till it comes to an oil, which, as it rises up, take off with a spoon; afterwards strain, and put to it three drachms of white lead powdered fine.

An Ointment for a Burn or Scald.

TAKE a pound of hog's-lard, two good handfuls of sheep's-dung, and a good handful of the green bark of the elder, the brown bark being first taken off; boil all these to an ointment: you must first take out the fire with sallad-oil, a bit of an onion, and the white of an egg, beaten well together; then anoint with the ointment, and in less than a week it will be well.

An Ointment for a Blast.

TAKE velvet-leaves, wipe them clean, chop them small, put them to unsalted butter out of the churn, and boil them gently, till they are crisp; then strain it into a gallipot, and keep it for use; lay velvet-leaves over the part, after it is anointed.

A rare green Oil for Aches and Bruises.

TAKE a pot of oil of olives, and put it into a stone pot of a gallon, with a narrow mouth; then take southernwood, wormwood, sage, and camomile, of each four handfuls; a quarter of a peck of red rose-buds, the white cut from them; shred them together grosly, and put them into the oil; and once a day, for nine or ten days, stir them well; and when the lavender spike is ripe, put four handfuls of the tops in, and let it stand three or four days longer, covered very close; then boil them an hour upon a slow fire, stirring it often; then put to it a quarter of a pint of the strongest aqua vitæ, and let it boil an hour more; then strain it through a coarse cloth, let it stand till it is cold, and keep it in glasses for use; warm a little in a spoon or saucer, and bathe the part affected.

For Obstructions.

PUT two ounces of steel-filings into a quart bottle of white wine; let it stand three weeks, shaking it once a day; then put in a drachm of mace; let it stand a week longer; then put into another bottle three quarters of a pound of loaf-sugar in lumps, and clear off your steel-wine to your sugar, and when it is dissolved, it is fit for use: give a spoonful to a young person, with as much cream of tartar as will lie on a three-pence; to one that is older two spoonfuls, and cream of tartar accordingly.

A Plaister for a Weakness in the Back.

TAKE plantain, comfrey, knot-grass, and shepherd's-purse, of each a handful; stamp them small; and boil them in a pound of oil of roses, and a little vinegar; when it is well boiled, strain it, and set it on the fire again, adding to it of wax four ounces, chalk, bole-armoniac and terra-sigillata, of each one ounce, boil all well, keeping it constantly stirring; then cool it, make it into rolls, and keep it for use; spread it on leather when you lay it to the back.

A Drink for the same.

TAKE four roots of comfrey, and of knot-grass and clary one handful, a sprig of rosemary, a little galangal, a good quantity of cinnamon and nutmeg sliced, and the pith of the chine of an ox. Stamp and boil all these in a quart of muscadine; then strain it, and put in six yolks of eggs; sweeten the caudle to your taste with double refined sugar, and drink a good draught morning and evening. Take of crocus-martis, and conserve of red roses mixed together, three or four times in a day.

The Stomach Plaister.

TAKE of Burgundy-pitch, frankincense, and bees-wax, of each an ounce; melt them together; then put in an ounce of Venice turpentine, and an ounce of oil of mace; melt it together, and spread your plaister on sheep's-leather; grate on it some nutmeg when you lay it on the stomach.

The Leaden Plaister.

TAKE of white lead three ounces, of red lead seven ounces, of bole-armoniac nine ounces; beat all into a fine powder, and put to them a pint of the best oil-olive; incorporate them over the fire, and let them boil gently half an hour, putting in one ounce of oil of Exeter; stir it continually, and when it is enough, make it up in rolls. This is a drying plaister.

A Plaister for the Sciatica.

TAKE of yellow wax a pound, the juice of marjoram and red sage, of each six spoonfuls, juice of onions two spoonfuls: let all these boil together till the juice is consumed; and when it is cold, put in two ounces of turpentine, and of nutmegs, cloves, mace, aniseeds, and frankincense, of each a pennyworth finely powdered; stir it well together, and make a plaister.

A Plaister for the Feet in a Fever.

TAKE of briony-roots one pound, tops of rue a handful, black soap four ounces, and bay-salt two ounces: beat all this in a mash, and out of this spread on a cloth for both feet; apply it warm, and sew cloths over them, and let them lie twelve hours; if there be occasion, renew them three times.

A Plaister for an Ague.

TAKE Venice turpentine, and mix with it the powder of white hellebore-roots, till it is stiff enough to spread on leather. It must be laid all over the wrist, and over the ball of the thumb, six hours before the fit comes.

An excellent Plaister for any Pain occasioned by a Cold or Bruise.

TAKE of the plaister of red leather and oxycroceum, of each equal parts; of the best Thebian opium one scruple; spread it on leather, and lay it to the part affected, after you have well anointed it with this ointment: take of ointment of marshmallow one ounce, oil of Exeter half an ounce, oil of spike, and spirit of hart's-horn, of each a drachm.

A Poultice for a sore Breast, before it is broken.

BOIL white bread and milk to a poultice; then put to it oil of lilies, and the yolk of an egg; set it over the fire again to heat, and apply it as hot as can be endured; dress it morning and night till it is broke: then dress it with the poultice of raisins.

A Poultice for a sore Breast, Leg, or Arm.

BOIL wheat-flour in strong ale very well, and pretty thick; then take it off the fire, and scrape in some boar's-grease, stir it well and apply it hot.

A Poultice to ripen Tumours.

TAKE half a pound of figs, white lily-roots, and bean-flour or meal, of each two ounces; boil these in water till it comes to a poultice; spread it thick on a cloth, apply it warm, and shift it as often as it grows dry.

A Poultice for a hard Swelling.

BOIL the finest wheat-flour in cream, till it is pretty thick; then take it off, and put in mallows chopped; stir it, and apply it as hot as can be endured; dress it twice a day, and make fresh every time.

To make Gascoign's Powder.

TAKE pearls, crab's-eyes, red coral, white amber, burnt hart's-horn, and oriental bezoar, of each half an ounce; the black tips of crab's-claws three ounces; make all into a paste, with a jelly of vipers, and roll it into little balls, which dry, and keep for use.

To make Pomatum.

TAKE a drachm of white wax, two drachms of sperma-ceti, an ounce of oil of bitter almonds; slice your wax very thin, and put it in a gallipot, and put the pot in a skillet of boiling water; when the wax is melted, put in your sperma-ceti, and just stir it together; then put in the oil of almonds; after that take it off the fire, and out of the skillet, and stir it till cold with a bone-knife; then beat it up in rose-water till it is white; keep it in water, and change the water once a day.

For the Piles.

TAKE galls, such as the dyers use, beat them to powder, and sift them; mix the powder with treacle into an ointment, and dip the rag into it, and apply it to the place affected.

Another.

TAKE of the tops of parsley, of mullet, and of elder-buds, of each one handful; boil in a sufficient quantity of fresh butter till it looks green, and has extracted the smell of the herbs; strain, and anoint the place with it three or four times a day.
See also Hemorrhoids.

Pills to purge the Head.

TAKE of the extract of rudium two drachms, and pill fœtida one drachm; mix these well together, and make into twelve pills; take two, or, if the constitution be strong, three of them, at six o'clock in the morning: drink warm gruel, thin broth, or posset-drink, when they work.

A fine Purge.

TAKE an ounce of liquorice, scrape it and slice it thin, and a spoonful of coriander-seeds bruised; put these into a pint of water, and boil it a little, and strain this water into an ounce of sena; let it stand six hours; strain it from the sena, and drink it fasting.

A purging Diet-drink in the Spring.

TAKE six gallons of ale, three ounces of rhubarb, sena, madder-roots, and dock-roots, of each twelve ounces; twelve handfuls of scabious, and as much agrimony, three ounces of aniseeds; slice and cut these, put them in a bag, and let it work in the ale; drink of it three or four times a day.

For a Purge.

TAKE half an ounce of sena, boil it in a pint of ale till half be consumed: cover it close till the next day; then boil it again till it comes to two spoonfuls; strain it, and add to it two spoonfuls of treacle, and drink it warm; drink gruel, or posset, or broth after it; keep yourself very warm while it is working; or else two ounces of syrup of roses, and drink warm ale after it in the working.

A good Purge.

INFUSE an ounce of sena in a pint of water, till half be consumed; when it is cold, add to it one ounce of syrup of roses, and one ounce of syrup of buckthorn; mix them well together. This quantity makes two strong purges for either man or woman, and four for a child.

A Purge for Hoarseness, or any Illness, on the Lungs.

TAKE four ounces of the roots of sorrel, of hyssop and maidenhair, of each half a handful; raisins stoned, a quarter of a pound, sena half an ounce, barley-water two quarts; put all these in a jug, and infuse them in a kettle of water two hours; strain it out, and take a quarter of a pint morning and night.

A Purging Diet-drink.

TAKE of garden scurvy-grass six handfuls, water-cresses, brook-lime, and peach-blossoms, of each four handfuls, nettle-tops and fumitory, of each three handfuls, monks rhubarb, and sena, of each four ounces, China-roots two ounces, sarsaparilla three ounces, rhubarb one ounce; coriander and sweet fennel-seed, of each half an ounce; cut the herbs, slice the roots,
bruise

bruise the seeds; put them in a thin bag, and hang them in four gallons of small ale; after three days drink a pint of it every morning; be regular in diet, eat nothing salt or sour.

An excellent Medicine for a Pain in the Stomach.

TAKE of tinctura sacra (or tincture of hiera-picra) one ounce in the morning, fasting an hour; then drink a little warm ale; do this two or three times a week till you find relief.

For a Pain in the Stomach.

TAKE a quarter of a pound of blue currants, wipe them clean, and pound them in a mortar, with an ounce of ani-seeds bruised; before you put them to the currants, make this into a bolus with a little syrup of clove-gilliflowers; take every morning the quantity of a walnut, and drink rosemary-tea, instead of other tea, for your breakfast; if the pain returns, repeat it.

To prevent After-Pains.

TAKE nine single piony-seeds powdered, the same quantity of powder of borax, and a little nutmeg; mix all these with a little white aniseed-water in a spoon, and give it the woman; and a little aniseed-water after it, as soon as possible after she is laid in bed.

For a Pleurisy.

LET the patient bleed plentifully, then drink off a pint of spring-water, with thirty drops in it of spirit of sal-armoniac; this must be done as soon as the party is seized. Approved by myself. S. C.

For a Pleurisy, if the Person cannot be blooded.

TAKE of carduus, the seeds or leaves, a large handful; boil them in a pint of beer till half is consumed; then strain it, and give it the party warm; they must be fasting when they take it, and fast six hours after it, or it will do them harm.

A Remedy for Pimples.

TAKE half a quarter of a pound of bitter almonds, blanch, stamp them, and put them into half a pint of spring-water; stir it together, and strain it out; then put to it half a pint of the best brandy, and a pennyworth of the flour of brimstone; shake it well when you use it, which must be often; dab it on with a fine rag.

Another

Another to take away Pimples.

TAKE wheat-flour mingled with honey and vinegar, and lay on the pimples going to bed.

For Weakness in the Hands after a Palsey.

TAKE of the tops of rosemary, bruise it, and make it up into a ball as big as a great walnut, and let the party roll it up and down in their hand very often, and grasp it in the hand till it is hot; do this very often.

Receipt against the Plague.

TAKE of rue, sage, mint, rosemary, wormwood, and lavender, a handful of each; infuse them together in a gallon of white wine vinegar, put the whole into a stone pot closely covered up, upon warm wood-ashes, for four days: after which draw off (or strain through fine flannel) the liquid, and put it into bottles well corked; and into every quart bottle put a quarter of an ounce of camphire. With this preparation wash your mouth, and rub your loins and your temples every day; snuff a little up your nostrils when you go into the air, and carry about you a bit of spunge dipped in the same, in order to smell to upon all occasions, especially when you are near any place or person that is infected. They write, that four malefactors (who had robbed the infested houses, and murdered the people during the course of the plague) owned, when they came to the gallows, that they had preserved themselves from the contagion, by using the above medicine only; and that they went the whole time from house to house without any fear of the distemper.

A Remedy for rheumatic Pains.

TAKE of sena, hermodactils, turpethum, and scammony, of each two drachms; of zedoary, ginger, and cubebs, of each one drachm, mix them and let them be powdered; the dose is from one drachm to two in any convenient vehicle. Let the parts affected be anointed with this liniment: take palm-oil two ounces, oil of turpentine one ounce, volatile salt of hart's-horn two drachms; afterwards lay on a mucilaginous plaister. Some that have been very much troubled with rheumatic pains, have by taking of hart's-horn in compound water of earth-worms, found mighty benefit.

For a Rheumatism.

LET the party take of the finest glazed gun-powder as much as a large thimble may hold; wet it in a spoon with milk

from

from the cow, and drink a good half-pint of warm milk after it; be covered warm in bed, and sweat; give it fasting abou seven in the morning, and take this nine or ten mornings together.

Another Remedy for the same.

LET the patient take spirit of hart's-horn morning and evening, beginning with twenty-five drops in a glass of spring-water, increasing five every day till they come to fifty, to be continued for a month, if not well sooner. By this I cured a woman that had this distemper to so great a degree, that she was swelled in her head and limbs that she could not lift her hand to her head; but taking this, in three days was much better, and in three weeks time went abroad perfectly well, and has continued so now for above seven years. S. C.

To cure the Dropsy, Rheumatism, Scurvy, and Cough of the Lungs.

TAKE English orrice-roots, squills, and elecampane-roots, each one ounce, hyssop and horehound-leaves, each one handful, the inner rind of green elder and dwarf-elder, of each one handful, sena one ounce and a half, agaric two drachms, ginger one drachm; cut the roots thin, bruise the leaves, and put them into two quarts of the best Lisbon wine; let these boil an hour and a half on a gentle fire in an earthen mug, very close stopped with a cork, and tied down with a bladder, that no air come to it, and set it in a large pot of boiling water; set it so that no water get into the mug, which must hold three quarts, that all the ingredients may have room to go in; when it is almost cold, strain it out very hard; take this for a week together if you can, and then miss a day; and if that does not do, go on with your other bottle of the same; take it in a morning fasting, ten spoonfuls at a time, without any posset-drink; it will both vomit and purge you; it is of an unpleasant taste; therefore take a lump of sugar after it; when it is quite cold, after it is strained off, let it stand in a flaggon to settle a night and a day; then bottle it up clear and fine for use: it is an admirable medicine.

For the Rheumatism.

TAKE one handful of garden scurvy-grass picked, two spoonfuls of mustard-seed bruised, two small sticks of horse-radish sliced, half an ounce of winter-bark sliced; steep these ingredients in a quart of mountain wine three hours before you take it, which must be three times a day; at eight, eleven, and five,

five, if your stomach will bear it; if not, then twice only, viz. at eight and five, eating and drinking nothing after it for two hours at least; you are to take a quarter of a pint at a time, which you must fill up out of another quart of the same wine; and so continue drinking till both bottles are emptied.

To make the right Angel-Salve.

TAKE black and yellow rosin, of each half a pound, virgin-wax and frankincense, of each a quarter of a pound; mastich an ounce, deer suet a quarter of a pound; melt what is to be melted, and powder what is to be powdered, and sift it fine; then boil them and strain them through a canvas bag into a bottle of white wine; then boil the wine with the ingredients an hour with a gentle fire, and let it stand till it is no hotter than blood; then put to it two drachms of camphire, and two ounces of Venice turpentine, and stir it constantly till it is cold: be sure your stuff be no hotter than blood when you put in your camphire and turpentine, otherwise it is spoiled; make it up in rolls, and keep for use: it is the best salve made.

To make Lip-Salve.

TAKE a quarter of a pound of alkanet-root bruised, and half a quarter of a pound of fresh butter, as much bees-wax, and a pint of claret; boil all these together a pretty while; then strain it, and let it stand till it is cold: then take the wax off the top, and melt it again, and pour it clear from the dregs into your gallipots or boxes: use it when and as often as you please.

A green Salve.

TAKE five handfuls of clown's all-heal, stamp it, and put it in a pot, adding to it four ounces of boar's grease, half a pint of olive-oil, and wax three ounces sliced; boil it till the juice is consumed, which is known when the stuff doth not bubble at all; then strain it, and put on the fire again, adding two ounces of Venice turpentine; let it boil a little, and put it in gallipots for use; melt a little in a spoon, and if the cut or wound be deep, dip your tents in it; if not, dip lint, and put on it, defending the place with a leaden plaister; dress it once a day.

For a sore Breast, when it is broken.

TAKE a quarter of a pound of raisins of the sun stoned, and beat them very small; then add to it near as much honey, and beat it together into a falve; fpread it on a cloth, and make tents, if occafion; drefs it once a day; when it is well drawn, ufe the yellow balfam, and black or leaden plaifter.

The Black Salve.

TAKE a pint of oil-olive, three quarters of a pound of yellow wax, of frankincenfe finely beaten and fearced, the beft maftich, olibanum and myrrh, of each two ounces; half a pound of white lead finely ground, and two drachms of camphire, boil thefe till they are black; then let it ftand a little; oil a board, and pour it on; oil your hand, and make it up in rolls for ufe.

A Salve for a Burn or Scald.

TAKE a pound of mutton fuet fhred fmall, melt it, and put into it thyme, fweet-marjoram, melilot, pennyroyal, and hyffop, of each a good handful chopt fmall; let it ftand together four days; then heat it, and ftrain it out, and put in the fame quantity of herbs again, and let it ftand four days longer; then heat it, and ftrain it out, and to that liquor put five pounds of white rofin, and two pounds of bees-wax fliced, and boil it up to a falve; when it is cold enough, oil a board, pour it on it, and make it up in rolls. This is an admirable falve, when the fire is taken out; you muft take out the fire with oil, then lay on the plaifter: it is good for a fmall cut, or iffue inflamed.

A Salve for a Blaft, Burn, or Scald.

TAKE May butter frefh out of the churn, neither wafhed nor falted, put into it a good quantity of the green inner rind of elder, put it in a pipkin, and fet that in a pot of boiling water; let it infufe a day or two; then ftrain it out, and keep it in a pot for ufe.

A Salve for a Cere-cloth for Bruifes or Aches.

TAKE a pint of oil, nine ounces of red lead, two ounces of bees-wax, an ounce of fperma-ceti, two ounces of rofin beaten and fifted; fet all thefe on a foft fire in a bell-fkillet, ftirring till it boils; and then try it on a rag, whether it firmly ftick upon it; when it does ftick take it off; and when you have made what cere-cloths you pleafe, pour the reft on an oiled board, and make it up in rolls; it is very good for a cut or green wound.

A

A Salve for a Sprain.

TAKE a quarter of a pound of virgin-wax, a quarter of a pound of frankincense, half a pound of Burgundy pitch; melt them well together, stirring them all the while till they are melted; then give them a good boil, and strain them into water; work it well into rolls, and keep it for use; the more it is worked, the better it is; spread it on leather.

A Salve for the King's Evil.

TAKE a burdock-root, and a white lily-root, wash, dry, and scrape them; wrap them in brown paper, and roast them in the embers; when they are soft, take them out, and cut off the burn or hard, and beat them in a mortar with boar's-grease and bean-flour; when it is almost enough, put in as much of the best turpentine as will make it smell of it; then put it in a pot for use.

The party must take inwardly two spoonfuls of lime-water in the morning, and fast two hours after it, and do the same at four o'clock in the afternoon; if there be any swelling of the evil, they must bathe it with this water a quarter of an hour together, a little warmed, and wet a cloth, and bind it on the place; but if the skin be broken, only wash it in the water, and spread a thin plaister of the salve, and lay on it; shift it once a day; if very bad, you must dress it twice a day.

To make the lime-water: Take a lime-stone as big as a man's head, it must be well burnt; put it into six quarts of boiling water, cover it close, but sometimes stir it; the next day, when it is settled, pour off the clear water, and keep it in bottles for use.

To make the Eye-Salve.

TAKE of fresh butter out of the churn, unsalted and unwashed, two pounds; set it in a glass jar in the sun to clarify three months, then pour very clear off about a quarter of a pound, and put to it an ounce of virgin-wax; when it is melted, put it into white rose-water to cool, and beat it in the water half an hour; then take it out from the water, and mix it with half an ounce of tutty finely powdered, and two scruples of mastich beaten and bruised as well as possible; mix all well together, and put it in pots for use; take a very little in your fingers, when in bed, shut your eye, and rub it over the lid and corner of your eye.

Sir Hans Sloane's Ointment for the Eyes.

TAKE of tutty and calamine, of each six drachms; of calcined lead and camphire, of each two drachms; of myrrh, sarcocolla, aloes, and white vitriol, of each one drachm: make them all into a fine powder. Then take of fresh butter twelve ounces, of white wax two ounces; and when they are melted together, by degrees shake in the fore-mentioned powders, and stir all together till the whole is cold and become an ointment.

All the ingredients that require powdering, ought to be reduced to the utmost fineness, and the whole made as smooth as possible.

To make Spirit of Saffron.

TAKE four drachms of the best saffron, put it in a quart bottle, pour on it a pint of the ordinary spirit of wine, and add to it half a pound of white sugar-candy beaten small; stop it close with a cork, and a bladder tied over it; set it in the sun, shake it twice a day, till the candy is dissolved, and the spirit of a deep orange colour; let it stand two days longer to settle, clear it off in another bottle, and keep it for use; give a small spoonful to a child, and a large one to a man or woman; it is excellent in any pestilential disease; it is good against colds, or the consumptive cough.

To cure the Spleen or Vapours.

TAKE an ounce of the filings of steel, two drachms of gentian sliced, half an ounce of carduus-seeds bruised, half a handful of centaury-tops; infuse all these in a quart of white wine four days; drink four spoonfuls of the clear every morning, fasting two hours after it, and walking about; if it binds too much, take once or twice a week some little purging thing to carry it off.

To make a Quilt for the Stomach.

TAKE a fine rag four inches square, and spread cotton thin over it; take mint and sweet-marjoram dried and rubbed to powder, and strew it over the cotton, pretty thick; then take nutmeg, cloves and mace, of each a quarter of an ounce beaten and sifted, and strew that over the herbs, and on that strew half an ounce of galangal finely powdered, then a thin row of cotton, and another fine rag, and quilt it together; when you lay it on the stomach, dip it in hot sack, and lay it on as warm as can be endured: this is very good for a pain in the stomach.

To disperse Tumours.

TAKE of yellow wax, frankincense, and rosin, of each four ounces; melt them together, strain it out, and when it is cold, make it into a roll, and keep it for use.

To cure a Place that is scalded.

TAKE linseed-oil, and put to it as much thick cream; beat them together very well, and keep it for use; anoint the place that is scalded twice a day, and it will cure it; put on it soft rags, and let nothing press it.

For a Scald Head.

TAKE three spoonfuls of juice of comfrey, two penny-worth of verdigrease, and half a pound of hog's-lard; melt it together, but let it not boil: cut off the hair, and anoint the place: it will cure it.

For the Falling Sickness.

TAKE of the powder of man's skull, of cinnabar, antimony, of each a drachm; of the root of male-piony, and frog's liver dried, of each two drachms; of the salt of amber half a drachm, conserve of rosemary two ounces, syrup of pionies enough to make it into a soft electuary, of which give the quantity of a large nutmeg every morning and evening, drinking after it three ounces of the water of the lilies of the valley; take it three days before the new moon, and three days before the full moon: to bring the patient quickly out of the fit, let the nostrils and temples be rubbed with the oil of amber.

To cure Spitting of Blood, if a Vein is broken.

TAKE mice-dung beaten to powder, as much as will lie on a six-pence; and put in a quarter of a pint of the juice of plantain, with a little sugar; give it in the morning fasting, and at night going to bed. Continue this some time, and it will make whole, and cure.

To take out the Redness and Scurf after the Small-Pox.

AFTER the first scabs are well off, anoint the face, going to bed, with the following ointment: beat common allum very fine, and sift it through a lawn sieve, and mix it with oil like a thick cream, and lay it all over the face with a feather; in the morning have bran boiled in water till it is slippery; then wash it it off as hot as you can bear it; fo do for a month or more, as there is occaſion.

To take out Spots of the Small-Pox.

TAKE half an ounce of oil of tartar, and as much oil of bitter almonds; mix it together, and with a fine rag daub it often on the face and hands, before the air has penetrated into the ſkin or fleſh.

For the Strangury.

TAKE half a pint of plantain-water, one ounce of white ſugar-candy finely powdered, two ſpoonfuls of ſallad oil, and the juice of a lemon; beat all theſe together very well, and drink it off.

For the Scurvy.

TAKE a pound of guaicum bark, half a pound of ſaſſafras, and a quarter of a pound of liquorice; boil all theſe in three quarts of water, till it comes to three pints; and when it is cold, put it in a veſſel with two gallons of ale; in three or four days it is fit to drink; uſe no other drink for ſix or twelve months, according to the violence of the diſtemper: it will certainly cure.

For the Scurvy or Dropſy.

STAMP the leaves of elder, and ſtrain the juice, and to a quarter of a pint of juice put ſo much white wine; warm it a little, and drink it off; do this four or five mornings together; if it purge you, it will certainly do good: take this in the ſpring.

A Water for the Scurvy in the Gums.

TAKE two quarts of ſpring-water, a pound of flower-deluce-root, a quarter of a pound of roche-allum, two ounces of cloves; of red roſe-leaves, woodbine-leaves, columbine-leaves, brown ſage, of each two handfuls, and one of roſemary, eight Seville oranges, peel and all, only take out the ſeeds; ſet theſe over the fire, and let them boil a quart away; then take it off, ſtrain it, and ſet it over the fire again, adding to it three quarts of claret, and a pint of honey; let them boil half an hour, ſkim it well, and when it is cold, bottle it for uſe; waſh and gargle your mouth with it two or three times a day.

An excellent Medicine for Shortneſs of Breath.

TAKE half an ounce of flour of brimſtone, a quarter of an ounce of beaten ginger, and three quarters of an ounce of beaten fena; mix all together in four ounces of honey; take the bignefs of a nutmeg night and morning for five days together; then once a week for fome time; then once a fortnight.

Another.

TAKE two quarts of elder-berry juice when very ripe, put one quart in a pipkin to boil, and as it confumes, put in the reft by a little at a time; boil it to a balfam; it will take five or fix hours in boiling. Take a little of it night and morning, or any time.

To make Syrup of Garlic.

TAKE two heads of garlic, peel it clean, and boil it in a pint of water a pretty while; then change your water and boil it till the garlic is tender; then ftraining it off, add a pound of double refined fugar to it, and boil it till it is a thick fyrup; fkim it well, and keep it for ufe; take a fpoonful in a morning fafting, another laft at night, for a fhort breath.

To make Syrup of Marfhmallows.

TAKE marfhmallow-roots four ounces, grafs-root, afparagus-roots, liquorice, ftoned raifins, of each half an ounce; the tops of marfhmallows, pellitory, pimpernel, faxifrage, plantain, maidenhair white and black, of each a handful, red chiches an ounce; the four greater and four leffer cold feeds, of each three drachms; bruife all thefe, and boil them in three quarts of water till it comes to two; then put to it four pounds of white fugar, till it comes to a fyrup.

To make Syrup of Saffron.

TAKE a pint of the beft Canary, as much balm-water, and two ounces of Englifh faffron; open and pull the faffron very well, and put it into the liquor to infufe; let it ftand clofe covered (fo as to be hot, but not boil) twelve hours; then ftrain it out as hot as you can, and add to it two pounds of double refined fugar; boil it till it is well incorporated, and when it is cold bottle it, and take one fpoonful in a little fack or fmall cordial, as occafion ferves.

To give Eafe in a violent Fit of the Stone.

TAKE a quart of milk, and two handfuls of dried fage, a pennyworth of hemp-feed, and one ounce of white fugar-candy; boil all thefe together a quarter of an hour, and then put in half a pint of Rhenifh wine. When the curd is taken off, put

the

the ingredients in a bag, and apply it to the aggrieved part; and of the liquor drink a good glass full. Let both be as hot as can be endured. If there is not ease the first time, warm it again, and use it. It seldom fails.

An approved Medicine for the Stone.

TAKE six pounds of black cherries, stamp them in a mortar till the kernels are bruised; then take of the powder of amber, and of coral prepared, of each two ounces: put them with the cherries into a still, and with a gentle fire draw off the water; which if you take for the stone, mix a drachm of the powder of amber with a spoonful of it, drinking three or four spoonfuls after it; if for the palsy or convulsions, take four spoonfuls, without adding any thing, in the morning fasting.

To give Ease in Fits of the Stone, and to cure the Suppression of Urine, which usually attend them.

TAKE snail-shells and bees, of each an equal quantity; dry them in an oven with a moderate heat; then beat them to a very fine powder, of which give as much as will lie on a six-pence, in a quarter of a pint of bean-flower-water, every morning, fasting two hours after it: continue this for three days together: this has been often found to break the stone, and force a speedy passage for the urine.

How to make the Lime-Drink, famous for curing the Stone.

TAKE half a peck of lime stones new-burnt, and put them into four gallons of water; stir it well at the first putting in; then let it stand, and stir it again; as soon as it is very well settled, strain off the clear into a large pot, and put to it four ounces of saxifrage, and four ounces of liquorice, sliced thin, raisins of the sun stoned one pound, half a pound of blue currants, mallows, and mercury, of each a handful; coriander, fennel, and aniseeds, of each an ounce; let the pot stand close covered for nine days; then strain it; and, being settled, pour the clearest of it into bottles; you may drink half a pint of it at a time, as often as you please: in your morning's draught, put a drachm of winter cherries powdered. This has cured some who have been so tormented with the stone in the bladder, that they could not make water, after they had in vain tried abundance of other remedies.

A Receipt for the Cure of the Stone and Gravel, whether in the Kidneys, Ureters, or Bladder.

TAKE marshmallow-leaves, the herb mercury, saxifrage, and pellitory of the wall, of each, fresh gathered, three handfuls; cut them small, mix them together, and pound them in a clean stone mortar, with a wooden pestle, till they come to a mash; then take them out, spread them thin in a broad glazed earthen pan, and let them lie, stirring them about once a day, till they are thoroughly dry (but not in the sun) and then they are ready, and will keep good all the year. Of some of these ingredients so dried, make tea, as you do common tea with boiling water, as strong as you please, but the stronger the better; and drink three, four, or more tea-cups full of it blood-warm, sweetened with coarse sugar, every morning and afternoon, putting into each cup of it half a spoonful, or more, of the expressed oil of beach-nuts, fresh drawn (which in this case has been experienced to be vastly preferable to oil of almonds, or any other oil) stirring them about together, as long as you see occasion.

This medicine, how simple soever it may seem to some, is yet a fine emollient remedy, is perfectly agreeable to the stomach (unless the beach-oil be stale or rancid) and will sheath and soften the asperity of the humours in general, particularly those that generate the gravel and stone, relaxing and suppling the solids at the same time: and it is well known by all physicians, that emollient medicines lubricate, widen, and moisten the fibres, so as to relax them into their proper dimensions, without forcing the parts; whereupon obstructions of the reins and urinary passages are opened, and cleared of all lodgments of sandy concretions, gravel and passable stones, and made to yield better to the expulsion of whatever may stop them up; and likewise takes away, as this does, all heat and difficulty of urine and stranguries; and withal, by its soft mucilaginous nature, cools and heals the reins, kidneys, and bladder, giving present ease in the stone-cholic; breaks away wind, and prevents its return, as it always keeps the bowels laxative.

A Wash for the Teeth, recommended by another great Physician, that makes them perfectly white, taking off all the black, ulcerated, and cancerous Spots, fastens the Teeth, and makes them of a beautiful Colour though ever so old, or ever so loose.

THE best thing to cure the scurvy in the gums is, every morning to wash the mouth with salt and warm water. Indeed it should be done every day after dinner with cold water, and the laſt thing at night. This cures the ſcurvy in the gums, and the waſh and powder will make them as white as ſnow, faſten the gums, and clear the mouth of all ulcers and cancerous humours, without any manner of trouble.

To preſerve and whiten the Teeth.

TAKE a quarter of a pound of honey, and boil it with a little roche-allum; ſkim it well, and then put in a little ginger finely beaten; let it boil a while longer, then take it off; and before it is cold, put to it as much dragon's-blood as will make it of a good colour; mix it well together, and keep it in a gallipot for uſe; take a little on a rag and rub the teeth, you may uſe it often.

A good Remedy for a hollow aching Tooth.

TAKE of camphire and crude opium, of each four grains, make them into three pills with as much oil of cloves as is convenient, roll them in cotton, apply one of them to the aching tooth, and repeat it if there is occaſion.

To cure the Tooth-ache.

TAKE half an ounce of conſerve of roſemary over night, and half a drachm of extract of rudium in the morning; do this three times together; keep warm.

Another Method.

LET the party that is troubled with the tooth-ache lie on the contrary ſide, drop three drops of the juice of rue into the ear on that ſide the tooth acheth, let it remain an hour or two, and it will remove the pain.

For the Teeth.

TAKE a pint of ſpring-water, put to it ſix ſpoonfuls of the beſt brandy; waſh the mouth often with it, and in the morning roll a bit of allum a little while in the mouth.

Pills to purge off a Rheum in the Teeth.

TAKE four drachms of maſtich, ten drachms of aloes, three drachms of agarick; beat the maſtich and aloes, and grate the agarick: ſearce them, and make them into pills with ſyrup of betony: you may make but a quarter of this quantity at a time, and take it all out, one pill in the morning, and two at night: you may eat or drink any thing with theſe pills, and go abroad, keeping yourſelf warm; and when they work, drink a draught or two of ſomething warm.

A Powder for the Teeth.

TAKE half an ounce of cream of tartar, and a quarter of an ounce of powder of myrrh; rub the teeth with it two or three times a week.

An admirable Powder for the Teeth.

TAKE tartar of vitriol two drachms, best dragon's-blood and myrrh, each half a drachm, gum lac a drachm, of ambergrease four grains, and those who like it may add two grains of musk; mix well, and make a powder, to be kept in a phial close stopped. The method of using it is thus: Put a little of the powder upon a china saucer, or a piece of white paper; then take a clean linen cloth upon the end of your finger, just moisten it with water, and dip it in the powder, and rub the teeth well once a day, if they be foul; but if you want to preserve their beauty, only twice a week is sufficient for its use. This powder will preserve the teeth and gums beyond any other, under whatever title dignified or distinguished; and what is commonly called a tainted or stinking breath, mostly proceeds from rotten teeth, or scorbutic gums; which last distemper, so incident and fatal to childrens teeth, this powder will effectually remove. Indeed there is no cure for a rotten tooth, therefore I advise to pull it out; and if this cannot be effected, the above powder will sweeten the breath, and prevent such tooth from any ill favour. The too frequent use of the tooth-brush makes the teeth become long and deformed, although it be a good instrument, and the moderate use of it proper enough. After rubbing the teeth with the powder, the mouth may be washed with a little red wine warm, or the like.

To make the Teeth white.

TAKE three spoonfuls of the juice of celandine, nine spoonfuls of honey, half a spoonful of burnt allum; mix these together, and rub the teeth with it.

An admirable Tincture for green Wounds.

TAKE balsam of Peru one ounce, storax calamita two ounces, benjamin three ounces, succotrine aloes, myrrh, and frankincense, of each half an ounce; angelica-roots, and flowers of St. John's wort, of each half an ounce, spirit of wine one pint; beat the drugs, scrape and slice the roots, and put it into a bottle; stop it well, and let it stand in the sun July, August, and September; then strain it through a fine linen cloth; put it in a bottle; stop it close, and keep it for use. Apply it to a green

green wound by anointing it with a feather; then dip lint in it, and put it on, binding it up with a cloth; but let no plaister touch it; twice a day wet the lint with a feather; but do not take it off till it is well.

For the Trembling at the Heart.

MAKE a syrup of damask-roses, and add thereto a small quantity of red coral, pearl, and ambergrease, all finely beaten and powdered; take this so long as your pains continue, about a spoonful at a time.

To kill a Tetter.

TAKE flour of brimstone, ginger, and burnt allum, a like quantity; mix it with unsalted butter, anoint as hot as can be endured, at bed-time: in the morning wash it off with celandine-water heated; while this is continued, the party must sometimes take cordials, to keep the humour from going inward.

For a Quinsey or Swelling in the Throat, so that the Patient cannot swallow.

TAKE a toast of houshold bread, as big as will cover the top of the head, well baked on both sides, soak it in right French brandy; let the top of the head be shaved, then bind it on with a cloth; if this be done at night going to bed, it will cure before morning, as I myself have had experience of. S. C.

For a sore Throat.

MAKE a plaister of Paracelsus four inches broad, and so long as to come from ear to ear, and apply it warm to the throat; then bruise housleek, and press out the juice; add an equal quantity of honey, and a little burnt allum; mix all together, and let the party often take some on a liquorice-stick.

For a Thrush in Childrens Mouths.

TAKE a hot sea-coal, and quench it in as much spring-water as will cover the coal; wash it with this five or six times a day.

A Vomit.

TAKE seven or eight daffodil-roots, and boil them in a pint of posset-drink, and in the working drink carduus-water a gallon or more; your posset must be cold when you drink it, and your carduus-tea must be blood-warm; if it works too much, put some salt in a dish of posset, and drink it off.

A good Vomit.

TAKE two ounces of the finest white allum, beat it small, put it into better than half a pint of new milk, set it on a slow fire till the milk is turned clear; let it stand a quarter of an hour; strain it off, and drink it just warm; it will give three or four vomits, and is very safe; and an excellent cure for an ague taken half an hour before the fit; drink good store of carduus tea after it, or else take half a drachm of ipecacuanha, and carduus-tea with it.

Another Vomit.

TAKE rectified butter of antimony, digest it with thrice its own weight of alcohol; a single drop or two whereof being taken in sack, or any convenient vehicle, works well by vomit: it was a secret of Mr. Boyle's, and highly valued; and by him communicated to the admiral Du Quesne: it is likewise recommmended by Dr. Boerhaave.

To stop Vomiting.

TAKE a large nutmeg, grate away half of it, and toast the flat side till the oil ouze it; then clap it to the pit of the stomach; let it lie so long as it is warm; repeat it often till cured.

Another Remedy.

TAKE half a pint of mint-water, an ounce of syrup of violets, a quarter of an ounce of mithridate, and half an ounce of syrup of roses; mix all these well together, and let the party take two spoonfuls first, and then one spoonful after every vomiting, till it is stayed.

Another.

TAKE ash-leaves, boil them in vinegar and water, and apply them hot to the stomach; do this often.

To provoke Urine presently when stopped.

IN a quart of beer boil a handful of the berries of eglantine till it comes to a pint: drink it off lukewarm.

To draw up the Uvula.

TAKE ground-ivy, and heat it well between two tiles, and lay it as warm as can be borne on the top of the head. The blood

blood of a hare dried and drank in red wine, ſtops the bloody-flux, though ever ſo ſevere.

A calcined Water to dry up Ulcers, and old Sores.

TAKE of the beſt Roman vitriol three ounces, camphire once ounce; beat them into fine powder, put them into the bottom of a crucible, and fix it in hot embers; cover it with white paper, and put a little tile on it; let it be well calcined, but not too much; when it is cold beat it into fine powder, and ſift it; then add to it three ounces of bole-armoniac, beaten and ſifted; mix all together, and to half an ounce of this powder, put a quart of ſpring or plantain-water; boil the water, and when it is blood-warm, put in your half ounce of powder, and ſtir it together in a pewter baſon till it is quite cold; then put it in a bottle for uſe; when you uſe it, ſhake the bottle, and pour ſome out, and uſe it as hot as can be endured, either by ſyringe or waſhing the place twice or thrice a day; and uſe the following plaiſter or ſalve.

For a Weakneſs in the Back or Reins.

TAKE an ounce of Venice turpentine, waſh it in red roſe-water, work it in the water till it is white; pour the water from it, and work it up into pills with powder of turmerick and a grated nutmeg; you may put a little rhubarb as you ſee occaſion; take three in the morning, and three in the evening, in a little ſyrup of elder.

A rare Mouth Water.

TAKE roſemary, rue, celandine, plantain, bramble-leaves, woodbine-leaves, and ſage, of each a handful; beat them, and ſteep them in a quart of the beſt white wine vinegar two days and nights; then preſs it well, ſtrain it, put to it ſix ounces of allum, and as much honey: boil them a little together ſoftly, till the allum is diſſolved: when it is cold, keep it for uſe.

For the Worms.

TAKE of wormwood, rue, whitewort, and young leeks, of each one handful; chop and ſtrip theſe herbs very ſmall, and fry them in lard; put them on a piece of flannel, and apply them to the ſtomach, as hot as can be borne; and let them lie forty-eight hours, changing the herbs when they are dry.

A Plaiſter for Worms in Children.

TAKE two ounces of yellow wax, and as much roſin; boil them half an hour, ſtirring them all the while; ſkim them well, and take it off, and put to it three drachms of aloes, and two spoonfuls of treacle, and boil it up again; rub a board with fresh butter, and pour the salve thereon; work it well, and make it up in rolls; when you make the plaister, sprinkle it with saffron, and cut a hole against the navel.

A Clyster for the Worms.

TAKE of rue, wormwood, lavender-cotton, three or four sprigs of each; a spoonful of aniseeds bruised; boil these in a pint of milk, let the third part be consumed; then strain it out, and add to it as much aloes finely powdered, as will lie on a three-pence; sweeten it with honey, and give it pretty warm: it should be given three mornings together, and the best time is three days before the new or full moon.

To know if a Child has Worms or not.

TAKE a piece of white leather, prick it full of holes with your knife, rub it with wormwood, spread honey on it, and strew the powder of succotrine aloes on it; lay it on the child's navel when it goes to bed; and if it has worms, the plaister will stick fast; and if it has not, it will fall off.

Excellent for Worms in Children.

TAKE fenugreek-seed and wormwood-seed one pennyworth, beat and searced; mix it well in a half-pennyworth of treacle; let the child take a spoonful in a morning fasting, and fast two hours after it; do this three or four days.

Another Remedy.

TAKE mithridate and honey, of each a pennyworth, oil of mace two pennyworth; melt them together, and spread upon leather cut in the shape of a heart; oil of savin and wormwood, of each six drops; of allum and saffron in powder, of each one drachm; rub the oils, and strew the powders, all over the plaister; apply it, being warmed, to the child's stomach with the point upwards.

An excellent Prescription for the Cure of Worms.

THE following receipt is an extraordinary remedy for the worms which breed in human bodies, and with which vast numbers of people of all ages and both sexes are afflicted, and some of them very severely, especially children, and other young persons, of whom abundance are carried off yearly by being thrown thereby into convulsions, epileptic fits, vomitings, looseneffes white or green sickness, and other disorders, which had been judged to have proceeded from other causes, when the occasion thereof was worms. But as there is such a variety of disorders proceeding from those intestine animals, representing other diseases, I shall, for the information of such as may little imagine their malady to be occasioned by worms, when it appears so plain to themselves and their physicians, that it is this or that other disease, first set down some of the many signs and symptoms of worms; and then prescribe the remedy to destroy, expel, and rid the patient's body of them; and this is a medicine so effectually adapted, and so innocent withal, that if it be pursued as directed, they that take it may depend it will not fail utterly and safely to do it, be the worm of any kind, or situated in any part of the body.

It is to be noted, that there are divers sorts of worms that breed in the body, and take up their residence therein, either in the stomach or bowels, and sometimes near the sphincter ani, or fundament, and often knit themselves together, and appear like a bag of worms, and are supposed to be bred from the ova or eggs of those animals swallowed down with the food, and encouraged and fed by viscidities in the passages; and according as they reside, or have placed themselves in the body, the symptoms and complaints which some people make are different both in kind and degree; in some to occasion looseneffes, in others costiveness, or frequent desires to go to stool, but cannot; in some to cause a fœtid or stinking breath, which is a shrewd sign of worms, as is also a hard or inflamed belly, especially in children, with a voracious appetite, and almost continual thirst, feverishness by fits, and intermitting pulse, and glowing cheeks; in some, a heaviness or pain in the head, startings in sleep, with frightful terrifying dreams; in some, a sleepiness representing a lethargy; in others, a nausea, or loathing of food, with or without motion to vomit, a pain and weight with a gnawing in the stomach, gripings and rumblings in the bowels, like the cholic; in children, a dry cough, and sometimes screaming fits and convulsions, with white lips and white urine; and in both old and young a weakened and lost appetite, giddiness in the head, paleness of countenance, with faintings and cold sweats of a sudden, indigestions, abatement of the strength, and falling away of flesh, as if dropping into a consumption; with many other symptoms, but these are the chief, which ever more or less, some or other of them always affect where worms are the cause; and for remedy of which the following receipt my be depended on, and very innocent, as well as powerful and effectual, as every one, when they read what it is, will believe, and when they try it, will find.

Take

Take tops of carduus, tops of centuary, Roman wormwood, and flowers of camomile (all of them dried, and of the lateſt year's growth that you uſe them in) of each a ſmall handful; cut the herbs ſmall, but not the flowers, put them with an ounce of wormſeed bruiſed ſmall into an earthen jar or pickling pot, and pour upon them a quart of ſpring-water cold; ſtir all about, and then tie the pot over with a double paper, and let it ſtand forty eight hours, opening and ſtirring it about five or ſix times in that ſpace; at the end of forty-eight hours ſtrain it through a cloth, ſqueezing the herbs as dry as you can, which fling away, and of the liquor give to a child from two to four or five years old half a ſpoonful, more or leſs, mixed with a quarter of a ſpoonful of the oil of beech-nuts, every morning upon an empty ſtomach, and to faſt for about an hour after it; and alſo the ſame doſe about four or five in the afternoon every day, for a week or ten days together: by which time, if the caſe be worms, and you make but obſervation, you will find them to come away either dead or alive: older children muſt take more, in proportion to their ages; and grown perſons from three or four to ſix or eight ſpoonfuls, or more, with always half the quantity of the ſaid oil mixed with each doſe, and it will keep the body ſoluble, and ſometimes, a little looſe.

This medicine has cured in ſuppoſed incurable caſes, when it has proved at laſt to be from worms, when neither the phyſician or patient have before thought it to be ſo; but if it be not worms, it cannot hurt, but may cure in caſes ſimilar to worms, eſpecially where the ſtomach and bowels are diſordered.

Note, The beech-nut oil may be had at moſt oil-ſhops; and the reaſon that that oil before any other is adviſed is, that it has a property, as has been often tried, of killing worms, of itſelf, when olive-oil and oil of almonds would not do it; and as a confirmation of it, Dr. Baglivi ſays, in a book of experiments upon live worms from human bodies, That he put worms into divers liquors, which were reputed would kill them, but did not under a great many hours; and that towards night he put others into oil of ſweet almonds, and found them alive the next morning; then after many other experiments, he put one into oil of nuts, where it died preſently: and Malpighi, another noted phyſician, ſays, That of all common oils, oil of nuts is the beſt againſt worms; and that at Milan, mothers have a cuſtom to give their little children once or twice a week toaſts dipped in oil of nuts, and to grown people ſome ſpoonfuls of it faſting: and many other authors ſay the ſame, particularly Dr. Nicholas Andry, of the faculty of phyſic at Paris, in his treatiſe of worms; who alſo ſays, if you dip a pencil in oil of nuts, and anoint the bodies of live worms that any one voids, tho' you never touch their heads, they will preſently grow motionleſs, and die beyond recovery; the reaſon, he ſays, they die ſo

ſuddenly,

suddenly, when anointed, is, because they breathe only by the means of certain little windpipes that run through their bodies; so that if you stop up those pipes with nut-oil, which hinders the commerce of the air (for that the parts of oil of almonds are more porous than nut-oil, and consequently less able to hinder the entrance of the air into the worms) of necessity the creatures must die for want of respiration, though neither the head nor any other part where the pipes are not, be anointed. This is so true, says Malpighi, that if you put nut-oil upon a worm in any other part but where the pipes are, though the head be not spared, yet the worm will live, and have its natural motion; and if you put the oil upon some of the pipes only, you shall see the parts where those pipes are become immoveable; but if you put, says he, upon all the tracheas or pipes, the whole worm becomes motionless, and dies in an instant: and I do assure the public, that the same has been many times tried, and found, both by myself and others, that no other oil whatever would do what this will. The late Dr. Radcliffe, in many of his prescriptions I have seen, ordered that oil preferable to all others, where he had reason to suspect the patient had worms; and in one very remarkable case of a young lady of thirteen I could name, who was at death's door with the green sickness, as supposed, and who, by the use of this very oil, and such bitters as he believed the case then indicated, once or twice a day repeated, was cured perfectly, upon her voiding clusters of small worms for several days together, some of which were inclosed in a cystis or bag.

This I was willing to observe, that people may be sure to get the oil of nuts, and not any other oil.

The following Receipt was inserted in the Carolina Gazette, May 9, 1750; and it is presumed that the Introductory Letter will be a sufficient Authority for adopting it into this Work.

From the CAROLINA GAZETTE.
To the PRINTER.

'SIR,

'I AM commanded by the commons house of assembly to send you the inclosed, which you are to print in the Carolina Gazette as soon as possible; it is the negro Cæsar's cure for poison; for discovering of which, and likewise his cure for the bite of a rattle-snake, the general assembly hath thought fit to purchase his freedom, and grant him an allowance of 100 l. per ann. during life.

May 9, 1749.   'I am, &c.
   'JAMES IRVING.'

The

The Negro Cæsar's Cure for Poison.

TAKE the roots of plantain and wild horehound, fresh or dried, three ounces, boil them together in two quarts of water, to one quart, and strain it; of this decoction let the patient take one third part three mornings fasting successively, from which, if he finds any relief, it must be continued till he is perfectly recovered: on the contrary, if he finds no alteration after the third dose, it is a sign that the patient has either not been poisoned at all, or that it has been with such poison as Cæsar's antidotes will not remedy, so may leave off the decoction.

During the cure, the patient must live on a spare diet, and abstain from eating mutton, pork, butter, or any other fat or oily food.

N. B. The plantain or horehound will either of them cure alone, but they are most efficacious together.

In summer you may take one handful of the roots and branches of each, in place of three ounces of the roots of each.

For Drink, during the Cure, let them take the following:

TAKE of the roots of golden-rod six ounces, or in summer two large handfuls, the roots and branches together, and boil them in two quarts of water to one quart (to which also may be added a little horehound and sassafras.) To this decoction, after it is strained, add a glass of rum or brandy, and sweeten it with sugar, for ordinary drink.

CHAP. II.
BROTHS, &c. for the SICK.

To make Broth of a Calf's-Head.

TAKE half a calf's-head, without the brains and tongue, wash it clean, cut it to pieces, put it into a gallon of water, set it over a slow fire. When the scum rises skim it clean, and put in one ounce of ivory shavings, one drachm of mace, one nutmeg sliced. Boil it till half is consumed, and then strain it. Drink three pints a day, either with sugar or a little salt.

To make Broth of a Knuckle or Scrag of Veal.

TAKE any part of a knuckle or scrag of veal, put it into a pot with as much water as will cover it, one ounce of hart's-horn shavings, half an ounce of vermicelli, two blades of mace,
and

and three cloves; boil it an hour and a half. If the patient be coftive, boil in it a quarter of a pound of currants, and fweeten it with Lifbon fugar.

To make a ftrengthening Drink for very weak Perfons.

TAKE one pound of filver-bellied eels; cleanfe them and cut them into fmall pieces, put them into a pot with five quarts of water, one ounce of fago, a cruft of bread, a top of mint, a fmall handful of pennyroyal, a drachm of mace, as much nutmeg, and a fmall ftick of cinnamon; boil it till half is confumed. Drink of it as often as thirfty.

To make Chicken Broth.

TAKE a chick juft killed, bruife it, put it into a faucepan with five quarts of water, a blade or two of mace, a fmall piece of lemon-peel, one fpoonful of ground rice; boil it till but two quarts remain.

To boil a Chicken.

WHEN you have picked and wafhed your chicken clean, put it into a faucepan with cold water, a little parfley, and fet it on the fire; a quarter of an hour will boil it. Then take a piece of bread and boil it in a fmall faucepan till the water becomes as thick as cream, ftrain it off, and mix it with the parfley chopped fmall, adding to it a bit of butter, and a little falt, and ferve it up.

To make Mutton Broth.

TAKE a pound of a loin of mutton, take off the fat, put to it one quart of water, let it boil, and fkim it well; then put in a good piece of upper-cruft of bread, and one large blade of mace. Cover it clofe, and let it boil flowly an hour; don't ftir it, but pour the broth clear off. Seafon it with a little falt, and the mutton will be fit to eat. If you boil turnips, don't boil them in the broth, but by themfelves in another faucepan.

To make Beef or Mutton Broth for very weak People, who take but little Nourifhment.

TAKE a pound of beef, or mutton, or both together; to a pound put two quarts of water, firft fkin the meat and take off all the fat; then cut it into little pieces, and boil it till it comes to a quarter of a pint. Seafon it with a very little corn of falt, fkim off all the fat, and give a fpoonful of this broth at a time. To very weak people, half a fpoonful is enough; to fome a tea-fpoonful at a time; and to others a tea-cup full. There is greater nourifhment from this than any thing elfe.

To make Beef Drink, which is ordered for weak People.

TAKE a pound of lean beef; then take off all the fat and skin, cut it into pieces, put it into a gallon of water, with the under-cruft of a penny-loaf and a very little salt. Let it boil till it comes to two quarts; then strain it off, and it is a very hearty drink.

A restorative Jelly for any one inclining to a Consumption.

TAKE four ounces of hart's-horn shavings, two ounces of erringo-root, one ounce of isinglass, two vipers, one pint of snails; the snails being washed and bruised, put all these into three quarts of pump-water, let them simmer till it comes to three pints, then strain it off, and add the juice of two Seville oranges, half a pound of white sugar-candy, and one pint of old Rhenish wine; drink a quarter of a pint fasting, and the same quantity an hour before dinner-time.

To make the Pectoral Drink.

TAKE of China-root one ounce, sarsaparilla, comfrey, and liquorice, of each half an ounce, orrice, and elecampane, of each one quarter of an ounce, yellow and red sanders, of each two drachms, aniseeds one drachm, Malaga raisins half a pound; boil these in a gallon of spring-water, till half is evaporated, then strain it off, and sweeten it with syrup of maidenhair.

To make artificial Asses Milk.

TAKE of pearl-barley two ounces, of eringo-root and China-root, of each one ounce, Japan earth one drachm, white maidenhair and honey of each one ounce, ten snails bruised; boil these in three quarts of water till half be wasted. Drink a quarter of a pint of it, mixed with an equal quantity of warm milk from the cow, and sweetened with syrup of balsam of Tolu, morning and night.

Another Method.

TAKE an ounce of French barley, and a pint of water, and let it have one boil up, then throw away the water, and boil it a second time in a fresh pint of water, which must be thrown away likewise; then put on three pints of fresh water, and boil it to a quart; at the same time add an ounce of candied eringo-root, and then drain off the liquor.

To make Bread Jelly.

TAKE a stale penny-loaf, lay it in cold water till thoroughly soaked, half an ounce of isinglass pulled in small pieces, and soaked twelve hours in water, put these in a saucepan with a gallon of water, a quarter of an ounce of mace and nutmegs, a race of ginger; boil it till you find it will jelly, which you may know by dropping some in a plate till cold. Then strain it, and drink a quarter of a pint of it twice a day, either mixed with white wine, sweetened with sugar, or milk.

To boil Sago.

TAKE two spoonfuls of sago, boil it gently in a pint and a half of water till thick, stirring it often; then take it off, and add to it a little wine, sugar, a bit of cinnamon, candied ginger, and grated nutmeg.

To make Sago Gruel.

TAKE four ounces of sago, give it a scald in hot water, then strain it through a hair sieve, and put it over the fire with two quarts of water and a stick of cinnamon; keep scumming it till it grows thick and clear; when your sago is enough, take out the cinnamon, and put in a pint of red wine; if you would have it very strong put in more than a pint, and sweeten it to your taste; then set it over the fire to warm, but do not let it boil after the wine is put in, as it weakens the taste, and makes the colour not so deep a red; pour it into a tureen, and put in a slice of lemon, when you are sending it to table.

To make Sago with Milk.

WASH your sago in warm water, and set it over the fire with a stick of cinnamon, and as much water as will boil it thick and soft; then put in as much thin cream or new milk as will make it a proper thickness; grate in half a nutmeg, and sweeten it to your taste.

To make Barley Gruel.

TAKE four ounces of pearl barley, boil it in two quarts of water with a stick of cinnamon in it, till it is reduced to one quart, add to it a little more than a pint of red wine; sugar to your taste, and add two or three ounces of currants washed and picked very clean.

To mull Wine.

GRATE half a nutmeg into a pint of wine, and sweeten it to your taste with loaf-sugar; set it over the fire, and when it boils take it off to cool; beat the yolks of four eggs exceeding well, and add to them a little cold wine; then mix them carefully with your hot wine a little at a time, and pour it backwards and forwards several times till it looks fine and bright; then set it on the fire and heat it a little at a time for several times, till it is quite hot and pretty thick, and pour it backwards and forwards several times.

To mull Ale.

TAKE a pint of good strong ale, put it into a saucepan, with three or four cloves, nutmeg and sugar to your taste; set it over the fire, and when it boils take it off to cool; beat the yolks of four eggs very well, and mix them with a little cold ale; then put it to your warm ale, and pour it in and out of your pan for several times; set it over a slow fire, heat it a little, then take it off again, and heat it two or three times, till it is quite hot.

To make Panada.

YOU must take a quart of water in a nice clean saucepan, a blade of mace, a large piece of crumb of bread; let it boil two minutes, then take out the bread, and bruise it in a bason very fine. Mix as much water as will make it as thick as you would have; the rest pour away, and sweeten it to your palate. Put in a piece of butter as big as a walnut, don't put in any wine, it spoils it; you may grate in a little nutmeg. This is hearty and good diet for sick people.

To make Barley Water.

TAKE of pearl barley four ounces, put it in a large pipkin and cover it with water; when the barley is thick and tender, put in more water and boil it up again, and so do till it is of a good thickness to drink; then put in a blade or two of mace, or a stick of cinnamon; let it have a walm or two and strain it out; squeeze in the juice of two or three lemons, and a bit of the peel, and sweeten it to your taste with fine sugar; let it stand till it is cold, and then run it through a bag, and bottle it up; it will keep three or four days.

To make Water Gruel.

TAKE a large spoonful of oatmeal, and a pint of water; mix them together, set it on the fire, and let it boil for some time,

time, stirring it often; then strain it through a sieve, and add to it a good piece of butter, and a little salt, stirring it constantly with a spoon, till the butter is melted.

To make Chicken Water.

TAKE a cock or large fowl, strip off its skin, and bruise it with a rolling-pin. Then put it into a saucepan with two quarts of water, a crust of bread, and an ounce of French barley. Let it boil till half the water is evaporated, then strain it off, and season it with salt.

To make Seed Water.

TAKE of coriander-seed, carraway-seed, cubebs, sweet-fennel-seed, and aniseed, of each half an ounce, bruise them and boil them in a quart of water; strain it, brew it up with the yolk of an egg, and add to it a little sack and double refined sugar.

To make white Caudle.

TAKE four spoonfuls of oatmeal, two blades of mace, a piece of lemon-peel, cloves and ginger of each one quarter of an ounce; put these into two quarts of water, and let it boil about an hour, stirring it often; then strain it out, and add to every quart half a pint of wine, some grated nutmeg and sugar.

To make brown Caudle.

TAKE six spoonfuls of oatmeal, a bit of lemon-peel, and two or three blades of mace, put them into two quarts of water, let it boil as before, and strain it. Then add to it a quart of stale beer, not bitter, and some sugar; let it boil, and then put to it a pint of white wine.

To make Beef Tea.

TAKE a pound of lean beef, cut it in very thin slices, put it into a jar, and pour a quart of boiling water upon it; cover it very close to keep in the steam, and let it stand by the fire. It is very good for a weak constitution, and must be drank when it is new-milk warm.

PART XI.

DIRECTIONS for BREEDING all Sorts of POULTRY.

As many of our readers amuse themselves with breeding their own poultry, &c. particularly in the country, the following directions may not be disagreeable to them.

Directions for managing and breeding poultry to advantage, &c.

TAKE particular care to keep your hen-roost quite clean; do not chuse too large a breed, they generally eat coarse. You may keep six hens to a cock. When fowls are near laying, give them rice whole, or nettle-seed mixed with bran, and bread worked into a paste. In order to make your fowls familiar, feed them always in one place, and at particular hours.

Take care to keep your store-house from vermin: contrive your perches not to be over one another, nor over the nests, which always take care to keep clean straw in.

When you design to set a hen, as you will know the time by her clucking, do not put above ten under her. March is reckoned a good month to set hens in; but if they are well fed, they will lay many eggs, and set at any time.

Wherever poultry is kept, all sorts of vermin naturally come. It would be well to sow wormwood and rue about the places you keep them in; they will resort to it when not well; and it will help to destroy fleas. You may also boil wormwood and sprinkle the floor therewith.

As to rats, mice and weasels, traps should be always kept for them, or you will never have any success.

Ducks usually begin to lay in February; if your gardener is diligent in picking up snails, grubs, caterpillars, worms, and other insects, and lays them in one place, it will make your ducks familiar, and is the best food you can give them. Parsley sowed about the ponds or river they use, gives their flesh a pleasant taste. Be sure to have a place for them to retire to at night.

Partition

Partition off their nests, and make it as nigh the water as possible, and always feed them there; it will make them love home, being of a roaming nature.

Their eggs should be taken away till they are inclined to sit; it is best to let every duck sit upon her own eggs; the same by fowls.

Geese. The keeping of geese is attended with little trouble, but they spoil a deal of grass, no creature caring to eat after them. When the goslings are hatched, let them be kept within doors. Lettuce-leaves and pease boiled in milk, is very good for them. When they are about to lay, drive them to their nests and shut them up, and set every goose with its own eggs, always feeding them at one place, and at stated times.

They will feed upon all sorts of grain and grass. You may gather acorns, parboil them in ale, and it will fatten them surprisingly.

Turkeys require more trouble to bring up than common poultry. The hen will lay till she is five years old. Be sure always to feed them near the place where you intend they should lay; in other respects they may be managed as other poultry.

They should be fed four or five times a day, being great devourers; and when they are sitting, must have plenty of victuals before them, and also be kept very warm.

To fatten them, you must give them sodden barley, and sodden oats for the first fortnight. Cram them as they do capons.

Pigeons, if you chuse to keep them, (being hurtful to your neighbours) take care to feed them well, or you will lose them all; they are great devourers, and yield but little profit.

Their nests should be made private and separate, or they will always disturb one another. Be sure to keep their house clean, and lay some hemp-seed amongst their food, they are great lovers of it.

Tame rabbets are very fertile, bringing forth every month; so soon as they have kindled put them to the buck, or else they will destroy their young.

The best food for them is the sweetest shortest hay, oats and bran, marshmallows, sow-thistle, parsley, cabbage-leaves, clover-grass, &c. always fresh. If you do not keep them clean they will poison themselves, and the person that looks after them.

Of feeding and cramming capons. The best way to cram a capon is to take barley-meal reasonably sifted, and mix it with new milk, make it into a good stiff dough paste; then make it into long crams or rolls, biggest in the midst, small at both ends; and then wetting them in lukewarm milk, give the capon a full gorge three times a day, morning, noon, and night, and he will in two or three weeks be as fat as any man needs to eat.

Of the pip in poultry. A pip is a white thin scale growing on the tip of the tongue, and will make poultry they cannot feed.

It is eafy to be difcerned, and proceedeth generally from drinking puddle-water, or want of water, or eating filthy meat. The cure is to pull the fcale with your nail, and then rub the tongue with falt.

Of the flux in poultry. The flux in poultry cometh with eating too much moift meat. The cure is to give them peafe and bran fcalded.

Of lice in poultry. If your poultry be much troubled with lice, (as is common, proceeding from corrupt food, want of bathing in fand, afhes, or fuch like) take pepper beaten fmall, mixing it with warm water, wafh your poultry therein, and it will kill all forts of vermin.

Of hens that eat their eggs. If you will not have your hen eat her eggs, lay a piece of chalk cut like an egg, at which fhe will often be pecking, and lofing her labour, fhe will refrain the thing.

Of making hens lay foon and often. If you feed your hens often with toaft taken out of ale, with barley boiled, or fifhes, they will lay often and all the winter.

PART

PART XII.

Of BREWING in General.

It is granted on all hands, that, according to the common saying, Good eating deserves good drinking: and as many ladies, and others, are fond of superintending the affairs of brewing, keeping, bottling, &c. their beer, ale, and other liquors, we shall here give directions concerning strong and small beer, and how to manage and bottle the same for keeping; likewise how to chuse the best hops, malt, water, cellars, &c. &c.

MARCH is esteemed one of the principal seasons for brewing of malt liquors for long keeping; the reason is, because the air at this time of the year is temperate, and contributes to the good working or fermenting the drink, which chiefly promotes its preservation and good keeping; for very cold weather prevents the free fermentation or working of liquors, as well as very hot weather; so that if we brew in very cold weather, unless we use some means to warm the cellar, while new drink is working, it will never clear itself as it ought to do; and the same misfortune will it lie under, if, in very hot weather, the cellar is not put in a temperate state; the consequence of which will be, that such drink will be muddy and sour, and perhaps never recover; or, if it does, perhaps not under two or three years. Again, such misfortunes are often owing to the badness of the cellar; for where they are dug in springy ground, or are subject to wet in the winter, then the drink will chill, and grow flat and dead: but where cellars are of this sort, it is adviseable to make your great brewings in this month, rather than in October; for you may keep such cellars temperate in summer, but cannot warm them in winter, and so your drink brewed in March will have due time to settle and adjust itself before the cold can do it any great harm. It is adviseable likewise to build your cellars for keeping of drink after such a manner, that none of the external air may come into them; for the variation of the air abroad, was there free admission of it into the cellars, would cause as many alterations in the liquors, and so would keep them perpetually disturbed and unfit for drinking. Some curious gentlemen in these things keep double doors to their cellars, on purpose that none of the outward air may get into them, and they have good reason to boast of their malt liquors. The meaning of the double doors is, to keep one shut while the other is open, that the outward air may be excluded. Such cellars, if they lie dry, as they ought to do, are said to be cold in summer and warm in winter; though in reality they are constantly the same in point of temper: they seem indeed cool in hot weather, but that is because we come into them from a hotter abroad; and so they seem to us warm in winter because we come out of a colder air to them; so that they are only cold or warm comparatively, as the air we come out of is hotter or colder. This is the case, and a cellar should be thus disposed, if we expect to have good drink. As for the brewing part itself, that is left to the brewers in the several counties in England, who have most of them different manners even of brewing honestly. What will be chiefly touched upon, besides speaking of cellaring, will relate to water, malt, hops, and the keeping liquors.

The best water, to speak in general, is river-water, such as is soft, and has partook of the air and sun: for this easily insinuates itself into the malt, and extracts its virtue; whereas the hard waters astringe and bind the parts of the malt, so that its virtue is not freely communicated to the liquor. It is a rule with some, that all water which will mix with soap is fit for brewing, and they will by no means allow of any other; and it has been more than once experienced, that where the same quantity of malt has been used to a barrel of river-water, as to a barrel of spring-water, the river-water brewing has excelled the other in strength above five degrees in twelve months. It must be observed too, that the malt was not only in quantity the same for one barrel as for another, but was the same in quality, having been all measured from the same heap; so also the hops were the same, both in quality and quantity, and the time of boiling, and both worked in the same manner, and tunned and kept in the same cellar: here it was plain, that the only difference was in the water, and yet one barrel was worth two of the other.

There is one thing which has long puzzled the best brewers; and that is, where several gentlemen in the same town have employed the same brewer, have had the same malt, the same hops, and the same water too, and brewed all in the same month, and broached their drink at the same time, and yet one has had beer extremely fine, strong and well tasted, while the others have hardly had any worth drinking. There may be three reasons for this difference: one may be the different weather, which

might

might happen at the several brewings in this month, and make an alteration in the working of liquors; or, secondly, that the yeast or barm might be of different sorts, or in different states, wherewith these liquors were worked; and, thirdly, the cellars were not equally good. The goodness of such drink as is brewed for keeping, depends upon the goodness of the cellars where it is kept.

The Dorchester beer, which is esteemed preferable to most of the malt liquor in England, is, for the most part, brewed of chalky water, which is almost every where in that county; and as the soil is generally chalk there, the cellars, being dug in that dry soil, contribute to the good keeping of their drink, it being of a close texture, and of a drying quality, so as to dissipate damps; for damp cellars, we find by experience, are injurious to keeping of liquors, as well as destructive to the casks. The malt of this country is of a pale colour, and the best drink produced in this country is where the cellars inclose a temperate air, and are of the nature before spoken of. The constant temperate air digests and softens these malt liquors, so that they drink as smooth as oil; but in the cellars which are unequal, by letting in heats and colds, the drink is subject to grow stale and sharp: for this reason it is, that drink, which is brewed for a long voyage at sea, should be perfectly ripe and fine before it is exported: for when it has had sufficient time to digest in the cask, and is racked from the bottom or lee, it will bear carriage without injury. It is farther to be noted, that in proportion to the quantity of liquor which is inclosed in one cask, so will it be a longer or a shorter time in ripening. A vessel, which will contain two hogsheads of beer, will require twice as much time to perfect itself as one of a hogshead; and it is found by experience, that there should be no vessel used for strong beer, which we design to keep, less than a hogshead; for one of that quantity, if it be fit to draw in a year, has body enough to support it two, three, or four years, if it has strength of malt and hops in it, as the Dorchester beer has; and this will bear the sea very well, as we find every day.

There is one thing more to be considered in the preservation of beer, and that is, when once the vessel is broached, we ought to have regard to the time in which it will be expended; for if there happens to be a quick draught for it, then it will last good to the very bottom; but if there is likely to be a slow draught, then do not draw off quite half before you bottle it, or else your beer will grow flat, dead or sour. This is observed very much among the curious.

One great piece of œconomy is the good management of small beer; for if that is not good, the drinkers of it will be feeble in summer time, and incapable of strong work, and will be very subject to distempers; and besides, when drink is not good, a

great

great deal will be thrown away. The use of drink, as well as meat, is to nourish the body; and the more labour there is upon any one, the more substantial should be the diet. In the time of harvest the bad effects of bad small beer among the workmen are visible; and in great families, where that article has not been taken care of, the apothecaries bills have amounted to twice as much as the malt would have come to, that would have kept the servants in strength and good health. Besides, good wholsome drink is seldom flung away by servants; so that the sparing of a little malt ends in loss to the master. Where there is good cellaring, therefore, it is adviseable to brew a stock of small beer either in this month or October, or in both months, to be kept in hogsheads, if possible: the beer brewed in March to begin drawing in October, and that brewed in October to begin in March, for summer drinking; having this regard to the quantity, that a family, of the same number of working persons will drink a third more in summer than in winter.

If water happens to be of a hard nature, it may be softened by setting it exposed to the air and sun, and putting into it some pieces of soft chalk to infuse: or else, when the water is set on to boil, for pouring upon the malt, put into it a quantity of bran, which will help a little to soften it.

We shall now mention two or three particulars relating to malt, which may help those who are unacquainted with brewing: in the first place, the general distinction between one malt and another, is, only that the one is high-dried and the other low-dried; that which we call high-dried, will, by brewing, produce a liquor of a brown deep colour; and the other, which is the low dried, will give us a liquor of a pale colour. The first is dried in such a manner, as may be said rather to be scorched than dried, and will promote the gravel and stone, and is much less nourishing than the low-dried, or pale malt, as they call it; for all corn in the most simple way is the most feeding to the body. It has been experienced too, that the brown malt, even tho' it be well brewed, will sooner turn sharp than the pale malt, if that be fairly brewed. A gentleman in Northamptonshire dried malt upon the leads of a house, and made very good drink of it: and the method of drying malt by hot air, which was once proposed to the public, will do very well for a small quantity, but it is much too tedious to be ever rendered profitable: however, any means that can be used to dry malt without parching it, will certainly contribute to the goodness of the malt. At Marlborough they dry their malt very tenderly, and brew with chalky water, and their cellars are dug in chalk.

It has been computed, that there has been above two hundred thousand pounds worth of ale sold in and about London, under the denomination of Nottingham, Derby, Dorchester, &c. in one year's time: but it is not in London that we must expect to taste these

these liquors in perfection; for it is rare to find any of them there without being adulterated, or else such liquors are sold for them as are unskilful imitations of them, and are unwholsome into the bargain. A gentleman of good judgment in this affair says, that the brown malt makes the best drink when it is brewed with a coarse river-water, such as that of the river Thames about London; and that likewise being brewed with such water it makes very good ale; but that it will not keep above six months without turning stale, and a little sharp, even though he allows fourteen bushels to the hogshead. He adds, that he has dried the high-dried malt to brew beer with for keeping, and hopped it accordingly; and yet he could never brew it so as to drink soft and mellow, like that brewed with pale malt. There is an acid quality in the high-dried malt, which occasions that distemper commonly called the heart-burn in those that drink of the ale or beer made of it. When malt is mentioned, as before, that made of barley is meant; for wheat-malt, pea-malt, or these mixed with barley-malt, though they produce a high-coloured liquor, will keep many years, and drink soft and smooth, but then they have the mum flavour. Some people, who brew with high-dried barley-malt, put a bag, containing about three pints of wheat, into every hogshead of drink, and that has fined it, and made it drink mellow: others have put about three pints of wheat-malt into a hogshead, which has produced the same effect. But all malt-liquors, however they may be well brewed, may be spoiled by bad cellaring, and be now and then subject to ferment in the cask, and consequently turn thick and sour. The best way to help this, and bring the drink to itself, is to open the bung of the cask for two or three days; and if that does not stop the fermention, then put about two or three pounds of oyster-shells, washed, and dried well in an oven, and then beaten to fine powder, and stirring it a little, it will presently settle the drink, make it fine, and take off the sharp taste of it; and, as soon as that is done, draw it off into another vessel, and put a small bag of wheat, or wheat-malt into it, as above directed, or in proportion as the vessel is larger or smaller.

Sometimes such fermentations will happen in drink by change of weather, if it is in a bad cellar, and it will in a few months fall fine of itself, and grow mellow.

It is remarkable, that high-dried malt should not be used in brewing, till it has been ground ten days or a fortnight; it yields much stronger drink than the same quantity of malt fresh ground: but if you design to keep malt some time ground before you use it, you must take care to keep it very dry, and the air at that time must likewise be dry. And as for pale malt, which has not partaken so much of the fire, it must not remain ground above a week before you use it.

As

As for hops, the neweſt are much the beſt, though they will remain very good two years; but after that, they begin to decay and loſe their good flavour, unleſs great quantities have been kept together; for in that caſe they will keep much longer good than in ſmall quantities. Theſe, for their better preſervation, ſhould be kept in a very dry place; though the dealers in them rather chuſe ſuch places as are moderately between moiſt and dry, that they may not loſe of their weight. Notice muſt be taken here of a method which has been uſed to ſtale and decayed hops, to make them recover their bitterneſs, which is to unbag them, and ſprinkle them with aloes and water, which, when it has proved a bad malt year, has ſpoiled great quantities of drink about London; for even where the water, the malt, the brewer, and the cellars, are each good, a bad hop will ſpoil all: ſo that every one of theſe particulars ſhould be well choſen before the brewing is ſet about, or elſe we muſt expect but a bad account of our labour. And ſo likewiſe the yeaſt or barm that you work your drink with muſt be well conſidered, or a good brewing may be ſpoiled by that alone; and be ſure to be always provided before you begin brewing, for your wort will not ſtay for it.

In ſome remote places from towns it is practiſed to dip whiſks into yeaſt, and beat it well, and ſo hang up the whiſks with the yeaſt in them to dry; and if there is no brewing till two months afterwards, the beating and ſtirring one of theſe whiſks in new wort will raiſe a working or a fermentation in it. It is a rule that all drink ſhould be worked well in the tun, or keel, before it be put in the veſſel, for elſe it will not eaſily grow fine. Some follow the rule of beating down the yeaſt pretty often while it is in the tun, and keep it there working for two or three days, obſerving to put it in the veſſel juſt when the yeaſt begins to fall. This drink is commonly very fine, whereas that which is put into the veſſel quickly after it is brewed, will not be fine in many months.

We may yet obſerve, that with relation to the ſeaſon for brewing drink for keeping, if the cellars are ſubject to the heat of the ſun, or warm ſummer air, it is beſt to brew in October, that the drink may have time to digeſt before the warm ſeaſon comes on: and if cellars are inclinable to damps, and to receive water, the beſt time is to brew in March; and ſome experienced brewers always chuſe to brew with the pale malt in March, and the brown in October; for they gueſs that the pale malt, being made with a leſſer degree of fire than the other, wants the ſummer ſeaſon to ripen in; and ſo, on the contrary, the brown, having had a larger ſhare of the fire to dry it, is more capable of defending itſelf againſt the cold of the winter ſeaſon. But how far theſe reaſons may be juſt, I ſhall not pretend to determine; but, in ſuch a work as this, nothing

ſhould

should be omitted that may contribute to give the least hint towards meliorating so valuable a manufacture; the artists in the brewing way are at liberty to judge as they please.

But when we have been careful in all the above particulars, if the casks are not in good order, still the brewing may be spoiled. New casks are apt to give the drink an ill taste, if they are not well scalded and seasoned several days successively before they are put in use; and for old casks, if they stand any time out of use, they are apt to grow musty.

There is but little more to say about the management of drink, and that is concerning the bottling of it. The bottles must first be well cleaned and dried, for wet bottles will make the drink turn mouldy, or mothery, as they call it; and, by wet bottles, many vessels of good drink are spoiled. But if the bottles are clean and dry, yet if the corks are not new and sound, the drink is still liable to be damaged; for if the air can get into the bottles, the drink will grow flat, and will never rise. Many who flattered themselves that they knew how to be saving, and have used old corks on this occasion, have spoiled as much liquor as has stood them in four or five pounds only for want of laying out three or four shillings. If bottles are corked as they should be, it is hard to pull out the corks without a screw; and, to be sure to draw the cork without breaking, the screw ought to go through the cork, and then the air must necessarily find a passage where the screw has passed, and therefore the cork is good for nothing; or if a cork has once been in a bottle, and has been drawn without a screw, yet that cork will turn musty as soon as it is exposed to the air, and will communicate its ill flavour to the bottle where it is next put, and spoil the drink that way.

In the choice of corks, chuse those that are soft and clear from specks.

In the bottling of drink you may also observe, that the top and middle of the hogshead is the strongest, and will sooner rise in the bottles than the bottom: and when once you begin to bottle a vessel of any liquor, be sure not to leave it till it is all completed, for else you will have some of one taste, and some of another.

If you find that a vessel of drink begins to grow flat whilst it is in common draught, bottle it, and into every bottle put a piece of loaf sugar, about the quantity of a walnut, which will make the drink rise and come to itself; and, to forward its ripening, you may set some bottles in hay in a warm place; but straw will not assist its ripening.

Where there are not good cellars, holes have been sunk in the ground, and large oil-jars put into them, and the earth filled close about the sides. One of these jars may hold about a dozen quart bottles, and will keep the drink very well; but the

tops

tops of the jars muſt be kept cloſe covered up: and in winter time, when the weather is froſty, ſhut up all the lights or windows into ſuch cellars, and cover them cloſe with freſh horſe-dung, or horſe litter; but is much better to have no lights or windows at all to any cellar, for the reaſons given above.

If there has been an opportunity of brewing a good ſtock of ſmall beer in March and October, ſome of it may be bottled at ſix months end, putting into every bottle a lump of loaf ſugar as big as a walnut; this eſpecially will be very refreſhing drink in the ſummer: or if you happen to brew in ſummer, and are deſirous of briſk ſmall beer, bottle it as above, as ſoon as it has done working.

SUPPLE.

SUPPLEMENT.

BEING of opinion that a book of this kind should contain every thing necessary and useful for the Complete Housewife, it has been thought adviseable to give her, by way of Supplement, some particulars that have been procured since the foregoing sheets were printed, which cannot fail of being matters of profit and pleasure to her, and will render this book so universal, that no other book on the subject of Cookery, &c. need be purchased or consulted.

To wash Gauzes, Book-muslin, and Blond-lace.

WASH them in three lathers, which must be pretty hot; then rinse them in good blue water; give them a shake, and hang them to dry; then starch them, bluing the starch well; give them a shake, and dry them again. Then take half a pound of isinglass, boil in three half pints of water till it come to half a pint, dip it into that, squeeze them out well, and roll them in a clean towel, and iron them directly; but the best way for all gauzes is to have a frame made, rather larger than an apron, and pin a clean cloth all over it tight; then pin on your gauze very smooth, even, and tight: and when it is dry it will look like new. It is a much better way than ironing them. Your aprons should never be bound. The best way for all sorts of gauze or muslin aprons is to hem them at top; then sew on a tape called Jacob's Ladder, full of holes, to run a bobbin through. Gauze ruffles should be made up very slight, and the seams only tacked and pinned on to a frame; it is less trouble to run them up than to iron them, and they will do twice the service. If fine weather, dry them in the air; if foul, by the fire. When you have not a frame, if you have a good carpet in a room where no dust comes, pin a table-cloth or sheet tight on it, then pin on your gauzes, and they will dry presently. You are to mind, that your starch is to be stiff and well blued, for you can hardly blue them too well, or starch them too stiff; the isinglass clears them, and stiffens them; and when you wash gauzes, you are to

do

do them up directly, for they must not lie; an iron is apt to fray or turn them yellow, and the other is the quickest and best method, and pulls the threads quite even, and with a little practice and care, you may come to great perfection; experience and practice teaches every body in time.

Wash your book-muslins the same way, and they will not only look as well again, but last as long again; and if they should be a little frayed, with great care in pinning them on the frame, they will come even again, taking a long fine needle and moving the threads, which is to be done with a very nice hand, as it must be supposed to be pinned very tight and even.

Wash your blond-laces the same way, and when on the frame, stick a pin into every pearl, and when dry, it will look like new. You may do the same if the blond be sewed on to the gauze or muslin. You are to mind that your muslins, after two lathers, are to be put into a scald; or thus, beat up a nice strong lather, blue it, put your muslins into a little bag for the purpose, or tied in a fine handkerchief, and boiled; then wash them out, rinse and starch as above, and clap them; wash and boil all your fine laces as your book-muslins, only no isinglass, but pinned on to a frame in the same manner, and when dry, take a red-hot iron, and make your box-iron very hot, throw out the heater, and iron the lace on the wrong side; if there is any thing to raise, have two fine ivory bodkins, one in each hand; lay the lace on a sheet of clean paper, and you may raise all the work presently; but those who would do them nicely, raise the lace with the iron, and others with their fingers, which makes them look like new. But these things cannot be taught without seeing them done; and yet practice and time, with endeavouring to try every way may at length attain the knowledge of doing them.

To make your muslins and lace look very clear, when you have starched them very stiff, and they are bone-dry, throw them into pump-water for a moment, then squeeze them well out, clap them, roll them in a clean cloth, wring them well, and iron them directly.

Another way to wash lace. Have a well seasoned flat board made of plain deal, that will not stain; sew a cloth on to it very tight and smooth; soap your lace well with soft soap, and roll it round this board very smooth and even, and that the pearl lie the same; when you have put on all your lace, sew another clean cloth over it, and put it into a very clean kettle for the purpose, with soft water; set it on the fire, and as soon as the water is scalding hot, take it out into your pan and pour the water into it; then rest one end of your board on the dresser or table, and your hand at the top on the other end, and with a hand-brush in your other hand, rub it well, dipping it into the water; not backwards and forwards, but press your hand with the brush downwards to squeeze out the soap and dirt; then set it on in another kettle of clean water, and when it boils, take it off again, and press it with the brush as before, for you cannot hurt the lace; when you have got out all you can, put into another water well blued, and boil it well, skimming the water till you find it quite clear; then take it up and brush it as before, and if you find there is still more dirt in it, you must boil it again till your water is quite clear; then make some good starch; lay the board in it, give it a boil, and squeeze it well, both to soak the starch in, and also to press it out again; when this is done, hang the board up in the air, till the lace is bone-dry, which you must be very sure of before you pull off the cloth; then lay your lace on a sheet of paper, and with your nails rub out the pearls, but not the ends of your nails, lest you scratch them; custom will teach you how to do it; then take a large book, and fold it very smooth in the leaves, in one leaf and over another, till all the lace is smooth between every leaf; then roll the book in a cloth, for fear the edges should be dirty, and lay a heavy weight on it all night; the next day your lace will look like new. You may iron it if you chuse it, but this is the best way; and with your fingers you may raise it so as to look like new.

To wash Cambricks, Muslins, and common Laces.

FIRST soap them well, and wash them in warm water; then soap them again, and wash them again in hot water; after this mix a little soap and blue together, rub a little on the clothes, and pour boiling water on them, covering them up for an hour or two, then wash them well out of that and rinse them in pump-water blued. Sometimes you will be obliged to boil them as the muslins above; then dry them, and starch them as stiff as you would have them; clap them in your hands, and half-dry them before a fire, then roll them in a cloth, and iron them; be very careful neither to singe or fray them, which you will do if you do not iron them the right way of the thread. Time and practice must make you perfect, for it is impossible by any receipt to speak so plain as one could shew you, but with these directions you may learn; and mind one thing, never wring fine things, but squeeze them well in your hand. When you boil any small things, first mix your soft soap and blue together, and beat it up with a whisk, then pour it in the water to boil the clothes; it keeps the blue from settling in the clothes; and put as much pearl-ashes in as will lie on a shilling; and when the clothes and stockings are boiled, they will look as white as snow. The best thing to make yellow linen or lace white, is to take a quarter of a pound of soft soap, and a quarter of an ounce of powder-blue, mix it well together, and rub it

C c thick

thick on the linen; then roll it up, and put it into cold soft water, with a spoonful of pearl-ashes, and boil them well; if the first boil or second don't do, boil them again, and they will come as white as snow. If in summer, soap as above, and lay them in the hot sun, then boil them, and that will fetch out stains and all.

How to make Starch for starching small Linen.

TAKE a quarter of a pound of starch; just wet it, so as it will bruise, and mix a little powder-blue with it; when it is bruised fine, add half a pint of water to mix it; then have on the fire a quart of water, and when it boils pour in the starch and stir it well, and let the starch boil at least a quarter of an hour, for it cannot well be boiled too much, nor will your linen iron or look well, unless the starch be well boiled. Dip your linen into the starch, and squeeze it out, but do not rub the starch as some do. Those things you would have stiffest dip in first, but you may add or diminish as you please, or as you want the starch thick or thin.

Always keep a bell-mettle kettle to boil starch in, as it is a thing which requires a great deal of boiling and is not so apt to burn-to, as in any thing that is tinned.

As to allum, gum-arabic, and candle stirring into starch as it boils, it is all wrong, and better without, the boiling of it well does the whole; allum rots the linen, and the gum does no good at all; mind to strain your starch when it is boiled.

If any thing be put into starch, isinglass is the best, about an ounce to a quarter of a pound of starch.

An excellent Way of Washing, to save Soap, and whiten Cloaths.

TAKE a butter tub, or one of that size, and, with a gimblet, bore holes in it about half way; put into your tub some clean straw, and over that about a peck of wood ashes: fill it with cold water, and set it into another vessel to receive the water as it runs out of the holes of the tub; if it is too strong a lye, add to it some warm water; wash your linen in it, slightly soaping the cloaths before you wash them; two pounds of soap will go as far as six pounds, and make the cloaths whiter and cleaner, when you by experience have got the right way: if it is too strong for the hands, make it weaker with water.

To take Mildew out of Linen.

TAKE soap, and rub it on very well; then scrape chalk very fine, and rub that in well, and lay it on the grass; as it dries,

dries, wet it a little; and at once or twice doing it will come out.

To take Spots or Stains out of thin Silks, &c.

TAKE white wine vinegar a pint, make it indifferently warm, then dip a black cloth into it, and rub over the stains; then scrape fuller's earth on it, and clapping dry woollen cloths above and beneath, place an iron indifferently hot, on the upper part, and it will draw out the spot, &c.

To refresh Hangings, Tapestry, or Chairs.

BEAT the dust out of them in a dry day as clean as possible, then rub them well over with a dry brush, and make a good lather of Castile or cake soap, and rub them well over with a hard brush; then take fair water, and with it wash off the froth, and make a water with allum, and wash them over with it, and you will find, when dry, most of the colours restored in a short time; and those that are yet too faint, you must touch up with a pencil dipped in suitable colours; and indeed you may run over the whole piece in the same manner with water colours mixed with weak gum-water, and it will cause it, if well done, to look at a distance like new.

To wash Gloves.

TAKE the yolk of an egg, and beat it, and egg the gloves all over, and lay them on a table, and with a hard brush and water rub them clean; then rinse them clean, and scrape white lead in water pretty thick, and dip the gloves in; let them dry, and as they begin to dry, stretch and rub them till they be limber, dry, and smooth; then gum them with gum-dragant steeped in sweet-water, and let them dry on a marble stone. If you colour them, scrape some of the following colours amongst the white lead; the dark colour is umber; for brick colour red lead; for a jessamy yellow oaker; for copper colour red oaker; for lemon colour turmeric.

To take Spots out of white Silk, green or crimson Velvet.

TAKE strong aqua vitæ of three distillings, and wet the spots, rubbing it up and down; then take the white of a new-laid egg, and spread it on the spot, and set it in the sun to dry; this done, wash it with clear water, and wring the spot well between your hands; do this twice at least, for the colour will not perish nor decay. Also for a cloth in grain, take allum-water, and wash well the spot with it, rubbing it hard, cloth against cloth; this done wash it again with clear water, and in twice doing the spot will be gone.

Also for the same effect, take roche-allum-water, tartar of tonnes, and white soap, of each of them three ounces, and make them into very fine powder, and two ox-galls; then take a new earthen pipkin, set the allum-water on a slow fire, and when it begins to simmer, stir in the galls with a stick, and by degrees the powders, and let it boil till one third or one fourth is diminished, then wash the spot three or four times, every time drying the cloth, then wash it in fair water, and it will take it out.

To take Spots of Ink or Wine out of Cloth.

TAKE the juice of lemons, and wet the spot with it divers times, letting it dry each time; then wash it with white soap and vinegar, and the spot will go out.

To take Pitch or Tar off Cloth.

TAKE spirits of turpentine, and, with a piece of cloth, rub it the right way of the cloth, and it will take it off.

To take a Spot of Oil out of Cloth.

TAKE oil of tartar and lay it upon the spot; after a while take it off again, wash it with lukewarm water, then three or four times with cold water, and the cloth will look as neat and clean as if new.

A Soap to take out all Spots from Cloth.

TAKE a pound of allum and burn it, six ounces of powder of Ireos, and let all be beaten into powder together; then take two pounds and a half of white soap, and half an ox's-gall, and the whites of two eggs, and incorporate them well together; afterwards take the allum and powder of Ireos, and incorporate them together, then put into them a little sal nitrum, or salt-petre; this done, put into it as much of the said incorporated soap, as will make it have such a substance or body as that you may be able to make it up into round balls; then dry them in the shade, not in the sun, which is contrary to it; and if you make them for sale, do it by measure and weight; and when you would take out your spot, wet the cloth first up and down, then rub it well with the soap, cloth against cloth; this done wash it with cold water, till the water grows clear; and if you don't think the spot quite out, when the cloth is dry do it again as before, and it will come entirely out.

To take out Greafe and oily Spots.

TAKE a pound of roche-allum, and as much frefh unflacked lime; fix ounces of alumen fecis, three pounds of white foap cut fmall, and four pints of clear water; let all boil foftly a quarter of an hour, or better, in a clean well-tinned pot, or bell-metal kettle, ftirring it with a ftick. When you ufe it, let it be lukewarm, and wet the cloth on both fides where the fpots are with the faid water; then wafh them with clear water and the fpots will difappear; then with foap and water, and the fecond or third time it will be clean and no fpots remain. Or for fpots you may take a quart of clear foft water, and the gall of an ox, four ounces of alumen fecis burnt, and three ounces of alumen fecis broiled, and two fcruples of camphire; put all together, and fimmer it over the fire, till half wafted, then ftrain it, and in two or three times wafhing they will come out.

To wafh Scarlet Cloaks, &c.

BOIL fuller's earth and water together, let it ftand till it is but juft lukewarm, then wafh them clean, and rinfe them in pump-water, and hang them to dry directly.

To wafh black Silks.

TAKE fmall-beer and ink and warm it, wafh them in it, and it will make them of a fine black; fo it does black leather-chairs to rub them well with fmall-beer and ink warm, and afterwards with a dry cloth.

To keep Englifh China clean.

WHETHER it is from the glaze, or what reafon, I am not a judge, but this I know, that both in cups and bafons, &c. if only wafhed in fair water, there will be a fettling on the infide, like fur or dirt, which muft be wafhed in hot foap fuds, and rubbed with fand both infide and out, once a week, to keep them nice. The above is the only way to wafh ornamental china, but then they fhould be boiled in the fuds.

To make yellow Varnifh.

TAKE one quart of fpirit of wine, feven ounces of feed-lake, half an ounce of fandarach, a quarter of an ounce of gum-anime, and one drachm of maftich; let thefe infufe for thirty-fix or forty hours: ftrain it off, and keep it for ufe. It is good for frames of chairs or tables, or any thing black or brown; do it on with a brufh three or four times, nine times if you polſh it afterwards, and a day between every doing; lay it very thin the firſt and ſecond time, afterwards ſomething thicker.

To make white Varniſh.

TO a quart of ſpirit of wine, take eight ounces of ſandarach well waſhed in ſpirit of wine; that ſpirit of wine will make the yellow varniſh; then add to it a quarter of an ounce of gum-anime well picked, half an ounce of camphire, and a drachm of maſtich; ſteep this as long as the yellow varniſh; then ſtrain it out, and keep it for uſe.

To boil Plate.

TAKE twelve gallons of water, or a quantity according to your plate in largeneſs or quantity; there muſt be water enough to cover it; put the water in a copper, or large kettle; and when it boils put in half a pound of red argol, a pound of common ſalt, an ounce of roche-allum; firſt put your plate into a charcoal fire, and cover it till it is red hot; then throw it into your copper, and let it boil half an hour; then take it out, and waſh it in cold fair water, and ſet it before the charcoal fire till it is very dry.

To clean and ſoften the Hands.

SET half a pint of milk over the fire, and put into it half a quartern of almonds blanched and beaten very fine; when it boils take it off, and thicken it with the yolk of an egg; then ſet it on again, ſtirring it all the while both before and after the egg is in; then take it off, and ſtir in a ſmall ſpoonful of ſweet oil, and put it in a gallipot; it will keep about five or ſix days; take a bit as big as a walnut, and rub about your hands, and the dirt or ſoil will rub off, and it will make them very ſoft; draw on gloves juſt as you have uſed it.

The Italian Waſh for the Neck.

TAKE a quart of ox-gall, two ounces of roche-allum, and as much white ſugar-candy, two drachms of camphire, half an ounce of borax: beat all theſe in a mortar, and ſift them through a fine ſieve, then mix them well in a quart of ox-gall; put all together into a three-pint ſtone bottle well corked; ſet it to infuſe in the ſun, or by the fire, ſix weeks together, ſtirring it once a day; then ſtrain it from the bottom, and put to every quarter of a pint of this liquor a quart of ſpring-water, otherwiſe it will be too thick; ſet it a little to clarify, and bottle it; put ſome powder of pearl in the bottle; waſh with it.

A Water

A Water to wash the Face.

BOIL two ounces of French barley in three pints of spring-water, shift the water three times; the last water use, adding to it a quartern of bitter almonds blanched, beat, and strained out; then add the juice of two lemons, and a pint of white wine; wash with it at night; put a bit of camphire in the bottle.

To whiten and clean the Hands.

BOIL a quart of new milk, and turn it with a pint of aqua-vitæ, and take off the curd; then put into the posset a pint of Rhenish wine, and that will raise another curd, which take off; then put in the whites of six eggs well beaten, and that will raise another curd, which you must take off, and mix the three curds together very well, and put them into a gallipot, and put the posset in a bottle; scour your hands with the curd, and wash them with the posset.

A Water to cure red or pimpled Faces.

TAKE a pint of strong white wine vinegar, and put to it powder of the roots of orrice three drachms, powder of brimstone half an ounce, and camphire two drachms; stamp with a few blanched almonds, four oak apples cut in the middle, and the juice of four lemons, and a handful of bean-flowers; put all these together in a strong double glass bottle, shake them well together, and set it in the sun for ten days; wash the face with this water; let it dry on, and do not wipe it off; this cures red or pimpled faces, spots, heat, morphew, or sun-burn, but you must eat the following diet for three weeks or a month.

Take cucumbers, and cut them as small as herbs to the pot; boil them in a small pipkin with a piece of mutton, and make it into pottage with oatmeal; so eat a mess morning, noon, and night, without intermission, for three weeks or a month: this diet and the water has cured, when nothing else would do.

A good Thing to wash the Face in.

TAKE a large piece of camphire, the quantity of a goose-egg, and break it so that it may go into a pint bottle, which fill with water; when it has stood a month, put a spoonful of it in three spoonfuls of milk, and wash in it. Wear a piece of lead beaten exceeding thin, for a forehead piece, under a forehead cloth; it keeps the forehead smooth and plump.

To make a sweet Bag for Linen.

TAKE of orrice-roots, sweet-calamus, cypress-roots, of dried lemon-peel, and dried orange-peel, of each a pound; a peck of dried roses; make all these into a grofs powder; coriander-feed four ounces; nutmegs an ounce and a half, an ounce of cloves; make all these into fine powder and mix with the other; add musk and ambergreafe; then take four large handfuls of lavender-flowers dried and rubbed; of sweet-marjoram, orange-leaves, and young walnut-leaves, of each a handful, all dried and rubbed; mix all together, with some bits of cotton perfumed with essences, and put it up into silk bags to lay with your linen.

To make the burning Perfume.

TAKE a quarter of a pound of damask rose-leaves, beat them by themselves, an ounce of orrice root sliced very thin and steeped in rose-water, beat them well together, and put to it two grains of musk, as much civet, two ounces of benjamin finely powdered; mix all together, and add a little powdered sugar, and make them up in little round cakes, and lay them singly on papers to dry; set them in a window where the sun comes, they will dry in two or three days. Make them in June.

To make Paste for the Hands.

TAKE a pound of bitter almonds blanched, and two handfuls of stoned raisins, beat them together till they are very fine; then take three or four spoonfuls of sack or brandy, as much ox-gall, three or four spoonfuls of brown sugar, and the yolks of three eggs; beat it well together, set it over the fire, and give it two or three boils: when it is almost cold, mix it with the almonds; put it in gallipots; the next day cover it close, and keep it cool, and it will be good five or six months.

The best Thing to wash Hands with instead of Wash-ball, Soap, Almond-powder, or any Thing that can be invented for that Purpose.

TAKE fuller's-earth, pick out the whitest, dry it before the fire, beat it fine, and sift it; take common sand, dry it, and sift it; take an equal quantity, mix them, and keep it for use. It washes the hands clean, making them smooth and fine. To beautify the skin, and wash the face and neck, use Cotlogon's wash, who, as a great physician, recommends as the safest and best thing which can be used (as is proved under his own handwriting.)

writing.) It takes off all tan, though ever so deep; all freckles, moss, and tetters in the skin; and though the neck be ever so brown, will, in a very little time using, make it perfectly white and clear, nothing in it being mercurial, or unsafe to use.

An excellent Liquid Blacking.

MIX a sufficient quantity of good lamp-black with an egg to give it a good black; then take a piece of sponge, dip it therein, and rub over shoes, &c. very thin; when dry, rub them with a hard brush, and they will look very beautiful. You are to take care the shoes are first well cleaned with a hard brush, otherwise they will not look near so beautiful.

To make Ink.

GET one pound of the best galls, half a pound of copperas, a quarter of a pound of gum-arabic, a quarter of a pound of white sugar-candy; bruise the galls, and beat your other ingredients fine, and infuse them all in three quarts of white wine or rain-water, and let them stand hot by the fire three or four days; then put all into a new pipkin; set it on a slow fire, so as not to boil; keep it frequently stirring, and let it stand five or six hours, till one quarter is consumed; and when cold, strain it through a clean coarse piece of linen; bottle it, and keep it for use.

A Receipt for destroying Bugs.

TAKE of the highest rectified spirit of wine (viz. lamp-spirits) half a pint; newly distilled oil, or spirit of turpentine, half a pint; mix them together, adding to it half an ounce of camphire, which will dissolve in it in a few minutes; shake them well together, and with a piece of sponge, or a brush, dip in some of it, wet very well the bed or furniture, wherein those vermin harbour or breed, and it will infallibly kill and destroy both them and their nits, although they swarm ever so much; but then the bed or furniture must be well and thoroughly wet with it (the dust upon them being first brushed and shook off) by which means it will neither stain, soil, or in the least hurt, the finest silk or damask bed that is. The quantity here ordered of this curious, neat, white mixture (which costs about a shilling) will rid any one bed whatsoever, though it swarms with bugs; do but touch a live bug with a drop of it, and you will find it to die instantly. If any bug or bugs should happen to appear after once using it, it will only be for want of well wetting the lace, &c. of the bed, the foldings of the linings or curtains near the rings, or the joints or holes in and about the bed, head-board, &c. wherein the bugs or nits

nestle

nestle and breed; and then their being well wet again with more of the same mixture, which dries in as fast as you use it, pouring some of it into the joints and holes where the sponge or brush cannot reach, will never fail absolutely to destroy them all. Some beds that have much wood-work, can hardly be thoroughly cleared, without being first taken down; but others that can be drawn out, or that you can get well behind, to be done as it should be, may.

Note, The smell this mixture occasions, will be all gone in two or three days, which yet is very wholesome, and to many people agreeable; you must remember always to shake the mixture together very well whenever you use it, which must be in the day time, not by candle light, lest the subtilty of the mixture should catch the flame as you are using it, and occasion damage.

To cure Bugs.

TAKE a quart of canary-seeds, boiled in a gallon of the best and strongest rape vinegar, till it comes to two quarts; first take the furniture down, brush well all the folds and bindings; see that no nits be there, which you can brush and rub off, unskrew the bedstead, and with the above ingredients wash well every part of the bedstead. A bedstead will take the whole two quarts; do this in February, before the bugs hatch, and in October, when they have laid their eggs, and there will never come another bug into that bedstead; and though it swarmed ever so bad before, this entirely clears it. If any in the wainscot, wash it with the same thing, and it will destroy them, or in the walls; this is a safe and easy thing; observe where the room swarms with bugs that you have your floors washed with hot lye and gall in it.

To kill Rats.

POUND some stone-lime, and mix it with oatmeal and coarse sugar, lay it about the house, set water by it, and they will eat it, which will make them very dry, so that they will drink till they burst; after which the rest will leave the place.

Though this seems but a simple thing, yet it will destroy them faster than any thing else, and do no other damage.

To prevent Weesels, and other Vermin from destroying Poultry.

RUB your poultry with juice of rue, or herb grace, and the weesels will not hurt them; and if they eat the lungs or lights of a fox, the foxes will not devour them.

What Things are to be kept in the House by small Families for Kitchen Use.

LAY in a store of spices, bought at some reputable grocer's, as nutmegs, cloves, mace, cinnamon, ginger, Jamaica pepper, black pepper, and long pepper, that you may have every one ready at hand; and for the sweet-herbs, you should always have them dry by you, kept in paper bags from the dust; such as red sage, thyme, sweet-marjoram, mint, pennyroyal, and all such others as you may want to season any dish you are about to prepare; neither ought you to be without eschalots, onions, and such like; beside orange and lemon-peel dried, capers, pickled walnuts, pickled cucumbers, cucumbers in mango, anchovies, olives, pickled mushrooms, or mushrooms dried and powdered, or kitchup, or mushroom juice, or mushroom kitchup; but if you have a garden, then most of the sweet-herbs may be gathered at any time, except the mint, or the pot sweet-marjoram, which last are not good in cold weather.

To cure a musty Pipe, Hogshead, or any other Vessel of Wine.

APPLY the soft part of a large fresh wheaten or houshold loaf to the bung-hole, and let it remain there five, six or seven days, which will certainly take away the must.

To make Pomatum.

TAKE a pound and a half of sheep's-heels, take the skin off, and lay it in spring-water a day; then take it out, and beat it well with a rolling-pin till it is white; put it into a clean pot, and put to it an ounce of camphire, and eight pennyworth of sperma-ceti; stop the jug very close, and set in a brass pot over the fire till it is dissolved; take care that no water gets into the jug as it is boiling; when it is all melted, take it out, and pour it into a clean earthen bason wherein is a little rose-water, and when it is cold it will be a cake; then keep it in white paper for fear of dust.

To make excellent Tinder.

TAKE three ounces of salt petre, put to it a pint and a half of fair water, set it on a fire in a kettle or pan to heat till the salt-petre be dissolved; then take a quire of smooth brown paper, and put them in sheet by sheet into the hot water till they are wet through, and then lay them on a clean floor or grass to dry. You may at any time tare a piece off, and put it in your tinder-box; it will catch like wild fire. By this means you may save all your linen rags in the family, keep them clean in a bag, and if you are careful of them, they may produce you a pair of shoes and stockings at the year's end; and by this frugality you will have the pleasure to think of encouraging the making of paper, and employing the industrious.

To boil up Plate to look like new.

TAKE of unflacked lime a pound, of allum the like quantity, aqua vitæ and vinegar of each a pint, and of beer-grounds two quarts; boil the plate in this, and it will set a curious gloss upon it.

To make any Linen on the first Appearance look like Diaper.

TAKE it when new washed, spread it upon a table somewhat damp, and sprinkle it over with a brush dipped in allum and rose-water, in form and manner as shall best suit your fancy.

A good Way to cement broken Glass or China Ware.

TAKE the whites of two eggs, half an ounce of quick lime beaten to powder, a drachm of the powder of burnt flint, and the like quantity of gum-sandarach; temper them well together, and add, for the better moistening, a little lime-juice, and with a feather anoint the edges of the broken vessels, and clap the pieces together by a warm fire; and if your hand be steady, the fracture will hardly be discerned. Or you may use white lead and oil, such as painters use.

To raise a Sallad in two Hours at the Fire.

TAKE fresh horse-dung hot, lay it in a tub near the fire, then sprinkle some mustard-seeds thick on it, lay a thin layer of horse-dung over it, cover it close and keep it by the fire, and it will rise high enough to cut in two hours.

A MARKETING TABLE,
By the POUND.

Beef, Mutton, Veal, Lamb, Pork, per lb.	Two Pound		Three Pound		Four Pound		Five Pound		Six Pound		Seven Pound	
d.	s.	d.	s.	d.	s.	d.	s.	d.	s.	d.	s.	d.
1	0	2	0	3	0	4	0	5	0	6	0	7
1¼	0	2½	0	3¾	0	5	0	6¼	0	7½	0	8¾
1½	0	3	0	4½	0	6	0	7½	0	9	0	10½
1¾	0	3½	0	5¼	0	7	0	8¾	0	10½	1	0¼
2	0	4	0	6	0	8	0	10	1	0	1	2
2¼	0	4½	0	6¾	0	9	0	11¼	1	1½	1	3¾
2½	0	5	0	7½	0	10	1	0½	1	3	1	5½
2¾	0	5½	0	8¼	0	11	1	1¾	1	4½	1	7¼
3	0	6	0	9	1	0	1	3	1	6	1	9
3¼	0	6½	0	9¾	1	1	1	4¼	1	7½	1	10¾
3½	0	7	0	10½	1	2	1	5½	1	9	2	0½
3¾	0	7½	0	11¼	1	3	1	6¾	1	10½	2	2¼
4	0	8	1	0	1	4	1	8	2	0	2	4
4¼	0	8½	1	0¾	1	5	1	9¼	2	1½	2	5¾
4½	0	9	1	1½	1	6	1	10½	2	3	2	7½
4¾	0	9½	1	2¼	1	7	1	11¾	2	4½	2	9¼
5	0	10	1	3	1	8	2	1	2	6	2	11
5¼	0	10½	1	3¾	1	9	2	2¼	2	7½	3	0¾
5½	0	11	1	4½	1	10	2	3½	2	9	3	2½
5¾	0	11½	1	5¼	1	11	2	4¾	2	10½	3	4¼
6	1	0	1	6	2	0	2	6	3	0	3	6

A MARKETING TABLE.

By the STONE.

Beef, Mutton, Veal, Lamb, Pork, &c. at per lb.	1 Stone or 14 lb. is		2 Stone or 28 lb. is		3 Stone, or 42 lb. is			4 Stone, or 56 lb. is		
d.	s.	d.	s.	d.	l.	s.	d.	l.	s.	d.
1	1	2	2	4	0	3	6	0	4	8
$1\frac{1}{4}$	1	$5\frac{1}{2}$	2	11	0	4	$4\frac{1}{2}$	0	5	10
$1\frac{1}{2}$	1	9	3	6	0	5	3	0	7	0
$1\frac{3}{4}$	2	$0\frac{1}{2}$	4	1	0	6	$1\frac{1}{2}$	0	8	2
2	2	4	4	8	0	7	0	0	9	4
$2\frac{1}{4}$	2	$7\frac{1}{2}$	5	3	0	7	$10\frac{1}{2}$	0	10	6
$2\frac{1}{2}$	2	11	5	10	0	8	9	0	11	8
$2\frac{3}{4}$	3	$2\frac{1}{2}$	6	5	0	9	$7\frac{1}{2}$	0	12	10
3	3	6	7	0	0	10	6	0	14	0
$3\frac{1}{4}$	3	$9\frac{1}{2}$	7	7	0	11	$4\frac{1}{2}$	0	15	2
$3\frac{1}{2}$	4	1	8	2	0	12	3	0	16	4
$3\frac{3}{4}$	4	$4\frac{1}{2}$	8	9	0	13	$1\frac{1}{2}$	0	17	6
4	4	8	9	4	0	14	0	0	18	8
$4\frac{1}{4}$	4	$11\frac{1}{2}$	9	11	0	14	$10\frac{1}{2}$	0	19	10
$4\frac{1}{2}$	5	3	10	6	0	15	9	1	1	0
$4\frac{3}{4}$	5	$6\frac{1}{2}$	11	1	0	16	$7\frac{1}{2}$	1	2	2
5	5	10	11	8	0	17	6	1	3	4
$5\frac{1}{4}$	6	$1\frac{1}{2}$	12	3	0	18	$4\frac{1}{2}$	1	4	6
$5\frac{1}{2}$	6	5	12	10	0	19	3	1	5	8
$5\frac{3}{4}$	6	$8\frac{1}{2}$	13	5	1	0	$1\frac{1}{2}$	1	6	10
6	7	0	14	0	1	1	0	1	8	0

A TA-

A TABLE to cast up EXPENCES, or WAGES.

Per Year.	Per Month.				Per Week.				Per Day.			
l.	l.	s.	d.	f.	l.	s.	d.	f.	l.	s.	d.	f.
1	0	1	6	2	0	0	4	2	0	0	0	3
2	0	3	0	3	0	0	9	1	0	0	1	1
3	0	4	7	1	0	1	1	3	0	0	2	0
4	0	6	1	3	0	1	6	2	0	0	2	3
5	0	7	8	0	0	1	11	0	0	0	3	1
6	0	9	2	2	0	2	3	2	0	0	4	0
7	0	10	9	0	0	2	8	1	0	0	4	2
8	0	12	3	1	0	3	0	3	0	0	5	1
9	0	13	9	3	0	3	5	2	0	0	6	0
10	0	15	4	0	0	3	10	0	0	0	6	2
11	0	16	10	2	0	4	2	3	0	0	7	1
12	0	18	5	0	0	4	7	1	0	0	8	0
13	0	19	11	1	0	4	11	3	0	0	8	2
14	1	1	5	3	0	5	4	1	0	0	9	1
15	1	3	0	1	0	5	9	0	0	0	9	3
16	1	4	6	2	0	6	1	3	0	0	10	2
17	1	6	1	0	0	6	6	1	0	0	11	1
18	1	7	7	2	0	6	0	3	0	0	11	3
19	1	9	1	3	0	7	3	2	0	1	0	2
20	1	10	8	1	0	7	8	0	0	1	1	1
30	2	6	0	1	0	11	6	0	0	1	7	3
40	3	1	4	2	0	15	4	0	0	2	2	1
50	3	16	8	2	0	19	2	1	0	2	9	0
60	4	12	0	3	1	3	0	1	0	3	3	2
70	5	7	4	3	1	6	10	1	0	3	10	0
80	6	2	9	0	1	10	8	1	0	4	4	2
90	6	18	1	0	1	14	6	1	0	4	11	2
100	7	13	5	0	1	18	4	1	0	5	5	3
200	15	6	10	1	3	16	8	2	0	10	11	2
300	23	0	3	1	5	15	0	3	0	16	5	1
400	30	13	8	2	7	13	5	0	1	1	11	0
500	38	7	1	2	9	11	9	1	1	7	4	3
1000	76	14	3	0	19	3	6	3	2	14	9	2

Note, In these two tables, the month is of 28 days.

A TABLE to cast up Expences or Wages by the Day, Week, Month, or Year.

By the Day.		By the Week			By the Month.			By the Year.		
s.	d.	l.	s.	d.	l.	s.	d.	l.	s.	d.
0	1	0	0	7	0	2	4	1	10	5
0	2	0	1	2	0	4	8	3	0	10
0	3	0	1	9	0	7	0	4	11	3
0	4	0	2	4	0	9	4	6	1	8
0	5	0	2	11	0	11	8	7	12	1
0	6	0	3	6	0	14	0	9	2	6
0	7	0	4	1	0	16	4	10	12	11
0	8	0	4	8	0	18	8	12	3	4
0	9	0	5	3	1	1	0	13	13	9
0	10	0	5	10	1	3	4	15	4	2
0	11	0	6	5	1	5	8	16	14	7
1	0	0	7	0	1	8	0	18	5	0
2	0	0	14	0	2	16	0	36	10	0
3	0	1	1	0	4	4	0	54	15	0
4	0	1	8	0	5	12	0	73	0	0
5	0	1	15	0	7	0	0	91	5	0
6	0	2	2	0	8	8	0	109	10	0
7	0	2	9	0	9	16	0	127	15	0
8	0	2	16	0	11	4	0	146	0	0
9	0	3	3	0	12	12	0	164	5	0
10	0	3	10	0	14	0	0	182	10	0
11	0	3	17	0	15	8	0	200	15	0
12	0	4	4	0	16	16	0	219	0	0
13	0	4	11	0	18	4	0	237	5	0
14	0	4	18	0	19	12	0	255	10	0
15	0	5	5	0	21	0	0	273	15	0
16	0	5	12	0	22	8	0	292	0	0
17	0	5	19	0	23	16	0	310	5	1
18	0	6	6	0	25	4	0	328	10	0
19	0	6	13	0	26	12	0	346	15	0
20	0	7	0	0	28	0	0	365	0	0

FINIS.

www.ingramcontent.com/pod-product-compliance
Lightning Source LLC
Chambersburg PA
CBHW022146300426
44115CB00006B/364